SCOTLAND'S SHANGRI-LA

SCOTLAND'S SHANGRI - LA

RAPTURE IN THE HIGHLANDS

BY

BEE JAY

Author of
And It Came To Pass, 1963
The End of the Rainbow, 1964
Sunset on the Loch, 1965
Highland Pearls, 1969

BARKER JOHNSON
STRATH · GAIRLOCH · ROSS-SHIRE
1972

PRINTED IN GREAT BRITAIN
BY R. & R. CLARK, LTD., EDINBURGH

CONTENTS

Dedicated
to all seeking relaxation and
opposed to those bent on shifting
the hills, the heather, the legends
and the history abounding
in the
Shangri-La Highlands.

CHAPTER I

SHANGRI-LA

Shangri-La . . .
    Scotland's Shangri-La . . .
        Rapture in the Highlands . . .

THIS book follows the general pattern of *Highland Pearls* (written and published by the author two years ago) so it may be looked upon as a companion to that most popular of all the author's works. This volume brings in many new facets connected with the scenic wonderland of Wester Ross and Sutherland as well as fresh chapters of deep concern affecting the peace and quietness of the Far North (including the Outer Hebrides) together with heart-throbbing accounts of the Covenanting and Eviction days.

        *   *   *

The guide was conducting a party of about twenty overseas visitors—mostly Americans—along the Great Hall of Halls and grouped them at one spot where there was a large scale map of Scotland stretching right up from the old oak flooring to the 20-feet high ornate ceiling. The map was no ordinary one, but was modelled to set out in bold relief the contours of all the many mountains, glens, burns and lochs with striking effect. Gathering his important visitors around him, he lifted up his long staff and pointed to GARVE, which he said was the gateway to Wester

Ross; then moving northwards, pointing to the little town of
BONAR BRIDGE, said that was the gateway to Sutherland; and
sweeping his magic wand embracing these two areas on towards
the westward seaboard, and the Inner and Outer Hebrides,
proudly told them all that territory could very well be called
SHANGRI-LA; its vastness and general tenor of life, a reality.
There was a hush, then a murmur here and there amongst a few
of his listeners. One American lady who was taking down full
accounts of everything in her notebook, nudged her husband
saying, 'Homer, what's he mean by Shangri-La?' Homer hadn't
a clue, but told his beloved Eleanor, 'You ask him.' So quite
unashamedly, she spoke up, 'Say, Mr. Guide, what do you mean
by "Shangri-La", for it's a new one on me, and all of us here, I'm
sure?' 'You may well ask, lady,' he replied, 'for there are few
Shangri-La's in this world today. It means a land or valley of
peace, contentment, happiness, godliness and beauty.' It was,
he went on to say, 'a land where no strife, no crime, no jealousy,
no covetousness or greed was to be found; only a confident
quietness whose people had a charm of manner embroidered with
smiles of warmth and cheer. It forgave another's faults, and
should any tears dim the eye, the heart would always sing. They
found a rainbow in the sky when each new storm had passed, and
they dreamed up songs when the sun went down behind their
high mountains, the same way as the leprechauns do when
peeping out from under every toadstool. The folk saw beauty
even in the falling snow and enjoyed the thrill of nature's charm
as the seasons came and went. In truth it all spoke so much for
their age-old traditions being so similar to those in Scotland's
north-west. The Shangri-La inhabitants lived the life God had
meant them to live.'

'Sometimes,' he said, 'though very seldom, you may come
across a house tucked away in solitude named after this valley of
ideal serenity; but I fear such ideals are lost to most of us in
today's self-seeking world. . . .'

A hush again descended on the company; rather more of a
deep soul-searching hush than was the case before, for this was
something quite unknown to them and their way of life; quite
unbelievable. In fact it seemed to rouse them all, as was the case
in Macaulay's time when 'the red glow on Skiddaw roused the
burghers of Carlisle'.

The party moved forward silently on its tour of the ancient Baronial Castle.

*   *   *

I would like now to take up the story (and the theme) from where our guide left off.

There is a novel written by James Hilton called *Lost Horizon*. James Hilton was a master at The Leys school, a public school for boys in Cambridge. Readers may perhaps remember he also wrote *Goodbye Mr. Chips*, *Random Harvest*, and many other epics. In 1937, the film of *Lost Horizon* had its premiere in London. I had just returned to England from the Far East, and went to see it. Magnificently screened, with a moving story, I was deeply impressed. Ronald Colman and Jane Wyatt appeared in the leading roles, the former as Conway (the hero), the latter as Lo-Tsen, an exquisite Chinese girl; a girl of infinite charm. As it is now nearly thirty-five years since I saw the film, I may be excused if I forget some of the details.

It is a world-famous story set largely in part of Tibet, called Shangri-La; a strange and mystical monastery hidden in a remote valley there, surrounded on all sides by its own wide expanses— its own world, its own sanctuary, so to speak. Those privileged and fortunate to live there, rich and poor alike, were a godly race, peaceful, contented, and what is more, they lived to a very old age 'midst such environments. In fact it could be said they lived for ever; but should any of them take a step outside the boundaries into the normal world they would almost shrink overnight and decline in age, stature and mind, and go hand in hand with Death. In short they passed from their dream-world into reality.

This, then, was the incredible secret of Shangri-La. Of course there was much more to the story than this; I have merely out-lined (from what I remember) the theme. Lo-Tsen, whom I have just named as a girl, was according to our earthly standards an old woman, but had all the appearance, vivacity and appeal of a young person. To filmgoers she would be looked upon as a galactic star. It may be asked what has all this to do with the Shangri-La that our guide had been pointing out to our visitors in that Great Hall of Halls—the country really known as Wester Ross and Sutherland?

I had better explain.

In the far north of western Scotland, there is to be found the peace and contentment of the Shangri-La of Tibet. It is the only part of Britain that can make such a claim; and an increasing number of folk are fast becoming aware of this. West of Garve, and north of Bonar Bridge you suddenly come across a new country that exudes simplicity and—so far as Sutherland is concerned—an unspoiled Paradise of vastness. A land, at times, of lonely grandeur extends right over this north-west region. In the many smallish villages there is to be found a restfulness and a feeling amongst the people, mostly crofters and fisher folk, to let the world go by. Although life in this far north may be hard to some extent and sometimes dreary in its manner by city standards, yet all the same the love of life lies lightly on their chiselled faces, and the real Highlanders, both men and women with whom you come in contact, live to a grand old age, far exceeding that of tensely living town dwellers. They may be, in some cases, poorly off compared with town workers, but they still live in *Tir nan Òg* . . . the land of the ever young, and should you get to know them well, their Gaelic salutation would be 'Slàinte Nach Teirig'— (here's health everlasting to you). A worthy, if not a wealthy people, and like Tibet's Shangri-La inhabitants, a godly people.

The folk, by and large, are not wrinkled-old; if anyone is, they will tell you that crow's feet under the eyes are but the dried-up beds of old smiles.

Readers may now see the similarity to *Lost Horizon*. Should these aged ones here leave their Highland fortresses, venturing south in visits to relations in towns, they quickly return home to live . . . and to live on; for there is happiness in the plain living and in the breathing in of an atmosphere that evokes the wave in the heart (young in heart) and the dream in the eye. So once in Scotland's Shangri-La one seldom wishes to step outside its confines. There is much poetry even in the place-names of the innumerable little hamlets that produce a golden ring in the soul; place-names strange to the Anglo-Saxon tongue that conjure up visions of clansmen in the days gone by, staunch in loyalty to their chief, following a proud piper to battle. Their descendants have dwindled and only those whose love for the land outweighs their desire for gold, stay to till the soil.

Here you come into close contact with the mountains and

lochs by day, and the stars by night. *Ionndrainn*—the longing for
things gone beyond recall; the most moving note in Gaelic
poetry. All have long memories, and as I have said, a long life. The
men have rosy cheeks and the young fair-to-look-upon maidens,
quiet eyes; eyes that speak softly in seconds. All are cheerful.

Shangri-La indeed, and in our own English-speaking country,
not 7000 miles away in the north of India. Here, there are
mountains, lochs and lochans; vast moorlands, glens, beaches
with sparkling waters rushing in from the Atlantic . . . and love.
Time, when even a minute takes longer is of small account, for
life just saunters along and can spare the time of day, for they say
'what is life if full of care, you have no time to stand and stare?'

> No time to stand beneath the boughs
>   And stare as long as sheep or cows;
> No time to see, when woods we pass,
>   Where squirrels hide their nuts in grass;
> No time to see, in broad daylight,
>   Streams full of stars, like stars at night;
> No time to turn at Beauty's glance,
>   And watch her feet, how they can dance;
> No time to wait till her mouth can
>   Enrich that smile her eyes began;
> A poor life this if, full of care,
>   We have no time to stand and stare.

(The Atlantic is so called because of the legendary continent
of Atlantis, which is supposed to lie beneath it.) Whatever the
clock says, it is morning—the morning of a new (Risen Christ)
day. Time in the Highlands has an elastic quality. Circumstances
may change generation by generation; the living of life does not.
And so I could go on and on, presenting a picture and a life of
these real Scottish Highlands and Islands which I am sure our
guide was right in calling same a veritable Shangri-La; for the
life, the love and the godliness met with, could not be more
alike. The Tibetan country however differs in one respect in that
it lacks the sea and coast line that our area has. It also lacks the
heather; the purple heather.

I am often asked about heather—the white heather, why is it
so scarce, how it came to be white and so on. Well, there is a
legend (and there are many up north) that when Oscar, an Irish
warrior, lay dying after a battle in Ulster, he gave one of his

followers a sprig of heather to take to his sweetheart, Malvina, as a token that his last thoughts were of her. When she received it, her tears fell on the sprig, and its flowers grew white. Ever since, white heather has been a token of faithful love and good luck. You see all down the ages and all through life, Love with a capital L predominates.

A new industry has now started in the Highlands which is termed *Heathergems*, manufactured by a completely new and patented process from specially selected heather stems gathered on the moors and hills of the Scottish Highlands. Each piece is hand-made by Scottish craft workers; no two are identical and each is a unique example of craft-skill. The heather stems are processed in a new way discovered by Hugh Kerr, a native of Glenlivet, and developed by him over the past twenty years. Cross sections of these heather stems are put together and polished to form colourful mosaics. Heather gems are mounted, or alternately hand-set into cross sections of real staghorn to form a variety of attractive brooches, pendants, ear-rings, tie pins, cufflinks and other articles. They are manufactured at East Kilbride.

It is true that over the centuries, the Highland people have been rent apart with problems, and their inherent contentment broken, not of their own volition, but brought upon them by grasping landowners. I refer to the Clearance days, and the dire trials and tribulations inflicted upon them. Sheep displacing humans, when thousands upon thousands of men, women and children were dumped like animals into stinking ships and sent overseas, regardless; whilst those who escaped the clutching hands and went to find some habitation on the rocky coast line where they thought they might exist, found no existence possible, and the only port of haven they found on the barren shore, was the port of Eternity.

Their devout and humble ministers declared it was the Will of God—*que sera, sera*—for they could do little to withstand the forces marshalled against them under the blazoned banners of 'Improvement', a word that was then paramount and used on every conceivable occasion. Glens of bitter weeping arose. However, in the long run, Faith helped them, and events turned full circle once more; their dawn of a new (not a lost) horizon broke through although families which had dispersed or died were not able to cherish this dawn to their bosoms. Those that were fortunate to be left alive, took over and saluted the new Dawn, and every tomorrow became a vision of the happy past. Where darkness was, light appeared; despair gave place to hope, and sadness to joy. . . . And Shangri-La came back.

It is said where a man has been given much, much will be expected of him. The Highland people were given much in their natural surroundings, and all through their history they have given much in return. The people were not chasing a a shadow, but the substance; and all have a love-affair with their (and their forebears') beloved land. The older generations still live contentedly; if they find the mountains impossible to climb —well, they have the valleys and the glens which hold such memories for them as are immortal, despite their tear-stained eyes; for their heritage is as ancient as the tablets of stone brought down from Mount Sinai. Is it not all so analagous to Tibet's sacred asylum where long life and every blessing prevail (*Beatha fhada leis gach beannachd*)? . . . They find a way of life, as well as an escape from it.

The ancient visionaries must have known there was such a land in the north, a land where you are suspended in an atmosphere of timeless incomplexity—a place of stillness. And they must have known that a gem was not polished without rubbing, nor a person or land perfected without trials. For the encouragement of those who with hope faced the task of recovering what they had lost, I would quote the Gaelic words of one of Scotland's oldest bards who said GUR FADO'N LA CHUALAS; 'CHA BHI BUAIDH MHOR GUN CHUNNART' (long since we have heard the saying 'There shall not be any great triumph without a bold venture'). After trials come Glory, and this word should be carved boldly in Gaelic on their hills.

The people live in a land where it would seem God is still busy at the work of Creation; thousands of square miles of moorland rolling down to the horizons. Yes, this land became a dream of man; and what he dares to dream, he endeavours to achieve. His path today etches the face of the moon, whereas his ancestors scratched their way across the face of the earth. What is happening in the space-age now, must be considered a victory for all men, especially so for those who went, and for those who in some way or another helped to send them. But we must hope the only purpose for these rockets and space-ships will be a search for new, real, and not lost, horizons. Truly, in little more than one generation we have moved from the pace of the ox to supersonic flights of fancy.

In some of the remote parts of the Highlands where even today man intrudes but rarely, we could say our Shangri-La is another Garden of Allah.

The unhurried mode of life is fully evident in the north-west where even the cockerels don't begin to crow till 10 o'clock in the morning. Cattle doze, sheep nibble, heather moths quiver in the grass as you pass by, and you look towards the hills and mountains, talking in whispers in case you break the spell. These mountains are satellites which bounce your thoughts back into ordinary-day words. Everything in the material surroundings may crumble, but Nature can never be overwhelmed. So it is with these folk's life, and such simpleness one feels is beyond death—it is part of the eternal hills. Happiness has its home 'midst simple things.

I have mentioned the word sanctuary a page or so earlier. A sanctuary means both silence and solitude, the two things which city life has never experienced. Yet to keep man's mind and soul in focus, every city dweller ought to have *some* natural sanctuary; a place within easy reach where he is not distraught by crowds; some secret spot where he can bathe his soul in silence, revel in the sights of Nature, and 'think on these things'. What better place in the United Kingdom than this north-west territory? A sanctuary of stillness and impressiveness as dusk begins to fall, just as from the minarets of the mosques one hears the high-pitched chant of the muezzin calling the faithful to prayer in his language 'There is no God but God, and Mohammed is the messenger of Allah. There is no God but God' (Mohammed was born at Mecca in 570 and died at Medina in 632, and was the Arab prophet and founder of Islam the Moslem religion). I have heard and seen this 'calling' in many Eastern cities, and believe me, it is magnetic.

As you journey through this country in the north, you pass such enchanting scenes and atmospheres as Loch Maree, the Torridons, the valley of Strathnaver, Strath Halladale and the Strath of Kildonan; the Kyles of Tongue and of Durness, Loch Eriboll, Eddrachillis bay, Kylesku; Loch Assynt, Loch Broom, and you find yourself inwardly and silently saying 'well, if this is not Shangri-La, what is?' And when you leave these boundaries you will be saying to yourself, *je reviendrai te chercher* (I shall come back to look for you—to fetch you); or in plainer language 'some day I'll go back'.

Each day the Highlander and his wife, as soon as they open the front or back door of their snug little croft house, look lovingly on their Shangri-La; they breathe in its air deeply, and going outside, their feet touch the sacred ground. Admiring the beauty and serenity they say to each other, 'well if the wrong side of Heaven is so wonderful as it seems from here what must the right side be like?' Another phrase deep down in their philosophy is 'as the tree falleth, so shall it lie', and that Heaven or Hell must be the eternal abode of all. Constantly do they say righteousness exalteth a nation, but sin is a reproach to any people (Prov. ch. 14, v. 34). As to the state of Britain today, they voice the opinion that as a nation, we have been sowing the wind, and now we are to reap the whirlwind.

As to the ordinary Highlander who may have left these shores years ago and died in a foreign land, or the soldier who may have lost his life serving abroad, I would remind you of the legend that runs through Scottish folk-lore, namely, that their souls return to the land of their birth (like the children in Maeterlinck's 'Bluebird of Happiness'; they may have gone away seeking happiness in the past and in the future, and then returned only to find it singing on their own front doorstep).

The last wish of those departed travellers was to come back to the ancestral surroundings in the great expanse of the Shangri-La they knew; for he is blessed to be able to call his own—even in death—*some* valley with green pastures, moorland and still waters. For to be born in a place of quietness and scenic beauty is to be sealed for life with the love of the countryside.

. . . and you hear the sounds of Silence in the far north . . .

In memory, he would revisit the scenes of his boyhood. As the shadow lengthened, his thoughts would turn more and more to the early days—the happy carefree days of youth—to the hills and glens he had roamed as a boy to the last resting place where his kinsfolk sleep, and where nearby, the waves break endlessly on the golden sands sounding an eternal requiem.

> Be it granted to me to behold again in dying
> The hills of home, and to hear again the call;

Hear over the waves the cry of the sea-mews calling
And hear no more at all.

Should our voyager be a Skye man, he would view his
beloved romantic isle in a mirage in the following lines:

Across the sea within my mind
A bright mirage I often find;
Mountains blue and silver-grey
Are shimmering for a future day;
When I shall turn back home to lie
Upon the mountain's lap in Skye.

I'll cross the wild Atlantic seas
To my beloved Hebrides;
For there the rough, gay-blooming heather
Shakes in the rains of tempest weather;
The swans will soar the day I die
Across the Cuillin, white and high.

And I will sweep, my soul set free
Across the isle to fair Portree;
Each hidden loch, brown bog, high tower
I'll visit in that shining hour;
There timeless moments I will pass
Listening to whispering bending grass.

Lay then my body deep to sleep
Not far from busy cropping sheep;
Let no bell toll for sign of grief
For death is joy and sorrow brief;
My soul will find in yonder cloud
A misty cool and tender shroud.

Oh, let me haunt a brief, bright while
Across the rough blue bay from Kyle;
I'll wail and tremble by Beinn Mhor
But bless each shieling's wooden door;
May I so live that I come nigh
To Heaven on the Isle of Skye!

*   *   *

In these years of the 70's and of rush and wonder, people are
looking for short-cuts and shouting themselves hoarse about
Human Rights, the Right to Live, Freedom Fighters and so forth,
whereas all the time, beauty in nooks and corners is eluding their

fast lives, and in their very anxiety for life, have no time to live.
It was that exact and argumentative Greek fellow called Euclid
who taught us that a straight line was the shortest distance
between two points. So it is. Therefore the straight line to the
Highlands is dead easy from London to Inverness and onwards.
I would say the secret of living happily in a city is to be out of it
as often as possible. Even be it spring, summer or autumn, the
Highlands is always a world of its own. (There are some folk
who will tell you there is no climate in the Highlands, only
samples of weather.) The *autumn*, with the mad rush of the
summer influx over, is one of the most human of institutions,
for it means that many people long for one more adventure into
the country before they finally turn back the hands of the clock
to winter. And the autumn colourings? Well, they have to be
seen to be believed.

> The Master of Painters looked down
> On the rugged contours below;
> With a sweep of His brush
> The colours laid on
> The greens, the purples, the brown.
>
> He added a frosty dawn
> With the mists in every hollow;
> And like as a crystal, they mirrored back
> His colours, by Time never worn.
>
> He signed the picture as Autumn
> Framed in a Highland setting
> So those who were tired of the maelstrom of life
> Could relax, and seek their fair portion.
>
> No human palette ever can hold
> Such blends as those of the Master;
> Very fortunate those with the wish to see
> Have the sight these secrets unfold.

The glories of autumn can be looked upon as the last fling of
Nature's gaiety before the trees stand naked against grey overcast
skies. The brilliant yellows and reds, subtle pinks and russets;
Nature giving herself a last reminder of the colours that will come
again, only with the sun. Then November; no fruits, no
flowers, no leaves, no birds, no vember! So sad it is for us to see,
the autumn leaves fall off a tree; with colours which so bright

and gay, drop down to earth and then decay. If darkness comes late to the Highlands, by mid-spring dawn comes as early.

In writing the following pages, readers will find a new wonder of Scottish beauty and life awaiting, together with its trials of the past, their legendary beliefs, their quiet achievements 'midst their priceless background. With the real Shangri-La perspective before me, the philosophy is, what can't be done today, can wait till tomorrow. These wonderful people live, not by the clock or calendar, but rather from sunrise to sunset; they say let the outside world have its interplanetary wars, its frustrations, its anxieties. In the sometimes windswept moorlands, these chosen people have attained the one elusive element that the so-called civilised world have rarely found—and perhaps will never find—peace of mind, body and soul. And unless we have all three, we have nothing. . . .

As you travel through this region, you come across many ancient burial grounds set in isolated spots. In many cases the wording and dates on the tombstone slabs have been obliterated by the centuries of Time. Some of the stones are leaning in all sorts of positions, others have fallen down, and in some instances they lie against the crumbling graveyard wall, buried in undergrowth; some are laid outside the hallowed area, being put there for some reason or other in orderly fashion. The writing on the headstones are often in Gaelic in so far as the epitaphs are concerned, and all embody love, faith and respect which their children's children will long remember and honour.

This is very like the story of Joshua we read in the Old Testament, chapter 4, which tells how Joshua commanded twelve men out of the people of Israel (one out of every tribe, a man) to carry twelve stones from the bed of the Jordan and to set them up on the bank, that 'this may be a sign among you, that when your children ask their fathers in time to come, saying "what mean ye by these stones" the answer will be that they were to be a memorial. . . .'

You and I may not leave much behind, only a headstone; but it's what we leave by way of ourselves and what we have done in our life-time in respect of being of help to others (even beyond our own kith and kin) that matters, and will continue to matter long after our epitaph has been defaced by the elements, and our name on the stone has surrendered to the weather, and we are apt to be forgotten. Like in Shangri-La, with such attributes we may faintly hope our name and our remembrance *may* last for ever. Certainly the old-type Highlander and his wife are remembered, not just for a day but for years to come.

The rugged country of the north-west is steeped in history and captures the visitor with feelings that the rest of England has no knowledge of, let alone those from overseas; and together with its host of legends, these Highlands haunt the exile with constant memories. To one and all, the country and the life of its dwellers here, is a pedlar or seller of Happiness (*le marchand de bonheur*).

Beauty? A seemingly endless variety of scenery is the true glory of the north-west. You meet different sorts of beauty absorbing different landscapes uncorrupted by man, with sandy bays stretching as far as you can see. Many of these sands are 'whiter than white'. And should you be favoured with a fine afternoon, then the sky will seem to be made of silk, the clouds mother-of-pearl; overwhelming revelations, which will suggest you are at Journey's End.

I would have you know this country of Shangri-La here should be labelled as A.O.B., and if you are not well-versed in official jargon, this means Areas of Outstanding Beauty, and as such should be under strict planning control; certainly not be developed as a Costa-something or other with spectacularly built pink-washed hotels; and deep in these sparsely-inhabited moorlands, speculative money must be thrown out, not thrown in; for to the urban dweller our A.O.B. is not only a sight for wearied eyes, but a breath of fresh wholesome air for fume-riddled lungs. There is no pollution in the Highlands as in the towns, where in most industrial centres, the air is so heavily laden with smoke, smog, dirt and grime, that if you 'shoot an arrow in the sky'—it sticks! It is Shangri-La, remember, and I have already remarked on there being *plenty of time*—and more. The crofter will tell you, he has no time to be in a hurry.

An old Highlander observing the day and all that was going on at the pier, lit his pipe, smiled a contented smile, and turning to me—knowing I was a visitor—said, 'You know, the real beauty of a holiday in the Highlands here, is that when you get fed up with doing nothing you can always relax.'

Highland philosophy at its best?

I recall an instance of a local from Cape Wrath-way driving down south, and coming to the ferry at Ballachulish on his trip to Oban, found a stream of cars ahead of him waiting to cross over. He just sat in his car saying to himself he'd get across sometime. Then the ticket man came along and asking for his fare casually told him he'd have at least half an hour to wait. 'Oh,' he said in his Shangri-La fashion, 'it doesn't take me long to wait half an hour.'

Motoring up here can be a joy if you are prepared to dawdle along at 30 miles an hour, for there is absolutely no point in trying to 'belt it'. If you do, then it's good scenery wasted. There are no traffic lights in Shangri-La. A section of our Planners up in Scotland have 'Bridges on the brain' (B.O.B. this time) and think only in terms of bridging first this Firth, then that Firth; so on *ad infinitum*. One now being built, and possibly completed by the time this book is published, is the one at Tongue, across that kyle to Melness, cutting out a beautiful 12-mile loop round the kyle itself, since it will, they say, close the gap on the route to Cape Wrath; perhaps they think an airport will be there one day, and that tourists must get there by a certain time. There is a new road also planned from the end of the kyle of Durness right up to Cape Wrath itself, so eliminating the crossing from the kyle mouth at Keodale in a little boat for cyclists and people only, to the opposite side, where you disembark to a mini-bus which takes you on to Cape Wrath lighthouse; a very enjoyable and novel way of getting there. But this is not good enough for our brainy chaps in St. Andrew's House, or in Whitehall. Oh, no; they have a mania to make everything easier and quicker to get there. To be 'with it'; so our overseas tourists, when remembering and retailing their holiday to their friends back home, can say they 'did Scotland on a Tuesday'. In my opinion all this will spoil completely the pleasure of ambling around the beautiful kyles and lochs of the wild west, and it would be best if such folk were encouraged to stay south of the border—Mexico way. Forsooth, some in authority say it is but a matter of time before even most of the inland ferries met with on the north-west coast will be replaced by bridges. If development persistently rings in these extra-clever planning ears, then for goodness sake and for the sake of Shangri-La, let these improvement potentials be confined to the regions

most suited to them. Let our area have the foresight to treasure
and protect the unique qualities and charm that we, and we alone,
possess. Some of course may say this is a selfish attitude in wanting to retain the old way of life up north. Maybe it is, but surely
this is not a crime when such beauty is at stake? As our towns
and cities tower upwards and sprawl outwards, as the business of
living in these man-made concrete environments becomes increasingly fretful and stressful, we must surely look more and
more longingly to the countryside, and to protect it for one's
children? It is the one and only sensible plan to adopt; and
since Britain is a comparatively small country with increasing
population, it is vital to safeguard the Highland countryside as a
safety-valve for relaxation. People cannot give of their best
unless they *do* have mental relaxation and a healthy atmosphere
at some periods of the year.

It is admitted one must respect and accept the good faith of
those in authority who disagree. This requires mutual forbear-
ance. Only in this way can the pursuit of national interest be
harmonised with the pursuit and preservation of the Highlands'
national heritage; that, coupled with a certain degree of progress.
We know that the Shangri-La of old cannot become a Utopian
area today.

Sheep (there are nearly eight million in Scotland), moorlands,
crofting, scenery and humans—all living peacefully together; long
may it remain so in this covetous country. However, I would
give our crofting friend Kenny a warning, for it came to my ears
some time ago, that round about Blair Atholl in Perthshire, there
are plans to make 100 grazing acres into a safari park for lions and
baboons. A century ago, as you'll know Kenny, it was you
crofters up north who were cleared off the land to make way for
sheep. Then the sheep were shifted to make room for deer, and
now the deer are being moved to make way for trees. A vicious
circle, eh! But the landowners haven't reached their limit, for
they think both sheep and crofters are spoiling the look of the
place; and so don't be thinking you've had one dram too much,
if one day you come across a man in a big stetson cowboy hat
(having left his bowler hat at St. Andrew's House) driving a
lorry-load of snakes on the road to Altnaharra going to Strathnaver or Ben Hope. Get in touch with the Prime Minister at
once, either by the telephone if there is a box at hand, and is

actually working and the post office is not on strike, or by the
grape-vine Radio 5. The man you have met on the road will
most likely tell you he is an official from the Ministry of Lands—
sheep abolition department; S.A.D. Section Baa Baa, instructed
to set up an experimental anaconda farm on, believe it or not,
your croft. You can take this as gospel truth, for I heard it straight
from the python's mouth—or perhaps it was making a rude noise,
having just eaten one of your own black-faced ewes—now turned
blue. Anyway they'll still let you keep your hens. And that
poses the question, Kenny, how many eggs should a white hen
lay this year (1971) on Monday, 16th June, when its wet and the
wind blowing in from the west? Well, the answer is none at all,
for Monday the 16th June is a Wednesday.

A few lines above I have been mentioning the chance of wild
game coming into the district; and this reminds me of the story
of the elephant and the tiger which a wealthy gentleman had shot
out East, bringing the heads back home to hang them up on the
wall of the library in his mansion, along with other trophies he
had collected over the years. In showing an honoured guest
over his big house one day, they stopped and looked at the two
beautiful heads, the elephant and the tiger. 'Yes,' said the Laird,
'I killed both of them with one shot.' 'One shot!' exclaimed
his friend? 'Yes, one shot,' said Sir Alec, 'I shot the elephant
first and it fell on the tiger.'

At this stage I think I should relate the following incident that
happened a few years ago up in Sutherland in the Ben Loyal
district. There had been a very convivial party at the Laird's
house which lasted until the early hours; however it had been
arranged that they should all set out in the morning as soon as
possible to stalk the deer on the Ben heights; and they set out
albeit after the previous night's celebrations, their heads were far
from clear and their eyes a bit bleary. They climbed up the
mountain and got to a point where the road wasn't really visible
down below but they could make it out in the distance. All went
well until one of the keepers chanced to look through his telescope and muttered, 'Michty, it canna be!' One of the gentry
on hearing him said, 'Let me look,' and then exclaimed excitedly,
'I don't believe it!' A third had a look and then yelled out, 'An
elephant! Snakes alive, surely not', thinking he was still under
the influence. But sure enough it was true. It was an elephant

trundling slowly along the road on its way to Thurso—part of a travelling circus.

*   *   *

Man must not be alienated from his environments, and again I say it would be a tragedy if Shangri-La, and its many thousands of acres, was turned upside down. Whilst there is a certain emptiness and hardness of some parts of the north-west, *that* is its beauty which one can still be proud of and visibly moved by all it holds.

If there is one thing that sets this land apart, it is the intensity of attachment to the remembered places. There are virtues still in smallness in local involvement, and if decisions are to be taken they should be taken in concert with the people who will be affected. As to visitors coming through the barriers to see us, they find the region so extensive they are apt to get lost at times. Some of them I have seen need to get lost permanently; and with them their litter.

LITTER. I find it hard to understand a person who travels miles to admire the scenery, then litters it with garbage. Special litter bins by the roadside, all at vantage points, are provided by the county council, and if a slogan such as YOU FILL THEM, WE EMPTY THEM were painted on the sides, it might help to focus one's eye more on this 'disease'. There was a sign posted at the entrance to the tropical gardens in Ceylon that I remember read thus:

> If you with litter will disgrace
> And spoil the beauty of this place
> May indigestion rack your chest
> And ants invade your pants and vest!

East, West, Hame's best is a familiar saying. Many Scots emigrated overseas years ago and stayed there, for money was not so plentiful as now for them to be able to return home, but those in later years did come back to their native Highlands— those who left with stars in their eyes returning with some knowledge of the debits of emigration; missing the mountains and the glens.

The exile returns, and when he lands in London he would undoubtedly feel lost at first in such a city of change, and long to hear a Scotch tongue; or tarry awhile at some Scottish rendezvous. In this connection I would bring to notice 'The Royal Scottish Corporation', better known as 'the Scottish Centre in London'.

This body, housed at Fleur-de-lis Court, Fetter Lane, London, E.C.4, was founded in the 17th century, and so has 300 years of history. It was on 30th June 1665 that it received from Charles II its first Charter, which declared, *inter alia*, 'it shall be called The Scottish Hospital of the Foundation of King Charles the Second, and that for ever after there should be eight able, honest and discreet men of the Scottish nation . . . who shall be, and be called, the Governors'. The Corporation's origins, however, stretch back fifty years further, for the accession of James VI to the throne of England in 1603 had resulted in a rapid increase in the Scottish community in London.

The Corporation has enjoyed the practical support of British monarchs since the reign of Queen Victoria; and H.M. Queen Elizabeth II is its present Patron. The premises comprise a large hall, committee rooms, a council chamber and offices. The building has become the headquarters of many Scottish Societies. The letting accommodation in the building also contributes to the Corporation's income; in fact, most of the income comes from that source.

In short, this building can be looked upon as a sort of 'Scottish embassy'—an oasis in the south for those of the north.

* * *

Wester Ross and north-west Sutherland is literally covered with mountains, and many of these peaks stand up in isolation—not just points in a massive range—and so can be seen in all their majesty.

Other writers may quite easily launch into more lyrical description of these mountains and their scenic beauty than I can; but in this respect I am reminded of the Glaswegian gazing up at everything, and saying, 'Whaur's yer Matterhorn the noo?' Surely this description is apt enough, devoid as it is of any high-brow fluency.

Regarding Scottish mountaineering one often comes upon the word MUNRO, which means a mountain of 3000 feet and over. On maps, mountains in Scotland are called Beinn so and so, but anglicised to Ben. The Munros have been tabled as such since 1890. Sir Hugh T. Munro, Bt., of Lindertis must have found his self-imposed task of card-indexing the three-thousanders a fascinating one, and he almost climbed all of them in the leisurely Victorian days. Not only was he breaking new ground in listing his discoveries, but he had to decide which should be considered distinct mountains, and which were subsidiary 'tops'. Today's figure is 276 'Munros' with a further 268 'tops'; a tally of 544 'bumps' above this magic altitude.

We have surmounted the decimalisation crisis, and the next thing I suppose, will be the metric system. This will be somewhat devastating, namely the conversion to metres of the heights of the Scottish Bens. Take the case of Ben Nevis, 4406 feet high; it will be reduced—if my arithmetic holds good—to a soulless 1342 metres; or Ben Lomond (3192 ft.) descending to the indignity of 972 metres. With the metric system swishing round my brain cells I suppose I'll be taking a 39 cm. collar, weigh out just a fraction too many kilos, drink coffee by the litre, drive a totally incalculable number of kilometres in a year; and for amusement, start assessing the weight of the paper used in this book in grammes per square metre! Am wondering if all this is coming about as an aid for people going abroad for their holidays; in the same breath as the government is spending more and more money in getting more visitors to come to Britain. If so, it seems a funny policy to me. And if my usual smiling face gets dimmed, I'll put it down to the faceless ones of Whitehall.

I hope now the first impact of decimalising (ugh!) is over, we are accommodating ourselves calmly to a new world; though it will not be the sacred world of Shangri-La. I suppose most of the Highland shops will have their vintage 1940 £.s.d. machines up on a backroom shelf under a polythene cover and carefully preserved; for who knows another Government might bring back the old pounds, shillings and pence régime? As it is now, these old machines look like something knocked up on a wet evening in the Ark, by Shem, Ham and Japeth. One day, perhaps in the year 2000, offers may be made from the Victoria and Albert Museum? One Highland shopkeeper told me he looked upon the change as 'dismalisation'.

*   *   *

There is the story of two Sutherland worthies discussing politics and the change-over in currency, sitting on a bench on a fine sunny morning in the old-world village of Tongue. 'Look here,' Hamish said to his pal Kenny after lighting his old clay pipe and having had a couple of drams over the Ben Loyal bar, 'how many pence are there in the pound?' 'Why, 240,' said Kenny, who had years ago gone to the old Tongue primary school. 'Right,' said Hamish, 'now how many are there to be in the new pound?' 'One hundred,' Kenny quickly replied, meaningly for he felt he was a knowledgeable fellow. 'Right again, my boy,' says Hamish, 'right again; well who's getting the 140 Kenny m'boy?'

* * *

Let us now turn over the pages written by a Colonial Englishman living in Gairloch, Wester Ross.

The book starts with Sutherland in the far north of Scotland. Of the Highlands and Islands of Scotland the former Chairman of the H. and I. Development Board once said that nowhere in the world had he found a landscape so beautiful or so sad. 'The country,' he went on to say, 'was one of the most ancient in the world fashioned by the interminable processes of geology, sculptured by the sea and the ice. The sadness had been made by man.'

It is true the ancient Caledonian forest was ravaged and burnt by successive generations from the Vikings onward; the people were harried and destroyed, not only by the Redcoats after Culloden in 1746, but by the landlords—often English—who took over the vast tracts of northern lands and drove the people out (the evictions) to make way for sheep, as I have said.

People with only a superficial knowledge of Scottish history think the martial exploits of the Highlanders (the Clansmen) were entirely confined to conflicts caused by feuds. This is wrong, for the Clans played a most important part in the historic battles which moulded the destiny of Scotland, and when the unity of the nation was at stake, the lesser differences of the clans were forgotten.

When the King of Alba called on Highland Chiefs, and the Chiefs on clansmen, the blood feuds of generations were laid aside, and the clans fought shoulder to shoulder, kinsmen in arms, in a common cause. The first instance of clan unity occasioned by a national crisis that appears in history, is found in the pages of Tacitus where an inspiring picture is presented to us, of all the tribes north of the Grampians combining under a common leader, Galgacus, to resist the Roman invaders.

Galgacus then appears at the dawn of history as a great national leader, ready to sacrifice everything for the sake of liberty, and independence. The inspiring spirit which he symbolised is found to run like a golden thread through the subsequent history of Scotland. The tale has it that the warriors before going to battle used to go to the nunnery so that the holy women might put a 'sian' or charm upon them against the dangers of battle. This was a living echo from the religion of the pagan past.

When the clansmen were gathering round the standard or marching into the fray, the pipes would always be playing the appropriate tunes, and long ago there would be one man who would recite battle songs of the noble heroes from which they sprung and telling of their great deeds of valour, so exhorting and inciting them to emulate the same. Even among so many brave heroes there would always be a redoubtable few; and so everyone was filled with determined vigour, and strained every muscle to the utmost so making heroic displays.

The decay of living tradition is a deplorable loss to our knowledge of the glorious past; and to the national character and culture.

Before reading further, I must let you into the big secret as to how to enjoy the Highlands of Scotland to the full. It is to take a three weeks holiday instead of a fortnight, in order to get ten days; if you see what I mean? I don't suppose you do, so I will explain. The first week is for settling-in to know the people, and winding down and getting all thoughts of work out of your mind; the last four days are for worrying about the arrangements for packing the car and the journey home. The fitting-in of all the small cases and the dozens of odds and ends collected on your holiday, is *some* job, believe me, and your sigh of relief when the boot of the car *does* finally shut, is worth all those last sleepless nights thinking if you would have to charter a local van as well as a trailer to take everything home to 75 Acacia Avenue, N.W. London. However, you've made it, as your wife said you would during those four anxious days; and as you finally drive off you'll be saying 'it's Scotland again next year'. And this is the prayer the landlady and the local shopkeeper will be saying too!

En avant then, to the Highlands . . . and after you have been and seen all I have to tell you, you'll come back again to be sure; or in the Gaelic THIG SIGH AIR AIS A RITHIST. In effect you'll be whispering 'absence makes the heart grow fonder'. And so it does.

The French have a saying *L'absence touche à l'amour comme un vent touche à une flamme; il souffle les petites, et il souffle en l'air les grandes*; the literal translation being 'absence affects love like a wind affects a flame. It blows out the little ones, and blows up the big ones'. In the Highlands, it's the 'big ones'.

Although in the north-west here, you may be motoring or walking alone, yet being engulfed by such scenic beauty and the vastness of the country you will assuredly have the feeling that '*you never walk alone*'.

In the summer months in many parts of the Highlands, you will come across banks upon banks of the sweet-scented flowering broom. Carpets of broom in some districts; so much so you'll think you are 'midst a perfume factory producing Chanel No. 5.

We must therefore do all in our power to preserve the Highland heritage; to go all out to rub out the faceless ones— the paid witnesses on behalf of developers. The boys with the bulldozers are behind them. They sit on committees and wait to see which side is going to win, and they cast their vote on the winning side. When they see woods in the spring they do not look at the leaves against the sky, but think of the price the timber will fetch. When they see an old house with a garden round it, they think of how many bungalows they can build on the site. They call that 'judicious infilling'. Open space to them is a gift from Heaven. They seize on the generosity of their forebears and build to overlook it, a monster slab of flats, offices or hotel.

THIS MUST NOT HAPPEN HERE . . .

When the Forestry Department open up new land and plant young trees, they erect a six-foot fence to keep deer from jumping over and eating the young shoots. I fancy we would need something like a ten-foot concrete wall to keep out unwelcome developers.

SUTHERLAND

... (a country of wide-eyed wonderment
that I count among my souvenirs) ...

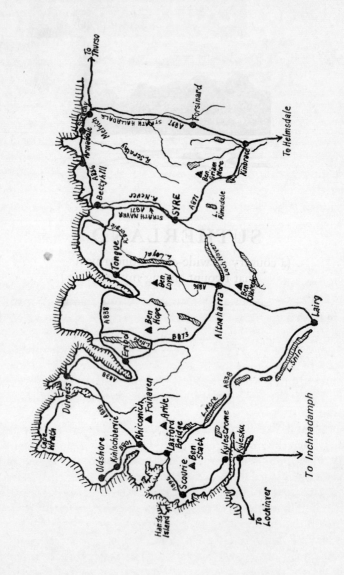

Sutherland

SUTHERLAND is an unspoiled paradise; its vastness is a reality. Its beauty is to be found in the feeling of space, coupled with its majestic mountains and moorlands engendering the feeling of freedom; a feeling of peace in its relaxing environments. All its surroundings stimulate quiet thought, and such an inborn spirit as this is surely more than welcome in this Concorde–Jumbo age in which we find ourselves living today.

In short it is a country of spectacular charm and haunting appeal to the transient visitors—yearly becoming more numerous. That the country holds an embarrassment of riches in all forms, is an understatement, for Sutherland is placed for ever in its wild and natural state. The mountains are a monument to the Creator's foresight. When Time or lightning crashes a tall fir or birch to the ground, there it must stay, untouched, to become first, part of the land and then a tree again in nature's own sweet way. This is the law. But the mountains never crash; they are there for all time.

Sutherland, like Wester Ross, is a rendezvous with history and legend; it has the fifth largest area of the counties in Scotland, but a very small population, and so this leaves plenty of room and plenty of open space for more people, either as settlers or visitors. It is a 3-coasted county, North, East and West. A relatively heavy rainfall in the western sea-board is balanced by a dry climate on the east.

It may be said Sutherland is not a county but a continent— a continent on one's own doorstep. The variety of its way of life stems not only from a rugged history but from the natural contrasts of the land and sea upon which Sutherland has depended. It is a paradox of nature that the finer the landscape the tougher it is to earn a living in it. But challenge in Sutherland has bred resourcefulness; lobsters are flown daily to Paris; tweed from the renowned Brora mills for fashioning in America; seed potatoes marketed in Spain and Cyprus. By workmanship, adaptability and the quality of its products Sutherland strives to be known— and not only by its exiles. The Forestry Commission's continuing investment (as also that of private landowners) is very evident in the large areas of new planting seen from the main roads. The fishing industry centred at Lochinver and Kinlochbervie has attracted the interest of major developments and continues growing month by month. There are great potentials in this line. The two ports named rank third in value to all the white fish ports in Scotland; this speaks volumes for the initiative shown; and is most praiseworthy. It shows there are still men of vision living in the county; and pier improvements at Lochinver and the comprehensive proposals at Kinlochbervie—a delightful rendez-vous for visitors—give every encouragement for the future of this prosperous industry.

Sutherland is a huge geographical slice of Scotland, with a very small overall population, as I have said; and so the administration of such an area has many headaches with which to contend. In a Government announcement (1971) of proposed alterations in Local Government administration as from 1975, TAIN and ARDGAY are to be brought under Sutherland's domain. Local Government, wherever it may be, *has* to concern itself with people—the people who dwell within its jurisdiction; its own people. And it is the duty of the governing authority (the County Council) to see to it that the people whom it governs, and who constitute this sparse population, whether from choice or by necessity, *are* given the utmost service and consideration they deserve.

There is still the feeling—and I know it from the host of letters I receive—that Sutherland is considered too remote, and too barren a land to visit. This needs correcting. It may be remote, but this remoteness has a charm of its own, believe it or not; but the services the ruling county authority extends are nigh one hundred per cent. This philosophy of remoteness has had its day. Its 'beyond-ness' and its attendant service can hardly be equalled anywhere in Britain. The communities in Sutherland are snug communities; and this is rare. In respect of the north and the western seaboard, it is *Shangri-La* at its best. The west and the north villages *are* villages; it is only on the east coast, like Dornoch and the others, that villages emerge as small towns; which in turn have their own particular attractions.

The roads throughout the county are excellent; there is no strain in motoring. This, surely, is a matter for comfort compared with English motorways, where speed is the order of the day— not the Order of the Road. When someone was told that a man was run over every day in Glasgow, he replied 'I don't believe it; no man could put up with that!' Up north, if you have an an accident and knock over a crofter, you could always get away with it by telling the village constable that although this happened the man admitted it was his fault, as he had been knocked down before! Should a cow barge up against your car, you may later on learn that it often did such things, for it was half-witted!

Sutherland may be called 'the sleeping giant', for it appears to have untapped mineral wealth. Sutherland of black Clearance memories; Sutherland of fond remembrance to its many famous exiles; Sutherland, the holiday haunts and land of loch and river and mountains; a land where so few people find a livelihood. This is Sutherland, a veritable Shangri-La until the Clearances came about (see later chapter). Those memories are still alive. A short time ago I was speaking to a dear old lady, a Mackay, in the Strathnaver valley, who with tears in her eyes told me she was the last of her own forebears. The last of the Mohicans. Her people had been forcibly driven out and sent overseas to America. Was she bitter? Yes, she was; and so would any right-thinking person be. Upon visiting the abandoned crofting areas in Strathnaver or in fact seeing any other of the dozens of districts that were subjected to those notorious brutalities, one cannot fail to sense the poignant atmosphere still lingering and still haunting those pitiful ruined crofts and steadings. Highland memories are long. If witchcraft were still practised—as it is in some parts of the East— then I am sure the curses laid upon the Clearance perpetrators would take centuries to evaporate . . . if ever. The Rape of the Highlands.

Though a sparsely populated Highland county, many enterprises in the commercial field can be quoted.

The Clynelish Distillery in Brora is now one of the most up-to-date and best equipped in the Scottish whisky industry. The Brora Brick Coy., recently taken over by an Aberdeen firm,

is now solely engaged in making farm drain tiles; the Brora
Colliery has found a new lease of life with the opening up of a
new seam. The name of T. M. Hunter of Brora is one associated
with tweeds, yarns and travelling rugs the world over. It is a
family concern, grown up from small beginnings in 1901 to be
one of the biggest employers of labour in that district. The
building and civil engineering firm of Alexander Sutherland,
Golspie, is the largest private employer of labour in the county.
Recently it took in hand the roadworks and bridge crossing the
Kyle of Tongue (Tongue to Melness); a contract worth something in the region of three-quarters of a million pounds, plus.

The family of Rapson has been associated with Helmsdale for
more than sixty years . . . at one time the only village store.
Unscrewing and giving out petrol from two-gallon tins, pouring
it into a funnel into a car's tank and then the single hand-operated
pump, was their first link with the internal combustion engine;
for in those early days one relied on the horse and cart for travel
and conveyance of goods. After the last war they embarked on
a haulage business, and today their fleet carries general merchandise, wool, and livestock all over the place. At Lairg, the focal
point of North and West Sutherland, the multiple firm of
Sutherland Transport and Trading Co. Ltd. serve that area,
operating one of the few privately-owned public bus services
remaining in Scotland. In fact the company, incorporating its
subsidiary Pulford (Scotland) Ltd., plays an integral part in the
life of the district and widely scattered areas. They run the
Royal Mail carriers, the ambulance; and at Lairg itself have a
large garage, repair shop, car showroom, radio and T/V sales and
electrical department. A case of you ask for it, we have it! The
company were responsible for bringing T/V to Lairg and Lochinver by installing piped television for these districts. From
Bonar Bridge too, they operate a long-distance haulage service
for general merchandise and from Kinlochbervie on the west
coast, a fish haulage service. The undertaking is owned by
Grosvenor Estates and trustees of the second Duke of Westminster.

All in all, Sutherland has seen tremendous development in the
last 20 years. This is a crofting county, and the many small
crofters are keen and hard working and take advantage of the
subsidies and grants which come their way. One has only to go

to the livestock markets (the chief one is at Lairg) in August, September and October to see how true that is. Usually more than 30,000 North Country Cheviot lambs are sold every August at a one-day sale in Lairg; and it is heartening to see the quality of the stock drawn from every corner of this vast county. Buyers come up from the Borders, and even from England. The growing tourist trade is also providing the crofters with a profitable sideline in the bed-and-breakfast business. I was amused at seeing one notice bearing the sign 'Bed. Find your own Breakfast.'

Then there is the shooting season that brings trade, though it is generally said by locals that the grouse season which attracts hundreds of guns from all over Britain heralds the end of summer in the North; and when October is over, one begins to hear the pheasant lamenting his absentee landlord!

In the Education field, Sutherland has gone ahead; one has only to see the magnificent school at Brora, to believe this. The new schools at Altnaharra, Bettyhill and Tongue must have cost over £1 million.

The approach to Sutherland on the west is by the route from Ullapool—along the coast road from Lochinver; a narrow tortuous road but one of scenic grandeur, by Stoer, Clachnessie, Drumbeg, Nedd to Kylesku Ferry; thence to Scourie with the wonderful bay of Eddrachillis on the left, where, if it is a fine day, you will linger for long enough admiring the scene. Thence to Laxford Bridge, Rhiconich and Durness taking in the many mountain peaks and countless lochans; a veritable rugged coastline with many sandy beaches to explore, and to laze on at leisure. At Durness you are near Cape Wrath and on journeying down both sides of Loch Eriboll, passing Ben Hope and Ben Loyal, and again down both sides of the Kyle of Tongue you reach this favourite old-time village, *Tongue*, where I have spent many pleasurable months the last few years.

As for fishing, the county of Sutherland has been aptly described as an angler's paradise. Lochs, rivers and estuaries provide sea trout and salmon fishing; and according to the opinion of acknowledged experts, the Oykel is the finest salmon river in Britain, if not in the world. The river Naver, and loch Naver in the Altnaharra and Strathnaver area, is another celebrated district for discriminating fishers.

As to this fishing business, there is a lake in America in the

state of Massachusetts which is called LAKE CHARGOGGUGOGG-
MONCHAUGG (for short!). Its name is derived from the Algonquin
Indian words meaning 'You fish on your side; we fish on our
side. Nobody fishes in the middle.' Quite a thought?

*   *   *

This, then, is a précis of what you can expect if you should
ever visit Sutherland. As I live peacefully in Wester Ross I have
no reason to exaggerate over another county!

I propose now to take readers along with me, in dealing more
specifically with the many aspects and pearls to be seen in journeying through this Shangri-La country.

*   *   *

In my last book, I started the journey to Bonar Bridge—the
gateway to Sutherland as I have mentioned earlier—from Inverness; but to eliminate repetition, we will just make for Dingwall,
the county town of Ross and Cromarty, turning off to the right
at the town's traffic lights . . . for the North. The road straight
to the Sutherland boundary is a main road, and one can easily
reach Bonar Bridge in just over one hour. After passing through
Evanton, you commence to see a little of the moorlands, but not
until you reach the Inn at Altnamain—a lonely spot and particularly desolate and bleak in winter—do you really come to
anything touching upon Highland-fare. You have come over
the Struie, a fairly steep, though gradual, climb, and at a welcome
vantage spot (made available by the A.A.) looking over the
Dornoch Firth, you get the first glimpse of Sutherland. It is an
exceptionally fine view on a clear day. To the left, the firth
stretches up past Bonar Bridge, where it turns into the Kyle of
Sutherland. Far beyond, the mighty hills break the skyline:
Ben More Assynt, Ben Loyal and many more. On your right
you can just see the spire of Dornoch Cathedral, apparently
surrounded by woods, rising from the flat links which border the
North Sea. The whole prospect is still something as unspoiled
by the hand of man as anything surviving in Britain today.
Shortly after leaving this vantage point we are soon at Ardgay,
where the big imposing bridge crossing over to Bonar Bridge
looms up, and crossing it—we are in Sutherland. The name
Bonar means 'the end of the ford'.

I think few motorists may be aware of the interesting plaque on the bridge spanning this kyle. It reads as follows:

'Traveller, stop and read with gratitude the names of the Parliamentary commissioners appointed in 1803 to direct the making of above 500 miles of roads through the Highlands of Scotland, and of numerous bridges, particularly those at Beauly, Scuddel, Bonar, Fleet and Helmsdale connecting those roads.'

The names of the commissioners are given, and the inscription states that the bridge was begun in September 1811 and finished in November 1812.

Thomas Telford was the architect. The stone was placed there by George Dempster of Dunnichen in 1815. The original bridge was destroyed by flood and ice in January 1892. Ross and Sutherland County Councils joined in re-erecting it. It was reopened in July 1893. William Arroll & Co. were the engineers. This firm built the Forth railway bridge. The bridge is giving rise to concern because of its structural weakness and its limited load-carrying capacity, and there is little doubt that in the very near future this old Bonar Bridge will need to be replaced by a bigger and safer structure parallel to the present bridge.

Turning left once over the bridge, we are on our way westwards to Lairg, which is the focal point to the north and northwest. In doing so we pass Carbisdale Castle (the scene of Montrose's final defeat by the Covenanters, described in more detail in a later chapter), Invershin and its notable (salmon) Falls. There are two roads from here to Lairg; the lower, and prettier run, and the higher road passing Altnagar Hotel (a former mansion house of Carnegie). This latter road is a quicker route.

Many roads lead out of Lairg: one to Tongue in the north; one to Lochinver and Inchnadamph and Ullapool; one to Overscaig and Laxford Bridge (estates belonging to Anne, Duchess of Westminster), Scourie and Kinlochbervie; one to Golspie by the new road through Rogart—a very pleasant run where you are within easy distance of Dornoch, Brora and Helmsdale. Yes, Lairg is a good central spot; a nice wee village and never crowded even at the height of the season. All posts for the north and northwest operate from Lairg.

I have often thought that years ago, if a light 2'-6" railway had been planned to operate along all these great scenic routes, what an attraction it would have caused and how profitable it

would have been.   Such a similar scheme (as has been in vogue in
Wales) would have paid off handsomely.   But now it is too late;
we have 'missed the boat'.   Our brilliant planners must have been
asleep at the time.

Without further comment, I am now making for Tongue at
a leisurely 30 or 35 miles an hour along a fairly straight and good
roadway, passing Crask and Altnaharra.   Lairg to Tongue is 37
miles, so it is an easy one and a half hour's journey.   There is just
an Inn at Crask set amidst the moors, and in winter it must be
an isolated spot.   From this 'Foreign Legion' landmark, it is a
pleasant journey to Altnaharra through Strath Vagastie, though
not very scenic except for its distant mountains.

Reaching *Altnaharra*, you seem to have arrived at an oasis in
the centre of Sutherland, for you come to one of the rare and
compact communities in the far north;   one of the 'snuggest of
snug' hamlets I know of in my many travels.   It is also an excellent centre from which to explore the northern Highlands.

Altnaharra, and its surrounds, is owned by Mr. Marcus
Kimball, M.P. for Gainsborough, Lincolnshire, who is well loved
by his tenants, being most co-operative and enterprising and—
as I know personally—far from being an absentee landlord.   Both
he and his wife spend many months up at their Lodge in the
summer, whilst he himself is invariably in residence for a few
days each month out of the summer season, despite his arduous
Parliamentary commitments.   Mr. Kimball continues to make his
estate more of a personal adventure, which not all landowners do.

Altnaharra is a Highland community in the *real* sense of the
word.   There are quite a few new houses, a new modern school
and a small post office 'manned' by a very pleasant lady, Jean
Ross.   The estate seems to have the right balance for the Highlands, viz. farming, forestry, tourism and sport (fishing and
stalking).

Altnaharra Lodge, a magnificent edifice (with an out-of-this-
world view of Loch Naver from the ornate dining room, lounge
and bedrooms) was burnt down in 1906.   It was rebuilt as the
best and the last, that the Sutherland estate built; and it was
erected to the tenants' specification, through architect J. W.
Baxendale.   With its stately staircase, the whole structure is far
and away above today's architectural standards.

Go where you will in the Scottish Highlands, you are sure to

come upon a private, or shooting lodge. Some hide themselves
away in woods of birch and pine; others survey their glen from
some vantage point on a hill slope like the tea plantation bungalows in India and Ceylon; whilst some are stuck in the middle of
nowhere! But many former shooting lodges are now no more
than empty shells, whilst others have been converted into hotels
or hostels. (Carbisdale Castle is now a hostel.)

These lodges are mostly a product of the 19th century, though
their origin is much earlier. In those fabulous days, a Highland
hunt was mounted like a military operation. The hunters rode
to the forest in cavalcade with bows and blunder-busses and might
be away a week or more. The gillies set up camps and field
kitchens; there was an abundance of food—venison, salmon,
hill hare, grouse, ptarmigan, and the cooks would have spits
turning on an open fire. As for drink, wine and whisky flowed
like water in a hill burn!

Queen Victoria had a great liking for Highland lodges and
such sports as deer stalking appealed to her romantic nature,
though she had no inclination to handle gun, rifle or rod. Mainly
it was the nearness of the hills and the feeling of freedom that
captivated her. It may be said, the rise and fall of the Highland
shooting lodges cover Queen Victoria's long reign; but lodges
were still being built as late as the turn of the century. Generally
speaking a decline of the ancient and aristocratic Scottish season
became very noticeable in the 20th century, and the reason was
largely economic. The upkeep costs of a Highland estate began
to soar. However, these lodges are not all left untenanted. Many
still serve in their original function; others have changed their
status, but are still useful in a variety of ways. They cannot be
written off as so much Victorian lumber. In its own glen 'The
Lodge' can still play an important part.

Reverting to Altnaharra, there is a very interesting and
descriptive Game Book, *A Veteran Sportsman's Diary*, written by
Mr. Charles H. Ackroyd (a Yorkshireman) who was born in
1848, and who in his day was one of the greatest sportsmen in
respect of shooting and fishing. He made many visits to Scotland
and particularly to Altnaharra where even as early as 1862 to 1871
he records phenomenal shoots totalling close on 7000 'game'
made up of grouse, blackgame, snipe, ducks, woodcock, great
plover, ptarmigan, partridge and others.

In 1856 his father took Altnaharra from the Duke of Sutherland. At that time the railway was open only as far as Perth, and so they had to drive from there by horse carriage, a distance of 230 miles. The Altnaharra shootings then were 15 miles by 12 miles (far less than now) and they had the whole of the river Naver fishing in spring. There was no regular lodge then at Altnaharra, and so they utilised some of the rooms in the then small Inn, having a dining room and a sitting room to themselves. In those far-off days they did not find it necessary to move about with a ton or so of luggage; just one suit on, and the other off, was about all they had. The few extra stores they needed, they got from a merchant at Lairg; as well as powder, shot, wads and caps, and their drink was the wine of the country.

In his diary he says when they first went up to Altnaharra in 1856, his father took an old gamekeeper from Yorkshire. He appeared in those days to be a typical Yorkshireman, always wearing a tall white beaver hat whilst out shooting. He and his wife had a grandson who used to come up and be with them in the summer. Going into the little house they occupied at Altnaharra, 'our Mr. Ackroyd' found the grandson reading the paper to the old man one evening. He listened for a while, but couldn't make head or tail of what the boy was reading out, but by watching his head, he found that he was reading the paper right across all the columns! The old people seemed to be quite satisfied. Those were the days!

Deer stalking was another sport of this great old-timer. The same gentleman went shooting in Switzerland, Turkey, Corfu, Italy, Norway, Iceland, Canada, Ireland; and indeed a host of other countries. But he always came back to Altnaharra; his oasis.

In all, this grand veteran, who lived for well over the allotted three score years and ten, shot just in Scotland and England alone, nearly 140,000 birds; to say nothing of what he shot in Ireland and all the other countries I have named; to say nothing of the fish he landed! Truly he was a Nimrod; a mighty hunter.

*   *   *

Carrying on from the Lodge, we come to Altnaharra Hotel, which is a famous fishing hotel, and ably managed by Charles McLaren and his very charming wife. This great 'Mine Host',

Charles, is a former British and Casting champion; and is the holder of the world record for Salmon Fly distance—namely, sixty-four yards. What a phenomenal cast; just short of three times the length of a cricket pitch.

Twenty-one miles from Lairg; sixteen miles from Tongue; and now I am hastening off from Altnaharra to that northern village Tongue. But before doing so, just think of Altnaharra's position. It is miles away in a sense from civilisation—and stands ALONE in its majesty 'mongst space surrounded by moorland. An oasis, as I have said, and perfectly restful, which city dwellers ought to welcome, in which to gather their scattered wits. I look upon Altnaharra as a replica of Shangri-La; and should a small monastery be built on a nearby hill, we would have to my mind, not a Lost Horizon, but a found and a very living horizon; with Ben Klibreck forming its southern skyline:

> . . . A dear little spot off the beaten track,
> Once you've found it, you're sure to come back . . .

Forestry is gripping the peat bogs around this area. Plantations, fenced against deer and sheep, are well established across the river Mudale. Against Altnaharra's background of Ben Klibreck (3154 feet)—and as you continue north to Tongue—the spectacular and beautiful Ben Loyal (2504 feet) comes into view, looking blue in the spring's morning sunlight. Although it is not the highest in Sutherland, it is one of those mountains which seems to alter shape, looking different from different places. Then further to the north-west is the red-sandstone cone of Ben Hope (3040 feet). Delightful surroundings. To see only these in a visit to Sutherland, is to have seen enough, and more than enough. Cattle graze, and sheep are gathered from the hills at shearing time. Sheep and the Highland Clearances? From 1790 to 1850 it was a sad, sad time for those crofters, as I recall at length in a later chapter. One observer, I find from old records, counted 250 fires on that evil night of the burnings. One minister at Achness at the end of Loch Naver, had tried to persuade his flock to accept the removals as necessary—but he was absent on that day! Later, his small church was dismantled, and some of the timber found its way into the structure of the Inn; now the Altnaharra Hotel.

It all makes sad reading; and this amongst a godly people who were content to work and mind their own business.

*   *   *

Mythology, legend and history intertwine with these ancient rocks in song and tale in this oasis; and in the hotel over the cocktail bar at night there will be only one topic—fish; those caught and those that slipped the gallows. One story I heard was of a fisher who caught a monster salmon, which took him more than an hour to tire out, and to gradually draw it near the bank. He had no gaff or landing net beside him, but somehow or other he managed to tether the mighty fish to a tree, whilst he rushed madly along to one of his pals fishing nearby for help. When the two of them got back, the tree was gone!

Glasses would clink over the bar that night, and such familiar requests as two ½ litres again, Charles; just when you have the time! In these fishing hotels, there is always a large fish weigh-scale on hand to weigh the catches, and a book to record them. Nowadays it will be a metric-scale of course, so the salmon will be going over to the kilogram. How much was it, Donald? A six-pounder, Lachlan; sorry, m'bhoy, I mean 3 kilos. Great is the march of progress.

In touring Sutherland, I must say I've never met so many cattle grids as in western Sutherland. There must be scores dotted around the countryside; and on coming to one, if you don't change down to low gear, you and your car will be bumped sky-high. Should you have children in the car, they just love to hear the 'Burrr' as you rattle over the rails, and look eagerly for the next one. I remember one motorist telling me, his small family excitedly asked him to reverse—and drive over it once more!

All over the Highlands, the roads are good with a tar macadam surface. John Loudon Macadam (1756–1836), an Ayrshire man, was a veritable Colossus of Roads, who invented the durable composition for roadways, which bears his name 'macadamised'.

In 1871 the first minister for a period of 52 years was or-dained at Altnaharra 'in the Heights of Strathnaver'. The former minister at Achness (Rev. Donald Sage) and 1600 of his people were evicted on a Tuesday—the Whitsuntide of 1819.

CHAPTER 3

TONGUE AND DISTRICT

WE have now arrived at Tongue, and will stay awhile, for like Lairg it is a focal point and a good centre for visiting many regions of special beauty. This little, old-time, unspoiled village is situate on the north coast of Sutherland and looks upon the lovely Kyle of Tongue. To the east there is Bettyhill, Melvich and Thurso-way. To the west, Loch Eriboll, Durness, the Kyle of Durness and Cape Wrath; then downwards to Rhiconich, Kinlochbervie, Laxford Bridge, Scourie . . . and a host of other interesting places in this real Shangri-La country.

Tongue is 16 miles beyond Altnaharra, along a good road; one that you can see for miles ahead at times.

A mile after leaving Altnaharra is a cross-road; to the right the road leads along Loch Naver to the Strathnaver valley, coming out near Bettyhill; the road to the left goes by Strathmore to Loch Hope and Ben Hope and comes out near Loch Eriboll.

Between Altnaharra and Tongue, you only come across one shepherd's house and the lodge bordering on Loch Loyal. Is there any other district in the British Isles where you are so alone and possess such a feeling of contentment in a 16-mile stretch?

As one approaches Tongue (the country of the Mackays, whose Chief is Lord Reay) one looks down on a lovely panorama—the Kyle of Tongue, with the village itself (a Norse name, TUNGA, meaning as one may imagine 'a tongue of land'; or as the Vikings saw it, the Kyle of Tongue itself being a tongue of water) lying snugly below. This kyle is one of the most pleasant of the northern sea-lochs. The best view of Ben Loyal is obtained from the west side of the kyle. Legend says that Ben Loyal is full of little men working in a big fairy foundry there. But I would

stress it was *not* those little men, but some of the evicted men from
Strathnaver and elsewhere who built the road from Tongue to
Durness.

The land around is green, rich and well-wooded. Out to sea
in the bay is Rabbit island. On an eminence not far from the
village, is the ruin of Castle Varrich—an ancient peel—a square
tower said to have been the residence of Kali Hundason who
made an effort to conquer Scotland on the death of Malcolm II.
Tongue, in earlier days, was named Kirkiboll, its Gaelic name
meaning 'the head of Mackay's salt water'; and its air smells
wooingly. Tongue House is now the seat of Elizabeth, Countess
of Sutherland. It was erected in Cromwell's time by Lord Reay
of those days. I have been through this beautiful mansion and
viewed many of the ancient mottos and crests adorning the walls.
The Duchess is seldom at Tongue, for her Highland home is at
Uppat near Brora, where she spends a great deal of her time,
when not in her London house.

As I have said, Tongue is an unspoiled Highland village, but
it has all the services one can wish. Two hotels—the Tongue
hotel as you enter from the south, the other the Ben Loyal hotel
in the centre of the village (opposite a newly created car park)—
provide excellent accommodation and splendid fare.

There is only one church in Tongue, a Church of Scotland
denomination. It is a perfectly sweet church built on the style
one might say of missionary churches I have seen in Ceylon and
South America. I gave a very full description of it in *Highland
Pearls*. It has the Rev. Alfred McClintock, B.D., as its able
pastor, who lives in St. Andrew's manse nearby. He and his wife
(who helps him considerably in all the church's many week-day
activities) are well loved by the Tongue people.

In the late 1700's there was much martial blood amongst the
inhabitants of the Tongue and Reay districts, and the Presbytery
and ministers had to take stern measures to suppress such heathen
conduct in their endeavours to instil into them the necessity of
worship. Although I have said this north-west Shangri-La
country has the sense of 'Timelessness', the people used to forget
the days, and which day *was* the Sabbath.

An amusing story is told of a few families who were so
thoroughly confused, or 'obfuscated' in intellect and careless as
to the flight of Time, that they frequently forgot when the

Sabbath came round; but they were reminded of it in the following manner: one of their neighbours, a man of some substance and superior intelligence to the rest—and somewhat of a casual friend of the pastor—kept a correct reckoning of Time, and had acquired amongst them the high title of 'Lord of Syre'. This personage every Sabbath morning regularly donned a long-tailed scarlet coat, and going to a small hillock near his house, stood there for about half an hour, to indicate to the community that the day of rest had come, when all labour, even to the grinding of grain on their lands, should be suspended. As soon as the signal was observed by neighbours, they would run in, exclaiming in Gaelic, 'Make haste, and lay aside your work. It is the Sabbath; his lordship is out in his red coat. So hasten and prepare for worship.'

*   *   *

The visiting Nurse lives at Melness, across the kyle. There is the usual-type small post office that you always find in the Highlands, with its chatty and obliging postmistress, who has a real sense of humour. Once when I was in, passing the time of day with her, she introduced me to her married daughter and husband; and being of an inquisitive turn of mind, I asked the old lady what her son-in-law did. 'Well,' she said, 'he's not with the County Council on the roads; he works!' (Talking of roads, during the winter months, with icy patches on them, the Council's men and lorries, shovel salt on to the surface; at least they do where I live in Gairloch, which quickly melts both snow and ice. Some districts had to stop this practice, and mix sand with the salt, for it was found all the local housewives were scraping up the salt to use it for boiling with their potatoes!)

Then there is the local resident banker, who will not turn a blind eye if you should want any ready cash; and of course the Doctor, who takes a very real interest in your ailments. Once, whilst staying in Tongue for a while, I suddenly developed acute rheumatics in the knee and lumbago in my back. Pals in distress I suppose? Two years later when I chanced to meet him in the village, I reminded him of that trouble, and of his having cured it. 'Yes, that's right, Bee Jay, I remember.' 'And you told me,' I said, 'to keep away from water.' 'Quite likely,' he replied. 'Well,' I retorted, 'do you think I could wash myself now?'

He is a most likeable doctor and his wife is very charming. (I think I have mentioned two charming folk; one in Altnaharra, and now one in Tongue. I must be more careful?)

Then last, but not least, I would mention the key-man of the village, Gordon R. Burr of 'Burr's Empire' as I call him. He and his wife, Jessie (yet another lady of charm) and family operate the large grocery store in Tongue. Additional to this the firm are general merchants, motor engineers, haulage contractors, coal merchants, and until recently operated the mail bus service for many years to and from Thurso. Their daily vans go all over the place. MacBrayne's of the north-west could well be another name for Burr's Empire.

Gordon, an Orcadian, was born in St. Margaret's Hope. The then small business was acquired by his father, Peter Burr, on 1st May 1913, nearly 60 years ago. It belonged to one Robert Garden of Kirkwall. At that time, his father was assisted by his two eldest sons, Peter and Charles, both of whom however made the supreme sacrifice in the First World War. The father was joined later by another son, Norman, who ultimately went into business on his own account in Stronsay in 1925, and died there in 1937. It was then that Gordon came into the business straight from school, and was later joined in turn by his younger brother Leslie. The elderly father retired to Tain in 1938, leaving these two brothers to carry on the good work. Then Leslie joined the Forces and saw service at Dunkirk, Tobruk, Salerno and the Rhine crossing, and came back to the firm in 1945. In 1956, he branched out on his own, like his brother Norman.

In the days before motor cars became common, one of the best known household phrases in these remote villages and straths of N.-W. Sutherland was 'THA MI DOLAIR BURR' (I'm travelling by Burr). And this is true, as for many years Burr's van up and down the glens was about the only direct means of communication between the scattered communities. Times may have changed but Gordon is still as large as life (and I'm not referring to his vital statistics!) in the van or behind the counter. He works as hard as any of his staff, and loves to move around. In the old days—I think Queen Victoria was on the throne—a horse-drawn cart was *the* thing; and Gordon had it. It was only in 1926 that the first motor van came into being. As I write these lines in 1971, Gordon and his wife celebrate their forty-first wedding anniversary. His wife was a former school teacher, is a fluent Gaelic speaker and a native of Skerray nearby.

Gordon finds time 'whiles' in shooting and stalking. He is the President of the Tongue–Altnaharra Gun Club which holds one of the north's most important clay-pigeon shoots annually.

This, then, is a short résumé of this great undertaking in the far north of Scotland; and a tribute to private enterprise. Gordon Burr's enthusiasm is infectious. With him in the business is his wife, his 37-year-old son Charlie, his daughter Joan and her husband George Mackenzie, and his nephew John Mackay. All told, they have a labour force of between twenty-five and thirty. Many of them have been in their employ since school-days. Besides being a sound, genuine businessman, Gordon Burr has an abiding interest in the county's economic welfare—a man of action, not just mere words. There are far too few people of his calibre about today. More's the pity. Verily, nationalisation is left at the post in the race when, as I have said, private enterprise steps into the arena. Yet, all over the country, these privately-owned concerns are being squeezed out of existence.

So visitors to Tongue will see this lovely village offers the fullest of service—and good service at that—to its people.

I must not of course omit saying Tongue has an indefatigable member on the County Council in the person of Mrs. Catherine Barbara Mackay, who lives in Loyal Terrace. She is a fluent speaker and is not bashful in telling the Council what she thinks of matters, not only affecting Tongue, but of the county as a whole. I have been connected with local authority work (as an 'outsider') for many years in Devon and Cornwall before coming north, and I know full well what a great deal of time is involved in such 'honorary' duties if one takes a real interest in local government work. Mrs. Mackay is one who *does* take such an interest; and enjoys it too. I consider Tongue and district are fortunate in having this lady as their representative.

There is also a very nice Crafts shop in Tongue set up a few years ago by J. & K. McIntyre. (Jimmy, and his wife Cathie, who in her spare hours from teaching in the school does quite a lot of fascinating knitwear.) He is a very good artist and always has a number of excellent paintings on show; he has quite an array of machinery for the means of making jewellery, stone cutting and polishing; and of course other handcrafts that make a visit well worthwhile.

The new bridge and causeway now (1971) in the 'muddy' throes of construction, is being thrown across the Kyle of Tongue, from Tongue village to Melness on the opposite side. The cost is well over £500,000. The complete causeway, the major part of which is on the Tongue side, is 6000 feet in length. The bridge, 600 feet long, comprises 32 feet concrete beams and steel piles up to 80 feet in length. In all these big constructional operations minor and sometimes major accidents crop up needing medical aid. In the building of this bridge, a very sad and fatal accident occurred on 20th November 1970, when 23-year-old Donald Ross Mackay of Melness was electrocuted whilst he was handling the steel sling of a crane, when the jib touched an overhead cable. The funeral at Melness was one of the largest ever seen locally; a compelling demonstration of sympathy.

This development will cut out the 12-mile detour round both sides of the Kyle. Here again we have an 'Improvement' which will take away all the scenic travel round the beautiful Kyle landscape; the road may be narrow and twisty, but up in the far north there is plenty of time and there are passing places at convenient spots. Whilst this road will be kept open, it will I suppose not be maintained to any real degree, so in the end it will peter away to its former track; and another Highland splendour will be lost. To my mind this is deplorable to cut out wide-eyed wonderment of such entrancing scenery as is the Kyle of Tongue. Admittedly, it will allow of the doctor, the nurse and the ambulance to dash through to the other side saving much delay and lives of those sick or dangerously ill—but at what a cost. Surely it would be more sensible to establish a nurse, a doctor and ambulance facilities on both sides of the Kyle? The new roadway approach to the bridge from Tongue is cutting through valuable arable farm land. But perhaps that doesn't matter? I am not alone in thinking that all this money could be better spent on better ideas elsewhere in the county. But there it is. If authority decides to go through with such a venture, then authority goes through. It is as simple as that. In saying all this from an entirely detached point of view, I may incur a little wrath from some Tongue/Melness residents, particularly the sitting County Councillor; but nevertheless I am pained beyond measure at seeing these so-called 'Improvements' coming along all over the Highlands that—in the long-term policy—are literally ruining the very nature, the very atmosphere, the very way of life of such a beloved country as the north-west; a country that lives by its own special attractiveness; an acknowledgment of which brings thousands upon thousands to visit and to participate in its uniqueness. I put the question fairly and squarely, are the Highlands to lose all this, and to irretrievably and irreparably sell its birthright over to Planners, whose battle-cry would appear to be 'What is that to thee? Follow thou me' (John ch. 21, v. 22) are we, like sheep, to follow all they plan? If so, we are more like asses than sheep. If there is money to chuck about, I would have thought in this particular case that a new and wider road should be made into Melness itself, and that it should have priority to any daft Cape Wrath road suggestion. For it would seem nothing has been done for donkey's years to the pretty Melness township road. Even the Councillor for Tongue and district is reported as saying in October 1970, that the Melness road was one of the worst; seven to eight feet wide in places, with no sidewalks or grass verges, and I quote him, 'there are the most terrible twists and turns'. Don't I know it, so much so, I don't go there! But as usual, authority speaks out, and in many cases everything is signed and sealed long before the general public know of it. Regarding this Melness road I have in mind the County Surveyor who said (and I quote from the *Northern Times* of 23rd October 1970) he 'doubted if they would get this improvement. The new road was a new road, whereas the access to Melness was very much a county road'. End of quote. Not a very reassuring comment?

*   *   *

Before leaving this delightful village of Tongue, there are two legendary stories I must tell you.

Many, many years ago, there was a woman who lived in that area, and said to be the most powerful witch in the north of Scotland. She was called CAILLEACH NA GAOITH—'the Old Wife of the Wind', because when she was travelling she could go as fast as the wind itself.

From Drumholliston, a ridge near the north coast on the

Sutherland/Caithness road, to Durness the people were in dread of her, and would never speak of her but in whispers; and if the Chief of the Mackays himself should happen to meet her, he would take off his bonnet and draw his horse into the side of the road to let her go on her way.

She had two servants, a lad and a lass—Callum and Effie, and she was very hard on them. Effie was the cleverer of the two. She used to keep a secret watch on the old woman when she was at her cantrips; and it wasn't long before Effie became as good at the witchcraft as her mistress—if not better.

They were being treated so harshly that they made up their minds to run away. Early one morning before the old Cailleach was awake, Callum took out the horse. He mounted and helped Effie to climb on behind him—and off they went.

The noise of the hoofs of the animal wakened the witch. When she looked out of her window and saw what was happening, she was hopping mad. After them she went on the wings of the wind. Callum put the horse to the gallop; but she was coming up on them fast.

The situation was tense.

'Callum,' said Effie, 'look in the horse's left ear, you'll see a splinter of wood. Throw it behind us.' There was the bit of wood. Callum threw it back; and at once it changed into a thick impenetrable forest that brought the witch to a halt. (A stirring story this?) 'If I had my magic axe,' said she to herself, 'I could soon cut a path through the wood.' Back to the house she sped and fetched her magic axe. In no time at all she was through the wood and hard on the heels of the couple. 'Callum,' said Effie, 'look in the horse's other ear and there you will find a chip of stone. Throw it behind us and be quick about it.' This Callum did, and the chip of stone rose up into a great long ridge of rock that stopped the witch following them· 'If I had my magic pick-axe,' said she to herself, 'I'd soon cut a passage through this.' Home she went again, and came back with her magic pick-axe, and broke a way through the ridge.

So in no time at all was she catching up on Callum and Effie again; although the horse was all the time galloping at its hardest, and in a lather of foam.

'Callum,' said Effie, 'take a drop of sweat from the

horse's neck and throw it behind us; and be quick, oh! be quick for she's just on us!' (This Effie sure knew the technique!)

Callum did this. And the drop of sweat changed to a long, wide loch that brought Cailleach na Gaoith to a halt again. 'If I had my great swan,' said she to herself, 'he'd soon drink up the water.' Home she sped again and almost at once was back with her big swan. He began to drink, and in a minute the loch was nearly dry. But it was too much for him. Suddenly he burst; all the water rushed out, and there was the loch as big as before. The old witch looked round, and she saw a fox sneaking through the heather. 'Hi!' she called, 'get me over this loch.' She got on his back and there he was swimming for all he was worth over the loch with her. 'You're putting my head under the water,' he complained, 'can't you get back a bit nearer my tail?'

She eased herself back and back; and then she slipped right over his tail and was drowned, and that was the end of the witch, the Cailleach na Gaoith.

When the news got round—as news in the Highlands travels fast—there was much rejoicing in all the homes. The story doesn't tell what happened to Callum and Effie. But if I know anything about life, I'm sure they married and lived happily ever after.

*   *   *

The second story that has 'gone the rounds' of Sutherland for over 200 years, concerns a bridegroom. When the party came out of the church, a stranger—a tall dark man—was standing nearby. He went up to the groom, saying he had something special to tell him, and asked him to go to the back of the church. The bridegroom, absenting himself from the wedding party, went round. The dark man had a short bit of candle, barely half an inch in length. He lit it, and asked the other to hold it until it burned out. The bridegroom saw it would scarcely last more than a minute; then he would run and catch up with the party. He took the candle in his hand and watched as it seemed to burn away rapidly. The dark man walked off.

In no time the stump of the candle was finished and the bridegroom hurried to catch up with his bride and the bridal party. There was a man cutting peat close by the road, and calling over to him, the groom asked if it was long since the wedding party had gone by. The man, in surprise, said no wedding party had gone past that day, nor for many a day. 'But I was married today; we came out of the church only a few minutes ago, and a strange dark man asked me to go to the back of the church and hold a bit of a candle until it burned out,' the groom said. 'What day are you thinking this is?' the man asked. The young man told him the day, the month, and the year. *And the year was 200 years before that time.* 'I remember', said the peat cutter, 'a story my grandfather told me, that he had from his grandfather, about a wedding in the church there, and the bridegroom mysteriously disappeared just after coming out.' The young man turned pale. 'I am that bridegroom,' he groaned; and the words were hardly over his lips when he shrunk and fell down, and all that was left of him was a small heap of dust.

From Tongue, we will first pay a short visit eastwards; then come back and go westwards.

There are many small coastal settlements off the main Bettyhill road such as COLDBACKIE, SCULLOMIE, SKERRAY, KIRKTOMY, ARMADALE, BORGIE, FARR, STRATHAY POINT and others; all nice quiet spots. SKERRAY is a particularly lovely hamlet, with a small secluded bay and stone pier, where one can spend many pleasant hours looking on to the great bluff headland. There seems to be a reef just at the entrance to the bay, with a narrow channel only for small boats to come and go. In former days it would be a regular Para Handy puffer harbour. About half a mile off shore is the historic small island NAOMH (Heaven) also known as COMB (Columba). On it are to be found the ruins of an old monastery, and a graveyard. The little hill opposite is known as the Hill of the Congregation. No doubt years ago services of worship were held there. Some say the island graveyard was there to prevent depredations by wolves. We are harking back some years now. About a mile off shore in a westerly direction is Island Roan which was inhabited until the 1920's when it was evacuated. Good stone and slated roofed houses still remain which were used by a medical team a few years ago in dealing with experiments against the common cold and influenza. Altogether Skerray is a sweet little Highland oasis.

> In surging tide the breakers shoreward race
> To cast o'er rocks their shawl of creamy lace;
> As wind and wave their changeless pattern weave
> Through every sunlit noon and starlit eve.

The above few lines give those who go and relax at Skerray a true impression of this priceless quiet refuge.

Coming away from Skerray, you join the main road after passing through BORGIE, a beautiful wooded part with its well-known fishing river; and carrying on, BETTYHILL (so-called after the Countess of Sutherland of the time) at the mouth of the famous river Naver. It is another small coastal township owing its origin to the Clearances. It is 30 miles from Thurso. In the churchyard at the west of the village is the famous Farr Stone, seven and a half feet high—one of the finest examples of Celtic art extant. Less than 10 miles on from Bettyhill is Strathy Point where a model lighthouse, taking the place of the old one, was built in 1958.

*　　*　　*

I now take you back to Tongue, and make the journey westwards to Durness, Cape Wrath and down Scourie-way.

About a mile out of Tongue, there is at the roadside, on your left, a plain granite stone about five feet high bearing the following inscription: '. . . Ewen Robertson, 1842–1895, Bard of the Clearances, died at this spot.' And lower down there is the epitaph, 'In place of the sheep there will be people; cattle at the shieling in place of stags'.

Proceeding at a leisurely pace round the beautiful Kyle we come to the fork of the road that leads to the MELNESS district I have already named. This includes the small townships of Skinnet, Talmine, Partvasgo and Achininver—where the road ends. All this strip looks across the Kyle to Tongue. There are beautiful sandy bays at Talmine and Achininver. Rabbit Island off shore can be visited on foot at low tide. In the days before the advent of motor cars the route from Tongue to Melness was across the small Tongue Ferry. This was discontinued when the road round the Kyle was made years ago.

Returning to the main road, we start crossing the bleak six miles of moor, known as the Mhoine—a road which was originally made by the Duke of Sutherland in 1830. Half-way along there is a lone, unoccupied derelict cottage once, I suppose, used by a shepherd; and known as Mhoine house. Its windows are all broken, yet the old dilapidated door is padlocked. In early times this road from Tongue to Loch Hope was but a desolate track through marshland. The house I name was built in the early 1820's, and later this wee cottage served as a halting place and rest for travellers. Few, if any, will today stop to look at it, but recently I looked it up and down and suddenly on the east end gable I saw a large marble-stone plaque, let into the wall, about 6 feet by 3 feet, in memory of the generosity of the builder who planned this 'haven' of rest. In places, the wording is difficult to decipher; the years and the elements have seen to that. I believe this 'memorial' was plastered over by those people nearby who felt so incensed by the perpetrators of the Sutherland Clearance days. So far as I could make out, the following is the inscription, chiselled out well over a hundred years ago.

> This house, erected for the refuge of travellers, stands to com-memorate the construction of the road across the deep morass of the Mhoine. . . . This road was made in the year 1830 at the sole expense of the Marquis of Stafford. . . . Those who feel the fatigue experienced over former days . . . can appreciate the present improved conditions and what it cost. . . . This plaque is put up . . . by James Loch, Commissioner on His Lordship's Estate . . . and John Horsburgh, factor for the Reay Country, Strathnaver and Assynt, under whose directions this work was undertaken. . . . Peter Lawson, Surveyor.

I would remind you (as you will read in a later chapter) the Marquis of Stafford had big estates in England. He was the husband of the then Elizabeth, Countess of Sutherland in her own right. Together they controlled enormous areas of land in Scotland, and were then absentee landlords for most of the year. It was those days that the crofters were evicted to make room for sheep. You will read in the chapter of the Clearances, James Loch was one of the factors, along with Patrick Sellar, both of whom were the chief officers in this dastardly affair. It is a wonder to me this memorial has been allowed to remain in evidence, and not hacked to pieces, for it has become an affront to the people of Sutherland.

We carry on and soon come to Hope Lodge, where one gets a lovely glimpse of Loch Hope; then very soon reach Loch

ERIBOLL the most beautiful sea loch in Scotland, and has the deepest natural anchorage in Britain. Motoring along the broad road hugging the loch (which you traverse both its sides on to Durness) will leave a lasting impression in your mind; its greatness and beauty is unsurpassed.

Loch Eriboll is set amidst mountains; and it is said that around its shore there is much dolomite and potassium to be found. One source puts the quantity of dolomite at twenty million tons; and with an abundance of sea water and power transmitted from Dounreay there would be no impracticability in the manufacture of magnesium metal. This Eriboll area is also nearer to the abundant and rich fishing grounds of the Arctic ocean—Icelandic, Norwegian and Russian coasts—than any other Scottish port. This loch with a 20-fathom (120 feet) channel running for $6\frac{1}{2}$ miles, and only 600 feet at some points from the shore, can take the largest ship afloat. It lies on the shortest sea route between America and Northern Europe. In short, it is strategically placed.

So who knows what Loch Eriboll may become in the not so distant future?

Coming down the lochside, and before reaching Eriboll Farm, you see the small isolated Church of Scotland building deeply wrapped up in an air of meditation. It comes under the jurisdiction of the Tongue minister, the Rev. Alfred McClintock. All around this area there are a number of 'hut circles' to be seen. During their occupation—probably in the Iron Age—a covering somewhat resembling a tinker's tent in basic design, would have been erected inside the circular walls, which are now all that remain.

It was at Loch Eriboll that enemy U-boats surrendered to the British Fleet at the end of the Second World War. The Brahan Seer, a noted Highland visionary, prophesied several hundred years ago, that a war would end in Eriboll. How right he was.

Up the other side of the loch, you pass the wee hamlets—superbly situated—of Laird and Portnacon; the latter having another Para Handy pier. At the former hamlet you might think you were in Holland, for almost every cottage has a small wind-mill pumping up water from their well. At Portnacon if you look closely on the right side of the road, a little distance from the pier, you will see two small cairns which indicate the approach to an Earth-house, or Souterrain. You will need a torch to enter down by the half a dozen steps to see inside; it is advisable to enter backwards. Many theories have been advanced to explain this and other similar 'houses' as to their use in bygone days. They were certainly not dwelling houses, neither were they illicit whisky hide-outs. They might have been hide-outs against invaders; 'funk-holes' if you like? They date from about A.D. 200.

From the mouth of Loch Eriboll it is not far to Durness and the Kyle of Durness. Shortly after entering the outskirts of the village, there is the well-known Smoo Cave, a huge cavern caused by the endless pounding of wind and waves on the cliffs. I gave a full description of this in *Highland Pearls*. History has it, that at one time the Chief of the Mackays wrestled successfully with the devil there.

DURNESS has a strong tourist appeal. It consists of an orderly arrangement of tidy crofting townships; it is the most north-westerly turning-point and halting place of those who may be touring that circuit of the Highlands. Durness is still basically Gaelic (its name means 'The Deer's Point').

In the village itself there is a nice attractive little square, with its tidily kept green in the centre; and a convenient clock at the roadside—though more often than not, it indicates yesterday's Time, not today's. The village has good stores and hotel; everyone is most obliging and anxious to help. In short, Durness lacks for very little.

The golden Kyle of Durness to the west of the village broadens into the Bay of Balnakeil. Here, overlooking two miles of white sand with sparkling blue waters rolling in (with an outlook to the Atlantic and Faraid Head jutting out as a sentinel) is a bay that you can gaze and feast upon for many an hour on a sunny day. It has quiet, perfect surroundings. The waters are shallow so one can wade out quite a distance. Beside the bay is an ancient burial ground with its roofless church walls of great antiquity. The foundations are said to have been Columban. It was a Catholic church built in 1619 on the site of an older one which was attached to Dornoch monastery. It is believed that an even earlier religious settlement on the same site dates back to early Celtic times. The old font, which can still be seen and known as the Stone of the Red Priest, is one of the genuine pre-Reformation church relics in Sutherland.

In the churchyard there is a monument to the Reay Gaelic Bard, Rob Dunn (or Doun), otherwise Robert Mackay of Durness (1714–1778). He spent the greater part of his life in or around Durness. The tall sculptured memorial was erected at the expense of a few of his countrymen in 1827—ardent admirers of his native talent and extraordinary genius. The inscriptions on the monument are in English, Gaelic and Latin. He inherited his gift of poetry from his mother.

Much visited in this old churchyard is the tomb of the scion of the Clan MacLeod, whose name was Donald MacMurchey. Although I have given this particular history before, I feel it is well worth repeating.

This tomb is built into the south wall, and the inscription above it can, even after the passing of the years, be faintly made out, viz.:

> Donald Makmurchov heir lyis lo,
> Vas il to his friend, var to his fo,
> Trve to his maister in veird and vo. 1623.

He was a remarkable man. He was a MacLeod from Assynt (near Lochinver) but was always known as Donald MacMhurchaidh Mhic Iain Mhor—or translated 'son of Murdoch, son of big John'. As a reward for some service he did for the chief of the Mackays, he was given the life-tenancy of much land near Hope in the parish of Durness and was therefore a vassal of Mackay. He settled at Hielam where one can ferry across Loch Eriboll. The tombstone inscription 'trve to his maister' must obviously refer to Mackay. Notwithstanding he had a dreadful reputation, a 'Rob Roy' of the north, with at least eighteen murders to his credit! Accordingly he had many enemies, and he learnt that some of them, daring not to touch him whilst he was alive, talked amongst themselves of taking vengeance on his dead body. At that time, 1619, the Balnakeil church was being built, so he used his friendship with the chief of the Mackays to have a place prepared for him in the wall, where no foe could get at his corpse or trample over his grave. He is supposed to have paid a thousand marks (about £50) for this 'privilege', and tradition has it that all that side of the church was built at

Donald's expense. By then he was getting an old man. A new minister, Rev. Alex Munro came to the parish in 1620. About three years later Mr. Munro was at Tongue, which was then the residence of the chiefs. The then chief, the son of the former chief (the 'maister') named previously had a premonition and gave Mr. Munro an armed guard to escort him on his homeward journey. Coming to Hielam he thought it his duty to call on Donald whom he had heard was very ill, thinking that a few words of the gospel might yet affect a change in his heart and save him from eternal punishment that was surely awaiting him on his death. But the old man was still fierce even on his death-bed, and only sheer lack of strength prevented him from laying violent hands on his minister; who in sadness left and journeyed on. Donald had two sons, wicked but not quite so courageous as their father. The minister was not long away when they came into the house. Donald ordered them to go after him, kill him and bring back his heart. They hurried out and soon caught up with Mr. Munro, expecting to fall upon one man alone; but when they spotted the guard of the chief's men, they were afraid to act. Instead they killed a sheep, cut out its heart and brought it back to their dying father. But the old die-hard recognised it for a sheep's heart, but did not wish to chastise his sons, and merely said, 'I always knew the Munro's were cowards, and no wonder now I see it's sheep's hearts they have'. He died shortly after he had spoken those words, and was duly buried by the Rev. Munro according to his wishes in an upright position in the wall of Balnakeil Church. And there is his tomb today. What a story; what an end. It may be mentioned that one of Mr. Munro's descendants became a President of the United States of America, who promulgated the Munroe Doctrine, the principle of which was an international policy held by the U.S.A., the root idea being 'America for the Americans'. This doctrine was first formulated in a message to Congress by President James Munro in 1823. He had been elected President, against Rufus King in 1816, and filled the high office for two terms of eight years. He died at New York on 4th July 1831.

The two essential points of his Doctrine were the following: (a) the American Continents were henceforth not to be considered as subjects for future colonisation by any European power, and (b) America should consider any attempt on their part to extend their system to any portion of their hemisphere, as dangerous to America's own peace and safety.

The Doctrine did not seek to prevent European Powers enforcing just claims under International law, as when the British and German fleets combined to blockade Venezuela in 1903, but both countries had given an undertaking that they had no ulterior motives in the political horizon. Britain on the whole has supported the Doctrine, making as it does for the security of Canada and other British possessions in the American continent.

Sitting many times on a sunny day at Balnakeil Bay, I used to ponder over questions aroused by the sight of what appears to be water majestically sweeping forward. But we have learned at school that it does not move forward, only up and down. And then the question of where and how the waves began, and where would they end if they had searoom to keep going? The smooth blue sea stretched to the horizon; no land that way save Iceland, Greenland and the North Atlantic, and of course farther down the globe to the Southern Seas, the South Atlantic, Cape Horn in South America, or Cape of Good Hope in South Africa. Although the sea was like a millpond, yet a few hundred yards from shore, long swells gradually arose and tumbling into the bay, broke from a height into the dazzling surf. Where *did* they come from? They had come thousands of miles from the many places, the many continents, I have named; there they may have raged onwards as forty-foot high 'greybeards', then they had flattened out to Balnakiel and had lost the appearance of waves; but the shallow water had made them rear up to appear once more as real waves. How many intimate thoughts can be conjured up over waves.

* * *

Now coming back to Durness, we pass the BALNAKEIL CRAFT VILLAGE, which is worthy of note, and of a visit.

On this site in 1953, during certain anxious periods of our war-time friend Stalin's imperialism, a fine new Radar station was built at a cost of some £2 million, to serve as a tracking station for the four-minute warning of Russian rockets. It was never used; in fact it became obsolete before it was wholly completed. I doubt if it should ever have been sited there in the first place for the stations at Unst, Shetland, and Lewis covered the area adequately. Stalin died and the menace receded. Ten years later the Sutherland County Council bought it all over for £500. Everything was written off as redundant. Looters came from all over Scotland with lorries at night taking away anything that could be wrenched out; and nobody there to stop them. It gradually became one more unsightly military ruin. The County Council with its Development and Planning Officer, decided it would be worthwhile to convert the buildings and make them adaptable for commercial purposes to attract new people to the area, help the local economy and attract tourist interests. It has been a long and slow process and there is yet a lot that remains to be done.

Housed in these confines there is a pottery workshop; a fabric design and craft unit; a coffee house; a craft shop; a Foto Art Studio; a guest house ; a Worm Farm Research building; and an hotel. But to my mind it all needs badly livening up. The area is all fenced in and reminds one of a concentration camp. It has a deserted appearance; the buildings are drab and everything could do with painting or distempering in attractive colour. As it stands there is no enticement at all for the visiting public; even when I have looked round in May and September, most of the places are shut. I could not even get a cup of coffee, for the coffee house was closed, bolted and barred. It is true there is a small stretch of grass—uncut; but the whole atmosphere gives one a sense of depression.

In the square at Durness, there is a Tourist Information Office, Mr. George Mackenzie being in charge. He was three years in the Cape Wrath lighthouse, retiring from there in November 1965 after completing forty-one years in lighthouse service. He is a very cultured person, has a wide knowledge of the Gaelic, an authority on Place Names, a broadcaster and for fifty years a freelance journalist. I look upon George as being the foremost officer in Sutherland's tourist organisation.

Leaving Durness, we will now take the road out south, and have something to say about Cape Wrath, the Land's End of Scotland, the northernmost tip of Sutherland and one of the loneliest lighthouses on the mainland of Britain. To the north lie the Faroes and the Arctic circle; to the west the sometimes turbulent waters of the Minch, and the misty, mysterious Outer Hebrides. Eleven miles of lonely moorland—the PARPH—separate the lighthouse from the little ferry boat which brings travellers and supplies across the Kyle of Durness.

Surrounding the lighthouse are cliffs that provide sea bird haunts for the delight of the ornithologist; and gneiss formations for the geologist; and a happy hunting ground for the botanist.

On the way out of Durness making for Rhiconich and about two miles along that road there is Keodale Farm and Cape Wrath Hotel signposted. Taking that road and within minutes you come to the ferry where a small boat will take you (but not your car) across the Kyle. A stalwart ferryman, Mr. Donald Morrison, carries you out to the boat should there be a low tide and within five minutes you are across to the other side. The boat, in the summer, leaves about 9.0 a.m. and runs backwards and forwards at frequent intervals till dusk. Then, the minibus takes you to the lighthouse; stays there about an hour, then brings you back again to civilisation. Since writing these lines, Mr. Morrison has now retired after 32 years plying his wee boat across the Kyle. What joy he must have given to many. There is a movement on foot by our planners to cut out this interesting and attractive service by making a new road from the end of the Kyle, right up along the west side of the Kyle to Cape Wrath. I think it's a mad idea. People enjoy crossing the Kyle by boat and then bumping over the rough road—and at times fording a wee burn or two—to the lighthouse. They like that kind of adventure; and who would be helped by the road? Nobody lives along it, so the authorities cannot say this idea and spending of money will be any social benefit to the community, when there is no community. We surely live and learn? I believe over 15,000 visitors make this ferry-cum-minibus trip each year.

Cape Wrath lighthouse is one of the most dreaded stations in the Scottish Lightkeepers' circuit, which ranges from Muckle Flugga in Shetland to St. Abbs on the east coast and the Calf of Man on the west coast. The name has no connection with wrathfulness or stormy; it is derived from an old Norse word, HVARF, meaning 'turning'—the turning point of the Vikings of old. The Gaelic name PARPH just named is also from the same source. The lighthouse flashes its white and red character every half minute. In the winter time gales up to 80 knots are commonplace, and thick pea-souper fogs with visibility down to a few yards are frequent; and then the quarter-million candle-power light can only be visible twenty yards away, but the strident fog-horn moos its way out to sea (what its cow-power is I cannot say!) and the radio beacon comes into play sending out its aerial signals to warn ships. In the summer, however, halcyon days compensate.

From Cape Wrath on clear days can be seen Lewis and the Long Island 40 miles away. North Rona too, 45 miles away, and the Ward Hill of Hoy 60 miles to the east. Of course a lighthouse keeper anywhere is constantly asked by visitors, 'Don't you find life terribly monotonous?' When told 'no', they shrug their shoulders, looking sceptically, thinking no doubt that it takes all sorts to make a world. These responsible, and all-important keepers, tell me that it is surely more monotonous to work in a factory or live in a city tenement day in and day out than live in a lighthouse, where the air is pure and undefiled, no smog or dust—or even flu germs—and where one can see nature in every imaginable mood.

Fiat Lux.

*   *   *

Continuing from the Cape Wrath junction with the main road south out of Durness, travelling along the Gualin road with its well-known salmon river, the Dionard (which empties into the Kyle of Durness) beside it, you eventually come to Rhiconich situated at the head of the extremely pretty sea-loch, Loch Inchard; but just before reaching Rhiconich, the road branching right takes you to Kinlochbervie, Oldshoremore, and at the end of the road, Sheigra.

Kinlochbervie, derived from the Gaelic meaning 'Head of loch fort', has two harbours. The ruins of the 'fort' are on the right bank of Loch Inchard; its occupants in days gone by are said to have levied tolls from shipping. The two harbours are a great attraction, where large catches of white fish are landed. In winter months, night falls early, and the dark waters reflect the multi-coloured lights of the harbour quay to great effect.

In the wee hamlet of Sheigra at the end of the road, one Alexander Gunn, a shepherd, is reported to have seen a mermaid at Sandwood bay on 5th January 1904. Whether he pulled her ashore by her hair and married her no one seems to know.

Sandwood bay is a pearl of beauty, like Balnakeil bay, and is full of strange tales. This bay can only be approached by a rough footway of some five miles. It is a perfect spot, a perfect seven-mile stretch of sandy bay, 'midst perfect quiet. Owing to strong tides it is not suitable for bathing; only for the frolicsome mermaids in their isolation.

Sandwood Bay! Its very name breathes romance and legend. Recently I had a letter from a lady in Warwickshire who in touring the N. West in the summer of 1970, walked with her husband to this wonderful bay. I now tell her story in her own words. 'Whilst we were there I was very restless and kept saying I didn't like the feel of the place, and I so much wanted to leave. I felt that something resented very much our presence. As it was a wonderfully sunny day there was no need for my feelings as far as I knew; none at all. As soon as we had left the bay, I felt normal again; my husband can confirm all this.' She ended her letter by saying how odd and strange it all was and talks of it to this day.

Although in my previous book, I have recounted some of the weird legends associated with this remote bay, they are so significant that I feel they should be mentioned again. The incidents are the most peculiar of any Highland loch or bay; and since the atmosphere felt and so plainly given a few lines above happened only a year ago, the experiences occurring years before then, can surely be looked upon as having some elements of truth in them, to say the least.

Late one summer afternoon before the Second World War, a crofter from Oldshoremore set out with a horse and cart to gather driftwood. He and his son were the only human beings on the beach as it grew dark. Suddenly the figure of a sailor in uniform appeared from nowhere and commanded them to leave his property alone. Terrified, they dropped their load of wood and fled. Some time later on, a farmer from Kinlochbervie was searching for some of his sheep in that self-same area with three local men. It was getting dark and the moon came out, when they saw the outline of a man on the rocks. Thinking it might be another of their village pals they went towards the figure, but as they drew near they realised he was a stranger who looked like a sailor, and as they watched, he disappeared amongst the rocks. Several weeks later there was a severe storm off the coast there, and an Irish vessel went aground at Sandwood Bay. A number

C

of bodies were washed up on the beach, and one of them was recognised by the four Kinlochbervie men as the sailor they had seen amongst the rocks, for he was a heavily built black-whiskered man, such as they had so closely observed before.

About fifteen years later, three Edinburgh men staying in a B. & B. house nearby to Sandwood Bay, decided to have a picnic there, and whilst halfway through, they felt they were being watched. On top of a hill was this mysterious sailor, who fled when they shouted out. They ran after him but he had vanished, leaving no signs of footprints. This was in broad daylight, remember. Now here is another peculiar 'twist'—if you can call it such, for I heard of a visitor and his friend fishing in the bay only two years ago. Suddenly they heard a shout and looking up they saw a very tall six-foot-odd man standing knee deep in the waves. He, too, was heavily built. As he was waving and shouting vigorously, they hurried along and saw he was in seaman's uniform. Just before they came up to him, he vanished into thin air, although the water at that spot was so very shallow!

At Sheigra, near Oldshoremore, there was a truly northland worthy by the name of Margaret MacDiarmid who was born about the year 1770, and died in 1842. She was seldom referred to by her married name; simply as BEAN A CHREIDIMH MOIR. Her descent from Abraham counted more than her MacDiarmid lineage, and her marriage to Christ more than her status as the wife of Donald Mackay of Sheigra. Margaret spent most of her life in Sutherland, but she was not a native of that county. She was born in Argyll of an Argyllshire mother, whose father, Colin Campbell of Glenure, held a high office in the religious and social life of the county. Her own father was of Perthshire stock. It was towards the end of the 18th century that Margaret removed to Sutherland. Her brother Colin had been appointed deerstalker in the Reay forest there, and Margaret had accompanied him. But a cup of sorrow was early filled for her in her new home. Her brother was drowned while engaged in his work. Already she had become engaged to Donald Mackay of Sheigra, and he was a source of comfort to her in her bereavement. The suddenness of her loss led her to the uncertainty of life and the need to prepare for death. Margaret thus began to seek the Lord.

The district where she resided was privileged at having the services of Rev. John Kennedy, the father of Dr. John Kennedy of Dingwall. He was missionary at Eriboll and Kinlochbervie, where Margaret lived nearby. And he held services there. It was at one of these services that Margaret passed from death to life.

Margaret's affections were now decidedly set on 'things above', and wherever there was a prospect of Gospel preaching in the vicinity she would do her utmost to be there. It was nothing unusual for her to walk barefooted through the moorland to Durness, fourteen miles away, to hear Rev. William Findlater who was minister there at the time. On one of those occasions she lost a boot on the moor, for she used to carry her footgear until she came near the church. What was she to do? Draw unwelcome attention to herself by going to church barefooted, or go home? The alternative she regarded as a temptation from the devil. Making the best of the situation, she pulled on her stockings and went to church in her stocking soles. She found the lost boot on her way home.

Margaret's conversion, to begin with, involved her in domestic friction, for her husband—though entirely dutiful and of a kindly nature—was a man of the world, and could not understand his wife's zeal for the things of God. Along with that, he disapproved of her frequent absences from home, for Margaret used to seek the fellowship of those like-minded with herself at the great communion gatherings in the Highlands. But after a sharp disagreement with him on one occasion, she sought the solitude of the barn to pour out her heart to the Lord. Donald, after a while, followed her and overheard as she pleaded with God for his conversion. The prayer appears to have been answered there and then. Donald Mackay began to pray for himself, and to seek the very blessing which his wife had been asking for him. No longer did he wonder at her thirst for the Gospel, nor did he put any obstacle in her way when she prepared for her communion pilgrimages. 'The grace he had not at first, has now been given him,' she said, 'and he will allow me to wander for bread to my soul wherever I can find it.'

This, then, is the story of that great woman of Sheigra.

* * *

Returning to the main road *en route* to Laxford Bridge, where the junction will take you to Scourie and on to Kylesku Ferry, or via Loch Stack and Loch More (the domain of Anne, Duchess of

Westminster) you then come back to the central spot I have mentioned, namely Lairg.

Rhiconich itself has a lovely view of Loch Inchard. Near this village is Skerricha and Ardmore where there is an Adventure holiday school and centre (referred to later), where you can take a boat trip into the Atlantic, visiting the famous bird sanctuary at Handa Island.

SCOURIE is the usual lovely type of Highland village. Its name signifies the 'place behind the rocks'. It is almost surrounded by hills and the journey on to Kylesku Ferry, though only about eleven miles, will take you an hour, for the road is very narrow and twisting and with all the lochans you pass and the scenery you suddenly come across round every bend will cause you to stop many times to admire everything. And all this takes time; the hour soon passes.

From Laxford Bridge—and it is only a bridge where the Duchess of Westminster's factor's house is situated—to Lairg provides an exquisite run; more so than Lairg to Tongue. You pass Loch Stack, reputed to be the finest fishing loch in Scotland, but I doubt if you will come across the fiercesome dog, said to guard the hoard of gold in its waters. On a wee island in the loch you will see a monument which was erected to the memory of a former Duchess of Westminster who loved to picnic there; I believe her grave is also on the island. Then comes Loch More where the Duchess has her Highland fortress, Lochmore Lodge; then to Loch Merkland where the Duchess's estate terminates going inland. After this, there is another loch, Loch Ghriama, and then you come in sight of Loch Shin, 18 miles in length, which more or less dominates this itinerary to Lairg—all along a good wide road, with scenery from all angles.

At Lairg, another road takes you to the Lochinver/Assynt district, by the Oykel river and valley, passing Altnacealgach (pronounced Alt-nar-kal-a-ger) and Inchnadamph—near the ruins of Ardvreck Castle. Shortly after here there is a branch road and a very good one, to Kylesku Ferry again. From there, you can turn left and take the coastal road via Nedd, Drumbeg, Clashnessie, and Stoer to Lochinver. This, again, is packed full of beauty which you are not likely to forget for many a year.

Since writing this chapter, the new Tongue bridge was officially opened on September 3rd, 1971.

In the shake-up of the Government's new proposals (to operate in 1975) for Scottish local government—announced in a White Paper on 17th February 1971—the parishes of Farr and Tongue are to come under Caithness district authority. I feel sorry over this, for Tongue is essentially a Sutherland village, and miles away from the Caithness border. To my mind, such scenic and historic an area should remain under Sutherland Council's jurisdiction.

CHAPTER 4

STRATHS OF BEAUTY

BY this caption, I refer to Strathnaver, Strath Halladale (and Kildonan) and Strathmore (Loch Hope). All these straths possess beauty of their own, and are within easy reach of Tongue. The Ben Hope strath, and Strathnaver, are also convenient to Altnaharra. Once seen, these three valleys are considered to be Sutherland's pride, and are truly meant for visitors as being 'richly to enjoy'.

Taking STRATHNAVER first, it is only half an hour's run from Tongue on the Bettyhill road, when you turn right—signposted Strathnaver. It was the scene, as you will read in a later chapter, of the awful Clearances. It stretches about 20 miles southward along the sweeping river Naver to Loch Naver at Altnaharra. It is a valley of infinite charm, fertile fields border the river, and snug crofts and farm buildings abound. What must it have been like years ago? As you travel through this enchanting countryside, you pass Skaill, owned by Miss Mary Mackay, the last of her long family history, who, as I have said before, weeps tears of remembrances. Near here is a stone at the roadside to commemorate the formation in 1799 of the 93rd Sutherland Highlanders, who formed the *Thin Red Line* at Balaclava. History did I say? All the way down this valley are earth-works of prehistoric men and fallen stones of Iron-age brochs. In a grove of birch trees beside the road at Skaill is the Red Priest's cell. It is said the priest used this megalithic tomb, and that his grave is somewhere near. On the opposite bank are the remains of one of the brochs.

Then you come to SYRE—just a house or two and a church. The 'big house' belongs to the Midwood family who own most of the land nearby. There is a bridge across the Naver here which takes you through moorland passing Garvault Hotel—an isolated spot—which caters for fishers and shooters, and leads on to Kinbrace (where there is a railway station) thence down Strath Kildonan connecting with Strath Halladale and on to Helmsdale on the east coast, north of Brora.

As you turn up the Strathnaver valley from Bettyhill, two or three miles up river on the east bank is Skelpick. One house in the small hamlet bears the date 1916, but other buildings date far older than this. There is a tiny corrugated-iron school complete with black-board and desks. But it is as dead as the bleached trees in the wood. These gaunt, white skeletons cluster like ghosts around the site of a broch, now only a grassy mound.

There must be some reason why Strathnaver has more Neolithic relics and Iron-age brochs than any other valley around the north coast. Orkney, 50 miles away to the north-east, and Shetland are rich in prehistoric sites. The seafaring Norsemen who raided along the coasts of Scotland left little but place-names on the mainland. Their 'wicks' and 'vicks', the 'ness' and the 'stra' are among the words used.

Strathnaver, of infinite charm as I have said. . . .

As you travel down the valley, and particularly nearing Syre and see the frame of Highland hills, Klibreck, Ben Loyal (the Queen of Scottish mountains) and their associates, and Loch Naver looming in front of you on a radiant summer's morning, you look upon the beauty of it all as one of special Creation. The whole landscape spreads out as great arms of welcome. The wholesome and familiar haze that accompanies summer may dim the mountains of the west further afield, but turns loch and hills, amethystine.

Coming face to face with this picture of glory, you will wish to pause and get out of your car; and with bowed head doubtless exclaim the words of the Psalmist 'This is my rest for ever; here will I dwell, for I have desired it' (Ps. 132, v. 14).

STRATH HALLADALE is beyond Bettyhill, turning off at Melvich which is just on the border of Caithness. The way down this strath, terminating at Helmsdale, is rich in every way. It echoes peace and quietness personified. None of the croft houses ever cater for bed and breakfast people. There are many lodges and estates en route. After passing Kinbrace junction, there is to be seen a sign by the roadside at Kildonan, 'BAILÉ AN OR'—Gold-town. Here in 1868 there were many huts and tents to house the men who came north to take part in the 'gold rush' of that year; for Scotland's little Klondyke had captivated the imagination. The story is quite interesting. Two brothers named Gilchrist returned from Bendigo in the gold-mining area of Victoria, Australia. They were up in Sutherland just jogging along on a holiday, when they leaned over a small bridge in Strath Kildonan and saw that there seemed to be gold grains being washed down the river. Word got around and in no time there was an immediate rush to Sutherland. A 'city of tents' sprang up almost overnight.

In this lonely strath, which was then still aching and groaning from the abhorrent Clearances, claims were staked and cradles mounted. The total amount and the value of gold dug and panned was in the region of £6000. Yields then began to dwindle and then the Duke of Sutherland again cleared his land, and only sporadic expeditions followed. However, over the years, geological surveys have nibbled at the hills and raked among the gravel. Recently, the Highlands and Islands Development Board suggested that panning for gold might prove a tourist attraction. Perhaps some enthusiastic visitors may start scratching the odd surfaces of the land like hens, expecting to expose a real gold seam. Some day, somewhere, someone, *may* strike it rich amongst the scurrying rabbits and the leaping salmon. On the other hand, 'Bingo' may not be heard.

Last year, the search for the precious metal was revived and engineering firms with up-to-date drilling apparatus were active in their explorations to find out whether there is any gold to be found in quantity to be of any commercial value to its diggers. I have not heard the result so far.

The Kildonan strath offers a wealth of scenic beauty and archaeological interest. Evidence of a continuous civilisation from the Stone Age exists the length and breadth of this fertile valley. Kildonan was the site of an ancient religious settlement, that of St. Dounan, a seventh century martyr. Other village names nearby also call to mind the sites of early Christian churches. Almost everywhere on the line where strath and hill meet, are antiquarian remains, or the stone outlines of the foundations of the simple turf houses that held the strath's last real

crop of people. Many went abroad during the eviction years—
they had to—some to Central Canada to found on the Red
River, the settlement of New Kildonan, where Winnipeg now
stands.

STRATHMORE, Loch Hope and Ben Hope. From Tongue this
is easily reached by going round the Kyle of Tongue, crossing
the Mhoine road, when you come to the Lodge at Hope, the road
then forking left 'To Altnaharra'. This is one of the most
beautiful runs I know of up north; at first you travel high up on
the road looking down upon Loch Hope on your right, and
overshadowing the landscape on the left is Ben Hope, 3040 feet
high. The road is certainly a narrow one, with passing places at
intervals; but the trees, the foliage and the general *ensemble* make
up for the road's narrowness. Loch Hope is simply super.
There are no houses or dwellings; you have it all to yourself,
until you come to a hamlet ALLTNACAILLICH (where the Bard,
Rob Doun was born) and by the roadside you see the broch of
DUN BORNAIGIL, better known as DORNADILLA. It is the finest
of its kind in Sutherland, or indeed in all Britain. It is of course
falling in ruins. The wall at its lowest point is barely six feet.
The low entrance has a large triangular stone for its lintel; and
the wall, still craftsmanship-made above the lintel rises to about
fourteen feet. It is really an ancient monument, and as such

should be preserved. The ground level has of course risen over the centuries, so the heights given would have been far greater than I have named in those days when it was built.

Dun Dornadilla is very like the illustration here, which is actually that of Dun Carloway in Lewis, mentioned in the chapter on the Outer Hebrides.

Across the valley is FEINNE-BHEINN MHOR. Nearly four centuries ago, the Brahan Seer said that some day a raven, dressed in a plaid and bonnet, would drink human blood on Binnebheinn. A strange prophecy that may have been unfulfilled unless he was referring to the Clearances? The seer also forecast the displacement of the plough, by sheep and emigration. Surely he *must* have had the Clearances in mind. The raven is a bird of ill-omen in the Highlands, for it was borne on the banners of the Viking raiders.

From Rob Doun's birthplace, and opposite the hill where the raven in a plaid and bonnet is still awaited, there is an excellent view of Ben Hope, buttressed and formidable.

BROCHS. Wherever you go in Sutherland, Orkney and Shetland you will find the remains of brochs and duns; once massive, fortified towers. They were built during the early Prehistoric Iron Age, probably between 200 and 50 B.C. Doubtless they were built as communal defensive forts, used by the surrounding farming community in times of attack and siege.

The essential features of a broch embody a circular wall of dry masonry about 15 feet in thickness, enclosing an area between 20 and 30 feet in diameter; and were about 40 feet high. Access was through a single tunnel-like entrance. There were narrow galleries inside leading to spiral staircases to the top for observation purposes. Apart from the main doorway, there were no openings in the outer wall, but there were narrow slits in the inner walls to allow of light. A central hearth seemed to be a common feature. These brochs were erected and positioned in the best defensive sites. They were built in the most excellent masonry—quarry-dressed blocks—which today is a lost art.

The *earth houses*, or 'weems', were almost certainly never used for regular habitation, but rather as 'funk-holes', where women and children sought refuge during brief raids for slaves and cattle. They were built beneath the normal houses. A sort of bomb-proof shelter in our late war-time days. Many are dated to the Roman occupation of Britain, but those in the Highlands are probably pre-Christian.

*   *   *

The three straths (valleys) I have mentioned are the most beautiful in the Highlands; indeed in the whole of Britain. Nothing approaches their isolated peaceful surroundings. This isolated timelessness holds you in suspense. You should come and see it for yourself; and if you do, you will feel bound to tell me that what I have said is true.

> . . . the voice of these straths may be sad
> strolling 'midst ancient trees,
> But there's still a song to be had
> and laughter heard in the breeze.

*   *   *

Of the three straths, I consider Strathnaver to be the sweetest. It has a Mackay family history going back to Kenneth Macalpin who defeated the Picts and created Alba, now Scotland.

I think this beautiful strath should be preserved by the National Trust, or some such body. Whilst the Trust has preserved such historic places as Culloden, Glencoe, Glenfinnan and Torridon, Strathnaver is overlooked. The ancient family of the Mackays presents an important part of Scotland's history, and should not be forgotten or obscured in years to come.

The Mackays were of the Protestant faith. It was General Hugh Mackay (who died in 1692) who continued the fight started by his ancestor, Sir Donald Mackay in 1626, for the Protestant cause in Germany. In October 1688, General Hugh Mackay sailed from Holland with William of Orange as commander of the English and Scottish troops who secured William's succession to the Crown as William III, causing James VII and II of England to flee to France, thereby securing the Protestant faith for England. General Hugh was killed in action in Holland. William III had intended to create him Earl of Scourie as a tribute to his birthplace.

Yes, Strathnaver is worthy of much recognition, honour and respect. The illustration heading this chapter is of Ben Hope and Loch Hope.

WESTER ROSS

... (where you may hold back the dawn) ...

Rubha Ré
Lighthouse

Melvaig

The Gairloch

Red Point

Loch Torridon

Isle of
Rona

Gruinard
Bay

Laide
Aultbea

Loch Ewe

Poolewe

Inverewe

Strath
Gairloch

Badachro

Ben Alligan

Dalbaig

Applecross

Loch Carron

Kyle of
Lochalsh

Kyleakin

Isle of Skye

Sound of Sleat

Ullapool

Dundonnell

An Teallach

Loch
Broom

Loch Maree

Letterewe

Slioch

Beinn Eighe

Kinlochewe

Torridon

Achnasheen

Strome Ferry

Loch Monar

Loch Mullardoch

Dornie

Loch Duich

Glenelg

Loch Affric

WESTER ROSS

N

Loch Clunie

Scale approx. 12 miles to inch

CHAPTER 5

WESTER ROSS

WE now turn to Wester Ross—a gracious land. This part of the Highlands is as ancient as Time; for Torridon stone is reputed to be the oldest known to geologists.

Wester Ross is in the county of Ross and Cromarty. The 1st Earl of Cromarty, Sir George Mackenzie of Tarbat, who was created earl in 1703, obtained the privilege of having his various estates throughout Ross created into a new and separate county of Cromarty. Therefore the County of Cromarty consisted of a number of 'pockets' surrounded by 'pockets' of Ross. This inconvenient arrangement lasted almost 200 years, but was ended in 1891, becoming 'Ross and Cromarty'.

GARVE, as I have said, is the gateway to Wester Ross, and once you pass this little village you come into a new country with all its mountains and moors beckoning you on—not to hasten but to take your time, remembering that on these roads up north you need the utmost attention, concentration and courtesy at all times, in or out of season. The majority of the roads are unfenced, and sheep graze freely.

Passing Garve you come to Achnasheen, where the railway (which is expected to be closed) continues to Kyle of Lochalsh. Mails for Gairloch and that direction are taken off to the waiting mail bus; those for Kyle and Skye carry on their way. Shortly after leaving Achnasheen ('Field of Storm') the road branches left to Loch Carron, Strome Ferry and Kyle. The ferry does not operate on Sundays and is always a source of much hold-up with streams of cars waiting to cross over; but now a new road has been opened, by-passing the ferry. It turns off at Strathcarron, proceeding along the south side of Loch Carron, coming out at Strome.

The road was opened on Monday, 5th October 1970, by the Scottish Secretary of State, Mr. Gordon Campbell. It cost something in the region of £750,000, and is almost eight miles long. The construction work suffered much delay on account of serious rock falls and landslides. As a guard against this danger of rock tumbling down during heavy winter storms, avalanche tunnels have been built on the Swiss-type avalanche shelters system— the first of their kind in this country. Such safety 'tunnels' can support a thirty-foot deep layer of fallen rock before showing any signs of strain. The shelter alone cost £100,000, and consists of twin tunnels each over 17 feet wide and 18 feet high. The walls and roof are two feet thick reinforced concrete and openings have been left in the outer and centre walls to provide natural lighting in the shelter, which is 210 feet long and follows the curve of the railway line. Quite a work of art.

The construction of this new roadway has been greeted by the Lochcarron people by more heartfelt sighs of relief than any other road schemes since General Wade opened up the Highlands two centuries ago.

* * *

I now give a hitherto unpublished report of the '*Stromeferry Riots*' which occurred in 1850 or just around that year. Two of the ringleaders were named Alexander Mackay and Alexander Gollan. As regards physical conditions they were poles apart; Mackay slightly built looked his age, while Gollan, older than Mackay, was of powerful physique, the embodiment of strength, as he strode along the village wearing a Balmoral, carrying a plaid over his broad shoulders. He must have been a worthy sight to behold. The trouble arose over Sunday work at Stromeferry railway station in loading herring. Events became so threatening that the military were summoned from Fort George to assist the police. The ringleaders were eventually arrested, with the exception of our friend Alexander Gollan whom no one could hold. They indeed surprised him in bed, but still with no better success, only damage and harm to themselves. Their efforts to handcuff him were fruitless. Eventually he consented to accompany his fellow-mates to Edinburgh for trial, but only on condition that, unlike the others, his arms should remain free. They were all tried and imprisoned in the Carlton Jail for some months, then liberated—returning to work at Strome, the Sunday dispute being resolved.

In a later chapter you will read of the horrors enacted in the eviction years in the north; and as I say therein, this cruelty was not confined to Sutherland only.

In mentioning Strathcarron here, in the year 1854, women were brutally maimed in truncheon attacks by police, as they defended their poor homes. Just at that time war was declared on Tsar Nicholas I of Russia. Britain was far more concerned as to the Crimea, and how many Russians were being killed by the Black Watch, conveniently forgetting that in the Highlands, people lost their memory, their reason and their all. The fact that a woman might be pregnant had no bearing on eviction orders. It was the word 'Improvement' that was uppermost; the economic argument was unanswerable—unassailable. Land which had produced 2d. an acre under cattle, yielded two shillings an acre under sheep.

*   *   *

Returning to Achnasheen joining the main road again to the west, we soon rise up to the summit of Glen Docherty, where you catch the first view of Loch Maree. A new lay-by has been made shortly after leaving the A.A. box summit; you should pull in there and tarry awhile, and if it be a clear day, you will look down this glen on to Loch Maree's shimmering waters, proudly. It is a compelling sight and you will perhaps feel you were a member of that company of original explorers, pioneers, argonauts, and empire builders who opened up this region of the north-west.

Travelling slowly down Glen Docherty (sometimes spelt Docharty), Kinlochewe is soon reached, a typical small Highland village. A few yards beyond the hotel there is a branch road on the left which takes you along Torridon to Loch Torridon—a sea loch—and from there, the magnificent mountain road to Alligin and Diabaig (pronounced Deer-beg) in one direction, and in the opposite direction along the large Balgy Gap motorway (opened on 9th September 1963) going towards Shieldaig and Applecross.

The journey along the terrific Torridon range takes you through wild scenery of loneliness. No sea-loch in Scotland is encircled by such terrifying massiveness. Passing the little jewel-village of Shieldaig and making for Strome, the turn-off for Applecross is at the signpost Tornapress; ten miles of real adventure climbing over the Bealach nam Bò ('pass of the cows') which rises 2000 feet in five miles with many hair-pin bends, you drop down to the sea—and Applecross. The Gaelic name is A'CHOMRAICH (the sanctuary) and so it *is* a sanctuary today. The village is arrayed along the shingle, its little stone houses looking out across the Inner Sound to Raasay and Rona, and beyond them, the northern end of Skye. The big glen of Applecross makes up the home farm of that English gentleman, Major John Wills (of the tobacco family), and here in recent years Major Wills has established a West Highland School of Adventure, run on outward bound lines financed by the Dockland Settlement of which the Major is Chairman. Major Wills' wife is a cousin of Princess Margaret. I refer to this 'Adventure' later.

I remember hearing of an 'adventure' in 1918, of a crossing from Kyle of Lochalsh to Stornoway in the *Shiela*, which was not much larger than a drifter. The captain stopped engines off Applecross, putting the mail and one or two passengers into a waiting rowing boat. The ship's rail was then lowered, and with a lot of shouting half a dozen cattle were herded overboard and made to swim to Applecross. Those were the days?

Since Applecross can often be cut off in winter and even in summer over the 'pass of the cows' road—in the winter it may be blocked by snow for many weeks, and in the summer blanketed out by swirling mist—I represented this matter to the authorities that a road, however minor, from Shieldaig round the peninsula to Applecross should be made. Through this route live some 50 old folk in the scattered 12 hamlets, and they can be cut off from the outside world for weeks, as there is only a rough track. In case of sickness or urgent surgical attention, patients had to be taken by stretcher up and down the tracks to be put into a small boat at Applecross (assuming of course the boat *could* put in to shore), then taken to Kyle and Inverness. What a terrible journey even in summer! I am glad to say the County Council have made a start on this road and are making good progress. Part of that new road Shieldaig–Kenmore was declared open by Princess

Margaret in May 1970 (see next chapter). Coming back to
Kinlochewe and the main road it is then ten miles to Loch Maree
hotel—a famous fishing hotel—situated in its beautiful surroundings at the loch's edge. The loch here presents itself more fully,
once you have left Kinlochewe, and begins to take shape. On
the opposite bank of the loch stands mighty, spear-headed Slioch,
rising to over 3200 feet sheer; a most natural sentinel for ever
like the rock of Gibraltar. When there has been a rainstorm,
waterfalls galore stream down its slopes.

I have made many references to Loch Maree, its islands and
the romances enacted there, in previous writings; so will not
repeat them here.

In the past two or three years considerable and heavy reconstruction work has been carried out on the main Loch Maree
road. And the work still continues, widening the old very
narrow roadway and ironing out many hazardous bends. Some
miles along from Loch Maree hotel, the loch road winds away
from the shore line across more or less open moorland through
plantations of fine timber, and then you find the little Kerry
river, where there is an attractively built Hydro-Electric Power
Station. These Hydro-Electric boys certainly keep the current
going all through the year. Particularly in the winter they are
called upon at all hours to effect major repairs caused by gales,
snow and heavy rains.

Soon you reach Gairloch and Badachro (this latter small
village on the south side of the big horse-shoe loch). These two
villages are the most attractive settlements on the entire west
coast here. The people are gentle, godly folk, and they continue
to live at a sensible pace, so different from the less fortunate who
live in the cities.

About six miles to the north of Gairloch is Poolewe, and here
you see the outlet of Loch Maree, through the short river Ewe,
to the sea; flowing out under the small road-bridge with a
rock-girt pool.

> . . . As daylight fades, the air is filled
> With the scent of flower and pine;
> A gentle peace enfolds the earth
> Soon evening stars will shine.

These few lines can very well depict the atmosphere felt in
travelling through Loch Maree's dreamland scenery.

CHAPTER 6

GAIRLOCH—AND DISTRICT

GAIRLOCH: the Gairloch of Wester Ross, the land of the FÀILTES and SLÀINTE MHATHS, a village and district of great charm—a 'resort with a difference'. The village overlooking the horseshoe Gair Loch, with its limitless stretches of golden sandy beaches (the safest imaginable), has a small sporting golf course, and is a typical hospitable Highland village; a friendly people still having courtesy and charm; a God-fearing Gaelic people who keep the Sabbath as few others do in this land of ours. And all this 'midst crashingly beautiful scenery. Could one ask for more?

Before reaching Gairloch, there is a small stone bridge (Kerry bridge) on your left where you turn off for Badachro, Port Henderson, Opinan, South Erradale and finally at the end of the road, Red Point, (eight miles from the bridge) where the County Council have made a very attractive view-point of Skye and the islands. All this area is known locally as the South Side; and the road is very good. Badachro (BAD-ACK-ROW) has much appeal to visitors for it has an old-world atmosphere of its own. Years ago this village had a large fishing station where curers purchased the herring, cod, ling, etc. from the fishing folk, and exported their catches in their own boats. It was said then, the cod fishery of Gairloch was historical. All that is now of a by-gone age. There is a grand stretch of sand and sand dunes at Opinan ('little bays') which stretch for miles and where you always find yourself alone, even in the peak visiting season; and where you look across to Skye. Red Point completes the last link with civilisation, where the stage-coach stops! High up on the cliffs of Red Point one looks down on Loch Torridon; and on the far side of Torridon, the Applecross forest mainland where you can see the pebble-whiteness of scattered cottages glistening in the sun; the hamlets of Fearmore, Fearnbeg, Kenmore and Ardheslaig where the new coastal road is being made.

Back to the main road again—and to Gairloch, a parish which extends to 200,000 acres. Just as you enter this ancient Gaelic stronghold, and upon passing the Factor's house you come to the Post Office, with the old Inn opposite; a very well appointed, non-licensed hotel with old-time hospitality extended and excellent food provided.

This Inn used to be a coaching station in the old days. Crossing the Flowerdale bridge, the pier is on the left, and Flowerdale House on the right is approached through an avenue of trees. This is the west coast residence of Brigadier and Mrs. Mackenzie 'of Gairloch'; the lairds. Their permanent residence is at Conon House, Conon Bridge, not far from Dingwall. They have a long-standing aristocratic connection. The first laird was Hector Roy Mackenzie, born 1440, who succeeded to the title in 1494. He died in 1528. It was he who received a grant of Gairloch from King James IV. The name Flowerdale is more or less self-explanatory; flowers were so plentiful in that no sheep were allowed to come near the grounds, except on a rope to the slaughterhouse. In previous writings, I have given a full genealogy of the 'Mackenzies of Gairloch'.

Proceeding up the brae we pass the Bank, the 9-hole golf course, and the Church of Scotland, and then up a further brae, the old and the new cemeteries. In the former is to be seen a monument erected to the 'Gairloch Bard', William Ross, a celebrated piper and poet, b. 1762, d. 1790 in Badachro. This monument was erected (in 1850) many years after his death by a few of his countrymen, in testimony of their respect and admiration of his genius. '*His name to future ages shall descend, while Gaelic poetry can claim a friend.*' His Gaelic scholarship was acknowledged as the foremost of his day. His monument is situate a little distance up the graveyard on the right side of the entrance gates. Outside this graveyard there stands another monument to the memory of John Mackenzie, who died at Poolewe in 1848 whilst preparing a new edition of the Gaelic bible. He composed, amongst many other poems, *The Beauties of Gaelic Poetry*. At the top of this brae is the War Memorial, commemorating the First World War, with sixty-three names thereon—men from Gairloch, Strath, Badachro, Red Point, Poolewe, Mellon Charles, Melvaig, Inverasdale and Kinlochewe. This imposing sentinel overlooking the bay was erected by Sir Kenneth and Lady Marjory Mackenzie in memory of their son Roderick I. Mackenzie, Lieut., Black Watch and the men of Gairloch who gave their lives, 1914–1919. Next we descend the road, passing the Free Kirk on the left and the manse (built in 1848) on the right; then comes the big hotel, Gairloch Hotel. This former mansion was built in 1872.

Today it is one of the foremost picturesque hotels in the west; perfectly situated overlooking the bay, the Cuillin range in Skye and on clear summer days, Stornoway in Lewis, and the south end of Harris. The hotel is ably managed and supported by an attentive staff. The food is excellent and the whole quiet atmosphere is just what one wants—and looks for—in the Highlands. Further along the road, the Company recently built a self-service grill room on a really posh scale. It is capable of serving 150 people up to 11 o'clock at night; and this is a great boon. Alongside is a block of twenty double bedrooms, all with a private bathroom. This building, which came into service in 1970, faces the bay, and each room has a balcony looking out to Skye. For meals, those who are in this annexe can go to the restaurant or to the hotel. These bedrooms have been fitted up 'regardless' and each has its own different colouring. A wonderful affair indeed; just the place for honeymoon couples!

All this, as well as the main hotel, embraces you with complete contentment; and looking out of your room on a perfectly still night with the sun going down in all its splendour 'across the bay to Mandalay', you could quite easily imagine you were in the tropics—even in Ceylon where I was for many years toiling, as ran the commandment to Adam, in the sweat of my brow (query?)—with the palm trees swaying and rustling in the gentle breeze and the wandering elephants making a crunching sound at 2 o'clock in the morning as they stripped the bark off the trees, chewing it up with noisy relish! But you must let them be— and go to bed!

A good garage adjoins the hotel, and you can be sure of a real prompt service given by Hamish and his mechanics.

Continuing, we come to a junction at the Wild Cat stores; the turning on the left takes you through the village of Strath to Melvaig, the road ending at the lighthouse, RUDHA-REIDH (Rue-Ray); in all nine miles. The road going straight on from the Wild Cat is the main road, taking you to Poolewe—and the Inverasdale district—Inverewe Gardens, Aultbea (Alt-bay), Laide, Gruinard, Dundonnell and Braemore where you join up with the road coming from Garve, and on via Loch Broom to Ullapool.

Taking the left turn at 'Wild Cat' corner, we come to Gairloch's only school, Achtercairn; then pass the old village hall, after that, the Free Presbyterian church (its manse nearby) where we reach the fine recently constructed promenade made by our own workmen. This has enhanced the amenities no end. Passing over a small bridge you are in STRATH, with its bakery and self-service shop; two other general stores further along in the small square (one known as the Centra Mini market owned by Mr. Donald Peacock, who recently took over the previously named 'Kowloon Stores' in 1970; the other store and paper shop owned by Mr. George Leask—formerly MacIntyres); then the ironmonger's, the Post Office, a drapery shop, the butcher's, an electrical shop—then 'Strathburn' which is an old folk's home and a very beautiful one in every aspect. It was opened by Sir John Stirling of Fairburn, then County Council Convener (Chairman) on 12th May 1960. Sir John's daughter, Marjory, is married to Brigadier Mackenzie, Laird of Gairloch afore-mentioned.

After this, there is very little but a few houses dotted here and there along the road, all having unrivalled views of the bay.

The Youth Hostel (CAIRN DEARG) is one and a quarter miles further on; next, the village of Sands with its fine up-to-date caravanning site and shop, North Erradale and finally Melvaig itself. In travelling this 9-mile road you get many beautiful views of the Minch from, at times, quite a good height above sea level.

Now, I am coming back to start this small route anew from the Wild Cat landmark, for there are one or two things of interest to mention.

The Village Hall. In this hall some twenty years ago I remember everyone looked forward to the 'cinematograph' show which trundled along about once a month to Gairloch, and we sat enthralled at real good old Westerns, sitting it all out on hard wooden benches. Whilst the general projection was far from perfect, we loved it, although it was hard going (I'm referring to the benches!) There was any amount of chatter going on. When the 'talkies' came along in later years, then we *had* to keep quiet and listen. These film shows were given by the Highlands and Islands Film Guild. There were naturally many hitches throughout the two hour display; such as the cable not fitting the plug or vice-versa; or it wasn't long enough to reach the plug-in; or some small piece of equipment getting lost in the van. But these were minor problems to us then, especially compared with the men who brought the apparatus to the many isolated communities and what they had to cope with; bumping over roads—or should I say 'supposed roads'—the like of which we have now forgotten; going through snowstorms, ferried through gales and working long hours to bring the only outside entertainment of its kind that could be expected in the Highlands and Islands. 'The show must go on' seemed to be their slogan. There was of course no TV those days, and I don't remember if the radio existed. If it did, you couldn't get any clear results on a set.

These film-men did a grand job for 23 years. But on the 31st August 1970, the body ceased to exist, for local audiences had dropped to almost nil, and so this mobile service could not afford to be mobile any more. The Guild had to wind up its affairs. At its peak in the mid-fifties, it employed a full-time staff of twenty-two, travelling all over Shetland, Sutherland, Ross-shire and Argyll. The year before they closed down there were only three of a staff. The old order changeth, giving place to new. In a way it is sad it had to close down after nearly a quarter of a century in business; for in that time it did an excellent job in the social field. However, in this age, if folk from Harris, Benbecula or Cape Wrath want to see 'the films', well they can take a 'plane to Glasgow to the cinemas there, and be back home again for their supper 'midst the smell of peat and Scotch broth. But I must say I spent many enjoyable, harmless evenings watching the flicks in the old village hall of Gairloch.

The hall has had its day, and not before time, for it is a ram-

shackle tin-roofed building, quite unworthy of Gairloch's prestige
—and is to be sold; what sum is realised is to go towards the
building of a new and up-to-date hall. Some years ago I seemed
to think it was infected with wood-worm, but I may be wrong.
However, I used to say to my young and dainty lassies sitting
beside me, it was good I hadn't a wooden leg, or else—! I still
look back on those silent film days with endless episodes of Pearl
White hanging on to life 'midst all the hazards of *The Clutching
Hand*. We had the same sort of hall in Ceylon, with a native
playing the piano dishing out appropriate music. Perched high
up on a narrow ledge near the ceiling he used to carry on the
whole two hours playing 'Destiny'; and that score seemed to fit
in to any parts of the film. Instead of wood-worm, we had
scores of cockroaches running in and out of the rotten open
floor-boards, and sometimes taking a fancy to our legs. When
you chanced to tread on one, going to your plush tip-up seat,
riddled with moth and other insects, there was a real 'squelch'.
I recall there were two particular cockroaches that seemed to be
a little above the common class. They were named Jellicoe
Jostler and Dead Sea Dora; and they apparently liked the darkness and the flickering screen. Jellicoe was a big, fine-looking
fellow, whilst Dora was petite, and so far as cockroaches go, a
loving sort of girl. They appeared to be the life and soul of the
party for a long time. Then—no sign of Dora; Jellicoe had
eaten her. 'Destiny' had stepped into her life, or rather eaten
into her life! You don't believe me?

So 'THE END' has to be written now over the Highland and
Islands Film Guild; in other words Good-bye.

Remarkable things happened during those 23 years of taking
the silver screen to remote places. People cycled, went by boat
or any other form of transport, just to have an innocent enjoyable
evening. In Foula, an 80-year-old woman often walked four
miles; she liked the cowboys best! The operators covered
200,000 miles a *year*; more than I reckon John Wayne's covered
wagons managed across the western prairies. One operator got
stuck in a blinding snowstorm at Dalwhinnie and kept himself
warm by brewing up tea with melted snow. They dug him out
after two days, and he said it was almost like the Yukon and the
fur-traders.

For 14 of those 23 years the boss of the Guild was Mr. Hugh

Ross. He was once a chief inspector in Edinburgh; a bomber pilot in wartime.

An era has passed; the last reel shown. But the memories of all these shows linger on in many a Highland village, even today.

The Ironmonger's Shop. Just before coming to the square at Strath there is a small bridge to cross, Strath Bridge. It may not be everybody who has seen a stone set in the bridge with the following Gaelic words cut into it: CEANN NA H-ATHAIN (head of the mill). In olden days there appears to have been a mill at this spot, motivated by the swift flowing burn.

The ironmonger's shop, owned by Kenny, serves a vital need to the community and is the finest equipped ironmongering store for its size north of Dingwall to Cape Wrath, or even on to Thurso. It is now a totally different store to what Simon Mac-Intosh had years ago, which catered for oil lamps, gas mantles for Tilly lamps and such like. In front of the doorway, buried at road level, is to be seen an old circular stone, where in the days of carts, cart-wheel iron tyres were heated over a peat fire outside on the square, then carried across, put on the stone's rim, and shrunk to the correct size by throwing water over it.

Simon MacIntosh, who died some ten years ago, was a lovable character and took life easy; and not all that particular as to keeping a check on cash sales, or on entering up goods taken and not paid for at the time. Simon had a small office at the back of the shop, where his niece attended to the books. When anyone came in and bought anything he would call out to her, 'Are you there, Margaret? Book out to Mr. Bee Jay 45 feet of quarter-inch rope for his flagpole at sixpence a foot, two pounds of one-inch nails at twopence, two tins of paint at three and sixpence each, half a dozen emery papers at a penny each', and a few more odds and ends. But lo! and behold, a few minutes later, Margaret, who had been across the way, came in by the front door, and Simon in all consternation said, 'Weren't you in the office when I shouted to you of all that sale?' 'No,' she said, 'I was out at the grocer's.' Collapse of poor Simon!

Simon was a Free Presbyterian. He was full of knowledge and well versed in local (and general) history, and on geographical matters. He was a most honest and straightforward man. Substantiating this, I would give you the following story. A stranger came in once and bought a knife from him. It was of a good make. Some weeks later he called in to show Simon that the knife he had sold him was no good; one of the blades had snapped in two . Simon looked it up and down and said, 'Well, I can't understand it, for it's made by a reputable firm and I've never had any complaints; you must have used it for something it was never intended for; cutting a piece of wood and coming across a nail, or something.' 'No,' said the man indignantly, 'and you'd better return me my money.' 'No,' said Simon, 'I can't do that; once a sale, always a sale.' With that the man threw the knife back on the counter in disgust, stalked out of the shop, slamming the door in anger. As the car drew off, Simon looked through a peep-hole in the window and jotted down the car's registration number.

Simon wrote the firm he had got the knife from and put the matter to them. Was there any fault in that particular consignment? Back came their reply that they had found several flaws in that lot, and if he would return the knife, they would send on a new one to him. When Simon learnt of this, he was sore at heart. He wrote the car-licensing authorities to find out who was the owner of the car. He wrote to the address only to learn it was a garage. He then wrote asking if they could give him details of the driver on that certain day. They told him the car was a 'hired car service' one, but upon further correspondence, he found out who the man was driving that car on that day. Having obtained the man's name and address, old Simon posted a new knife on to him, with his sincere apologies.

Would any shopkeeper in a town do the same today? I am sure they would not. Readers may now realise to the full what I say in this book as to the out-of-this-world genuineness found in the Highlander. As to their characters and dealings, Shangri-La has been their background; so Shangri-La it will be, for ever and a day. An Englishman's word is his bond; and in this generalisation, we must embrace the Highlander. His uprightness need never be queried.

Next is the Post Office, generally bombarded in the season as all these Highland P.O.'s are, with visitors seeking accommodation. Kenny and his wife, should they happen to be full up themselves, will generally manage to fix up these itinerant last-minute visitors one way or another. The P.O.'s in all these villages are looked upon as centre-pieces of information, gossip and what have you. The postal arrangements up north operate with clock-work precision all the year round; and even if the roads become heavy-going in the winter months due to snow and ice, the slogan is 'the mail must get through'. The postie himself is always greeted as a real friend bringing news from the outside world.

A crofter was asked by a visitor what his son did, and was told he was a postie; it was a good job, for in his own words he said, 'I have a job for life and then a pension!'

A new firm, Gordon's of Alford, Aberdeenshire, have recently opened up a store in the square. Their main attention is given to drapery and all its allied service and it is a most useful shop up here. Gordon's travel the north-west and Skye with their big vans, stopping at various places setting out their wares. They generally come around April when the B/B and guest-houses need various things before the season steps in; and in October they come round again—like a travelling circus—to display other goods ranging from furniture to carpets and rugs. They provide an invaluable service up north, where the people don't readily go into Inverness or Dingwall to shop.

The Wild Cat has recently opened up a self-service store, and I have already said the Bakery has one; also the Centra market. It is of course not everyone that relishes a self-service store—not even in towns. Some like to make their purchases from a general grocer's shop, feeling it has more of a personal flavour. In some stream-lined supermarkets where you get lost in finding what you want, and you ask a passing assistant to help you, if she is of the 'can't care less' make-up, she will say she's 'no' sure; wait 'n ah'll see.' 'Assorted biscuits?' she says frowning. She comes back biting her nails, 'nae assortit; will mixed dae?' Ask for a pound of currants and you're told there's fourpence off the roly-poly! And so some people go to the grocer's shop to ask for the dog food their cat's daft about!

The small butcher's shop in all these villages is literally besieged by visitors, May to September. I overheard one day, a lady meaning to buy skinless sausages, asking for a pound of seamless sausages. You see how one can get carried away up in the Highlands? And another woman driver stopping to ask a local for directions, was told, 'Turn right at the road end, go past where the police station used to be before they pulled it down, and you'll come to a bridge that isn't there now. There's a road on the left just beyond it, but that's not it. Go on to the next one and ask again.' Simple enough, if you see what I mean.

On the 11th May 1970 Princess Margaret honoured us with a visit. 'Royal visit to the West' were the headlines. She was carrying out a day's programme of engagements connected with the Festival of the Countryside, during which time she opened the Shieldaig–Kenmore road (mentioned earlier) that when completed will link up with Applecross, eliminating all the exacting and nerve-wracking years when that village was often cut off from the world in the winter time. She also cut a ribbon at the start of a new mountain trail in Beinn Eighe Nature Reserve in the Torridon range. The Princess had spent the week-end at Applecross House as the guest of Major J. L. Wills and the Hon. Mrs. Wills, a cousin of the Princess. The recently commenced road to Applecross is so far seven miles long. It is not a double carriageway; merely a minor road to enable all the old folks in that outlying area to reach civilisation. The road has still another 12 miles or so to go before finally reaching Applecross; so there is every hope of this route being completed before this decade is out! At Shieldaig the Princess unveiled a plaque commemorating this auspicious event. I might mention this small stretch of road has taken five years to make; so on this basis my reckoning for the final link-up being a *fait accompli* about 1980 may not be wide of the mark.

From this point, the Princess came to Gairloch, where outside the Hotel she said a few words stressing the importance of the conservation and preservation of areas of natural beauty, and emphasised that this was not incompatible with the properly controlled use for visitors. It was a sunny day, and I hope our Planners took to heart this pointed reference to 'preservation'. The Princess recalled the visit to our area nearly 100 years ago in 1887 of her great-great-grandmother, Queen Victoria, who was so attracted to these parts whilst she was staying at Loch Maree. The Princess went on to say that Wester Ross was renowned as one of the most beautiful places in Great Britain, far removed from the industrial south. Its peace and remoteness gave it a magical charm and a rare value as an area to which people can escape for a while from the pressures and stresses of daily city life. These words from a member of the Royal family.

The main concern of the 'Festival of the Countryside' was to increase the visitor's knowledge and understanding *of* the country-side.

> . . . So many scenes of beauty lie
> In this our land so fair,
> Each one's enough to fill our hearts
> With joy beyond compare . . .

It is to be hoped Gairloch and district will not be desecrated of its priceless pearl of quiet contentment; of its Shangri-La background.

*   *   *

Each and every year in the Gairloch parish, some sad and sudden death occurs; some tragedy or other is recorded.

There was one fatal accident that shocked the whole village on the afternoon of Tuesday, 18th August 1970, when young 16-year-old Andrew Anderson, riding his motor cycle on his way home to Strath from the nearby garage where he worked, crashed into a rock-face just beyond the hotel when he swerved to avoid a dog crossing the road. He was taken at once and in record time by ambulance to Inverness, but died in the early hours of the following morning, 19th August. This was a major tragedy and as I have said, shocked and cast a gloom over everyone. He was the only son of Margaret and Roderick Anderson, who are now left with three young girls. The funeral at the Church of Scotland, Gairloch, was on the following Friday (21st). It was one of the largest and most solemn I can remember here; there must have been over 500 present, half of whom could not get into the small church.

The service was led by the C. of S. minister, who was assisted by the Gairloch Free Church minister. Psalm 103 from verse 13, 'Such pity as a father hath, unto his children dear' was sung in all reverence, which was followed by Psalm 23, 'The Lord's my shepherd'. The reading of the Scriptures was from the last chapter of Ecclesiastes.

The day was warm and sunny.

Things 'come to pass' it is true; and those who remain have a duty in their life to carry on; although in thoughts one can never forget. 'Not just today, but every day, in sorrow we remember.'

Here was a youth standing at the threshold of a goodly future, for whom the sun went down 'ere yet it was day.

*   *   *

In no way am I possessed with Second Sight, which is common to many old folk in the Highlands; but here I would record my own experience in connection with the above fatality, which I have, until now, never spoken of to anyone. And it is true; I write these lines just as it occurred to me, without any attempt at trimmings or eloquence or choosing of words.

About two months before this accident took place, I was on my way, alone, in my car to the Free Church Sabbath evening service held at 5 p.m.; and it would be about twenty minutes to five when on passing the Wild Cat shop at the junction of Strath and the main road, I came close to an articulated lorry with its flashing lights on the driver's cabin; as is the usual practice. I thought it very strange that such a vehicle should be along the road on the Sabbath. As it came to a dip in the road before the Hotel, it swerved to the right still flashing its lights. Thinking there must be some obstacle in the way, I changed into lower gear and went on cautiously. There was nothing in the way; and when I carried on I could see *no* sign of the lorry at all. I looked if it had gone into the Hotel grounds, or into the Garage entrance, but no; neither did I see it in front of me as I came in view of the kirk's entrance gates and the clear stretch of road beyond.

There was not the slightest sign of the vehicle or its flashing light anywhere; and the distance involved was only a matter of a few hundred yards. The vehicle and its lights had simply vanished.

The spot where I first saw the flashing light was the spot where poor Andrew met his death. Beyond this, I have no explanation to offer; except to add that the time I saw this 'incident' around 5 p.m., more or less corresponded with the time of the fatality weeks later.

*   *   *

Now, we take the journey along the main road from the Wild Cat, up the brae to Poolewe—just another wee village, where if you go through it (off the main road) you come to

Inverasdale, and Cove which is the end of the road. A delightful run, looking over Loch Ewe. At Poolewe there is a lovely little church, Episcopal Church of Scotland denomination, that well deserves seeing, even if not attending worship. It is known as St. Maelrubha. This church is the first Episcopal church to be built and dedicated on the north-west coast of Scotland since the Jacobite rebellion of 1745. It was built in 1964 and dedicated a year later on April 8th and consecrated in 1966 by the Bishop of the Diocese of Moray, Ross and Caithness, the Right Rev. Duncan MacInnes. It was dedicated to St. Maelrubha who played a very important part in the spread of Christianity to Wester Ross and the North-West Highlands. He was responsible for this introduction in the 7th century. He was born on 3rd January 642 A.D., and closed his labours on 21st April 722 A.D.— at the good old age of 80 years.

The name Maelrubha is compounded of MAEL, 'a servant', and RUBHA, signifying either 'patience' or a 'promontory'. He received his early training at the monastery of Bangor, Ireland, where he rose so much in esteem that he became the Abbot, or Prior. In A.D. 671, he left his native country and withdrew to Scotland—then known as Alba—following in the wake of St. Columba. He first settled at Applecross (then named Apurcrossan) where he founded a church. He also lived for a time on Isle Maree in Loch Maree. Maree is probably a corruption of his name. Tradition points to the Isle of Maree being a place of worship before the Christian epoch and of course there are records of the sacrifices of bulls there. St. Maelrubha with his seat in Applecross, used to travel to his cell in Loch Maree via Glen Torridon, and there is a stone on which he is reputed to have rested, which is known as St. Maelrubha's Seat. There is another legend concerning his death, namely that he died at Ferrintosh, whilst discharging his sacred duties, and that his body was removed to Applecross and there interred.

The site upon which this Episcopal church was built in Poolewe was granted by the landowners, Sir Reginald and Lady Macdonald-Buchanan.

A very interesting and informative booklet of this church and the historic background of St. Maelrubha, was written by my friend the veterinary surgeon, Mr. F. H. Kelsey, M.R.C.V.S., who lives near to me in Gairloch. The 8-page booklet can be had at the church, or from Miss M. V. Brown, Headmistress of Bishop Eden School, Inverness.

*   *   *

I know a loch above Poolewe where turquoise and sapphire dragonflies might be mistaken in shimmering summer for the little people of legends; the fairies, or leprechauns. One day, a sensible, rational woman sat there watching children coming to play by the lochside, laughing and shouting among the reeds. When she called to them to be careful, they did not seem to heed, and when she got back among her village people she discovered that there could have been no children there in the first place. Nobody laughed. And neither did she. There is an acceptance in such places that the mirror of yesterday is strangely reflected in the looking glass of tomorrow.

In the Episcopal Church of St. Columba at Portree, Skye, there is a beautiful stained-glass window dedicated to the memory of Skye's heroine, Flora Macdonald.

Leaving Poolewe, six miles from Gairloch, another six miles brings us to AULTBEA (Alt-bay), where there is an Admiralty depôt, for during both world wars the district was a great naval base. There was a boom across Loch Ewe; and this can still be operated if needs arise. In the Second World War, Poolewe was used as a merchant harbour. Ships would come in either to unload tons of war material, or to assemble whilst waiting for a naval escort. Many a convoy to Russia left from Poolewe. Some days there would be 20 or 30 steamers in the sea-loch. Come morning, and they were all gone.

Storms were often a feature of this bleak western coast. One American ship which had discharged her cargo, lay empty in the bay. Suddenly a storm blew up out of the darkness and smashed the vessel on to a tip of an uninhabited island—little more than a rock—just off the shore. Her crew were flung into the angry waters. The blizzard continued unabated till the next day. Rescue parties did their utmost, but only 12 out of a crew of 74 survived this disaster. This is just one of many such sea tragedies around here, during those dark days of World War Two.

A few miles ahead is LAIDE, a small hamlet, and then we come to Gruinard Bay, one of Wester Ross's beauty bays, with Gruinard island off and the Summer Isles (comprising eight small islands)

D

afar off. At Gruinard there is a steep drop at Cabeg Hill, about
1 in 7, to sea level. Rounding the bay near Gruinard House,
there is a War Department notice, warning people to keep away
from the little island just off shore as it is contaminated. It is
Gruinard Island, and was used during the last war for experiments
on anthrax which was to be an answer to Hitler's germ warfare.
Government officials say the island will not be clear of these
germs for at least 100 years. I simply cannot understand how it
came about that some idiot, who by having a severely twisted
mind, gave the order to scientists to impregnate this island of
Gruinard with lethal bacteria. This island has been a death trap
ever since. I can think of many other places where such filth as
anthrax might have been germinated to a far greater effect. But
it had to be Gruinard Island. Should you be out sailing in a small
boat for pleasure, be sure to steer clear of this contaminated
tragedy. Anthrax is a disease fatal amongst farm animals, and
can claim human victims also. And all this to be found in dear
old Shangri-La.

Leaving here and via Little Loch Broom, we reach Dundonnell with AN TEALLACH ('The Forge') towering at 3483 feet
in the distance. This area is supposed to be unsurpassed as a field
for geological research; as is the Torridon range. After Dundonnell—only a small hamlet with a good hotel—we come to
Braemore, the junction with the trunk road Garve–Ullapool,
which one reaches along lovely Loch Broom itself, a distance of
some 12 miles. Just after the Braemore junction, one should not
fail to stop and see the Corrieshalloch Falls, known also as the
Falls of Measach, a 300-feet sheer drop and a most remarkable
defile, the water tumbling over like the graceful drapery of a
Shetland shawl. This gorge is one of the finest examples of a
'BOX CANYON' in Britain, and is spanned by a spectacular suspension bridge. The surrounding mass of trees are wych elm, birch,
hazel, sycamore, Norway maple and beech.

Once in Ullapool you are not far from the Sutherland border
at Ledmore, going through the villages of Ardmair, Strath-
kanaird and Elphin; and from Ledmore you are well on the way
to Inchnadamph, Loch Assynt and Lochinver.

Ullapool has been chosen as the mainland terminal for the
proposed £460,000 fast roll-on, roll-off ferry service for Stornoway. This Wester Ross fishing village was backed by 27 out of

44 members after a two-hour debate at Ross and Cromarty County Council on 21st October 1970. An attempt to have the terminal at Kyle of Lochalsh or in Loch Ewe, near Aultbea, failed.

As I have said, we are just near the Sutherland border, so I will close this chapter; however, before doing so, I feel I must describe a journey taken in the autumn of 1893 from Lairg to Lochinver (by stage-coach) by a gentleman who had travelled up by train from London, and whose train from Inverness was late in reaching Lairg. I came across the following vivid description purely by chance. It will give readers what conditions of travel were in those days. I record it in the first person; I believe the passenger was a Mr. Wyndham.

Here then is the saga of that memorable journey . . .

My train was very late so that I only left Lairg Hotel at 4 p.m. on the box seat of a buggy in the teeth of driving rain and gusts of icy wind. Even under those conditions, a rough road and rising storm, I dropped off to sleep after we had made 10 Scotch miles and was not awoken till the thick snow began to sting my face after 16 miles. There were 10 more to the inn where the second pair of horses awaited me. The storm increased and night fell, so that we made the inn at 8 p.m. The new driver and innkeeper did their best to make me stay. But I insisted on going on, and for a moment the moon soared out of the storm clouds and was reflected in the loch. But only for some three minutes, as ahead of us the night became impenetrably black, the snow increased and the horses, flinching and wincing from it, swayed from one side of the road to the other.

We pulled up at a small wayside inn by Loch Assynt, the place being known as Inch-na-damph. I decided to go on; but the local would have none of my insolence. The wind suddenly whistled and howled round the bleak house, the hail threshed the horses, and the thick snow suffocated the night air, so I gave up at twenty minutes to ten and turned in.

I was frozen through, but found a bright little Highland maid, immensely surprised and amused at receiving a stranger out of the storm. I felt exactly like 'the stranger' in a novel, having, from the nature of my journey, no very clear idea of its object. I was merely 'the stranger' conceived for the first time by the storm and delivered into the warm room.

The nice little Highland maid fried me eggs and bacon, and tried to show the place on the map, but with no success, as she said, 'It sometimes catches my ee'.' But not that night. She prefaced most of her answers to my orders with a startled 'ooch' and informed me gratuitously that she was born at Rosehall.

The announcement that I meant to start at five in the morning brought out a stronger and longer 'ooch' than ever, and, the cook having declined to act, offered to make tea for me. So I went up to a tiny draughty room full of peat smoke and, putting my dressing-gown between the bedclothes and my sopping overcoats, I soon got warm and dropped off to sleep.

Woke before 5 and found capital tea prepared by the little hand-maid. In return for her brightness I presented her with 3s. and a small book, a love story, for she said she was fond of reading story books.

Well, I was rewarded for having given in to the driver. A wonderful morning; dazzling snow on the high hills; Suilven white as the sugar-loaf he resembles, pointing up into the shifting clouds; snow sprinkled over all the tufted bent and heather and peatbogs down to the water's edge. A great deal going on in the sky; excursions and alarms of white and grey and sombre storm-clouds, fleeting and meeting with shining spaces of blue above them, down from which the shafts of light walked over the hills warming the greens and ruddy red piercing through the snow, and passing in blue and gold over the dulled waters, the loch studded with islands and eyots, on one of which the ruined castle of the Macleods of Ardvreck, and hard by, on the shelving shore, the ruined castle of the Mackenzies burnt, as my driver informed me, out of the ignorance of a later and darker age, with all within it who were dancing on a Sabbath morning.

Soon I was driving along the river Inver shining as a sapphire between woods or dwarfed birches, or rushing with a haze of spray hanging about it in a concentrated torrent between grey walls, until it debouched into the sea, with fishing smacks riding at anchor in rows, and far out on an island in the open sea with the white foam of Atlantic breakers leaping and disappearing above its weather-end. . . .

Surely this is a most exciting, vivid account of a journey up in the Highlands, nearly 80 years ago. When one thinks of the easiness of travel today, we have no cause to complain should we be held up on a Highland road for half an hour by a lorry or car becoming ditched and blocking the roadway.

*   *   *

There is the story of a young couple who got married. He

was from Poolewe; the dainty pretty girl from Ullapool. He was fond of porridge; she was not used to cooking it. However, she mixed it up and put it on the cooker and boiled it vigorously, and of course that is not how porridge should be made. When his lordship came down for breakfast and saw what was happening, he just said to his bride, 'that's not the way to make porridge; it needs to be simmering not boiling fast. As you have it, it's boiling away making a noise like *Ull*-a-Pool; *Ull*-a-Pool; whereas it should be boiling gently, like the sound of Pool-*Ewe*; Pool-*Ewe*; Pool-*Ewe*'. (As to Ullapool, the accent should be on the first letters *Ull* and spoken rapidly; for Poolewe, the *Ewe* is drawn out and spoken softly.)

*   *   *

In most of the villages in the Highlands, you come across a wee shop 'Highland Home Industries', which is a unique kind of institution; a shop window for crafts and handwork done in isolated villages and remote islands. Over the years, 'Highland Home' has done a great amount to encourage the old crafts to keep going by ensuring that there will be a ready market for the work done in the long winter evenings. It was over a hundred years ago that the idea started when some of the county ladies, wives of the lairds and landowners, were concerned that the traditional industries should not die out They began to help the local women find markets for their knitting and weaving, and then in 1921 the various groups became co-ordinated and Highland Home Industries Ltd came into being. As business started to expand, the original small shop in Golspie, first a room and then a large shop in Edinburgh, were all outgrown.

So from small beginnings, Highland Home is found dotted about all over the Highlands and Islands. Looking in at the small shops you will find a whole range of beautiful knitwear and craftwork which is bound to add greatly to your souvenirs of the Far North.

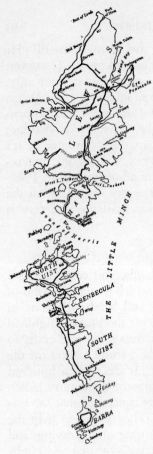

CHAPTER 7

THE
OUTER HEBRIDES

THERE is not much doubt that bands of fierce sea rovers known as Northmen, Norsemen or Vikings stealed away from the Capes of Denmark and sailed far and wide, centuries before Columbus discovered the New World; but once upon a time before the Long Ships ventured to the far side of the Atlantic and to the Mediterranean (and even Ceylon in 1620), the western isles of Scotland were thought, even by the Vikings, to be on the edge of the world. By coincidence, in Celtic legend there is the tale in which the Long Isle is talked of as FIOR IOMALL AN DOMHAIN MOR—the True Edge of the Great World. But today the Hebridean isles are no longer on the edge of the universe.

The whole of the Outer Hebrides can be looked upon as a real yachtsman's paradise, for it is really only they who can easily visit the remoter areas. In this respect the yachtsman has a different world on his doorstep. There are some 250 islands included in the county of Inverness-shire alone, and if one adds those embraced by the counties of Argyll and Ross and Cromarty the total is over 500. Of these, only 100 are inhabited; many of these so-called islands are insignificant dots of rock in the ocean.

The Hebrides comprise a fascinating string of isles and islets, which no visitor, time permitting, should miss seeing. There are several roll-on, roll-off car ferry steamers that one can take to make a comprehensive tour. I receive hundreds of letters from tourists of all races, telling of their various happy tours of the

Highlands, and many mention the Hebrides. I have one before me from a young Sheffield lady, and as it is very typical, I would like to quote what she says:

I have just returned from fourteen days away from it all, away from wars and memories of wars, electioneering, football and TV. Not in a far corner of the world, but in the isles on the edge of the sea—the Outer Hebrides.

I found old-world kindness, wonderful hospitality and friendly people with time to chat, which made up for the rather chilly weather of the first week. With the aid of MacBrayne's steamers and buses, I visited eight islands: Coll, Tiree, Barra, South Uist, Benbecula, North Uist, Harris and Lewis. Also Skye, to find primroses, bluebells and birds. In Harris I was shown Harris tweed in the making, and was allowed to try the weaving myself. To my delight Gaelic was still in everyday use. In Lewis, I visited the Standing Stones at Callernish and the Pictish broch at Carloway. I would like to thank all the islanders for a very memorable holiday.
. . .

How's that for a nice tribute? 'Old-world kindness, wonderful hospitality, friendly people'; and so on. I am privileged to know this bright, young lady; and wish her many more memorable journeys to Shangri-La.

All this brings to my mind the following lines:

So many gods, so many creeds,
So many paths that wind and wind,
When just the art of being kind
Is all this sad world needs.—

THE OUTER HEBRIDES. The isles of the Hebrides (Pliny's Hebrides) stretch from Barra Head in the south to Butt of Lewis in the north, a distance of 130 miles. According to tradition they originally formed one undivided stretch of land—hence the name 'Long Island' which many call it even today. Centuries of buffeting by Atlantic seas have worn away parts of low-lying ground and resulted in the fascinating chain of islands. These, from south to north, include Barra, Eriskay, South Uist, Benbecula, North Uist, Harris and Lewis ('The Lews'). Geologically, the islands are composed of grey-pink archaean gneiss, the oldest known rock, found nowhere else except in Sutherland and the St. Lawrence district of Canada, and they have existed from the time the Himalayas were still beneath the seas. Harris is the only island that one can say has any mountainous landscape; and the few there are, are of a barren rugged nature. In general the island's surface is flecked with innumerable lochans. The white sands provide marvellous sea-bathing, and with the flowery machair and the few isolated hills, these form the most fascinating landscapes. Most of the tourists who come to the islands are anglers, artists, yachtsmen; or just lovers of wild nature. The numerous early antiquities include chambered cairns, earth-houses, standing stones, brochs. The crofters are Gaelic-speaking though partly of Norse origin, for the Hebrides were under Norse domination until 1266. The beauty of their Gaelic folk-songs and folk-poems was discovered by Mrs. Kennedy-Fraser. Agriculture, the herring and lobster fisheries, and sea-weed burning for iodine, and of course tweed-weaving are among the principal occupations. Of late years minor small light industries, bulb-farming, etc., have developed.

During the eviction years, large numbers of the crofters emi-grated to Canada and America, and the *Song of the Exiles*, a Canadian boat-song of unknown authorship, expresses their nostalgia. . . .

> . . . From the lone shieling of the misty island
>   Mountains divide us, and the waste of seas;
>   Yet still the blood is strong, the heart is Highland,
>   And we in dreams behold the Hebrides. . . .

*   *   *

Most Americans like to assure everybody that they could trace their ancestry to the *Mayflower*. What a size of boat it must have been, surely? I once read of a Sioux student who knew the history of Scotland even better than that of the U.S.A. I recall a popular American actor with Cherokee Indian blood in his veins who, when asked if his ancestors had come over on the *Mayflower* too, always said, 'Oh! dear no. My ancestors *met* the boat!'

*   *   *

The Butt of Lewis, the northerly point of the island is thirty miles from the Sutherland coast; Barra Head at the south of the string of islands, is fifty-four miles from Ardnamurchan Point, the most westerly point on the mainland of Scotland. The area of the Western Isles is 810,000 acres, including inland waters, salt marshes, etc.; 1270 square miles. What it may be in the metric system, I leave that to readers to figure out! The acreages of the islands is made up as follows: Barra isles, 23,000; N. Uist, 75,000; S. Uist and Benbecula, 91,000; Harris, 124,000; Lewis, 405,000. Inland waters, salt marshes and foreshore and tidal waters make up the full total of 810,000 acres. Only a small fraction of this area is cultivated at the present time.

The 'Long Island' in the south, ends in a string of small islands before reaching the medium-sized island of BARRA; namely Berneray with a lighthouse and Barra Head the southernmost point of the Outer Hebrides and one of the wildest and grandest spots in Scotland with cliffs nearly 600 feet high; then uninhabited MINGULAY with the weirdest and most startling cliff scenery; then PABBAY ('priests' isle'); SANDRAY; VATERSAY; then BARRA.

BARRA lies almost due west of Mallaig. It is named after St. Barr, a Saint of the old Scottish Church, commemorated before the Roman religion spread to the island. Today, the principal village and seaport is Castlebay, the name being derived from Kishmul, Kisimul or Kiessimul Castle, ancient rock fortress of the MacNeills, looking incredibly old and romantic, which still stands as a prominent landmark in the bay. VATERSAY, lying to the south, across the narrow sound, was the scene of one of the tragedies following the Highland clearances. An emigrant ship tossed by storm, was driven against the rocky coast and wrecked. The burial of the 400 bodies washed ashore presented a problem to the aged, half-starved inhabitants. Scarcity of soil added to the difficulties. Barra, like most of the southern Hebrides, is almost wholly Roman Catholic.

To the north of the island of 'Barra the Beautiful' is the Eoligarry peninsula, where primroses and many other wild flowers flourish in the flat machair.

Heaval is the highest hill on Barra; 1260 feet. Anyone who has sailed into the harbour of Castlebay must have raised his eyes to Heaval, and its great green and grey mass. There is also to be seen Ben Tangaval (1092 feet) on the island's west coast. This side of the island is gentler in aspect than the east. However, Heaval holds the real picture. It is most spectacular viewed from the north-west, when the rocky knob of its peak is particularly striking. Unlike Tangaval, it has little heather.

Most of the east and south-east coast is jagged and rocky—a sailor's nightmare in fact; and as for the waters off this coast, the official word is 'foul'. There are more rocks and shoals off the S.-E. coast of Barra than are found off any other part of the eastern side of the Outer Hebrides.

The central region of Barra is hilly, indented with glens—all of them empty. The folk are clustered in townships round the coast. The island's population is about 1300.

A marble statue of the Virgin and Child looks out to sea from below the summit of Heaval, erected in 1950 by the Catholic church to mark 'Marian Year'—The Year of Our Lady. The biggest of the four churches was built in the 1880's at Castlebay, and dedicated to 'Our Lady, Star of the Sea'. At Borve Point on the western coast, there is a walled burial ground where the crumbling remains of the ancient chapel of St. Brendan now lie almost submerged in the sand. There is to be a new luxury hotel built in the Borve area sponsored by the H. and I. Development Board, facing the bay; a grand view to be sure on a good day, but the winds can be very violent along that part of the coast, with frequent gales, blowing up heaps of sand blocking the road sometimes. This hotel is the second in a chain of five to be built by the Board in the Western Isles.

A small perfumery factory was started early in 1969; but I think the real future for Barra is bound up with the herring, white fish and lobsters. The great fishing days of 1925 are no more, but possibly a revival of this profitable industry may come about during this decade.

Yes, Barra, with its green and blue Atlantic waters tumbling into the many splendid bays on its west coast, is well worthy of the name 'Beautiful'; though its economic prospects appear to be clouded. The optical works mentioned later, has folded up. MacBrayne's freight charges have again been raised; the new time-table for the car ferry service has aroused anger and dismay, as has the decision by the H. & I.D. Board that Castlebay should not be designated as a port for landing herring catches. All in all, the islanders have a stiff fight ahead of them for their place in the sun which they deserve.

ERISKAY (pronounced *Erris-Kay*), a familiar name in romantic song and story, lies north-east across the Sound of Barra. It was here on 23rd July 1745 Bonnie Prince Charlie (Prince Charles Edward Stuart) first set foot on Scottish soil. Today, after the passing of over two centuries, men and women still come from overseas to visit this place of memories.

Eriskay still has a virile population and appears to thrive and improve its prosperity, whilst other islands fade away. Its crofts are well tended and the homes of the people are kept in good repair. Their harbour is the home port of one of the best fishing fleets on Long Island. Fascinating and enchanting are words that can be applied to Eriskay. There is a tiny church, St. Michael's of the Sea, which was built on Spanish lines. The Eriskay pony is still to the fore. They carry creels of peat and seaweed daily. Eriskay supports about 250 people.

SOUTH UIST (pronounced *You-ist*) is separated by the narrow Sound of Eriskay. Its principal port, Lochboisdale, is built on the north of a sheltered bay of the same name, where passenger ships (carrying cars also) connecting with the mainland, call regularly. There is a main highway running up the island, parallel with the west coast from which it is only two miles distant. The island provides good sport for the angler, salmon and trout being plentiful in the streams and lochs. Two mountains, Ben More and Ben Hecla rise to near 2000 feet. In the cave on the shore below Hecla, Prince Charlie hid for several days in 1746 after the battle of Culloden. The ruins of Flora Macdonald's birthplace at Milton are about seven miles N.W. of Lochboisdale. It was in a hut near Ormaclett three miles farther north that she first met the Prince and agreed to take him over to Skye. The Prince spent twenty-two days (15th May to 5th June 1746) in a forester's cottage in Glen Corodale at the foot of Ben More.

Talented artist Miss Kathleen Wylie, who had a studio at Balnakeil Arts and Crafts Village, near Durness (mentioned a few chapters earlier), has now taken up residence in South Uist at the village of Carnan at the northern end of the island, and opened a large studio there. She also has a studio in Edinburgh, High Street, near St. Giles.

Early 1971, the Hydro-Electric Board commenced to build a diesel power station near Loch Carnan, the first stages of the plant being scheduled for completion in 1973; and by 1974 it is expected the final station's capacity will be 7600 kW. There is an increasing demand for electricity in South and North Uist, and the nearby islands.

BENBECULA is connected with South Uist by a causeway built across the sands during the early days of World War II, and completed in 1942. A good road stretches north to the ford at Gramisdale. On the right is Loch Uckavagh, where Prince Charlie embarked with Flora Macdonald on that memorable crossing to Skye. Benbecula is now an important airport. A century ago the island was the scene of sordid evictions, when many of its best men were compelled to find shelter in Canada. The antiquarian will be interested in the remains of Danish forts or circular DUNS. One of the largest is the Tower of Elvina, named after Elvina, the daughter of Rory, a Danish Chieftain.

NORTH UIST is an interesting and enterprising island. Loch-maddy, its 'capital', occupying a good position on the east coast, has a sheriff, court-house—and an empty prison! A level road-way encircles the island. There is a car-ferry service from Uig in Skye. There are several ruins of Druid Temples and Danish forts. The latter were frequently built on rocks in the centre of fresh water lochs, accessible by a causeway. Others were built on high ground in various parts of the island, possibly for the purpose of signalling.

When the Atlantic beats against the western shores, it washes up great masses of seaweed. A hundred years ago there were 400 families in Uist employed at the kelp industry, working all through the day. The seaweed was collected, dried and burnt in shallow pits, the ash or slag remaining being called KELP. In those days kelp was the principal source of iodine and potash; and the industry proved profitable. Then a newer and cheaper source was found in the salt-petre of Chili. However, seaweed is especially good on the light, sandy machair lands. Machair is the name given to the low-lying sandy plains fringing the Atlantic side of the Outer Hebrides.

In the north-west of the island lies the great bay called the Valley Strand. The ebbing of the tide almost empties the bay of water, and some 1500 acres of sand are exposed. There are plans to transform this area into a vast and colourful bulb field—the biggest in Europe.

ST. KILDA, or Hirta, is the largest of a lonely group of about sixteen islets in the Atlantic, 40 miles west of North Uist, but forming part of Harris. Cruising steamers call there at rare intervals. The islands, now National Trust property, belonged from time immemorial to the Macleod of Macleod, but in 1930 the last of the permanent population, thirty-six of them, were evacuated at their own request. I believe a few have returned lately. The superb cliffs of the main island, rising to 1200 feet on the north-east side, are the home of innumerable sea-birds; fulmars, puffins, guillemots and a host more; the gannets breed on the neighbouring islet of Boreray.

HARRIS is the southern portion of the Isle of Lewis, North Harris being separated from the portion known as South Harris by an isthmus of half a mile wide at TARBERT, where the steamers call. A motor road crosses and connects the two. SCALPAY, a small island at the mouth of East Loch Tarbert was a frequent refuge of Prince Charlie during his wanderings in the Hebrides.

The parish of Harris and all the islands of the Hebrides farther south are included in the county of Inverness. Lewis, alone, is in Ross-shire. The traveller proceeding northward from N. Uist must await a boat to carry him to RODEL, the nearest port in Harris. From Rodel the road connects with Leverburgh, formerly known as the village of Obbe, but renamed, replanned and enlarged by the late Lord Leverburgh (or Leverhulme). The Highway stretches north to Tarbert, then on past the deer forest of Ardvourlie, and soon one comes to Loch Seaforth curving down to the open sea.

On this Hebridean island where the tweed comes from, a boy used to help his crofter father with the peat-cutting. One clear day the father pointed across the Atlantic to smudges on the horizon, and told his son that those were the Flannan Isles, inhabited only by a few unattended sheep, a lighthouse and its keepers.

The boy was Finlay Macdonald, and one day he discovered a poem written about the lighthouse men; 'Three men alive on Flannan Isle who thought of three men dead. . . .' This poem by W. W. Gibson told the true story of the three lighthouse-keepers, who mysteriously disappeared 70 years ago in December 1900. Our crofter's son is now attached to the Scottish BBC's production of documentaries. Today, the lighthouse on Flannan is automated, and there are now no lighthouse-keepers there.

LEWIS. We now come into Lewis, 'the Lews'; it is the

northern and largest portion of the northernmost island, and is part of Ross-shire. Stornoway is its largest town. The most important shipping port in the north, it possesses a fine sheltered harbour. It is the seat of a sheriff court, and has a provost, bailies and town council. The daily passenger ship, the *Loch Seaforth*, connects with the mainland at Kyle of Lochalsh and Mallaig. There is an air service direct to Inverness. Stornoway kippers are renowned. Stornoway is called the 'Queen of the Hebrides'.

Lewis castle, modern, with wooded grounds was presented to the town by the late Lord Leverhulme, who bought Lewis and Harris in 1918 and made vastly expensive, but unavailing, efforts to improve the economic condition of the islanders by the development of the fishing industry. Many of the people living in distant parts of the island come to see the castle and its policies. In olden days they were accustomed to exclaim, 'Great Stornoway of the Castle! It is a wonder the King himself does not come to live here!'

Lord Leverhulme (the 1st Lord Leverhulme, founder of the 'Unilever' empire) was nicknamed in Lewis as 'the wee soap mannie—BODACH ANT-SIAPUINN. In 1918 he attempted at his own expense to introduce industry to the Hebridean isles of Lewis and Harris, hoping to stem the flow to the south by providing work for the people. His vision for the isles was of a model paradise thriving on the basic fishing industries and ancillary industries like fruit, flax-growing, peat-processing—and soap. The paradise he was to create would retain all the traditional virtues of Highland kindness, hospitality and Gaelic culture.

But it didn't work out that way.

Why did it go wrong?

According to all accounts, Leverhulme failed because the islanders he was dealing with were 'a crowd of stone-age peasants, work-shy oafs who didn't want progress, preferring to live in squalor'. That was legendary talk; but we all know legend can be wrong. The main problem was finance, as Leverhulme was caught up in the recessions of the 1920's at a crucial time in the development (which was estimated to take ten years to complete) and so he was forced by lack of funds to call a halt.

There was another problem though. Leverhulme found it hard to understand the grim determination of the island crofters to hold on to their own small plots of land, their traditional unique life and independence. He failed to see how important that independence was to them, and he tried to lure them from their land to jobs in industry. That was the main cause of failure. It was, indeed, a sad cause, but quite believable to the islanders. Crofting and industrial efficiency were, he was led to realise, incompatible; and so were the views of the islanders. Lever-hulme became more stubborn as he grew older, and would brook no interference or opposition and tolerated no compromise. All this led to the break-down of understanding between the islanders and himself. He was fond of them, and they of him; but there it rested. All his schemes fell through, and today there are only the sad remains; a stretch of railway in Lewis, a whaling station, and an overwhelming sense of regret. The only successful ven-ture which emerged and survived to this day is MacFisheries, which Leverhulme started, to sell fish to the rest of Britain.

The irony is that today, some 50 years later, the Highlands and Islands Development Board is attempting in those islands just what Leverhulme tried to do.

He lived before his time. He bought an island but failed to buy its people.

*   *   *

Stornoway with a population of nearly 6000 is the hub from which roads radiate to all parts of the island.

Eastward, across a narrow isthmus, is the Eye peninsula, where at Knock a stone in the ruined chapel is supposed to mark the grave of 'the last of the MacLeods'. Despite this, it is cheering to know the MacLeods are still alive and kicking! Because Lewis is so big, landing at Stornoway does not give one the impression that Lewis is an island at all. Indeed you can travel some 80 miles from north to south and still be unaware that the sea is anywhere near. But the roads, as all island roads do, peter out at a shore, a sandy beach or a small pier. Only then does it come home to one that Lewis is an island, sharing its land with neighbouring Harris.

Much of Lewis is peatland; and peat is still forming. *Peat* is a post-glacial deposit, and in the long ages past with the weather cool and wet, the growth of sphagnum moss would be encouraged and this is the main formation of peat. So it grew and accumu-lated over the long, long years. The usual impression of peat is that it is a very modern growth and quickly formed. Nothing could be further from the truth. Forest upon forest; peat upon peat—and so it came to pass. More than 1,600,000 acres in Scotland are covered with deep peat, and workable deposits are put at 600 million tons of peat solids, equivalent to 500 million tons of coal.

Away back during the Napoleonic Wars a local minister suggested that some moorland could be sweetened and thus reclaimed as pasture by the liberal addition of peat and of shell sand from the shore; and in recent years the Lewis crofter has been doing much on the lines of that former minister's idea. Some 10,000 acres of waste moorland have been reclaimed and re-seeded; and today visitors can look at plush green pastures, where before grew only heather and bracken. It is the Harris Tweed industry which has provided the most outstanding example of native initiative. It started as a cottage industry in neighbouring Harris, but at first Lewis was not terribly interested as crofting and fishing were the mainstays of the island economy. But then a series of depressions, boating disasters and threats of starvation caused Lewis to take a closer look at cloth-making. In 1899 only 55 looms in Lewis were turning out tweed. By 1911 almost 300 looms were 'clacking, clacking' along the way to lay the foundation of what is now a giant industry earning millions of pounds in dollars alone. There are nearly 3000 men and women employed, and the product is said to use over one-third of the Scottish wool clip.

Lewis is five times bigger than the Isle of Wight, and three times bigger than the Isle of Man.

Sixteen miles due west of Stornoway brings you to Callernish.

Here on a knoll, its base washed by the Atlantic, is spread out the famous Druid Circle, or *Standing Stones of Callernish*. The massive circle, sixty-two feet in diameter, is about 4000 years old and is ranked second only to Stonehenge among British megalithic monuments. In the centre of the circle stands a boulder 15 feet high, with an altar in front. Stretching north and south of the circle are two rows of upstanding stones extending to 392 feet; east to west, forming the cross, a single row extends to 141 feet. Callernish was obviously an important centre of worship at one time; there are numerous smaller circles in the vicinity all, of them within sight of the main circle. A few miles north from Callernish is a well-preserved dun or broch, DUN CARLOWAY, whose double walls, with a spiral stair between, provide endless fascination for the visitor. Southwards from Callernish, the road winds round the head of Loch Roag, and westward to Uig district. Here, in the beautiful Glen Valtos, Kenneth Mackenzie, better known as the Brahan Seer, was born.

Out of all proportion to its size, the island has contributed a significant element to the development of Britain and the Commonwealth. Even European and American history have Lewis niches, carved by the emigrant and ever-roaming sons of the island. Lewis can boast of Sir Alexander Mackenzie, who discovered the Mackenzie river in Canada; Lt.-Col. Colin Mackenzie who left Stornoway to become Surveyor-General of all India. The MacIvers of Liverpool were a Lewis family who took a leading part in the development of regular steamship travel across the Atlantic and in the foundation of the Cunard Line. Kenneth Morison who founded the Railway Clearing House was born in Stornoway in 1805. W. E. Gladstone's mother was a native of that town. And the list can go on. Today there are many sons of Lewis who are prominent in economic, industrial, scientific, political and religious fields and are found in all corners of the earth.

*   *   *

Having given you a fair account of Lewis and Harris, brings to my mind the following story.

A crofter and his wife had a small plot of land in Lewis near the Harris border. They had a cow and about twenty sheep. One of the latter was a real pet and they called her Betsy. Although a pet she had the bad habit of wandering around from croft to croft, and even from village to village; and one time she crossed over the border to Harris, and seemed to want to stay there. But the Harris people being God-fearing folk sent her back in a van to the Lewis crofter, for they knew his sheep markings as well as their own. Betsy was glad to see the old surroundings and to be made welcome again.

Some time after this the crofter's wife gave birth to a son; and Betsy had twins. Andra was very pleased about these great events, and walking down the village came across the minister, who, seeing the beam in Andra's eye, said to him, 'You're looking very pleased with yourself, my man. What's the reason?' 'Yes,' said Andra, 'I am indeed happy, minister; and why not, for my wife has had a son, and Betsy twins.' 'My, my! That's great news, and you should give thanks to the Lord,' the minister replied. Then he looked at Andra a bit puzzled, saying, 'And who's Betsy?' 'Why, the sheep, minister, the pet sheep.' 'Oh! of course; now I remember,' said the reverend Sir. 'Well, there's all the more reason for you to be thankful to the Almighty, Andra.' 'I've done that,' he replied, 'and I thanked God that it was Betsy that went to Harris and not the wife!'

* * *

And now, what about the women of Lewis, and of the Hebrides in general?

I recall some time ago the *Stornoway Gazette* commented as follows: 'One cannot understand a people and why they act as they do, unless one knows the content of their memories. One cannot understand also the paradox of the naturally gay in heart, seeking religious consolation in grim Calvinism; neither can one understand why Lewis, which clothes the world in such colourful tweeds, clothes most of its womenfolk in black.'

Isleswomen are seldom in the news. Apart from reports of presentations to District Nurses and school-teachers on retiral, they figure but infrequently—even in the columns of the *Stornoway Gazette*! They are not politically minded and rarely attend rural election meetings no matter how heated the campaign. They are never 'strike-minded' as so many women workers are in English works.

The Hebridean woman is at her best in her own home—organising it, running it, raising a family and welcoming people.

It is her field of operations. The Lewisman is very much the head of the household, and the women with the wisdom of experience are outwardly content with this. She achieves what is best for all in her own quiet, unobtrusive way.

Over the last decade there has been much upheavals in the homes, eliminating the old-time drudgery. Electricity, water supply, TV and a lot more modern conveniences have come about. Only those who began their wash-day by having first to carry every drop of water from well or burn, knew what real drudgery was. The middle-aged island woman knew and mastered this; the young woman housewife today would not countenance it, and the very old would have been thankful had drudgery been all the harshness she knew. Life in the islands has never been easy for its women-folk. Even today, though work inside the home is less back-breaking, outside the peats still wait to be cut, the potatoes to be garnered, the animals to be fed. They are practical, industrious, self-effacing women and they make a virtue of any hard work for its own sake. Brought up in an age when strength and endurance were, of necessity, almost as attractive assets in the marriage market as rosy cheeks and flaxen hair, they find it hard to accept that today's well-groomed, expertly made-up slim wisps of girls can so successfully take over. One trait above all has always marked out the Island women. Hard times and a harsh environment breed resourcefulness. The women have always been able to cope. They coped with confinement after confinement, with being left on their own with the brood while the husband went south or east to the fishing; they coped with illness, and there were plenty of home-made remedies. When their daughters grew up, these young girls went over to the mainland and found work in the domestic line in England. They were new to the job, new to the surroundings but they were not bewildered or over-awed. They watched and they learned and they kept their mouths shut. But when they came back home for holidays and got together in Lewis and Harris and the other islands, how they talked and how the Gaelic flowed! and how they would sing, not only to the golden splendour of Shangri-La, but in their own unique golden Highland voices, 'making their way to Stornoway' which Calum Kennedy has made famous by *his* golden voice (the words and music emanate from himself and Bob Alfin).

Make your way to Stornoway,
    On the road to Orinsay,
Where my thoughts return each day,
    By lovely Stornoway.

Where the folk are truly kind,
    Where you leave the world behind,
Where each cloud is silver lined,
    By lovely Stornoway.

And no matter where you are,
    Hitch your wagon to a star,
Heaven can't be very far,
    From lovely Stornoway.

I think this beautiful lilting song could very well be clasped
with the one 'dancing in Kyle':

When the sun has gone down in the dark Western Isles,
    our work is all done for a while,
Then we gather together, whatever the weather,
    and drive to the dancing in Kyle.

*   *   *

There are two pictures of Island women, one of sorrow, one
of joy, that I call to mind.

The first, over fifty years ago of a widow, a small bent figure
in black, working in the fields. She heard shouts. Someone is
running in the village road proclaiming, '*Tha e seachad. Tha an
cogadh seachad.*' (It is ended; the war is over.) The little figure
straightens slowly, for she is tired and widowhood means hard
work and privation. She is crying softly as she beats her breast
and moans, '*Tha e seachad. Tha e seachad. Ach de ni sin dhomhsa?*'
(It is ended; it is ended; but what will that do for me?) Her
son, her only child, is buried in France.

The other is a quarter of a century later. A woman pressed
against the barrier at the quayside as the mailboat comes in,
strains to catch a glimpse of someone on board. And there they
are—painfully thin and deeply tanned, waving, shouting, crack-
ing jokes to hide their emotion across the ever-decreasing gulf
that separates them from shore. She does not wave or shout
back, but the naked intensity of that gaze as it searches and rests
on one of those lean faces, stilled me to silence as I watched. She

is repeating the same phrase over and over again. It is, '*Mo gràdh air na balaich. Mo gràdh air na balaich.*' (My love to the boys.)

There, in the warm-heartedness, the rejoicing in her neighbour's good fortune as well as her own, the gratitude for blessings received, speaks the Lewis woman.

* * *

There are many legends to be found, connected with the Outer Hebrides and Lewis in particular.

There was a famous Lewisman, the Rev. John Morrison, minister of Petty, near Inverness, from 1759 to 1774. He is known in history as the Petty seer, because he had that weird faculty of seeing into the future, called in the Highlands, the Second Sight. He was also a Gaelic bard; and his name is well remembered in Lewis.

One morning a newly-born baby was found on the doorstep of the manse at Petty. Mr. Morrison was told of this, and he gave instructions for the child to be brought in and given every care. Weeks and months went by, yet no one came to claim the child. A year elapsed and this reverend minister called a meeting of the Session, at which two of the elders were appointed to go with him to find the parents of the child. They set off one morning accompanied by a nurse woman carrying the baby. None of them had any idea where they were going, save the minister. They walked to Inverness, then to Port Kessock, where they got the ferry across to Kessock village in the Black Isle, and from there went to a small hamlet, Drumderfit. At this place they saw three men working near the roadside, and the minister sent one of the elders to ask the middle one of the three to come and take charge of this child which he had abandoned a year ago on the steps of the manse at Petty.

The man came in fear and trembling and confessed all to the minister. He said that his wife had died giving birth to the child, and being a poor man he did not know what to do, and got into a panic. He then remembered the reputation of the minister of Petty for softness of heart, so he carried the baby there and left it on the doorstep where he was sure it would be well looked after at the manse.

On another occasion, as there was a special well near the manse, Mr. Morrison was very fond of drinking its excellent water. One Saturday evening the maids forgot to take in the Sabbath water as was their custom. The well was a slight distance from the manse but a good short-cut to it was through the churchyard. On the Sabbath evening, the minister asked for a drink of water, and one of the maids ran with a pitcher in a great hurry to the well. The minister asked why no drink was forthcoming; 'You'll get a drink in a moment, Sir; it is coming,' said the other maid. 'Indeed I won't,' said the minister, 'for the pitcher is broken and the water is spilt, and you had better go and lift Mary out of the newly-dug grave, into which I see she has fallen.' The maid went off, and there was Mary in an open grave, dug the day before, just as the minister had said.

Then again: one wild wintry night with a depth of snow on the ground, Mr. Morrison ordered his man to saddle his horse and to come with him, but the man, seeing the fierceness of the weather, refused to go, whereupon the minister set off alone. He battled on towards a small loch on the south side of Petty, called Lochan Duntie, and whom should he see crouching by the lochside but a young woman trying to conceal a bundle under her shawl. 'What have you got there?' he said. 'Nothing,' said the girl. 'Don't you tell me any lies. I know very well what that bundle contains,' the minister said, 'but before you part with him, kiss him and say "May God bless you".' The girl kissed the child and asked God's blessing on it, and then confessed she had come to the loch to throw the child in, and so hide the evidence of her sinful folly. She returned home and reared the infant with great love and care, and it turned out to be a useful member of his congregation.

One day a group of the women of Petty went into Inverness to sell their fish, and when they had disposed of them, they gathered at a pub and drank more than they ought to have done. When they got back to their village at Petty they were well liquored-up, and upon passing the manse they were more rowdy than usual. Mr. Morrison went out to deliver a homily to them on the evils of drink, but one of them more lively and younger than the rest, asked him to play them dance tunes on his fiddle. The reverend minister was a good hand at the fiddle and very musical, so he went into the manse and soon had the whole company dancing reels to his playing. One of the elders heard about this display and came a few days afterwards to give the minister a piece of his mind, for was it not an awful offence for a minister to be playing the fiddle on the high road to a lot of drunken women? 'How could I refuse to play for the poor woman who asked me to do so, when I know that the holy angels of God will soon be tuning their harps to welcome her home. I wish I could hear the sweet music they will play to welcome her in Heaven.'

The elder shrank away, still full of self-righteousness, but the young fishwife who had asked the minister to play for her, was dead within the week, though she looked blithe and bonny when she made the unusual request.

'Second sight'; and from a Lewis minister of the Gospel!

*   *   *

About the year 1800, there lived at Holm, a wee village south-east of Stornoway and facing the Eye Peninsula, an old man whose reputation for white wizardry and wise forecasts had become known all over the Long Island. He was known as the Holm Wizard.

At that time there lived in the hamlet of Miavaig in Uig (on the west side of Lewis), a very knowing man named Iain Mac-avidh, who in his young days had been a sailor and had visited most of the countries of the world. He it was whose cows one morning suddenly went dry and acted in a peculiar manner without any visible cause. The evil eye of some neighbour or passer-by was suspected, and after a family conclave had discussed the loss of the milk for some time, it was decided that Iain himself must go and put the case before the skilful Wizard of Holm.

There was no road from Uig to Stornoway in those days, but he set out to walk all the 39 miles to Holm. He had to take two ferries to get across to the point of Callernish and then had to walk 16 miles further along across a moorland track to get to Stornoway and then to Holm. Reaching there, he found out where the wizard lived, and told him what had happened to his cattle and wished him to give him a cure; and if envious eyes had caused the trouble would he please name the party who had so badly treated him. The wizard said, 'You are a sensible man, Iain, and have met many people in your travels, yet you have never harmed anyone knowingly, so I can tell you that your cows have been subjected to the black magic, but I will not tell you the name of your envious enemy, for that would do no good, but I can tell you he lives in the township of Crowlista.' This was a place nearby Iain's.

The old wizard went to a battered ancient sailor's chest and took out a packet from which which he extracted roots, pliable stems, leaves and other vegetable products, and with these he made an entwined circlet, which he handed over to Iain, saying an incantation in Gaelic over it. (The story does not say whether he crossed the old man's palm with silver or not!)

Iain returned home and put the circlet in a large wooden *cist* where the milk basins were usually kept, and soon the cows got back their milk and everything in Iain's household went on as before; but the magic circlet of stems and leaves was always kept in the milk chest.

After many years, the good wife of the house noticed that the circlet was becoming damp and sticky, so she had a brainwave, and hung it on the pot-chain that hung from a rafter above the fire so as to dry it. She was very busy with her household duties, and for a time forgot the precious circlet of leaves given to her husband by the famous wizard; and then with a shock she remembered it, but when she went and took a hold of it to put it back in the chest again, the whole thing crumbled into nothingness. However, the milk was never again taken from their cows.

*   *   *

How many people know that in 1739, six years before the '45 rebellion and Bonnie Prince Charlie, disgraceful deeds were enacted in the Isles.

In September 1739, a vessel named the *William* from Ireland with William Davidson as Master, put into Loch Bracadale in Skye, on the pretence of discharging a cargo of brandy. The real purpose of her visit was soon made apparent, when about 60 persons, men, women and children, were torn from their homes and bundled aboard like so many cattle.

Then the vessel went to two ports in Harris, where she received on board some twenty or thirty persons, similarly forced from their homes, and in some cases, from their beds.

In all, the *William* had on board about 120 persons—men, women and children, when she sailed back to Donaghadee in

Ireland. She arrived there on 20th October of that same year, 1739. *En route* a few of these people had been dumped ashore on the islands of Rhum, Canna, and Jura, with not the slightest provision being made for their sustenance. They were thought to be too weak to endure the voyage to Pennsylvania.

On the arrival of the ship at Donaghadee, to rig and victual, the men were taken up from the vessel's hold where they had been stowed and the women and children from another part of the vessel. They were all marched ashore under guard, to two barns, which were duly guarded day and night; but the prisoners by some means or other, managed to escape on Sunday, 4th November, and dispersed throughout the country.

They were pursued by Davidson and his men, and some of them were captured, bound and brought back to the ship; Davidson cudgelling brutally those who failed to move as quickly as he wished. They were labelled as convicted felons fleeing from justice, and the magistrates had therefore issued warrants for their arrest, and as a result there appeared before them on the next day nearly thirty women and children; many of the latter seemed to be only about ten years of age. They were all the most miserable objects of compassion and the most helpless creatures that had ever appeared before the magistrates.

They told their tale of woe as best they could, and later an official inquiry was set on foot, which could only have one result, namely—the captive Highlanders were released and allowed to go where they chose. Probably there are descendants of these Highlanders in County Down to this day.

The chief partners in this iniquitous scheme were William Davidson, the master of the vessel as I have said, and Norman MacLeod, son of Donald MacLeod of Bernera, Harris, and when a warrant for their arrest was made out after the inquiry it was found they had both fled the country and were never brought to justice.

* * *

In the past, histories of the Highlands and Isles have been written and forced upon the Scots by historians of the south, who of course did not speak Gaelic and who looked upon the Highlander as the 'hairy wild Hielanmen ignorant of grace and of culture'.

Cattle raiding, traditionally known as 'Lifting the cattle'—
TOGAIL NAM BÓ—was a common custom in the Hebrides and
the North for many generations. It was common to every race
of mankind really, and probably dated back to the days when men
ceased to be primarily hunters and began to be more and more
dependent on their tamed herds for subsistence. Wherever men
were grouped together in tribes, mutually exclusive, there arose
inevitably a conflict of interests and rights—real or imaginary—
and as a consequence there followed blood-feuds, which recognised no law but retaliation on life and property. To this day in
the Arabian deserts, where the tribal system still survives in its
original pastoral form, raiding is still carried on—though the
livestock lifted are usually camels and horses. Cattle raiding was
a natural consequence of the right of feud; the right to protect
oneself and one's kinsmen, and punish injuries received.

One of the most heroic exploits in the sagas of the Gael is the
famous 'TÀIN BÓ CUAILGNE'—the cattle raid of Cooley, which
took place in Ireland. The story is to be found in the 11th and
12th century manuscript, 'The Book of the DUN COW', one of
the finest and most extensive pieces of Gaelic literature in existence. Cattle lifting was a task for the strong and the brave (we
used to witness a lot of this in the many rousing Western films,
made in America, years ago; and still hashed up now and then
today), demanding courage, skill and daring, and the exercise of
warlike drama. The time usually chosen for these forays was
the second full moon in September, which, in Gaelic, was traditionally known as 'the fattening yellow moon'.

Cattle lifting can never be placed in the same category as
sheep-stealing; the sheep stealer was a man of treachery and
deceit, for his was a nefarious trade, carried out in secret and
darkness, demanding not the heroic qualities, but the base and
the mean. Sheep are weak, timid to some extent, and inoffensive
creatures, incapable of putting up a fight to save themselves. In
the case of cattle-lifting, to the natural stubbornness of cattle,
their tendency to stampede at critical moments, their bellowing
which prevented the raid from being carried out in secret, add to
the possibility at any moment of armed retaliation by the raided;
so it can be understood a cattle raid was an enterprise demanding
every skill. It was no light task to drive half-wild Highland
cattle and it can be appreciated that to try an argument with the

horns of a fierce Highland bull can be as terrifying, as paralysing
to mind and body as any encounter with any other wild beast in
any hunter's territory.

*   *   *

I would now tell you of the mutineers of the ship *Jane* in 1821,
and of the Spanish silver, at Stornoway, Lewis.

The schooner-brig *Jane* of Gibraltar, 90 tons burden, belonged
to a Jew, Moses Levy of that part, and left for BAHIA in Brazil on
19th May 1821, commanded by Thomas Johnson (my own
father's name—but no connection so far as I know!) an Englishman, with a crew of seven. Peter Heaman was mate and François
Gantiez, a Frenchman, served as cook. She carried, along with a
mixed cargo, 38,180 Spanish silver dollars. These were packed
in small canvas bags, which were put in sawdust in casks, six of
eighteen gallons each, one of nine gallons and one of seven
gallons: in all one hundred and twenty-four gallons of silver
dollars. (The plot thickens!) There was no strong room in those
days on a ship, and the casked dollars were simply put in the
ship's hold.

From Gibraltar to Bahia was a distance of 4000 miles. Gantiez, the French cook, started to covet these dollars, and Heaman
was won over and tried to get the crew to fall in with their plans,
but they refused. Paterson, the one responsible seaman, was
openly antagonistic to any schemes for this thieving and looting.
He was at the wheel one night while Heaman was officer of the
watch. The cook crept into the cabin and shot the captain in his
bunk with a loaded musket (reminiscences of our hi-jacking
days) while the mate attacked Paterson at the wheel and clubbed
him to the deck with a musket. The bodies were thrown overboard, and aided by an Italian and the Maltese cabin boy, they
cleared away all signs of the struggle.

Two others, Smith and Strachan, and two Scotsmen were
locked in the forecastle. This cold-blooded murder took place
a few degrees north of the Equator, and five days west of the
Canary Isles. Then the ship's course was altered for the west
coast of Scotland. They sighted Barra Head and the mate went
ashore at Barra, calling himself Captain Rodgers. He purchased
fresh supplies and an open boat. They then cut holes in the *Jane*
and tried to sink her, taking the boat with the casks of dollars

aboard and tried to make for the mainland. But a gale drove them back, and they put ashore at Swordale, on the EYE peninsula off Stornoway. The *Jane* did not sink but went aground at Tolsta Head not far away. Mr. Maciver of the Custom House questioned the men, and the Maltese cabin boy gave them away. They were arrested and the cart load of dollars taken to Storno- way where the Revenue cutter took them to Leith. Gantiez and Heaman were tried, condemned and hanged on the sands of Leith; but odd Spanish silver dollars kept floating around Stornoway for many a year.

*   *   *

It might now be of interest to relate how the renowned Brahan Seer, Coinneach Odhar Fiosaiche—or Kenneth Mac- kenzie—got the 'Seeing Stone'. I have mentioned the Brahan Seer in many of my books.

Kenneth's mother was watching the flocks by night, and as she sat on CNOC EOTHAIL, which looks down on the ancient mound and commands a wide view of sea and moorland and mountain, she occupied her time by spinning with her distaff and spindle. As she watched the flock, looking over the graveyard, she saw the graves open and the ancient mound became thronged with a great concourse of spirits. Then one and all sallied into the stilly night in all directions. Before cock-crow the spirits returned, fluttering into their own places, but then she noticed one grave was still open. The old lady decided to watch for the late-comer and put her distaff across the open grave, when at last she saw the spirit approaching from the ocean regions to the North. In a moment a vision of beauty stood before her, and a young woman, graceful as a fawn, 'golden-haired and fair as the young morn', entreated Kenneth's mother to allow her entrance. 'Remove, I pray thee, thy distaff from my grave and let me enter into my rest.' 'Neither prayer nor pity,' the old lady replied, 'will make me remove my distaff until you tell me who you are, and where you have been.' 'In the dark days of my earthly life,' said the spirit, 'my name was Gradhag, the daughter of the King of Lochlinn. In those far-off days my people ruled the seas, and few were the dwellers in the Southern Isles who had not reason to dread when the white sails of the ships of Lochlinn appeared on the horizon. There were burnings and slaughter and spoils wherever my fierce kinsmen descended, and often my heart was sore within me at the thought of the red ruin these sea-reivers left in their wake, for I had the gift of seeing the dreadful things that were done. One day when the croaking ravens moved the warriors to leave the fiords to make a descent on the coasts of the Lands of the Scots, I hid myself on board one of the ships, hoping that being a king's daughter, and favoured of the gods, I might perhaps be able to stay this senseless slaughter. The voyage was not favourable to the Northmen, for before they sighted these Southern Isles (Sudreys) our ship went down and all perished. My body floated about the ocean currents until it was left at the foot of this mound by a high spring tide. When it was discovered by the people, they carried it up here and buried it among their own kindred. That is why I have been so long in getting back to my place of rest, for I have to travel far over seas and through gales and currents of air to distant Lochlinn, to commune with the spirits of my own people. One thing more let me tell you. When I was in the world of living breath, the gift of vision which I had was in virtue of a stone of prophecy which was given to me by an ancient 'SGALD'. This stone fell from my bosom as I lay in yonder pool, and there it still is with all its pristine virtue, waiting for a finder who is worthy to look into the things that are hidden from the natural vision of man. He who seeks will find it and he will be a famous man, but he who will neither seek for it nor find it, will be a much happier man. Now, I beseech thee, remove the distaff from the mouth of my grave, and let me enter into my rest. . . .'

When Coinneach came to relieve his mother at sunrise, she told him of the strange happenings of the night. Scarcely conscious of what he was doing, he searched diligently amongst the pebbles in the shallow pool, putting each one to his left eye; but no vision came. Eventually he picked the fatal talisman, for an agonising pain shot through his eye, and to his dismay he discovered that his sight was gone. The sight came back gradually, and whenever Coinneach put his left eye to the hole in the stone he could see what was happening in other places, or what was to happen in the future.

The foregoing is the version current in Uig, Lewis, at ceilidhs in the old days.

I leave all this to readers to form their own conclusions.

Personally, and having many years ago read very full accounts of all this Brahan Seer said and prophesied—most of which 'came to pass' centuries after the time the prophecies were made—I am convinced he definitely was gifted with the Celtic second sight, so often come across in the Highlands. It would be ridiculous to discount it all; for they really were uncanny to say the least. Perhaps 'The Stone' may have been illusionary—a gimmick as we would term it today. All the same I am sure he *had* the power of insight into future happenings. How else?

He was born at the beginning of the 1600's at BAILE-NA-CILLE in the parish of Uig 'in the isle of Lews'. If there is a psychical element in man, if there is something more than a mechanical result of physical processes in nerve, brain and blood, then we cannot set any limit to the range of knowledge super-normally acquired. As one philosopher said years ago, 'Time and space are only hallucinations'; we are daily finding this to be true, and it is becoming frightening to say the least. Such hallucinations may be transcended by the spirit in man, *et voilà pourquoi votre fille est muette*. (This is why your daughter is dumb.)

*   *   *

As I have given much space to the Isle of Lewis, it might be fitting, and of much interest to readers, if I gave an account of 'THE FIFE ADVENTURERS' in Lewis; so here it is:

His needs pressing, his coffers empty, and, only too often, His Majesty disregarded by the more unenlightened of his subjects, King Jamie the Saxt looked out on the closing years of the 16th century with a jaundiced eye. And yet, so simple was the cure for all his worries and troubles. Money was the panacea. Money he must have. But from whence was money to come? Where, in all his kingdom, was there an extra groat to be gathered?

North, south, and east he looked, to see only a land squeezed empty of gold. To the west—to the west, what? The Highlands, the narrow Minch and the islands beyond. The islands beyond! The islands beyond! He mused over the question they posed, remembered again the travellers' tales of the Long Island of Lewis, its reputed fertility, its richness in fish, in cattle and sheep—and its wild and uncivilised inhabitants.

Of these people one of his Council had written describing them as 'voyd of ony knawledge of God or his Religioun, and

naturallie abhoiring all kynd of civilitie, quha hes givin thame-
selfis over to all kynd of barbarietie and inhumanitie occupying
in the meantime and violentlie possessing his Hienes proper landis
without payment of maill or gressum thairfore.'

Surely such a state of affairs was an insult to His Majesty. No
longer should the island be allowed to continue a black spot in his
realm. Civilise and develop must be the new watchword for
that part of his kingdom. But how? How to bring the island
and its people within the Glory of God and his own tight fist.
How? Again, how?

Civilise and develop was the only answer. And who more
fit to do the work than those already proven commercial missionaries, the Gentlemen of the Kingdom of Fife and of the Lothians
around his capital? Who better able than they to squeeze gold
from the sunset, even if they might leave behind an afterglow the
colour of blood?

The Gentlemen agreed—for a consideration, a considerable
consideration, formed a Syndicate of Adventurers, and, on a raw
December day in 1598, landed on the bleak shores of the new
El Dorado with five hundred fighting men at their back.

The Adventurers' landing in Stornoway Bay was stoutly
opposed, for, although old Ruari Mor MacLeod, once paramount
Chief of Lewis, was dead, he had left behind a full quiver, born
on both sides of the blanket. Two of the less blessed led the
resistance, Murdo and Neil, but they were swept aside by the
trained mercenaries. Murdo took with his boat to the waters of
the Minch, while Neil and his fighting-men withdrew westwards
to the moors. Their way cleared, the invaders built a stockade,
unloaded their stores, and looked round eagerly for the riches to
be picked up.

But there were no riches. There was not even food for the
men or sustenance for their beasts. Neil and his followers in their
retreat had adopted the scorched earth policy. The days were
short, wet, and cold, fevers and fluxes struck down the incomers,
and, with both the long heel of winter and the bleak days of
spring still ahead, the colonists were forced to send one of their
leaders, Leirmont of Balconie, back to the mainland to tell the
tale of hardships and bring in fresh supplies.

As Balconie sailed out into the Minch, Murdo, with a galley
and two birlinns, was waiting in the shelter of Kintail for just

such a sortie. The fight was short and sharp. Balconie was taken prisoner, most of his followers killed, and a ransom demand dispatched to the King and Council.

The winter wore on, and the plight of the colonists worsened as they waited for the much-needed supplies which never came. Colonel Stewart and Spens of Wormiston took another ship to the south on the same errand and, seeing the garrison thus weakened, Neil MacLeod struck in with his men from the hinterland. His army of 'two hundred bludie and wiket' Lewismen killed more than twenty of the Fifers and, retreating again to the wilds of the west, took with them most of the horses, sheep, and cattle.

News of this disaster was a bitter blow to the King's pride and purse. Infuriated, he appointed the Duke of Lennox and the Marquis of Huntly as Justices over the island, ordered them to assist with all their power the Syndicate of Adventurers and to 'prosequite with fyre, sword and all kinds of hostilitie' those who, openly or secretly, worked against the scheme of colonisation.

That there were secret enemies of the project was suspected by many, and most saw in MacKenzie of Kintail the chief antagonist. It was believed that he had aided Murdo in his attack on Balconie's ship and it was known that he held, more or less a prisoner, Tormod MacLeod, the younger brother of Torquil Dhu, who, before he was murdered, had been one of the Chiefs of the island. But to the unhappy colonists Murdo was enemy number one and, when news came to them of the death of Balconie, they swore to have his life.

Safe and strong on the waters of the Minch or under the shadow of Kintail, Murdo could not easily be laid by the heels, but where direct attack showed little promise, treachery might succeed. It was common knowledge that there was little love lost between Neil and Murdo, so, approaching the former with promises of a free pardon and a grant of land, they got his word that, in his own way, he would bring Murdo in. Arranging a meeting with Murdo, he laid an ambush, seized him and twelve of his followers, and brought the captives in to Stornoway.

The less important prisoners were given short shrift, strung up on the spot, their heads severed from the bodies, packed in a sack and shipped to Edinburgh as proof that, at length, the colonists were breaking down the hard core of resistance. Murdo, sent prisoner to St. Andrews, was accorded a more formal trial by the Fife Justices there. They, perhaps not wholly unbiased, and having been directly briefed, found him guilty, and for his heinous crime of local patriotism he was hanged, drawn, and quartered.

While awaiting his trial, Murdo had spoken with a certain carelessness of some of his exploits, proving that Kintail was seriously involved in the misfortunes of the colonists, but, with the dumb head now fixed on the Nether Bow at Edinburgh, MacKenzie not only refuted all the charges but also entered into a compact to help the Syndicate. Encouraged by this, they entered the new century with high hopes, planned a new town, parcelled out the lands of Lewis amongst themselves, and took their rightful place as the master class. The natives were looked on and treated as slaves, segregated from the rulers, and success at last seemed about to bless the venture.

However, while Neil was alive there could be no tranquillity. Since betraying Murdo, he had seemed to work into the scheme of things, but he was not a man who could be content in the role of underdog. After a trifling quarrel with Spens of Wormiston he took once more to the moors and the old way of life.

The Adventurers realised that the only way to complete success was over Neil's dead body, and a strong force was organised and set out from Stornoway to surprise and capture him. But he still had friends around the camp. They sent him warning. Instead of hiding deeper in the moors, he took the bold course. Mustering his men, he led them close to Stornoway, watched the punitive expedition set out to effect his capture, slipped in behind them in the dark, and attacked from the rear. They panicked at the unexpected attack, put up a poor fight, and, although some of them won back to the shelter of the stockade, sixty were left dead on the moor.

From across the Minch Kintail looked on unmoved at this development. His compact with the colonists was no load on his conscience and, sure now that their venture was doomed, he sent Tormod MacLeod over to Lewis to join Neil.

His arrival decided the fate of the Fifers. Every free man in the island rallied to the resistance and, in the spring of 1602, they struck. The camp was stormed, the fort burned, the majority of the colonists killed and the remainder taken prisoner. Flushed with this success, Tormod and Neil spared the lives of the captives

E

on condition that they would secure from the King a free pardon for all the misdeeds of the MacLeods, resign their rights and claims in Lewis to the victors, and leave behind as hostages for the King's mercy Spens of Wormiston and Monypenny of Kinkell.

So, their dead, their hostages, and their ruined hopes left behind, the few survivors of the first attempt to civilise and develop the island sailed sadly eastwards across the Minch to explain to an impoverished and angry King that there were still men in his realm who valued freedom above life itself.

King James's first action was to redeem the hostages by granting pardon to Tormod and Neil, but, Spens and Monypenny safely home, he immediately planned another expedition, not merely to civilise and develop the unwilling natives but to exterminate them. Then, as before, James's empty Treasury was his greatest stumbling-block. The Convention of the Estates refused to sanction grants for the purpose and, to their credit, also turned down the King's personal plan to cut the costs of an expedition by paying the troops involved in base coin. So, with a fine diplomatic gesture, James put the onus of repossessing the island back on the thoroughly disillusioned Syndicate, ordered each member to hire and equip thirty soldiers, lay in sufficient provisions for a year, and complete the work of development and civilisation within twelve months of again landing in Lewis. But before the expedition was ready to set out Queen Elizabeth of England died and, in the glory and excitement of a dual crown, James let the affairs of Lewis rest in the pending tray.

It was two years before he again found time to devote to the problem of that now more than ever outlandish fragment of his kingdoms. In July 1605 he appointed Spens of Wormiston, Hay of Nethercliff, and Ker of Hirth as Justices and Commissioners in Lewis for a period of one year, enjoining them not to be sparing in the use of 'fyre or ony warlyke ingyne' that might hasten the process of developing and civilising.

That August the new expedition set out, and so imposing was its strength that Kintail decided on a personal policy of insurance by sending with it some of his fighting-men. Tormod MacLeod, overawed by the new force deployed against the island, and ignoring the advice of the lionhearted Neil, decided not to oppose the landing. But Neil would have no truck with any appeasers and once more withdrew west to the moors, while Tormod, putting his trust in the word of the King, journeyed to London and spent the next ten years in prison for his credulity.

Through the remainder of that summer, all winter, and into the following spring Neil kept up an unrelenting guerrilla warfare against the new settlement. Their crops were spoiled, their cattle and sheep harried, and this cold war, livened by hotter spells, preyed on the nerves of the settlers, who gradually lost heart and hope. But in the summer, to their relief, Neil came forward with an offer of peace, professed to have seen the error of his ways, and happily promised the services of all his men to promote a new era of prosperity.

Overjoyed, the settlers welcomed him with open arms, seeing at long last the end of their troubles. Neil himself was given a position of some importance, his men were employed in and around the settlement, and all went on happily till in the dark of a night the poor deluded colonists woke to the sound of shots, the clash of swords, the smell of burning, and the screams of death. When morning came there was only ruin and ash, dead men, and, shrinking in nooks and crannies where they had hidden, a few cowering panic-stricken survivors.

Then, the tide of success running high, Ruari MacLeod of Harris threw in his lot with Neil. Together they hunted and harried the few 'foreigners' still at liberty in the island. Coming in once more on the side of the King, Kintail gave an undertaking in September to recover Stornoway Castle, but the colonists still alive had had enough. Completely ruined and discouraged, they sailed east and, for the second time, the King's policy of development and civilisation by fire and sword proved a dismal failure.

But even then his Royal obstinacy refused to recognise defeat. While in parts lying farther south he modified his former policy of bringing peace to the island outposts of his kingdom 'not be agreement with the people bot be the extirpatioun of thame', he had no intention of relaxing in Lewis. Others might respond to more gentle ways, but not those who opposed his pet colonists from Fife.

A new landing was made at Stornoway, and Kintail, now my Lord Mackenzie of Kintail, was charged with the task of providing the settlers with adequate protection. This in no way agreed with his lordship's personal plans. If the third settlement met with the same fate as the others, there was more than an even chance that the rich prize of Lewis would fall, by default, into his own hands. But the command of his King had to be obeyed, so he sent his brother Roderick with four hundred men to act as garrison. In addition, he was also required to supply such necessaries as the settlers might require till they were self-supporting, and, obeying this order, he loaded a ship with supplies and sent it west into the Minch. But, at the same time, he informed Neil MacLeod of the sailing-date and he, nothing loath, intercepted the vessel, looted it, and the settlers were left in a sorry plight.

Without supplies their chances of surviving the winter were slight, so Sir George Hay and Spens of Wormiston withdrew the majority of the colony back to Fife, leaving only a small garrison to hold the fort till they would return in the spring with reinforcements and stores.

It was all as Kintail had planned. Neil struck at once, overran the weakened garrison, slew all who resisted, and, generous in victory, sent the prisoners home unharmed to the kindlier east.

For Hay and Spens that was the last straw. No matter how great the riches of the Lews, they resolved to cut their losses, and they found a ready buyer of their interests, at a bargain price, in my Lord Kintail. At long last his game of waiting, of playing both ends against the middle, of double-dealing, and lip-service to King and colonists paid off. Lewis was his.

Still in the offing hovered that fiery patriot Neil, welcoming the men of Kintail no more than the men of Fife. Tactfully he retreated to the island of Birsay at the mouth of Loch Roag as the Mackenzie grip tightened. His hopes of winning back by the sword the lands of his father were slight, almost non-existent. But there was always a chance that by some accident of fate the light of the King's smile might yet shine on him. Always the optimist, always the unconquered, he bided his time.

Opportunity came in a strange guise. Crippled, many of her crew wounded, desperately in need of a refit, the pirate craft *Priam* drifted into the shelter of the narrows between Birsay and Bernera. Neil welcomed her captain, Peter Love, as a brother outlaw, admired greatly the cargo of rich spices, hides, precious stones and gold in the *Priam*'s hold, and gave all the help in his power to hurry the corsair back to her nefarious trade.

Captain Love, grateful for the help, saw in the quiet anchorage an ideal base for his future operations, and in the eyes of one of

Neil's kinswomen he saw another promise. To his proposal of
marriage Neil gave his full support and, for once on the side of
Church and State, declared that the union should be solemnised
with due ceremony. The first of the feasts was an engagement
party, and perhaps Captain Peter's eyes were dazzled by the
beauty of his loved one so that he failed to notice that very few
of the male MacLeods were amongst the guests. In the morning
he realised why. He woke to the bite of irons on wrist and ankle,
the knowledge that his ship had been captured, many of the crew
killed and the others prisoner like himself.

Immediately Neil sent news of his important capture abroad.
The Privy Council were delighted at the evidence of poacher
turned gamekeeper and had his name taken off the roster of
outlaws for a period of six months, by which time they had hopes
that complete redemption might take place.

Officers were sent from Edinburgh to take over the *Priam*
and her rich cargo, but while they found the spices and hides in
her holds there was nothing to show that she had ever carried gold
or jewels. Perhaps she never had. Perhaps Captain Love and
his men strung up on the sands at Leith with the tow at their
throats were merely venting their spite when they accused Neil
of having hid the treasure. Anyway, what were a few pieces of
gold between friends? It may only have been coincidence but,
about two hundred years later, in 1813, a pot of gold was dug up
at Kirkibost in Bernera near where the *Priam* had berthed.

Now all seemed set fair for Neil. The King and the Council
were smiling on him kindly for ridding the seas of a pest, and
almost immediately afterwards, in February 1611, my Lord
Kintail was gathered to his fathers and Lewis descended to his
son, Cailean Ruadh, a minor of only fourteen years. Looking
after the young Lord's interests on the island was his uncle, Ruari,
and, at once, Neil decided to test the strength of the new régime.

His first foray was his last. None of his old friends on the
main island gave their support and Ruari, the tutor of Kintail,
chased the unsuccessful raiders back to their Birsay stronghold.
To capture Birsay by force, the tutor saw, would mean a long
blockade and a desperate assault. There was a simpler way.
Rounding up all the women and children kin to Neil and his men
from the main island, he marooned them at low-water on a rock
within earshot of the besieged. Then he delivered his ultimatum.

If, before the next high-water, Neil surrendered with all his followers, the hostages would be set free. If not, the tide would do its grim work slowly.

For the only time in his wild life Neil gave in. The tutor's terms were generous. Neil and his men were free to go where they would outwith the lands of Lewis. Before the next tide made, he and they moved sadly southwards to seek refuge with their kinsman, Ruari MacLeod of Harris.

It was this same Ruari who had helped Neil to bring to an end the second venture of the Fife Syndicate, and from him he expected at least shelter and succour. But in Harris there had been a change of heart. Ruari lost no time in handing over to the tender mercy of the Privy Council the last hero of a lost cause. For this he had his reward. Back from his shameful journey to Edinburgh, he came no longer Ruari Mor, but the bold and well-beloved Sir Roderick of Harris.

On the 30th of March 1613 Neil stood his trial on a long calendar of charges, each a capital one. He did not deign to offer any defence, and there could be only one verdict. At the Mercat Cross in Edinburgh he kicked away the last of his life high above the jeering crowd. His head was struck from his body and stuck above the Nether Bow Port. And so Sir Thomas Hamilton was able at last to write to his King that the one who had been for so long his sworn enemy had gone to his last account 'verie Christianlie'.

The last ledger of the Syndicate of Gentlemen Adventurers of Fife was closed.

*   *   *

Scotland has always been a maritime nation of necessity, and her sailors have won renown through all the ages. Few of her native sailors though have won such fame as John Paul Jones, hailed as the founder of the United States Navy in the country of his adoption, and described as a 'desperate buccaneer, closely akin to the Fife Adventurers'. Another name given him was 'Paul Jones, the Rover of the Seas'.

In 1779 Paul Jones (those acquaint with dancing will know there is often a 'Paul Jones' dance, where at intervals everyone grabs hold of another partner) appeared in the Firth of Forth, and spread alarm and despondency all around the East Coast. The minister of Kirkcaldy took his flock out on to the sands to pray for winds to drive Paul Jones away. Many of the coastal harbours still show the defences that were hurriedly built to withstand a possible attack from this master mariner.

And all this, 190 years ago.

In August 1779 this famous American privateer was reported prowling among the Western Isles and the Hebrides; and word was passed along the coast to keep a sharp look out for him.

On 30th August, Norman MacLeod of Waterstein reported a large ship between his place and Barra. There was a strong gale blowing from the west, and the ship appeared to be making for Skye. When nearing Feist Point (now miscalled Neist) the wind began to slacken and so Norman MacLeod, thinking the ship might be Admiral Paul Jones's, sent messengers along the coasts to Bracadale and Waternish warning the people to be constantly on the alert while he himself along with others of the gentry went post-haste to Dunvegan.

Meantime, that evening the ship rounded Dunvegan Head. MacLeod's fisherman, Allan MacLeod, happened to be fishing and as he saw the strange boat rounding the Head he became suspicious and so lost no time in reporting all this to the Factor at Dunvegan. At this time General MacLeod was in North America serving with the British Army, leaving the Castle in charge of the Factor, who promptly arranged for the safety of the plate and valuables to be packed into three creels and loaded on to two ponies; his own baby boy was placed in a fourth creel to balance the third; and off they went with two men in charge of this precious cargo, and with some women and children they all went to the hill of 'SGRIAIG' not far away. This done he set about defensive measures for the Castle in case of attack. Meantime the movements of the ship were closely watched by eagle eyes from the Castle battlements as the morning of the last day of August 1779 dawned. As the ship, with Paul Jones aboard, was approaching the anchorage in the bay of Dunvegan (Loch Dunvegan), the Admiral was preparing to man his gig boats for landing, the sound of bagpipes was heard, and looking in the direction from which it came, he was alarmed to see a column of people with pipers playing at its head marching along the shore from the north, apparently making straight for the Castle. Believing that this was a force of Clansmen gathering to the defence of the Castle and having no doubts at all of the warmth of the reception in store for him from such a formidable-looking force, he immediately put about without casting anchor, or firing a shot, and made all haste to escape from the trap into which he imagined he had got himself. But this so-called formidable force was none other than the funeral cortège of Donald MacLeod, tacksman of Swordale, who had died three days previously, and which was wending its way to the burial ground of Kilmuir, about a mile south-east of Dunvegan.

The identity of the raider was established as the *Richard*, for in entering the loch Paul Jones intercepted two local men in their wee boat, and took them on board to pilot the ship safely to anchorage. (It was Calum Ruadh—Red Malcolm—and his brother who were returning home from visiting friends at Bore-raig the previous evening. Calum heard one of the ship's officers refer to the Commander as Admiral Jones. Later when Paul Jones hastily sailed away, Calum and his brother were dropped off to their own wee boat again and given payment for their services. Calum knew that the long column of men they had all seen was Donald MacLeod's funeral; but he never enlightened the Admiral as to this. The laugh was surely on the Admiral!)

After leaving Dunvegan, the *Richard* made towards Barra, and next day was seen off the Butt of Lewis, being chased by two other warships.

This story of the abortive raid on Dunvegan by Paul Jones was told for many years at ceilidhs 'midst great hilarity accompanied by many drams going down the hatch; and how that one MacLeod, and a dead one at that, defeated the American navy!

*   *   *

In the chapter on Highland Fisheries, I have devoted much to the hazards the fishermen have to risk. Many small tragedies occurred off the Hebridean coast, but the worst of all was in December 1894 when 19 fishermen died in the great drowning at BACK in the Broad Bay area east of Stornoway.

Broad Bay on the east coast of Lewis, between the northern mainland and the Eye Peninsula, used to be one of the richest fishing grounds in the United Kingdom. Last century, for the hundreds of crofters who lived around its shores, it was their

larder. They lived on potatoes, meal—and fish. The land occasionally cheated them of its harvest, but the sea, never. But they
had to pay dearly for the bay's bounty, sometimes with their lives.

In the 30-year period to 1894, sixty-nine fishermen from
villages in the BACK area were drowned within sight of their
crofts. The 'great drowning at Back' forms the story of the
worst of these tragedies.

On an ominously calm December night in 1894, ten open
sailing boats, ranging in size from 14 to 24 feet, put to sea to fish.
A sudden hurricane from the north-east struck the little fleet, and
drove them helplessly towards the rock-strewn sands at the head
of the bay. Three boats crashed to disaster, seven were saved.
Nineteen men from the same little village street at BACK, including fathers, sons, and three brothers, perished. The whole area
grieved as the people searched the shores for days afterwards,
looking for the bodies. Some were found only weeks later,
wedged in rocks at MELBOST. As so often happened, one body
was never recovered.

The periodic sacrifice was complete—until the next time.

CHAPTER 8

HIGHLAND CUSTOMS AND BELIEFS

THERE is an old Highland saying, 'Better a good funeral than a poor wedding'.

A cheerful note on which to start a new chapter, surely!

Funerals and Second Sight—or 'The Sight' as it is generally called in the Highlands—can form very interesting reading in the North. Even today incidents *do* occur which would seem to suggest the existence of a sixth sense. It is said this strange phenomenon is a heavy burden to be borne, made heavier by the knowledge that the possessor will, in all probability, pass it on to the children or even grandchildren.

Second Sight is a gift, or curse, which cannot be controlled or switched off at will like the wireless. There are two kinds of the True Sight. Those who see something at a distance, like an accident, illness or sudden death; and those who see the future which is unknown to others living. This latter is more commonly found in the Hebrides. At one funeral, as the neighbours assembled round the house of death where the coffin had been placed on chairs outside the door so that the service might be held in the open, one man stumbled out of the gathering obviously ill. Two friends helped him into a nearby house. When recovered he told them that as they were all coming to the house he had seen, not the old man's coffin on the chairs, but a tarpaulin in which was wrapped the still-dripping body of a young man drowned in the sea. He knew it to be the young owner of the croft. A year later, that young man was drowned and his body brought back for burial.

Then there were seers in the Highlands (such as the renowned Brahan Seer) who acquired the art or gift of telepathy. I have also mentioned the name of the Rev. John Morrison, the Seer of Petty, and there was also the Rev. John Kennedy of Killearnan, father of Dr. Kennedy of Dingwall, who saw events coming.

One Sabbath morning Mr. Kennedy, preaching from his pulpit at Killearnan, warning sinners of their danger in a Christless state, suddenly paused, and in a subdued and solemn tone said, 'There is a sinner in this place very ripe for destruction, who shall this night be summoned to a judgement seat'. Next morning the neighbours observed flames issuing from a hut (not far from the meeting house), which was occupied by a woman notorious for immorality, and in which, when they were able to enter, they found but the charred remains of the miserable tenant.

On another occasion he was preaching at Contin on a Communion Sabbath, when a certain man from Kiltarlity, who was a church member, for some reason kept his seat after the other members had taken their places at the Table. The minister said, 'There is still one communicant here who has not come forward, and until that person takes his seat at the Table I cannot proceed with the service'. Another verse was sung, but the man from Kiltarlity did not come forward. Mr. Kennedy then said, 'I implore you to come forward, for this is your last opportunity of showing forth the Lord's death till He come, for if I am not greatly mistaken, you will not reach your home in life after the service'. The man then came forward and the minister proceeded with the service. On the dismissal of the congregation on the Monday, the man set off homewards, but on crossing some ford on the Orrin, he was carried downstream and drowned.

The Rev. John Morrison (the Petty Seer) once was accompanied by his servant lad, when he was riding into Inverness to officiate at a Communion. 'You see a large number of people there," remarked Mr. Morrison, 'yet only six of them will go to Heaven. As proof that I know the truth of what I say, the innkeeper there (pointing to the inn at Milton) who is now in good health, will be in eternity when you return.'

When the lad was passing Milton on his return journey, he was horrified to find that, under the influence of drink, the innkeeper had fallen down the stairs a short time previously and died immediately.

One of Mr. Morrison's parishioners was a fisherman noted for his bad life and utter disrespect for the admonitions of his good pastor. Walking one summer evening in the garden of his manse in earnest conversation with one of his Elders, the reverend gentleman suddenly paused in the middle of a sentence, and stood staring before him with unseeing eyes. The Elder, alarmed, asked if he was unwell, but received no answer. In a minute or so, however, the minister drew a long breath, shivered slightly and turning to his friend with a horror-stricken face, said, naming the fisherman, 'Well, that poor unhappy man has often scoffed at my teaching, but he will never do so again, for he is at this moment lying drowned at the new pier at Inverness, and his body will be taken into the Gaelic Church tonight and kept there until it is claimed by his relatives'.

This vision came strictly true in every particular. The Elder hastened to the friends of the fisherman and told them of what the minister had said. They, having the most implicit belief in his supernatural powers, immediately hastened to Inverness and found the body of the drowned man lying in the Gaelic Church, which at that time was used as a sort of mortuary in cases of sudden death, until the relatives came forward to claim the remains.

On another occasion, this minister had some cattle grazing on the fields near Culloden. He sent his manservant one day to see how they were getting on. On his return to the manse the man reported that he had seen all the cattle, and that they were getting on well. 'Have you seen them ALL today, William?' asked Mr. Morrison, 'Yes, every head of them,' answered the man. 'Well, William, you will go as fast as you can, and take a horse and cart with you and bring the dun stot home. He is at present lying on his back in a ditch with two of his legs broken. Get some men to go along to help you. You have told me a falsehood, for you have not seen the poor dun stot today' (a *dun stot* is a black, young bullock). The man afterwards confessed that he had not seen the dun stot, but on proceeding to the ditch indicated by the minister, he found the animal just as described.

These few incidents I have named are surely extraordinary?

I had a letter from a lady in Stafford written early in 1970 telling me that her grandmother had often recounted the Clearance days and Patrick Sellar. She also told me of a story, very similar to one I wrote of in *Highland Pearls* as to the men and women getting lost in the mist at Slioch, Loch Maree, and therefore stayed where they were overnight to proceed next morning to Aultbea, after being some months away at the east coast for the herring season there. Her grandmother told the following story: namely, that on one journey from the east coast, the returning party consisted of all young men—about a dozen of them. They too were cut off by a swirling mist on Slioch, and so decided the only sensible thing to do was to stay put in an old bothy till morning. This they did. One of the lads had his bagpipes with him, and he said all we need now is a girl each, and we could have a dance and keep us warm and cheery through the night. At midnight some lovely girls *did* come along, so they started to dance and have a real good ceilidh. The piper's girl sat beside him, holding his hand best she could, but as he was playing he noticed that all the girls had horse's hooves instead of feet. He tried to convey in his music, telling the boys about it, 'Heigh-ho they have horse's feet' (in Gaelic). These maidens were called 'Hoofies'. But his compatriots took no heed, so he said to his girl that he wanted to go outside for a wee while. She said, 'You won't run away, will you, because I love you'. So he left his pipes with her, and when he got outside he ran as fast as he could away from the bothy and spent the remaining hours of darkness in hiding in the heather. When dawn broke, he returned to the bothy; and all that remained was a pile of bones and the bagpipes; so he knew there had been a midnight feast. His pals were never seen again.

Dense Scotch mists can produce weird spectres, as the following story will show. It occurred to a visitor who went for a walk high up Ben Loyal (Sutherland) one fine autumn day, but on his way back to Tongue later in the day, a mist suddenly shut everything down completely. He happened to be near some sheep fencing and so decided to follow its direction downhill. After going a little distance he looked back and saw a large man silhouetted against the mist and he hailed him several times, but getting no answer went back the fifty yards or so to investigate. There was no one to be seen. Starting off down again, and looking back from about the same point, he again saw the man's figure. Again retracing his steps, there was no sign of anyone or anything. He then imagined he had seen a spectre, and taking fright, soon made his way back home.

The next day he questioned the head keeper and one or two shepherds around Ben Loyal estate, but they were all quite certain nobody had been up where he had walked that day. The answer to this peculiar and somewhat nerve-racking experience can be explained, that the man had seen his own image. The shadow of the observer is thrown up by a low sun against an opaque wall of mist. It is thus magnified enormously and is sometimes distorted into grotesque forms. So that's your ghost story!

Another tale the aforementioned grandmother used to like telling about, was people who used to dig up graves for gold, for it was said fishermen wore gold earrings, as it was supposed to give them good eyesight. Her grandmother said that when anyone was ill and they had to stay up with them at their bedside, they always put plenty of blankets on the windows to keep any light from showing, as there was usually a man prowling around, a doctor, and if he thought anyone was ill and dying, he liked to get the body. No doubt it was sent to Edinburgh for the students to practise on; and he was supposed to have a black shiney horse and trap, and was often seen passing the iron bridge, between Golspie and Brora, at midnight—in fact they still say his ghost passes even today.

These authentic stories cannot be too outdated even today?

Another elderly married woman, a friend of mine living in Muir of Ord, near Beauly, told me in all seriousness, that whilst she did not have Second Sight, she had Second Hearing. Not so many years ago, her daughter (about nine or ten years of age) and she were staying in a small cottage near the Free Church at Muir of Ord at the time. Her husband was on night shift at a nearby works, so her daughter and herself were sharing the same bed. She used to get up at 5.30 a.m. or so to unlock the door for her husband coming in at 6 a.m. and then went back to bed. It was late spring time. Her daughter and she were talking in bed, when suddenly, she says, 'We heard a most glorious choir of voices, beginning low and, when the sound was directly above us, the singing rose to a high crescendo, and then dwindled away into the distance. Now, at that time,' she tells me, 'there were few if any radios nearby and certainly no transistors. My child and I said, "What was that?" And we talk about it to this very day (1971).' She continues in her letter, 'It certainly was no earthly choir; I shall never forget it as long as I live, because it was *so* beautiful, and my own personal opinion is that it was some soul going to Heaven in Glory. I mentioned it to our minister at the time, but his only comment was "Very interesting, yes, very interesting indeed".' And that was all.

These things certainly make one think.

There was a ferryman taking an English passenger from one of the small islands back to Lochmaddy in North Uist. They had been to visit a sick woman, but she made a remarkable recovery. As he disembarked his passenger at Lochmaddy he chanced to say that he had seen in a vision a crowd of people around her doorway as they left. The passenger paid no heed to this remark of an otherwise quiet, silent ferryman. Later that year the woman's husband died. Hence the crowd of folk; a 'host of witnesses'.

I now tell you about a dog, a spaniel breed, who seemed to delight in attending funerals and howling his head off. A postie, Gillie Munro, lived near Onich, ten miles from Fort William, and he bought this mongrel pup for company's sake. As I have said, the dog was mad on funerals; he seemed to smell them, and people remarked upon his strange 'Smelling Sight'. One day there was a very big funeral taking place at Fort William, ten miles away, as I have told you, yet the animal appeared to know of it, and was there, howling his lament the whiles. Then he trotted back home. When this dog, with obvious uncanny smell, died it was reported all the dogs in Fort William attended his burial in the postie's wee garden, and howled to the moon.

Funerals. Funerals were big social occasions for the men on an island in the Highlands, where people took a long time about dying. Father and sons left ploughs, sheep and fish hooks and came eagerly to renew old acquaintances, to exchange news and views, to spit reflectively and enjoy the unaccustomed wearing of a gold watch and chain. Uniformity of wear was observed only in bowler hats, and a half bottle of whisky fitting snugly in the hip pockets. Islanders wore bowlers only for funerals and their own marriages, so that a nonogenarian might go to his rest without having had it on his head more than, say, a dozen times. The eldest sons then came to wear these bowlers.

But the funerals today are not the same as they were in days gone by. In olden times, it was necessary to take provisions when men had to travel long distances on foot and had to carry the coffin across rough and hilly country to the place of burial. And of course the provisions which were obtainable and easily carried were home-made oatcakes, cheese and whisky. The more important the person, the bigger and better was the banquet. There is related the story of one Chief dying in Kintail who was buried in Beauly Priory, about a year or so after Waterloo. There was a great feast set out for the gentry, who were to have foreign wines and liqueurs, and for the hundreds of ordinary folk, many of whom had walked from Glenelg, eight bolls of oatmeal were baked into oatcakes, and this, together with large quantities of cheese washed down with 170 gallons of whisky, made the folk so light-headed that they took part of the drinks reserved for the gentry. The result was that one man and two women died. Perhaps the poor souls drank on empty stomachs! The story of that funeral was often told at ceilidhs for many a day. Some years later when Colonel Grant of Moy died, it was said that 4000 people attended; and it took several days for some of the mourners to return to their respective homes.

These days are gone; and in far-off districts motor hearses come and go, and the people are gathered to their fathers with as little ceremony as possible. You would think at times that the living cannot get rid of the dead quickly enough. Many Americans come to the Highlands and take a look at churchyards seeing if they can trace a tombstone or such like where their ancestors might be. But the poor and the proud of yesterday, rest in these hallowed spots side by side as the dust of today.

*   *   *

I think myself as to Second Sight and whatever anyone else has to say about it, even learned psychologists and the like, or however much some may scoff, it is best to keep an open mind on the subject for 'there are more things in heaven and earth than are dreamt of in our philosophy'.

One comes across stories of Phantom Funerals in bygone times. Some people are specially gifted to hear sounds which are inaudible to others. In respect of phantom funerals it must give one a very eerie feeling if, when going along a road at night talking unconcernedly to somebody, you are suddenly told to keep quiet and to take to the side of the road as a funeral is passing, when indeed nothing is seen by you. You were told that if you did not step aside, and kept to the roadway, you were obstructing its way, the consequences to you might be serious.

There was a man in the Newtonmore district, whose family had migrated from Wester Ross years ago. He possessed the second sight to a remarkable degree. He never failed to see a spectre funeral before the death of someone in the neighbourhood, and as he told people what he saw, they ultimately endeavoured to keep out of his way, not knowing what doleful news he might have to communicate to them. On one occasion he was walking along the public road, near his house, when a spectre funeral met him as he was about to cross a bridge. Just at the moment when he stepped aside to let the funeral pass, he received a severe kick on the leg from a horse that happened to be ridden by one of the funeral party. There could be no doubt that he got the kick— he felt the pain, and actually limped back home. He told his household what had happened, but on looking at his leg, they could see no mark of any kind that would show he had received a kick from a horse. However, he persisted he *had* been kicked, and complained of severe pain in the leg the remainder of the night. Next day, though, he was up and about as usual, and having cause to pass along the same road and over the same bridge, he this time met a real funeral at the very spot where the phantom funeral had passed him the previous day. He saw that the funeral party was the same; the same horse and its rider were there, and then suddenly, as it passed him, the horse shied, kicking him severely on the leg in the exact spot where he had received the kick from the spectre horse. He limped home again as he did before, and was obliged to keep to his bed for some time owing to the severity of the blow he had received; but he assured his friends that the pain was no more severe than he felt after the kick he got the previous day. His household did not laugh at him this time.

There are many instances of this peculiarity to be heard of in Sutherland; too many to record here. But I will give two examples. An old lady used to frequently see what she described as the spectre of people known to her; and after the vision, she would invariably tell her friends that such a person was to die. Once, she said, she saw the spectre of a person then abroad, and sure enough some weeks later, there came the news of that person's death, which had actually taken place on the very day the old lady had seen the spectre. On another occasion, she said that she saw what looked like a human eye coming out of a certain house in the evening and proceeding along to the church-yard. And although there was no case of illness at the time, a few days afterwards a death occurred in that very house, and the funeral took place to the churchyard indicated in her vision.

*   *   *

The ancient worship of the Sun is still commemorated in the common practice of 'circumambulating' anything three times in the direction of the sun, the beneficent power, or by taking water to be used in charming and turning it three times round a lighted candle. This invitation of the action of the sun, called DEASIL, is supposed to bring good fortune as a matter of course. The ancient sun-god of the Celts was named GRANNOS, sometimes GRUAGACH—the fair-haired. In pagan times, wells or springs were believed to be inhabited by a spirit or divinity which caused the waters to have healing properties to those who drank, or bathed in them, at the same time propitiating the divinity with an offering. In Christian times such useful properties could not be discarded and the spirit of the well was still vaguely believed in, or its power transferred to some local saint in whose charge the well was supposed to be. The ritual observed, the offering made, and the benefit expected, were the same for the Christian Celt as for his pagan ancestors.

Parts of the rowan have the occult powers of the whole growing tree. A rowan wand placed over the door of a barn or byre keeps off witches and evil spirits; a twig bound in a circlet and placed beneath a vessel of milk prevents its being spirited away; while a fire of rowan-wood is three times sacred.

A man at Kyle-Rhea once said he saw a sea-serpent; 'Yes, yes, one day I saw the fearful head of the beast go down the kyle; and indeed it was a week after before its tail had passed!'

In 1900, when it was sought to remove the crofters of Sconser (in Skye) to better land in the south of Skye, among the reasons alleged by them for having to remain in their unhealthy township was this, namely that the ground was cursed because of former evictions which had taken place there, and so it was impossible to expect them to settle on it.

A woman frequently saw a double of herself walking close

by her. To make sure that it *was* her own double, she went out on different days in different articles of dress, which she found to be exactly copied by her spectral companion. This was or course regarded as a warning of her speedy death.

* * *

I come now to Highland belief in strange cures.

Belief in strange and wonderful cures was very prevalent in the Highlands not so very long ago; and indeed they may still be found here and there. Many of the cures, as previously mentioned, were effected by water, which usually came from some well or other generally associated with the name of a saint, who in the dim and distant past pronounced his blessing over it. Usually some votive offering had to be given to the spirit of the well; and that is the reason why at such wells pieces of cloth, coins and such like were either affixed to some tree in the vicinity or actually put into the well; generally described as wishing wells. We see this even today in the 'Clootie well' at Culloden, where hundreds of people go there each year in May to keep up the ritual. The same thing happens on Isle Maree in Loch Maree. I have many times plugged a coin (or a nail) into the old birch tree at that famous well—and wished!

Near Cromarty, there is a well, known as the 'Fiddler's Well'. Two young men of the place who were very much attached to each other, were seized at nearly the same time by consumption. One died very shortly afterwards, but the other, though wasted away almost to a shadow, was able to follow his friend's remains to the grave. The survivor's name was Fiddler. During the night he was haunted by thoughts of coffins, and graves, but towards morning slept and had the following dream. He thought he was walking along the seashore when he heard the voice of his late companion say, 'Go on, Willie, I shall meet you at Stormy'—the name of a rock. On hearing the voice, he turned round, but seeing no one, he got up and went on to near the rock, in the hope of seeing his friend, and sat down on a bank to await his coming. Suddenly he remembered he was dead and burst into tears, but at this moment, a bumble bee came buzzing round and round his head. Although he brushed it away, still it came back, and at last its buzzing seemed to resolve itself into the voice of his dead pal, saying, 'Dig, Willie, and drink.' No sooner had he lifted and torn off a sod than a beautiful spring of clear water gushed forth, and the bee flew away in triumph— after which he woke. Rising up, he proceeded to the spot, dug the well, drank the water and recovered. To this day, it is said the well still possesses its virtues, for though the water may only be simple water, it must be drunk in the morning, and with pure air, exercise and early rising as its helpers, it continues to work cures.

There is a little mountain loch, or tarn, in Sutherland, not far from Ben Loyal, which was reputed to cure, not by drinking, but being immersed in it; and in addition to dipping in the loch it was necessary for the patient to climb the neighbouring hill so as to get out of sight of the loch before the sun rose. The loch in particular is named Lochan Manar, which means 'For shame'. It is said the cures it effects are not limited to any one kind, and are effective for all persons, except those of the name of Gordon; and for this reason: a woman from Ross-shire came to Sutherland and gave out that she could cure diseases by means of water into which she had previously thrown some pebbles which she carried with her. In her progress through the land she stayed on one occasion in the house of a man called Gordon, and he made up his mind to get hold of the wonderful pebbles. She discovered his designs and fled. He followed, and as she drew near this little loch, she saw that she could not escape, so she threw the pebbles into the loch, crying, 'Mo nar! mo nar!' ('for shame, for shame'). From this, the loch got its name and so the pebbles were thus supposed to give its waters their healing powers.

The patients had to come to the loch about midnight on the first Monday of May or August, wait for the first streak of dawn and then strip themselves in silence. As they enter the loch they throw in a coin and then allow the waters to close over their head three times, and as they are doing this, they earnestly wish that they may be cured of the malady from which they are suffering. They must dress in silence, and if possible walk round the loch sun-wise. They then depart, taking good care to be out of sight of the loch before sunrise. It has been said that people actually were known to have been carried on horse-back to the loch if they were too old or too infirm, to walk there.

In mentioning Isle Maree on Loch Maree, the Holy Well there was supposed to have been blessed by St. Maelrubha, and

near by is the altar stone on which bulls were sacrificed; this is
recorded by the Presbytery of Lochcarron in the years around
1660 to 1680. Its waters were said to be a cure for madness. The
well is dry now, but the tree I have spoken of is still laden with
coins and nails.

In days not so long gone by, some people seemed to go to
extraordinary lengths in endeavouring to cure human ailments by
human sacrifices. There is the story, handed down by tradition,
how in the Black Isle (Easter Ross) they did not hesitate at these
human sacrifices, and that to save their cattle. A large number of
the cattle were attacked with a strange malady, which invariably
ended in madness and death. The disease was particularly de-
structive on two neighbouring farms and estates, which since
I don't know the names, I will call them A and B. The owners
offered a large reward of money to anyone who should find a
remedy. An old worthy belonging to the parish agreed to cure
the cattle for the sum offered, if they provided him with a human
sacrifice, and to this ghastly proposal the lairds at length agreed.
A barn in a secluded place was chosen for the horrid crime, and
here a poor friendless man, who lived not very far away, was
requested to appear on a certain day. The unsuspecting creature
obeyed the summons of his superiors, and upon arrival he was
instantly bound and disembowelled by the wizard. Various
organs of his body, such as the heart, liver, pancreas, were then
dried and reduced to powder, of which the wizard ordered a
little to be given to the diseased animals, sprinkled on water.
Before the unfortunate victim breathed his last, he uttered this
curse . . . 'May the day never come when the family of A shall
be without a female idiot, or the family of B without a fool.'
History does not tell us what effect the cure had on the cattle, but
it was true of the families concerned in the curse that to some
extent it was realised; and it is also said that Coinneach Odhar—
the Brahan Seer—years before, knew and predicted that it would
be made, and that his prayer would ultimately be granted. One
can scarce credit that such a horrible thing could happen within
about three or four miles of Conon.

The virtues of the ivy leaf, the leaf of the Common Lady's
Mantle, a wild flower plentiful in the north, with regard to
festering sores and cuts, are no doubt known to many, while the
application of a fine fat slug for curing a boil may also be known.

As a lad, I can testify that rubbing a wart with the slimy slug, *does* effect a cure. It may, however, not be so well-known, the melted fat droppings from slugs hung up before the fire and mixed with the marrow of bones, was looked upon as a specific cure for troubles of the lungs and bronchial tubes.

Another cure connected with a horse which had a bad knee has been told me. Its owner was seriously thinking of destroying it, when a certain wise man of ancient belief and who was fond of whisky, said he would cure the horse for the price of a few drams. This being promised, he went to near the sea-shore, and after hunting for and getting a frog, he split it open and applied the parts to the animal's knee. The horse was cured.

*   *   *

I now come to tell you of one Lachlan Stewart who lived in Broadford in Skye. One balmy summer's morning in 1936, he milked the cow, locked up the stone-built and slated cottage on his croft, and walked down the lane to the main road at Broadford. He carried a valise and wore the suit he wore for visiting the minister, the church and the local ceilidhs; he stopped outside the post office at the foot of the lane, and waited for the local bus. Neil Mackinnon 'the post', noticed him at the road end—and wondered. Lachlan, 42 years of age, unmarried, a stocky, lively man with a shock of early grey hair, just stood there waiting patiently for the bus. He spoke to no one. He looked back once or twice towards the house he had left and which he had built himself. The massive bulk of the Ben Blaven mountain across Loch Slapin glowered down.

When the bus came, Lachlan stepped inside, and it rattled off towards Kyleakin and the ferry to the mainland.

Since that day no one has heard of Lachlan Stewart.

Over the years—at ceilidhs, weddings, funerals, in gossip, church socials, the folk of his village always came round to the subject: 'what became of Lachlan Stewart?' What was known was that Lachlan was the younger of two sons of Angus and Mary Stewart, and they were brought up in the picturesque little village near Broadford. There was John, the elder, who went off to work at the aluminium factory at Fort William. Lachlan stayed behind on the croft, looked after his aged mother when his father died. As I have said, it was Lachlan who built the cottage on the rented croft. It was Lachlan who looked after the half-dozen cattle and the few sheep they had. He was a friendly soul, founder of the local debating society, boon companion of the minister, Mr. Anderson; and the school master. Lachlan was always his mother's favourite. When his mother died the brothers quarrelled over ownership of the house and succession to the croft. But John was the elder and legal heir to both croft and house. It was because of that quarrel that Lachlan, who had lived there all his life, packed a few things, walked down the lane and got on the bus thirty-five years ago. The stone house lay derelict for years, until John retired and took up his birthright. In January 1969 he died in an Inverness hospital.

He left a will, leaving the house to a neighbour—an Elder in the Church—and his wife who had shown him great kindness whilst he lived there. Not once had he spoken about his long-lost brother. Rumours had it that Lachlan had gone to London; that he had got married; that he was killed in the blitz; that he had emigrated; that he had been seen by a Skye man in the Metropolitan Police years ago on a London street; that he was still alive. Skye police cannot help; no one ever reported Lachlan was a missing person. The minister, the only one whom Lachlan may have confided in as to where he was going, kept his secret—and is dead. Neil, the post, would never speak about it—and now he is dead. Although the home that Lachlan built is now left to others, he has still a rightful claim to it. Should he be still alive he will now be nearing 80. A distant relative, Mr. John Mackinnon, now living in Glasgow, has no knowledge as to Lachlan's whereabouts—or if he is alive. Lachlan simply got up and walked away all those years ago; and there is not a trace of him.

In years to come, who knows, Lachlan may become one of the myths and legends that abound in and around the black Cuillin. Should he be alive—well, the croft is still awaiting him. Queer? I would hazard a guess that there might have been a woman in the background.

*   *   *

Athole brose. You may ask what this has to do with beliefs, second sight and legends. Well, in the instance I am about to relate, it has quite a lot to do with it. Athole brose figures largely in almost every celebration of any real Scottish character, though it belongs more particularly to Hogmanay. (Incidentally in Scotland, the adjective 'Scotch' is frowned upon; 'Scottish' or 'Scots' is preferred. But 'Scotch' is always allowed when speaking of whisky, and of course 'Scotch broth'.)

The legend in connection with this powerful Athole brose is interesting.

Some hundreds of years ago, a wild man of the woods haunted the precincts round about Blair Atholl, and the beautiful heiress of the district was greatly alarmed. As a reward she offered her hand in marriage to the man who would be brave enough to rid her of this menace.

A stalwart Highlander accepted the challenge and laid his plans well. At a small pool where the wild man was wont to refresh himself, he set to work. The pool was emptied and filled with honey and whisky (although not perhaps known as such in those days), with just enough water added to disguise it. The wild man duly drank of this potion, and with the usual results of such a draught, fell into a deep sleep. The young Highlander captured his prize, and took him to the fair heiress, who readily gave her hand to marry him.

Hence we have Athole brose, a mixture of honey, whisky and water, although oatmeal and cream are sometimes added to emphasise its Scottish character. It can be made according to the following recipe and should be served in a quaich: 14 oz. medium-cut oatmeal; 2 pints cold water; ¼-pint whisky; 4 dessert spoonfuls of heather honey and ¼-pint single cream.

And to make it: put the oatmeal in a bowl and pour over the cold water; stir well, and leave the bowl for at least an hour, covered with a plate or board. Strain through muslin, then mix with the whisky and honey, and lastly the cream. Serve at room temperature.

This recipe, I may say, was given me in confidence as it was a safely-guarded recipe; but as the lady who kept this secret all her life is now dead, I feel there is now no breach of confidence.

It is, I can assure you, an energy-giving drink if taken in small doses!

*　　*　　*

In some of these eerie ghost and phantom stories which have passed down from generation to generation, there can be some rational explanation, which the following story can illustrate. It was given me by Mr. Graham Paterson, owner of the West End garage, Lairg, one September afternoon in 1970. Here is what he told me.

As a lad he used to fetch milk at night in a pail from a nearby farm at Loch Shin. One night it was dark, but he got his pail filled with milk and went on his way back home. Turning off the main roadway, the path up to his parents' house was narrow, with stone-wall dykes on each side. As he was going merrily on, he suddenly felt something tickling or stroking the back of his head and his hair stood on end in fright. He carried on a little further, but still the sensation persisted, and being young and believing in ghosts and getting more and more frightened, he dropped his pail of milk and ran as fast as he could home. However, nearing home he knew that what he had done in spilling all the milk and giving the reason why to his father and mother he would only be scoffed at, and probably have been given a spanking for being so foolish. So he turned back, picking up courage to redeem the pail and get another lot of milk from the farm. As he neared the pail, the moon was showing through, and then he discovered how and why he had felt his neck having been stroked a few minutes before, and how he had imagined he had been pursued either by a witch or an evil spirit. The walls of the path were low, and in the field at his left side there was a horse—a pet pony in fact—and this beast had had his neck overlooking the wall as he had passed by. The pony stretched out and with his tongue had licked Graham's neck, and continued to do so as he kept pace with Graham; thinking he was doing a friendly action and requiring a stroke or two. That was the answer to the supposed witch; and if, as Graham told me, he hadn't gone back to get his pail, he would maintain to this very day that he *had* had contact with a witch or evil spirit in his young days.

Americans in their travels to Scotland just love to visit castles, mansions or even habited houses, which they have read up from their guide books over in the States, as having had some connections with ghosts or legends in the dim past. One such traveller, when he was visiting a family, said, 'Have you no ghosts in this house?' 'No,' said the man, 'but there are fine spirits in the Inn.'

Before this I have mentioned the subject of the 'little folk'; the fairies. Ireland I think has more belief in these 'little things'

than have the Highland folk; although in Wester Ross there are
people who believe in a stone, charm, or spell called the *sian*.
This so-called charm could—by means of certain incantations—
render any object that it was wished to conceal, invisible; and
it could re-appear at will. The following story bears on this
interesting belief.

It is connected with the manufacture of illicit whisky, very
prevalent during the first half of the 18th century. This was not
considered as serious a crime as smuggling, and penalties were
surprisingly light. Actually, the confiscation of their distilling
apparatus was a greater misfortune to the law-breakers than the
paltry sums they were fined.

This is a true story about the revenue cutter *Fada* which
landed a lieutenant and six sailors at Stornoway, en route to
Shawbost at the western side of Lewis (there was not a suitable
harbour to put in there), to search the croft of an Irishman who
was suspected of making contraband spirits. They walked the
twelve miles by foot, and sure enough they caught him red-
handed distilling whisky. Patrick O'Flannagan had a young
Scots lad assisting him from a nearby house. Everyone around
was keen on this industry of course.

The lieutenant and company duly arrived as I have said; and
it was pretty plain what their mission was. 'Ho, ho,' Pat greeted
them coolly. 'Come in, me Scots bhoys; 'struth, ye have caught
me nately at me work. But all the materials will now belong to
ye, me bhoys; all the whisky and the still, and the worm-head.
It'll be yours, me bhoys.' Meantime his Scots laddie Hamish,
seeing the soldiers coming, fled out of Pat's back door according
to plan, and sat on the heather, watching and listening; and
waiting. 'But, dear me, bhoys. I am now running the lovely
stuff'—meaning he was just in the act of distillation—'and it
would be a terrible shame, and a wickedness to destroy it all.
And so, me fine bhoys, if ye'll rest a while until this lot is finished
distilling, then ye'll have all the spirits and me as well; and I will
leave them all outside the door for ye, ready for ye to be taking
away—and me with them. But now, m'bhoys, business is business all the world over, but why should it stop us from enjoying
ourselves while we are able? So instead of spilling out the
precious stuff, which would be sinful, I would ask ye to be making
yoursel's comfortable-like, till the whisky is ready. And here are

some nice easy chairs for ye, me foine bhoys, where ye can sit at ease and be watching me at work. I'll teach ye all the secrets o' me trade for 'chust nothing at a', if ye'll treat me lightly. And not to be idle yersels', here's some noice employment for ye, a bumper o' whisky to ye a'; so let us be happy while we may— you and me—although duty is duty a' the same.' So said Pat.

The lieutenant and his men were greatly amused with the rascal and, as they were not indifferent to a tot of strong drink (what sailors are?), they sat around at leisure while Pat went among them with a large jar of the 'craitur', plying them with refreshments after their long walk across Lewis.

They relished this, and sat drinking good-naturedly while Pat went on with the distilling, running off the spirits whilst he cracked jokes and telling anecdote after anecdote.

When he had got all his whisky off he dismantled the head of his still and all the other parts, carrying the lot outside the door. And this was Hamish's cue

'Now, me bhoys,' he said, 'I've shown ye how to make good potheen, and taught ye all me secrets—just for the fun o' things. So if ye are going to take me away, let's have another wee dram, to keep us good friends.' So they took a parting glass merrily and went outside to collect all the apparatus. It had vanished. (Hamish was good at his job!)

'What did you do with it?' they all asked him. With a sly and puzzled look he answered them. 'Well now, me dear bhoys, that's most peculiar, that is indeed; most strange. They must have been taken away by the little folks; they're always around, ye know. I put all the stuff outside as you saw, and oi left it there; and if they're not there now, why then, it is the fairies who have stolen it all, and it is sure I have lost everything as well as ye.'

They searched around the barn, but could find nothing. Hamish had hidden everything in a hollow of the hill, well screened by heather.

The enemy had to drop the whole thing, having no proof; and to admit they had themselves to blame when they got back to the revenue cutter, that the reports given had been quite wrong, and that the man they were sent to arrest was truly a good and upright citizen of Lewis.

* * *

In another chapter 'Ardvreck and Montrose', I refer to the little village of Inchnadamph; and in my previous book, related several legends accredited to that district.

About four years ago there was an article about Inchnadamph by Mr. William Morrison of the editorial staff of the *People's Journal* (Inverness office); and quite by chance I met his father and mother—George and Jessie Morrison—who live in a charming house, 'Ardvreck', at the southern outskirts of Durness. Noticing the name of the house being 'Ardvreck', I called out of curiosity. His father had been the chauffeur and handyman at the Inchnadamph hotel for many years.

Mrs. Morrison told me the Inchnadamph postmistress, Miss Munro, who died in November 1970, was cycling along the road near Stronechrubie, when she felt her cycle getting heavier and heavier to pedal, and latterly felt she was cycling through a ploughed field and as if the road was—to use her own words—'coming up to meet her'. This was a case of second-sight in that it was the forerunner of the major reconstruction of the road that was undertaken *several years later* from that point to Lochinver.

Only fifty years ago, Jessie said, there were many stories told her of that area, but unfortunately these absorbing and precious legends were not written down—and so they went to the grave with those who told them. Truly around Inchnadamph, the ghosts outnumber the people; but still, there are many living today who will tell you the ghosts are still alive.

Mrs. Jessie Morrison has two younger sisters, Ruby and Barbara. Ruby (Corbett) is the local schoolmistress at Inchnadamph and told me she had definitely seen, more than once, in the light of her bicycle lamp, a fearsome 'black dog' that haunts the road near Stronechrubie House which was a former shooting lodge; and I understand quite a number of other locals claim to have seen this evil monster that disappears as suddenly as it appears. I can vouch for all these people being sensibly minded (and surely a schoolmistress would be!) and not given to imaginary visions. Now, with the roads being reconstructed and people motor, rather than walk or cycle, these apparitions are not so noticeable.

The other sister, Barbara, as a girl once stayed in Stronechrubie with a friend. One night they heard a dreadful racket coming from the huge kitchen below, as if all the crockery in the place were being smashed to bits. When the two girls investigated, they didn't find a single dish out of place. They often heard the door bell ring in the middle of the night for no apparent reason. Mice?

A late cousin of William's grandfather used to spend his summer holidays fishing the Loanan burn that flows through Inchnadamph to Loch Assynt. Sometimes he would patrol the banks of the wee river at night, and he seriously maintained he could hear the fairies crooning from the numerous little knowes that dot the burn between Inchnadamph and Stronechrubie. Duncan was a very level-headed man, but he was also of that very psychic clan, the MacGregors, so there is little doubt that he did hear something out of the ordinary.

Since the motor car first appeared on Sutherland roads about 65 years ago, there have been numerous instances of phantom cars and ghost headlights in this Assynt area.

William's brother David and his friend Charlie MacCuish were walking along the road in the gloaming one evening not so many years ago, when they saw what they took to be the dipped headlights of a car at a passing place not far away. As they came nearer the lights suddenly disappeared, leaving no trace of a car.

Several generations ago, the farm known today as Stronechrubie belonged to a very greedy woman whose husband died. A few miles further up the road at Lyne lived a very poor woman who had only one cow, but that cow was the best milker for miles around. Probably the cottage where this poor old soul lived belonged to the farm, because it wasn't long till the covetous widow cast her eyes on the cow, and one morning very early she sent one of her men to take the beast out of its byre, so that she could have that morning's milk. This was done. The animal was dragged away from its poor home and taken to the lush pastures of Stronechrubie. All went well for some little time, but then a series of misfortunes came along. Things went so far wrong that the greedy widow was forced to seek advice from a God-fearing woman in Elphin. This wise person, after hearing her story, told her she must visit her husband's grave by night in the Inchnadamph cemetery. 'Well,' said the widow, 'I'll go, only if you will come with me.' Said the other woman, 'I'll come, but only as far as the gate, and wait there for your return.'

Upon reaching the cemetery, the farmer's widow went forward and stood at the grave. The one who waited heard the murmur of voices coming from the direction of the grave. Eventually, the widow came out of the churchyard, rejoining her 'adviser'. What transpired at the grave is not recorded, except that it was noticeable her future life's story and outlook was a kindlier one after getting advice—so it would seem—from her dead husband.

Long years ago, the lovely daughter of an Assynt laird fell in love with a sea captain from Gairloch (Wester Ross) called Currie. In a fierce gale Currie's ship went aground near Kylesku, and there he met this beautiful girl. They became engaged and were to be married the next time the captain returned to Assynt. In the meantime, however, another suitor came on the scene in the person of the Laird of Achmore, near Ardvreck, and after some persuasion on her father's part, she married him.

Some time later Captain Currie returned and was told about the marriage. In anger he took a gun and set out for Achmore; but the laird seeing him coming, hid. The story goes on to say that the laird left his hiding place, got Currie at a disadvantage, and shot him, dumping his body in a lochan near Kylesku. He then returned to Achmore, shot his lovely bride and then himself. Legend says that people passing by Achmore at dead of night often see the ghost of the murdered bride.

*   *   *

THE DURBAN STORY

I am now able to record for the first time ever a further extraordinary, sinister story given me by a charming lady whom I know, living in Durban, South Africa. It certainly has a deal of bearing on premonition, second sight or call it what you will; and I give it very much in her own words. The incidents happened and culminated in September 1964—nearly eight years ago.

The lady has Scottish blood. Her grandfather was John Stewart of Perth, and he went out to South Africa in the 1890's, taking the first dredger to Durban. He never returned to Scotland, and married her grandmother who was a Hilder. Her own father was born in Durban, and although he never visited Scotland, he was very Scottish in both thought and tongue.

My friend whom I will call Mrs. X is aged forty, married

an Inspector of Mines out there and has a daughter of sixteen and a son of twelve; so readers will realise she is of a mature mind. Her husband was killed in a car crash on 6th September 1964.

Now to start the story proper.

About eighteen months before the accident she had a feeling her husband was going to die; for about four years previous he developed a heart condition. In 1961 she started to get premonitions; feelings of forebodings and of impending death. She felt as though a big black cloud was for ever hanging over her, and wherever she went she had the feeling of death. She told none of her friends, because they—like ordinary folk—seemed to scoff at such matters. She did, however, tell her sister-in-law that someone near and dear was going to die, but never indicated it was to be her husband. On 28th April 1963 her father died suddenly, and when this happened she thought 'well that's the death I've been thinking about'. But it was not. The feelings persisted and were getting daily stronger. And then another strange thing. 'Every night I would have the same dream, seeing myself and my two children and mother on a ship going overseas.' And this dream persisted for over a year. Eventually she felt she *had* to tell someone, and who better than her mother who was living with them after her father had died. Her mother was a very understanding person, and tried to reassure her.

The week before her husband died, he went to the Free State, and was due back home on 6th September (1964) two days before his thirty-eighth birthday. During that week she and her mother had premonitions of a death. Her mother had a dream of him hitting a bridge and landing on the railway line.

Her husband said he would be back home about 7 P.M. At precisely that hour, her mother sat down at the piano and subconsciously started to play *Abide with me*. This she did twice, when suddenly she realised with anguish what she was doing. Both were taken aback at such a hymn being played. At 8 P.M. they all retired to bed. She (Mrs. X) fell asleep and woke up at 12.30 A.M. with a knocking at the front door.

Instinctively she knew! She went to the door where two police officers were standing outside. They asked to come in, and at once she said, 'You've come to tell me my husband is dead.' In their own way they tried to explain there had been an

accident at a bridge. From that moment her 'cloud' lifted. The
officers told her the accident had happened at 7 P.M..

After that tragedy, she, her children and mother *did* go overseas to Scotland, and by ship. That dream, too, 'came to pass'.

Verily, Truth can be stranger than Fiction.

*   *   *

THE MAN FROM THE SEA

There is an equally strange story, with perhaps a different slant,
happening over a hundred years ago to a young man which has
an eerie feeling about its details.

This sea-faring man after being away seven years landed back
at his native Lewis one New Year's day to see his aged parents
and friends on the west coast of the island near Carloway and
Shawbost. Later on, and to pass away the time, one grey day
when a biting north wind was gusting out of the Atlantic, he
thought he would walk over the moors and visit friends in another
part of the island close by. He reached them safely and had a
good ceilidh with them of old times and yarns, and of course a
few drams around the peat fire. Late though it was, he said he'd
better be making tracks for home despite the growing storm,
though his hosts pressed him to stay the night. So back he
trudged over the moorlands, but as the blizzard became worse
and he was fast becoming exhausted, he was relieved to see a dim
yellow light of a wee croft, and making for it as fast as his poor
legs would carry him, he banged on the door, which was soon
opened by an old man he vaguely remembered from his boyhood
days.

The old man led the sailor into a tiny warm room lit by an
oil lamp, where an old woman, whom he also recognised, was
sitting by the blazing fire. He was warmly welcomed by the
couple, and they soon made him take off his drenched clothes,
whilst the old man took out a bottle of whisky from the corner
cupboard.

They talked on and on exchanging news of years past. The
peat fire and the whisky soon made the sailor so warm that he
loosened his collar and took off his fine silk cravat, and tossed it
over on to the window sill.

After about two or three hours, the storm abated somewhat

and our sailor friend decided to continue his journey homeward to Shawbost. So he thanked the old couple for their hospitality and bade them goodnight. It was well into the sma' hours of the morning. Reaching home his parents were not in bed, for they had worried about what might have happened to him on such a dreadful night. Where had he been, and what had he been up to when the snowstorm was raging? He told them he had come across Johnnie and Jeannie's wee croft about four miles back, where he took shelter and had had a grand old yarn talking of the years ago.

His parents looked at one another and then at their son in blank amazement, saying 'Ye couldna' ha' been in yon hoose,' his father said, 'for both Johnnie and Jeannie ha' been deid for o'er five years.' In vain did their son protest. He was quite certain he'd been with that couple whilst the storm raged; his parents were equally adamant that the old folk had been long in their graves, and their wee but an' ben was empty, and partly in ruins.

So what? He said that in the morning he'd go off and again check up. When he got there, he found the house deserted; the door off its hinges, windows broken and so forth. He was astounded, but went inside for curiosity's sake thinking that perhaps he *had* been wrong considering the excesses in drink he had indulged in at the other folk's house prior to trundling back home, and that he might have sheltered somewhere else. Turning to leave the empty house, his eye caught a flash of colour on the window-sill.

It was his own silk cravat.

*   *   *

SANDEMAN SHERRY.

In my last book I wrote of the most extraordinary true story bordering on the supernatural, that occurred to a friend of mine in 1952 near Dornie on the way to Kyle. I now recount a very similar experience given me by an acquaintance that took place quite close to Dornie four years later, in the summer of 1956; and I give the story more or less as told me . . . 'while employed as a salmon fisherman on Loch Duich, near Dornie, I often walked along the driveway leading from Inverinate Lodge by way of Kintail Church, to the main road. This short cut from the cottages at the lodge had a big locked gate across the drive to

F

stop vehicular traffic, but pedestrians could pass through a small wicket gate. Whilst visiting friends at the gardener's cottage, I stayed till shortly after midnight. It was a fine early morning, quiet and peaceful, with a glint of daylight showing. As I approached the wee gate I saw a dark man about seven feet tall, apparently waiting for me to go through the gate. He was dressed in a wide-brimmed black hat and a long flowing black cape, looking just like the figure depicted on a Sandeman sherry label. Afraid to go on, I started walking backwards with my eyes firmly fixed on this jet-black silhouette. Taking a few paces backwards, the 'form' suddenly vanished without any flash, light or noise. Being still shaken, I returned via the Lodge and the salmon station to the main road, a detour of some two miles, all the time shaking like a leaf, for I was convinced I had seen the devil. I may add that not far distant from the wicket gate are the remains of an old pier, known locally as Coffin Pier. This dates from the time when funeral processions from the surrounding parishes brought the coffins ashore at this point *en route* to the church and thence to Clachan Duich burial ground. Other locals to whom I have spoken of my 'encounter' have said they too, have experienced similar apparitions at odd times near the wicket gate . . .'

I would say my friend, still a young man, is a very level-headed person, and holds a responsible post in Glen Shiel.

CHAPTER 9

THE COVENANTING
AND
CLEARANCE DAYS

I AM now going to combine two centuries into one; not very
hard these computer days, when by pressing a button every
subject, every question of the age can be answered within a
split second, and all works out smoothly, we hope!

I refer to the 1600's and the 1800's, when the Covenanting and
Clearance era took pride of place. These two strife-torn events,
one can say, turned Shangri-La into a Shambles-La. The stories
of those sad days are stories one is almost ashamed to tell today.
But it is true history and should therefore be recorded. After
reading this chapter one should pause and think on these things;
what tribulations, what lamentations the Scots went through.
The charge of rebellion against the State is one that has constantly been brought against Christians down through the ages,
for almost every persecution carried out against them. 'If a
Jezebel wants a Naboth's vineyard,' one old writer points out in
an apt illustration, 'and he stands up for his rights and property,
she will not want sons of Belial to bear witness that he "blas-
phemed God and the King".' To the Romans, Christians were
rebels because they would not swear by the life of Caesar and
adore his image. Therefore, *Christianos ad Leones*; to the lions,
Christians.

I will first deal with the *Covenanters*.

Those perhaps not well-versed in 17th century Scottish history
may ask, what were the Covenanters? Well, this trouble
between them and the Royalists arose about 1637 when Charles I
and his bishops attempted to impose English Episcopacy, by force

if necessary, upon the people of Scotland. The great majority of Scots declared their determination to defend their own form of worship, which at the Reformation had been brought straight to Scotland from Geneva by John Knox and subscribed by King James VI. In order to resist Charles' impositions as incompatible with the civil and ecclesiastical laws and constitutions of Scotland, the leaders (including the Earl of Seaforth) drew up a Covenant of mutual defence against any that should oppose them; and the Covenant was generally subscribed and sworn through the whole kingdom. Preparations for war, civil war at its worst, began on both sides. This, then, was a solemn League and Covenant. According to this agreement, both countries were to strive for the uprooting of Prelacy and Popery, and to labour for the reformation of religion in the Kingdoms, in doctrine, worship, discipline according to the word of God and the example of the best reformed churches. The liberty of Parliament and people was the aim of the chief political principle. This alliance was ratified on 17th August 1643 by the Scottish Convention and General Assembly, and soon after received the sanction of the Assembly of Divines then sitting at Westminster as well as that of both the English Houses of Parliament.

Many heart-rending stories can be told of these Covenanting days. I will limit myself to but one or two. There are many more of course, all of which make one furiously to think; *cela donne beaucoup à refléchir.*

THE CROSS OF DALGARNOC. Dalgarnoc is a quiet little God's acre standing in green meadowlands a mile or so south of Thornhill in Dumfriesshire. Dalgarnoc tells the tale of brave men who gave their lives for Christ's cause and covenant in 1684. Looking on these lettered memorials we are reminded of the dearest loyalties of our souls—the Faith of our fathers, freedom of conscience and that patriotism which must ever be set above all else, the good of this motherland. Within the iron gateway of the churchyard there stands a tall cross of grey granite which is unique. On the top of the eastern side are carved in large letters these words, 'The Nithsdale Martyrs'. Below that moving title are recorded the names of fifty-seven men. On the western side there are symbols which are dear to every Scotsman's heart—the thistle, the crown, the open bible, the sword of justice, the scroll of the Covenant, and the words, 'For Christ, Church, Coven ant'.

The martyrs' monument in Greyfriars churchyard, Edinburgh, commemorates about one hundred noblemen, gentlemen, ministers and others who gave their lives for Christ's sake. But as to Dalgarnoc there is no other monument commemorating so many men of the Covenant from *one* district who died for their Faith. Fifty-seven. . . . Truly Nithsdale was drenched in the blood of the martyrs. The cross was not erected till 1928.

After the defeat of the Covenanters at Bothwell Bridge on a summer Sunday, 22nd June 1679, twelve hundred prisoners were penned up in an inner yard of Greyfriars kirkyard, and the place is still called the Covenanters' prison. Through five months of summer heat and winter cold, ill-clad and ill-fed, their only bed was the damp earth—the good earth. Some escaped; four hundred were released on taking an oath of non-resistance. Many died. By the 15th November only 257 of the 1200 remained. One morning these men were marched down in stumbling fashion to the Port of Leith where they were put on board a ship called the *Crown*, to be sold as slaves in the American plantations. The hold had accommodation for a hundred, but the 257 were crammed into that terrible floating prison. For twelve days they remained at Leith; then after another twelve days on stormy seas, the captain was forced to land at Scarvating, which is about 1½ miles from Mull Head in the district of Deerness, part of the mainland of Orkney. To allow the sick to lie down, the strong had to stand up, day and night. Intolerable thirst drove many of them to dreadful extremities. One letter from a prisoner named James Corson came through by an escaped man saying, 'Our uneasiness is beyond words; yet the consolation of God over-balances all, and I hope we are near our port, and Heaven open to us'.

On 10th December 1679, the ship was driven on the rocks and broke in two. The captain ordered the hatches to be battened down despite the cries of the prisoners. When the ship foundered about fifty of the Covenanters managed to get out and either swam or scrambled ashore. Even then the brutal captain ordered his men to thrust them back into the surf. Not more than forty got ashore and two hundred were drowned under hatches like rats in a hole. All this, and much more, is miserable memory, and if it were possible to undo history, we would blot it out.

So today, in far-off Scarvating there stands a tall square

monument beside the restless cruel sea with an inscription on it which tells the sad story of those who were drowned at that point. Every year on a summer Sunday many gather at this lonely memorial to worship God, to sing a psalm, to hear the Word and to give thanks for the blessed dead. Leal (loyal, faithful) hearts have long memories and we dare not forget those who by their death long ago *bought for us Freedom of Faith*, and left us a legacy of Liberty, which is, to us, most dear.

As we stand at the Martyrs' Cross at Dalgarnoc there burns within us this self-same sense of identity with the dead, and soothing, inspiring words come wafting with the wind to seal our faith: 'I have a tryst to keep, it was plighted long ago, with some who lie asleep. I have a tryst to keep. . . .'

* * *

I would now relate the facts as to another sad Covenanting memorial, situate 25 miles or so north of Dalgarnoc in another county, Ayrshire, at Priesthill near Muirkirk. A small farm road leads off the main road, and from the farm it is a moorland walk to the memorial, the last resting place of John Brown, a Covenanting martyr.

Before giving the story, I would like to make some notes on John Graham of Claverhouse, Viscount Dundee, who lived 1648–1689. The 'Great Dundee'. Sir Walter Scott called him 'Bonnie Dundee'. But he had another by-name in his day, 'Bluidy Claver'se'; a man with the face of an angel and a devil's heart; full of pride and ambition and loyalty to the Royalists. Claverhouse was a King's man for life. He was stern and competent. As a soldier, he was defeated at Drumclog; it was the Covenanters only victory, and after that he was ruthless against them, as will be seen as my story unfolds.

The Grahams were one of the great families of Scotland—the gallant, proud Grahams. The family was descended from the Royal line of Stuarts. He admired Montrose and endeavoured to emulate his exploits.

Now for the sad story . . . '*A moorland Memorial*'.

You need to trudge a desolate moorland to find it; a lonely grave at Priesthill. The pilgrimage is worth the pains, for as you stand there you have the feeling of being on holy ground—the last resting place, as I have said, of John Brown.

The story of his martyrdom is in many ways unparalleled in Covenanting history. No fanatical firebrand was he, this godly tiller of the soil. But he was a Covenanter by strong and en-lightened conviction, and he made no secret of it. His humble home was in a sufficiently remote spot to serve as a hospice for fugitive co-religionists, and his approval of their manifestoes was well known. All this notwithstanding, it might reasonably be thought that the persecutors of the Covenanters would take a light view of John Brown's non-conformity to royal require-ments. But John Brown himself had a presentiment to the contrary—so much so that when he proposed marriage to Isabel Weir he felt it right and just to warn her that if she accepted she might be marrying a man who would soon be put to death for his faith.

But Isabel quietly made her reckoning, 'If it should be so,' she said, 'through affliction and death I will be your comfort.' Her marriage vows were taken soon after, under the shadow of a similar caution. The marriage took place in a hidden spot on the moorland and the officiating minister was Alexander Peden. Taking the bride aside, Peden said, 'You have got a good husband —value him highly. Keep linen for a winding-sheet beside you; for in a day when you least expect it, thy master will be taken from thy head. . . . But fear not, thou shalt be comforted.'

And now I have to bring on the stage, John Graham of Claverhouse—the 'Great Dundee'.

Early in the morning of 1st May 1685, John and Isabel Brown joined in family worship, as was their wont (and as is the custom amongst Highlanders to this very day), and sang the opening verses of Psalm 27. No empty words these:

> Against me though an host encamp
> my heart yet fearless is;
> Though war against me rise, I will
> be confident in this.
> One thing I of the Lord desired,
> and will seek to obtain,
> That all days of my life I may
> within God's house remain.

John Brown then went out to cut his peats.
There, Graham of Claverhouse found him.

A brief examination revealed where the peat cutter's sympathies lay, and he was promptly marched back to his house. When search was made there, some bullets and 'treasonable' papers were found. There was nothing to suggest that the bullets were there for any infamous purpose, nor any papers indicating loyalty to the Covenant could be regarded as 'treasonable'. But Claverhouse being quick to seize on such, quietly ended his investigations.

'Go to your prayers,' he commanded, 'for you shall immediately die.' And there in the presence of his wife, the godly cottager of Priesthill knelt before God, committing his family to the sustaining grace of God. A brief farewell to his wife was allowed, and then the muskets rattled and John Brown passed to be 'with Christ', which is 'far better'.

With a parting sneer, the great Claverhouse left the young widow, with her babe in her arms and her husband's body at her feet. Where he fell, there she had him buried, and there in better days, men raised a memorial to mark his moorland grave.

Brave John Brown! Brave Isabel Weir! Brave all the men and women of the moss-hags who in days of persecution lost their lives and battles, but vindicated their cause, bequeathing to us, who live today, our priceless heritage of spiritual and civil freedom.

As one stands before this memorial our mind turns to a verse written by Robert Louis Stevenson in far-off Samoa as he was thinking of such scenes as this; and softly we repeat these lines:

... Blow the wind today and the sun and the rain are flying,
   Blow the wind on the moors today and now,
Where about the graves of the martyrs the whaups are crying,
   My heart remembers how!

*   *   *

My eyes are dimmed as I write these lines, for surely there cannot be found a more callous, inhuman, pitiless, merciless—indeed, barbarous—action as this, destitute of all feeling as it was, and enacted by a so-called great man in this country of ours. And not so long ago really, as Time goes.

Claverhouse died four years after this incident, being shot at Killiecrankie at the moment of his triumph in smashing the

King's Enemies there. Though his ghost walked for half a century, the cause of the Stuarts really died with Claverhouse at Killiecrankie.

There are of course many more horrific stories to be told of this Covenanting period; but I have said enough. Many martyr stones stand four-square on many a windswept moor to this very day.

Yes, the story of the Scottish Covenanters has a significance far beyond that of a local squabble in a provincial backwater of civilisation in the 17th century. Limited though it was in space and time, it focused attention upon a crucial issue as I have said, which the Christian church has had to face throughout its history; for the issue was nothing less than the Crown Rights of Christ the Redeemer to be King of His people, Master of His household, and Lord of His Church. The blood of the martyrs is the seed of the church.

THE CLEARANCES (or the Rape of the Highlands). I now leave these heart-rending references to the Covenanting age, and turn to the equally appalling—though perhaps not so 'bloody'— Clearance days of the 1800's. Years of gloomy memories when people were replaced by sheep, and enforced Highland emigration by the tens of thousands resulted. Truly, the Rape of the Highlands.

It was around 1780 that this brutal period began; people evicted to make way for the new economies of sheep and deer. It was all done in the name of progress. Landowners found that sheep paid better than people—and so the latter had to go; they had no rights and the law upheld the landlords. To this very day the Highlander refers to these Clearances as barefaced stealing. But wool gave better returns than paltry rents. 'Improvement' was then the operative word, and the economic argument was unanswerable. Land which produced 2d. an acre under cattle yielded two shillings under sheep, so how could there be any argument. The human or humane element didn't come into it at all. The first families ordered out sadly picked up their belongings, left the land and homes they loved, and trekked towards the barren coast. They tramped and carried all their meagre belongings miles and miles on their backs just like snails.

This episode ended in 1854, little more than a hundred years ago.

Most of the young able men in the Highlands were overseas fighting for their country in the Napoleonic wars, fighting for the very people and government that were clearing out their ancestral homes; and when they returned, what did these men find? The croft homes and their people gone. Just that. It was too late, the damage had been done. The crofters in the far north said—'There was neither sin nor sorrow in the world for us, but the Clearances came upon us with such suddenness, destroying all, turning our gladness—our Shangri-La—into bitterness, our blessings (and we had many) into blasphemy and our Christianity into mockery. . . .' Sadness and weeping; death and eternity.

Their ministers, as I have said, did little to help them, except to say it was God's will. The people dared not complain openly in force, for were not their oppressors also the administrators of the law? The seventeen parish ministers in Sutherland, with the single exception of the Rev. Donald Sage (later of Resolis, Easter Ross) took the side of the powers that were exhorting the people to submit, and to stifle their cries of distress told them that all their sufferings came from the hand of their Heavenly Father as a punishment for their past transgressions. These ministers have since rendered their account, and I am left wondering if they have been forgiven for such cruel and blasphemous conduct? One cannot help noting to what awful shameful uses these men in Sutherland and elsewhere prostituted their sacred office and high calling.

Then came the Crimean War, when in 1854 additional Highland blood was needed to fight for the British Empire against the Russians. But the men of Sutherland said . . .

We have no country left to fight for. You robbed us of our country and gave it to the sheep. Therefore since you have preferred sheep to men let sheep defend you. . . .

Even the pompous Duke of Sutherland (a Sasunnach), George Granville Leveson-Gower, who bore no blood kinship to the once-proud Clan Sutherland, journeyed north from London to assist in the recruitment. Over the previous twenty years he and his Duchess-Countess had been partly responsible for nearly emptying their lands of Sutherlands, Mackays, Gunns and Rosses, exporting them like cattle to the four corners of the earth to make room for Lowland Scots, sheep and deer as I have said. Now that the Duke wanted to replenish the famous 93rd Sutherland Highlanders with new men, he went to a meeting of his wife's tenants at Golspie, near stately Dunrobin Castle. The meeting was held on the Mill Brae at Golspie Burn, ancient rallying place of the Clan Sutherland. (This spot can be seen today very close to the Sutherland Arms Hotel.) The Duke was unsuccessful in getting more recruits enlisted 'to put down and keep down the tyrant Czar in Russia'. (No mention of the Clearance tyrants?)

After the recruitment drive had ended in failure, the men of Sutherland (lest their reasons be misunderstood) drafted a notice to the Press explaining the wrongs done to the people of Sutherland which 'will be remembered by every true Highlander as long as grass grows and water runs'.

Nevertheless, Sutherland men who were already with the 93rd regiment made history for themselves as 'The Thin Red Line, tipped with steel', defeating a Russian cavalry charge on the plains of Balaclava. The 93rd thereby became the only infantry regiment with 'Balaclava' as a battle honour.

When the regiment had been formed in 1800 (as an outgrowth of the old Sutherland Fencibles) it numbered 630 men and sergeants, 400 of them men from Sutherland and many having the surname Sutherland. Traditionally, the early chiefs of the Clan Sutherland—the ancient Earls of Sutherland—were descended from Freskin de Moravia (Moray), progenitor of the Clan Murray. In the 12th century King William the Lion gave to Hugh de Moravia, a grandson of Freskin, a grant of lands in the southern portion of Caithness. Subsequent Earls became chiefs of men who took the surname Sutherland, mainly from being resident of the 'Suderland' area. The Clan Sutherland grew in power, and as a fighting force it was a good match for further invasions by Norsemen or for feuds with the Mackays, Rosses, Gunns and Sinclairs.

The old Earls of Sutherland used the surname only until the time of John, 8th Earl, who went mad in 1494. His son also suffered mental illness and died in 1514, being succeeded by his sister, who married Adam Gordon of Aboyne, son of the 2nd Earl of Huntly. Their descendants, the Gordons, Earls of Sutherland, never took the surname Sutherland until the time of William, 16th Earl, who was Hanoverian in his political allegiance. He was a strong advocate of the Union of the Scottish and English Parliaments.

Suderland, or Sudrland (the southern land) is the Norse word for Sutherland which the Norsemen conquered and where they settled. With the evictions, thousands emigrated to America, Canada and Australia, as I am to relate further on. Many went to Red River (Winnipeg) in Canada, where the spiritual leader of the Selkirk Colony was James Sutherland, known in Gaelic as 'Seumas Buidhe' (pronounced Shame-us Boo-yuh), or yellow-haired James. He had earlier lived at Ceann-na-Coille on the Helmsdale river.

*   *   *

Having made a passing reference to the Sutherland family I will now deal more specifically with the Clearance tales of woe.

There are many who look upon the Clearances as involving Sutherland and Sutherland alone—particularly the Kildonan and Strathnaver areas. But this is not so. The Clearances affected Inverness-shire mainland, Ross-shire, the Hebrides (N. Uist, S. Uist, Barra), Rum, the Isle of Skye (Boreraig and Suisinish), Argyll (Mull, Tiree, Coll, Ardnamurchan, Morven, Glenorchy. This latter was owned by the Marquis of Breadalbane), Arran and Perthshire (Rannoch and Breadalbane). But what was true generally of the Highlands was, with the county of Sutherland, carried to the greatest extreme.

It is quite impossible for me to recount all the happenings in these various places, but the overall pattern is the same. The districts were ruthlessly cleared of their whole native population. It was very akin to the slave trade that finally roused the national conscience, as many of us may remember, and under William Wilberforce (1759–1833), born in my home town Hull, Yorkshire, the famous advocate of the abolition of slavery, the slave trade ended.

The Clearances embodied the tearing of human beings (with hearts as warm and affections as strong as dwell in the bosom of the white man) from their homes and families; the packing them into the holds of over-crowded foul and unwholesome ships. The finger of guilt, deep-dyed guilt, has been levelled against the perpetrators ever since. By degrees the power of the latter in those days, assisted by Saxon legislation, encroached upon the liberty of the people. Highland chiefs became feudal lords, the people were robbed to increase their power, and the fruits were eventually reaped in the Clearance evictions. The cry seemed to be 'do away with the people'; this was the shorthand manner of doing away with the Gaelic. Ruined homes, ruined hamlets; hamlets on fire in the mountain glens, the hills red with burning houses. Sorry, sad, lamentable sights wherever one went those days. And all this enacted in a country that had not a nobler class of people than the Highland people, or a set of people better worth preserving. How warped can some minds become.

One might ask, and I ask it too, why there was no one like Wilberforce to ventilate and bring everything to light in the open in Parliament all the wrongful on-goings in the far north? What a story the Press would make of such happenings today. But it would appear everything was done to conceal and whitewash the atrocities. Everything that was done was to glorify the 'Improvements'. The people really could not voice any grievances, save in their native Gaelic tongue.

The Sutherland clearances were commenced in a comparatively mild way in 1807, by the ejection of ninety families from Farr and Lairg. In 1809 several hundred were evicted from the parishes of Dornoch, Rogart, Loth, Clyne and Golspie under circumstances of greater severity.

In all this sad affair, the name of Patrick Sellar stands out in bold relief. He was the factor to the Duke of Sutherland at Dunrobin Castle, and he looked upon the district of Strathnaver to become a great sheep farmer and make a fortune. STRATH-NAVER was a Celtic country and few of its inhabitants understood any language except Gaelic. Actually the agent the Sutherland's chose to transform their northern estates was William Young (from Morayshire) who had put forward a Plan for Development. He was appointed commissioner of the estate to supervise this improvement (of clearing the land of inhabitants, except on coastal strips, and giving it over to sheep), but Patrick Sellar who joined him (also from Morayshire) acted as legal agent and accountant, though he was really the factor and full agent with unlimited powers and was the moving spirit. The partnership began in 1810 and prospered so much that Sellars was himself able to bid in 1813 for the huge sheep farm in the district between Loch Naver and Badenloch. William Young resigned from his

position the year of Sellar's trial in 1816, when Sellar appeared
before the Circuit Court at Inverness, charged with culpable
homicide, and with 'wickedly and maliciously setting on fire and
burning'. Sellar was the man who personally supervised the
burning of Strathnaver. There was a jury of fifteen men, eight
of them being landed proprietors! Nine witnesses were called
for the defence. These were sheriff-officers and servants who
had accompanied Sellar to Strathnaver and they would have been
stupid not to realise that they were on trial too. Sellar was acquitted on 23rd April 1816.

Patrick Sellar did not remain long in control, and in the end
he died the death he richly deserved in 1851. His place was taken
over in 1855 by one James Loch, from Bloomsbury, London,
whose father at that time had written a book in eulogistic terms
on the improvements being carried out on the Estate of Sutherland. Improvement was on everyone's lips and in his book Loch
defined its cause . . . 'to emancipate the lower orders from slavery
has been the unceasing object of the Highland Proprietors'; and
for his father's sake he became General Agent of the Sutherland
Estate.

I have already referred to the Rev. Donald Sage. In those days
he was in charge of the parish of Achness and Kildonan and he
left on record a full account of the evictions which consisted of
hundreds of his flock, the Sutherland aborigines who had from
time immemorial been in possession of their mountain tenements.
What blind hatred can man conjure up in the name of God, when
God is supposed to be a God of Love.

Whilst this sweeping desolation extended over every parish,
it fell most heavily on the Kildonan and Strathnaver areas. It was
the device of William Young, whom I have just named, a successful corn-dealer and land-improver. He rose from indigence, but
was a man of taste, of an ingenious turn of mind and a shrewd
calculator. After realising some hundreds of pounds by corn-
dealing, he purchased from Sir Archibald Dunbar of Thunder-
town, a small and valueless property in Morayshire, called
Inverugie. It lay upon the seashore and like many properties of
more ancient date, it had been completely covered with sea-sand
which had drifted upon its surface. For this small and worthless
spot he paid a correspondingly small price—about £700; but
tasking his native and vigorous genius for improvement, he set

himself at once to better his bargain. Making use of ploughs of peculiar construction, he turned the sand down, and the rich old soil up, and thus made it one of the most productive properties in the county. This, with other necessary improvements how-ever involved him in debt; but just as it became a question with him to pay it all off, his praise in the north as a scientific improver of land reached the ears of the Stafford (Sutherland) family, who in connection with their immense wealth were racked with the anxiety to improve their Highland estate. As William Young had been so successful on the estate of Inverugie, they thought he could not but be equally so on the Sutherland estate. Young introduced the depopulating system into Suther-land ('Clearances' had, however, been effected in some parts of Sutherland previous to this period (1813) although to a smaller extent. From along the banks of the river Oykel for instance many families were evicted in the year 1800). This system during his tenure of office as Commissioner on the Sutherland property was just at its commencement. It was first brought to bear on the parish of Kildonan, as previously indicated. The whole north and south sides of the Strath from Kildonan to Caen on the left bank of the river, and from Dalcharn to Marrel on the right bank were at one fell sweep cleared of their inhabitants. The measures for their ejectment had been taken with such promptness and were so suddenly and brutally carried out, as to excite a tumult among everyone.

Young had as his associate in the factorship Patrick Sellar as I have said, who acted in the subordinate capacity of legal agent and accountant, and who by his unprincipled recklessness in con-ducting the process of ejectment, added fuel to the flames. It was said that the people rose *en masse*, that the constables and officials were resisted and their lives threatened and the combination among the peasantry was represented as assuming at last so alarm-ing an aspect that the Sheriff-Depute of the county was under the necessity of calling in the military to quell the riots. A detachment of soldiers was accordingly sent for from Fort George. The 21st Regiment was marched to Dunrobin Castle with artillery and cartloads of ammunition. A powder magazine was erected at Dornoch and every preparation made as for the commencement of a civil war. A great farce was staged; the people were sent for by the factors to the Castle at a certain hour. They came peaceably, but the farce had to be gone through, and the Riot Act was read; a few sheepish, innocent Highlanders were made prisoners, but nothing could be laid to their charge, and they were almost immediately set at liberty. The chief magistrate of the county shrewdly and wisely ordered back the military, and came himself alone among the people and instituted a cool and impartial enquiry into their proceedings. The result was that the formidable riot which was reported to have for its object the murder of Young and Sellar, the expulsion of the store-farmers and the burning of Dunrobin Castle, amounted after all only to this, that a certain number of people had congregated in different places and had given vent to their outraged feelings and sense of oppression in rash and unguarded terms. It could not be proved that a single act of violence was committed.

The demonstration, however, had the desired effect in cowing and frightening the people into the most absolute submission. They became dismayed and broken hearted and quietly submitted to their fate. I have made mention of the clergy already and I do so again in saying that all this time they were assiduous in preaching that all the misfortunes of the people were fore-ordained of God and denouncing the vengeance of Heaven and eternal damnation on all those who would presume to make the slightest resistance. What humbug talk in the land of Shangri-La.

Sellar himself laboured hard to involve the Rev. Donald Sage's father and mother in the criminality of these proceedings but he utterly failed. The peasantry, as fine as any in the world, were treated by the owners of the soil as 'good for nothing but to be cast out and trodden under the feet of men' while the tract of country thus depopulated was divided into two large sheep-farms, one of which was given in lease to William Cluness of Cracaig, and the other to a Mr. Reid from Northumberland.

During these days, the Stafford family only treated Dunrobin Castle as a summer residence.

A second Clearance began in 1819 when the reckless lordly proprietors had again resolved upon the expulsion of their long-standing and much-attached tenantry from their widely extended estates, and the Sutherland Clearance of 1819 was not only the climax of their system of oppression for many years before, but the extinction of the last remnant of the ancient Highland peasantry in the north. As violent tempests send out before them many

a deep and sullen roar, so did the advancing storm give notice of
its approach by various single acts of oppression. Mr. Sage was
then church minister at Achness and one day about the beginning
of October 1818 news reached him of the wholesale removal of
his poor flock. A tenant from the middle of the Strath had been
to Rhives, the residence of Mr. Young, the commissioner, paying
his rent. He was informed and authorised to tell his neighbours
that the rent for the half year ending May 1819 would not be
demanded, as it was determined to lay the districts of Strathnaver
and Upper Kildonan under sheep. This intelligence when first
announced was indignantly discredited by the people. Notwithstanding their knowledge of former clearances they clung to the
hope that the 'BAN-MHORAIR-CHATTA' (as the Duchess was
called) would not give her consent to the warning as issued by
her subordinates and thus deprive herself of her people, as truly a
part of her noble inheritance as were her broad acres. But the
course of a few weeks soon undeceived them. Summonses of
ejectment were issued and despatched all over the district. These
must have amounted to upwards of 1000, as the population of
the Mission alone was 1600 souls and many more than those of
the Mission were ejected. The summonses were distributed with
the utmost preciseness. They were handed in at every house and
hovel alike, be the occupiers of them who or what they might—
minister, catechist or elder, tenant or sub-tenant, out-servant or
cottar—all were made to feel the irresponsible power of the proprietor. The enormous amount of citations might also be accounted for by the fact that 'Mr.' Peter Sellar had a threefold
personal interest in the whole matter. He was, in the first place,
factor on the Sutherland estate at the time; then he was law agent
for the proprietors; and lastly the lessee or tacksman of more
than a third of the country to be cleared of its inhabitants. It may
easily be conceived how such a three-plied cord of worldly interests would bind him over to greater rigour and even atrocity,
in executing the orders of his superiors on the wretched people
among whom he was thus let loose like a beast of prey. It is a
wonder he was not waylaid at night and stabbed through the
heart.

The Rev. Mr. Sage records distinctly remembering the effects
produced by these specific measures. He, in common with the
rest of his people, received one of the notices, and resolved that

at the ensuing term of Martinmas, he would remove from Achness and go once more permanently to reside under his father's roof, although he would at the same time continue the punctual discharge of his pastoral duties among the people till they also should be removed.

I now take up his story as he tells it:

I left Achness about the middle of November 1818, sold my cow at the Ardgay market and got my furniture conveyed to Kildonan by my father's horses and my own. The people received the legal warning to leave for ever the homes of their fathers with a sort of stupor—that apparent indifference which is often the external aspect of intense feeling. As they began, however, to awaken from the stunning effects of this first intimation, their feelings found vent. The truly pious acknowledged the mighty hand of God in the matter. In their prayers and religious conferences not a solitary expression could be heard indicative of anger, revenge or vindictiveness, but in the sight of God they humbled themselves and received the chastisement at His hand. Those however who were strangers to such exalted and ennobling impressions of the gospel breathed deep and muttered curses on the heads of the persons who subjected them to such treatment. The more reckless portion of them fully realised the character of the impenitent in all ages and indulged in the most culpable excesses, even while this divine punishment was still suspended over them. (But what wrong had they done? Surely God could not be held responsible to their being God-fearing?) These last however were very few in number. To my poor and defenceless flock, the dark hour of trial came at last in right earnest.

It was the month of April 1819 and about the middle of it, that they were all—man, woman and child—from the heights of Farr to the mouth of the Naver, on one day, to quit their tenements and go —many of them knew not whither. For a few, some miserable patches of ground along the shores were doled out as lots, without aught in the shape of the poorest hut to shelter them. Upon these lots it was intended that they should build houses at their own expense, and cultivate the barren ground, at the same time occupying themselves as fishermen, although the great majority of them had never set foot in a boat in their lives. Thither therefore they were driven at a week's warning. As for the rest, most of them knew not whither to go, unless their neighbours on the shore provided them with a temporary shelter; for on the day of their removal they would not be allowed to remain, even on the bleakest moor and in the open air for a distance of 20 miles around.

On the Sabbath, a fortnight previous to the fated day, I preached
my valedictory sermon in Achness, and the Sabbath thereafter at
Ach-na-h'naighe; both occasions were felt by myself and by the
people from the oldest to the youngest to be among the bitterest
and most overwhelming experience of our lives. In Strathnaver, we
assembled for the last time at the place of Langdale on a beautiful
green sward overhung by Robert Gordon's antique romantic little
cottage on an eminence close beside us The still-flowing waters of
the Naver swept past us a few yards to the eastward. The Sabbath
morning was unusually fine and mountain, hill and dale, water and
woodland among which we had so long dwelt and with which all
our associations of 'home' and 'native land' were so fondly
linked, appeared to unite their attractions to bid us farewell. (I
would ask my readers to pause and think deeply over this whole
and tremendous soul-reaching Gethsemane.) *'The sore scene of
parting caused me pain beyond endurance.'*
I selected a text which had a pointed reference to the peculiarity
of our circumstances, but my difficulty was how to restrain my
feelings till I should illustrate and enforce the great truths which it
involved with reference to Eternity. The service began. The very
aspect of the congregation was of itself a sermon and a most impressive one. Old Achoul sat right opposite to me. As my eye fell
upon his venerable countenance bearing the impress of eighty-seven
winters, I was deeply affected and could scarcely articulate the psalm.
I preached the Gospel and the people listened, but every sentence
uttered and heard was in opposition to the tide of our natural feelings,
which, setting in against us, mounted at every step of our progress
higher and higher. *At last all restraints were compelled to give way.
The preacher ceased to speak, the people to listen. All lifted up their
voices and wept, mingling their tears together. It was indeed the place of
parting and the hour. The greater number parted* never again to behold
each other in the land of the living. Their only port of haven on
the coast would seem, as I have said, to be the Port of Eternity. My
adieu to the people of Ach-na-h'naighe was scarcely less affecting,
although somewhat alleviated by the consideration that I had the
prospect of ministering still to those among them who had leases
of their farms and whom Sellar, the factor and law agent, had no
power to remove. Sellar earned a name perhaps unrivalled in the
annals of Highland villainy.

The middle of the week brought on the day of the **Strathnaver Clearance of 1819**. It was a Tuesday, at an early hour
of that day 'Mr.' Sellar, accompanied by the Fiscal and escorted
by a strong body of constables, Sheriff-officers and others, com-

menced work at Grummore, the first inhabited township to the
west of the Achness district. Their plan of operations was to
clear the cottages of their inmates, giving them about half-an-hour
to pack up and carry off their furniture, and then set the cottages
on fire. To this plan they ruthlessly adhered, without the slightest
regard to any obstacle that might arise while carrying it into
execution. At GRUMBEG, lived a soldier's widow Henny Munro.
She had followed her husband in all his campaigns, marches and
battles in Sicily and in Spain. Whether his death was on the
field of battle or the result of fever or fatigue, I forget; but his
faithful helpmate attended him to his last hour, and when his
spirit fled, closed his eyes and followed his remains to their last
resting-place. After his death she returned to Drumbeg, the
place of her nativity, and as she was utterly destitute of any means
of support, she was affectionately received by her friends who
built her a small cottage and gave her a cow and grass for it.
The din of arms, orders and counter-orders from headquarters,
marchings and counter-marchings and pitched battles, retreats
and advances, were the leading and unceasing subjects of her
winter evenings' conversation. She was a joyous, cheery old
creature; so inoffensive moreover and so contented and brimful
of goodwill, that all who got acquainted with old Henny Munro
could only desire to do her a good turn, were it merely for the
warm and hearty expressions of gratitude with which it was
received. Surely the factor and his followers did not personally
know old Henny, or they could not have treated her as they did.
After the cottages at Grummore were emptied of their inmates
and roof and rafters had been lighted up with one red blaze,
Sellar and his iron-hearted attendants approached the residence
of the soldier's widow. Henny stood up to plead for her furniture
—the coarsest and most valueless that well could be, but still her
earthly all. She first asked that, as her neighbours were so occupied with their own furniture, hers might be allowed to remain
till they should be free to remove it for her. This request was
curtly refused. She then besought them to allow a shepherd, who
was present, and offered his services for that purpose, to remove
the furniture to his own residence on the opposite shore of the
loch, to remain there till she could carry it away. This also was
refused, and she was told, with an oath, that if she did not take
her trumpery off within half-an-hour, it would be burned. The

poor widow had only to task the remains of her bodily strength and address herself to the work of dragging her chests, beds, presses and stools out at the door, and placing them at the gable of her cottage. No sooner was her task accomplished than the torch was applied; the widow's hut, built of very combustible material, speedily ignited and there rose up rapidly, first a dense cloud of smoke, and soon thereafter, a bright red flame. The wind unfortunately blew in the direction of the furniture, and the flames lighting upon it speedily reduced it to ashes.

In their progress down the Strath, CEANN-NA-COILLE was the next township reached by the fire-raising demon evictors. An aged widow lived there who, by infirmity, had been reduced to such a state of bodily weakness that she could neither walk nor lie in bed. She could only, night and day, sit in her chair, and having been confined for many years in that posture, her limbs had become so stiff that any attempt to move her was attended with acute pain. She was the mother-in-law of Samuel Matheson and had, with her family, been removed by 'Mr.' Sellar from Rhimisdale some time before. His treatment of her and others on that occasion had brought Sellar into trouble, but now she was once more in his power. 'BEAN RAOMASDAIL', or 'the good wife of Rhimisdale' as she was called, was much revered. 'In her house, I have held diets of catechising and meetings for prayer and been signally refreshed by her Christian converse.' When the evicting party commenced their operations in her hamlet, the aged widow's house was among the very first that was to be consigned to the flames. Her family and neighbours represented the widow's strong claims on their compassion and the imminent danger to her life of removing her to such a distance as the lower end of the Strath, at least ten miles off, without suitable means of conveyance. They implored that she might be allowed to remain for only two days till a conveyance could be provided for her. They were told that they should have thought on that before, and that she must immediately be removed by her friends, or the constables would be ordered to do it. The good wife of Rhimisdale was therefore raised by her weeping family from her chair and laid on a blanket, the corners of which were held up by four of the strongest youths in the place. All this she bore with meekness and while the eyes of her attendants were streaming with tears, her pale and gentle countenance was suffused with a smile. The change of posture and the rapid motion of the bearers, however, awakened the most intense pain and her cries never ceased till within a few miles of her destination, when she fell asleep; a burning fever possessed her of which she died a few weeks later. And this in the year Queen Victoria was born.

> During these proceedings I had occasion to visit the manse at TONGUE. On the way thither I passed through the scene of the campaign of burning and extinction. The spectacle presented was hideous and ghastly. The banks of the loch and the river, formerly studded with cottages, now meet the eye as a scene of complete desolation. Of all the houses, the thatched roofs were gone; but the walls, built of alternate layers of turf and stone remained. (Many of these can be seen to this day, but of course the walls are almost laid to the ground.) The flames of the preceding week still slumbered in their ruins and sent up into the air spiral columns of smoke; whilst here a gable and there a long-side wall, undermined by the fire burning within them, might be seen tumbling to the ground, from which a cloud of smoke and then a dusty flame slowly sprang up. The sooty rafters of the cottages as they were being consumed filled the air with a heavy and offensive odour. In short nothing could more vividly represent the horrors of grinding oppression and the extent to which one man, dressed up in a little brief authority will exercise that power without any feeling or restraint, to the injury of his fellow-creatures.

I have taken these extracts from a close research of the Rev. Donald Sage's MS. of 1840. This and much more was only published for general release in 1890. And the happenings only eighty years ago; it seems incredible.

*   *   *

Now I will bring to notice other sinister cruelties taken at random, but as I have said before, they all bear the same hallmark pattern woven amongst the beautiful countryside of Kildonan and Strathnaver.

John Mackay's wife, of Ravigill, in attempting to pull down her house in the absence of her husband, to preserve the timber from being burnt, fell through the roof. She was in consequence taken in premature labour, and in that state was exposed in giving birth to her child, to the open air, and to the view of all the by-standers. Donald Munro, of Garvott, lying in a fever, was turned out of his house and exposed to the elements, and died. Donald Macbeath, an infirm and bedridden old man, had his house unroofed over him, and was in that state exposed to the wind and rain until death put an end to his sufferings. At the pulling down and burning of the house of William Chisholm, Badinloskin, in which was lying his wife's mother, an old bed-ridden woman of nearly one hundred years of age, none of the family being present. The persons about to set fire to the house were told of the circumstances and prevailed upon to wait until Sellar came in person. On his arrival, he was told of the poor old woman being in a condition unfit for removal; but he replied, 'Damn her, the old bitch, she has lived too long—let her burn.' The same old story. Fire was immediately set to the house, and the blankets in which she was carried out were in flames before she could be got out. She was placed in a little shed, and it was with great difficulty they were prevented from firing it also. The old woman's daughter arrived while the house was on fire, and assisted the neighbours in removing her mother out of the flames and smoke, presenting a picture of horror one can never forget and difficult to describe.

Within five days she was a corpse.

Evictions were carried out from 1814 down to 1819 and 1820, pretty much of the same character as those before. But the removal of Mr. Young, the chief factor, and Mr. Sellar from power was hailed with delight by the whole remaining popula-tion. Their very names had become a terror; in fact their appearance in any part of the county caused such alarm as to make women fall into fits. One woman became so terrified that she became insane, and whenever she saw any one she did not recog-nise, she invariably called out in a state of absolute terror— '*Oh! sin Sellar*'—'Oh! there's Sellar.'

It is officially recorded by well educated persons that the people's wretchedness was so great that, after pawning everything they possessed to the fishermen on the coast, such as had no cattle were reduced to come down from the hills in hundreds for the purpose of gathering cockles on the shore. Those who lived in the more remote situations of the county were obliged to subsist upon broth made of nettles, thickened with a little oatmeal. Those who chanced to have cattle (and they were few) had recourse to the still more wretched expedient of bleeding them, and mixing the blood with oatmeal which they afterwards cut into slices and fried. Those who had a little money came down and slept all night upon the beach, in order to watch for the boats returning from the fishing, that they might be in time to obtain a part of what had been caught for a mere pittance. They would relish the fish guts that were being thrown overboard. In some parts of the coast constables were stationed to prevent the starving people from collecting shellfish.

The whole of the inhabitants of Kildonan, numbering nearly 2000 souls, except three families, were utterly uprooted and burnt out, and the whole parish converted into a solitary wilderness. Suffering was intense; many understandably lost their reason.

The same applied to Strathnaver, where the fine population was burnt out. The church, like the parish church at Farr, was no longer in existence; it was razed to the ground and its timbers conveyed to construct one of the Sutherland improvements, namely the Inn at Altnaharra, while the minister's house was converted into a dwelling for a fox-hunter.

Another cruel factor was visiting a hamlet and going towards a small thatched cottage met an old great-grandmother as she was returning from milking the cow carrying a wooden vessel of milk. Brutally he snatched it from her, and to use his words, 'drowned for ever the fire of her hearth with it', and then drove her and the children to search through great privation for some foothold on rugged ground beside the western coast-line. When this factor died, his body was carried through another, equally hard dealt with, township. The sympathy of the folk was conspicuous by its absence for they all remembered his cruelty. One old woman expressed the general, but hitherto suppressed, feeling of the community when she said, 'CHA DEACH AM MAOR RIAMH TROIMH NA BHAILE CHO SAMHACH SA CHAIDH E AN DUIGH' (the factor never went through this township so peacefully as he went today).

I have to repeat that one of the worst features of these Clearances was the method in which they were perpetrated; sick people carried, or even thrown, out of their homes and left on the wayside seeing their houses going up in flames. Perched on rocks and moorlands these people were driven from the inland valleys and had to build themselves shelters from the turf and stones of the hillside and carve out of barren land with infinite toil and under the constant menace of famine, some miserable hovel as a home. These patches of over-cultivated land can be seen today as evidence of their labours. Others were forced to emigrate and the sufferings of those who survived well-nigh baffle description. The horrors of the small emigrant sailing ships of those days; people packed like sardines in a tin regardless of anything approaching comfort (a word unknown then) and the decencies of life and without sufficient food. And all this equalled only by the terrible privations and struggle for existence that awaited those who landed on the frozen lands of the north of Canada, to be assailed by hostile Indians, the rigours of the weather and the desolation of an unfriendly country.

Altogether it is a tale of barbarous action unequalled in the annals of agrarian crime.

*   *   *

Prior to the start of the Clearances proper, an idea was set on foot to try and induce these ignorant people by misrepresentation and falsehoods to leave their homes for new pastures abroad. There was one notable ship, the *Hector*, which sailed between Scotland and Pictou, Nova Scotia. This ship was owned by two men, Pagan and Witherspoon, who bought a small share of land in Pictou, and they engaged a Mr. John Ross as their agent, to accompany the vessel to Scotland, to bring out as many colonists as could be induced to leave their homes. They offered a free passage, a farm, and a year's free provisions to their dupes. On his arrival in Scotland, Ross drew a glowing picture of the land and other manifold advantages of the country to which he was enticing these people.

The Highlanders, sad to leave their Shangri-La homeland, knew nothing of the difficulties awaiting them in a land covered over with a dense unbroken forest—not a land of milk and honey; and, tempted by the prospect of owning splendid farms of their own, they were gullible and imposed upon by his promises, and many of them agreed to accompany him across the Atlantic and were keen to embrace his proposals. Calling first at Greenock on the Clyde, three families and five single young men joined the vessel at that port. She then sailed to Loch Broom near Ullapool in Wester Ross, not far from Gairloch, where she received 33 families and 25 single men, the whole of her passengers numbered about 200 souls. This poor lot in July 1793, bade a final farewell to their native land, not a soul on board having ever crossed the Atlantic, except of course, the agent, Ross. As they were leaving a piper came on board who had not paid his passage; the captain ordered him ashore, but the strains of the national instrument affected those on board so much that they pleaded to have him allowed to accompany them, and offered to share their own rations with him in exchange for his music during the passage. Their request was granted, and his performances aided in no small degree to cheer the noble band of these pioneers in their long voyage of eleven weeks, in a miserable hulk across the ocean.

This pilgrim band kept up their spirits as best they could by song, pipe-music, dancing, wrestling and other amusements through the long and painful voyage. The ship was so rotten that the passengers could *pick the wood out of her sides with their fingers.* They met with a severe gale off the Newfoundland coast, and were driven back by it so far that it took them about fourteen days to get back to the 'point of no return' at which the storm met them.

The accommodation was wretched, smallpox and dysentery broke out amongst them. Eighteen of the children died, and were committed to the deep amidst such anguish and heart-rending agony as only a Highlander can understand. Their stock of provisions became almost exhausted; the water was scarce and bad; the remnant of food left consisted mainly of salted meat which, from the scarcity of water, added greatly to their sufferings. The oatcake carried by them became mouldy, so that much of it had been thrown away before they dreamt of having such a long passage. Fortunately for them, one of the passengers, Hugh Macleod, more prudent than the others, gathered up the despised scraps into a bag, and during the last few days of the voyage, his fellows were only too glad to join him in devouring this refuse to keep body and soul alive.

At last the *Hector* dropped anchor in the harbour, opposite where the town of Pictou now stands. Though the Highland dress was then proscribed at home, this band of emigrants carried theirs along with them, and in celebration of their arrival many of the younger men donned their national dress—to which a few of them were able to add the *sgian dubh* and the claymore—while the piper blew up his pipes with might and main, its thrilling tones, for the first time, startling the denizens of the endless forest, its echoes resounding through the wild solitude.

Scottish emigrants are admitted upon all sides to have given its backbone of moral and religious strength to Nova Scotia, and to those brought over from the Highlands in this vessel is due the honour of being in the forefront—the pioneers and vanguard.

But how different was the reality to the expectations of these poor creatures, led by the plausibility of the emigration agent, Ross, to expect free estates on their arrival.

As I have said, the whole scene, as far as the eye could see, was a dense forest. They crowded on the deck to take stock of their future home, and their hearts sank within them. They were landed without the provisions promised, without shelter of any kind, and were only able by the aid of those few before them, to erect camps of the rudest and most primitive description, to shelter their wives and their children from the elements. Their feelings of disappointment were most bitter, when they compared the actual facts with the free farms and the comfort promised them by the foul-lying agent. Many of them sat down in the forest and wept bitterly; hardly any provisions were possessed by the few who were before them, and what there was among them was soon devoured, making all—old and newcomers—almost destitute.

It was now too late to raise crops that year. To make matters worse they were sent some three miles into the forest, so that they could not even take advantage with the same ease of any fish that might be caught in the harbour. The whole business appeared an utter mockery. To unskilled men the work of clearing the forest was hopeless; they were naturally afraid of the Red Indians and of the wild beasts roaming in the jungle, and without roads or paths, they were frightened to move for fear of getting lost.

Can we wonder that in such circumstances, they refused to settle on the company's lands? and the agents refused to give them any provisions when food did arrive. Ross quarrelled with the Company and he ultimately left the newcomers to their fate. The 'pioneers' were forced to exchange their clothes for food; but the greater number had neither money nor clothes to spend

or exchange, and all were soon left totally destitute. Driven to
extremity, they determined to have the provisions retained by
the agents, right or wrong, and two of them went to claim them.
They were positively refused, but they resolved to take what they
could by force. They seized the agents, tied them up, took their
guns from them, which they hid at a distance; told them they
must have food for their families. They then carefully weighed
or measured the various articles, took account of what each man
received (as they said they would pay for everything once they
gained any money) and left, except one man, a powerful and
determined fellow, who was left behind to release the two agents.
This he did, after allowing sufficient time for his friends to get a
safe distance, when he informed his prisoners where they could
find their guns. Intelligence was sent to Halifax town that the
Highlanders were in rebellion, from whence orders were sent to
a Captain Archibald nearby to march his company of militia to
suppress and pacify them; but to his honour, be it recorded, he
point blank refused, and sent word that he would do no such
thing. 'I know the Highlanders,' he said, 'and if they are fairly
treated there will be no trouble with them.' Finally, orders were
given to supply them with provisions.

It would be tedious, as well as sad, to describe the sufferings
which they afterwards endured. Many of them left. Others,
fathers, mothers and children, bound themselves away as virtual
slaves in other settlements, for mere subsistence. Those who
remained lived in small huts, covered only with the bark of
branches of trees to shelter them from the bitter winter cold, the
severity of which they had no previous conception. They had
to walk some eighty miles, through a trackless forest, in deep
snow to the nearest village (named Truro) to obtain a few bushels
of potatoes or a little flour in exchange for their labour, dragging
everything all the way back again on their backs. Endless cases
of great suffering from actual want occurred.

The remembrance of these terrible days sank deep into the
minds of that generation.

In the following spring they set to work. They cleared some
of the forest, and planted a large crop. They learned to hunt the
moose (a large deer). They began to cut timber, and sent a cargo
of it from Pictou—the first of a trade very profitably and extensively carried on ever since. One of the modes of laying up a

supply of food for the winter was to dig up a large quantity of clams or large oysters, pile them in large heaps on the sea-shore, and then cover them over with sand, though they were often, in winter, obliged to cut through ice more than a foot thick to get at them. Hardships piled upon hardships.

In Prince Edward Island, emigrants from Lockerbie in Dumfriesshire fared even worse in the late 1700's. They commenced operations on the Island with fair prospects of success, when a plague of locusts and field mice broke out and consumed everything, even the potatoes in the ground—almost overnight—and for eighteen months the settlers in this Lost Horizon experienced all the miseries of a famine. The winter brought them to such a state of weariness that they were unable to convey food a reasonable distance, even when they had the means to buy it.

In this pitiful position they heard that the Pictou people were making progress that year and even had some provisions to spare. They sent one of their number to make enquiries. An American settler, when he came to Pictou, brought a few slaves with him, and at this time he had just been to Truro to sell one of them, and brought home some provisions with the proceeds of the sale of his Negro. The messenger from Prince Edward Island was putting up at this man's house. He was a bit of a humorist, and continued cheerful in spite of all his troubles. On his return to the Island, the people congregated to hear the news. 'What kind of a place is Pictou?' enquired one. 'Oh, an awful place. Why, I was staying with a man who was just eating the last of his niggers,' and the poor creatures were reduced to such a point themselves that they actually believed the people in Pictou to be in such a condition as to oblige them to live on the flesh of their coloured servants! They were told, however, that matters were not quite so bad as that, and a few families left for that earlier settlement, where for a time they fared very little better, but afterwards became prosperous and happy. A few of their children and thousands of their grandchildren are now living in comfort and plenty.

But even so, who of us today can think of these early terrible hardships and cruel existences without condemning—even to hating point—the memories of the harsh and heartless Highland and Scottish lairds, who made existence at home even almost as miserable for those noble fellows, and who then drove them in thousands out of their native land, not caring one iota whether they sank in the Atlantic or were starved to death on a strange and uncongenial soil? Retributive justice demands that posterity should execrate the memories of the authors of such abject misery and horrid cruelty.

It may seem uncharitable to write these lines of the dead; but it is impossible to forget their inhuman conduct, though no thanks to them—cruel tigers in human form—it has turned out for the better, for the descendants of those who were banished to what was then infinitely worse than transportation for the worst crimes. Such criminals were looked after and cared for; but those poor people, driven out of their homes by the Highland lairds, and sent across there, were left to starve, helpless and uncared for. However, the descendants of the evicted from Sutherland, Ross-shire, Inverness-shire, and elsewhere, to Canada, Australia and New Zealand, are today producing enormous quantities of food and millions of cattle. The sheep farmer— the primary and original cause of the evictions—in due time suffered.

*   *   *

The Highlander loves his past and his native land with a passionate attachment, and the story of the great wrongs of the day of the clearances is still *today* deeply embedded in his mind. Many evil deeds have been associated with the abuse of the monopoly power of land-ownership, but it is safe to say that nowhere within the limits of these islands, or indeed anywhere else at any time have blacker or more foul deeds been committed in the sacred name of property than in the Highlands of Scotland. It has always been a matter of astonishment that such a brave race should ever have submitted to them. This becomes all the more remarkable too, when one remembers that during those years regiments raised in these very districts of the finest soldiers who ever marched to the stirring strains of the bagpipes, were gaining for the empire and for British arms the most noted achievements ever won in the Napoleonic wars. But it is true, as I have said, and it is an eternal discredit, that many of these brave fellows came back wounded and war-scarred to find, not that a grateful country had taken care that the homes and the helpless ones they had left behind were kept sacred and immune from the greed and ruthless savagery of the landlord or his hirelings, but that their hearths and homes were desecrated and destroyed, and every moral law of patriotism and honour had been violated. Their humble dwellings were of their own rearing. Far beyond the reach of history, they had possessed their mountain holdings; they had defended them so well of old that the soil was still virgin ground which the invader had found only a grave.

The silence with which men of that calibre met these hardships and cruelty might well remain an enigma to anyone who does not know the Highlands. They knew that for centuries their ancestors had tilled those lands and lived free and untrammelled. By every moral law, if not by the law of the land, they had a right to the soil which had been defended with their own right arm and that of their ancestors. But after the '45 men were no longer assets to the chief, for his territorial jurisdiction had been broken. It was money, not men, that was needed and the lonely silences of the hills, instead of merry laughter and the prattle of children singing graces by the wayside. And these men bore the change which meant so much to them with patience. The Highlands were permeated then, as now, with a deep religious sense. They lent a willing ear to the teachings of the ministers of the Gospel, who wielded the power of the iron hand which left its deep impress on the social life and literature of the Highlands. They regarded the minister as the stern oracle of Truth and the strict interpreter of the meaning of the ways of God to man. *What happened was right*, so their pastors said.

If a singularly well-conditioned and wholesome peaceful district of a country had been converted into one wide ulcer of wretchedness and woe, it must be confessed that the sore had been carefully bandaged up from public and national knowledge, and whilst little had been done for its cure, much was done for its concealment. Plenty indeed, even to this day.

The circle turned, and deer and sporting rights soon became more profitable than sheep, and it is astonishing to find historians attempting to show that evictions never took place on account of deer forests. What trash! Evictions took place for the object that was at the moment most profitable. The Napoleonic wars made sheep runs temporarily more profitable; but the moment there was more profit to be obtained from sport and deer forests, then deer forests were to a large extent substituted for sheep.

From the knowledge I have, it is indisputable that the worst feature of the Clearances was the method in which they were perpetrated.

*   *   *

The facts recorded in this chapter will possess for many Englishmen an almost startling novelty; the tales of oppression and cruelty they reveal read like one of those hideous stories peculiar to the dark ages, rather than a simple record of events happening upon our own land and not so very long ago.

For a parallel to this monstrous power of the landowner, under which life and property were entirely at his mercy and counted for nought, we must go back to mediaeval times, or to the days when serfdom not having been abolished, the Russian noble was armed with despotic authority; while the more pitiful results of this tyranny, the wide devastation of cultivated lands, the heartless burning of houses, the reckless creation of pauperism and misery out of well-being and contentment, could only be expected under the rule of Turkish Sultans or greedy and cruel Pashas. Yet these deeds were perpetrated in one of the most beautiful portions of our land. They are not the work of uncultured barbarians or of fanatic Moslems, but of so-called civilised and Christian men.

In my last book, *Highland Pearls*, in dealing with this Clearance subject, but not in such a comprehensive manner as here, I referred to the terrible happenings in 1843 at CROICK, a small village near Ardgay (before you cross over to Sutherland at Bonar Bridge) where the entire population—through the unscrupulous factor, Gillanders—were made to seek refuge in those agonising days, under the raised flat tombstones in the churchyard exposed to all weathers, and of their names scratched in copper plate style on the panes of the east window of the little church. I paid a visit to Croick two years ago and these names are there for all posterity to see as plain as the day they were written— indelible evidence of those days of tribulation. Should you visit this wee church, approached by a good (though narrow) road and situated in a lovely peaceful glen, you will stand spellbound as you gaze at that window and think upon a lost community and maybe bow in reverence to their fortitude—men, women and children—and pour down curses upon the factor and his superior.

The experiences and incidents I have recited in this chapter should be sufficient, and more than sufficient, for any soul-possessing human person, to realise what a terrible state of affairs then existed.

*   *   *

In a speech delivered at Inverness on 18th September 1885, Mr. Joseph Chamberlain ('Joe' Chamberlain, 1836–1914, of that illustrious family) ten years before he became Colonial Secretary, said:

> The history of the Highland Clearances is a black page in the account with private ownership in land, and if it were to form a precedent, if there could be any precedent for wrong-doing, if the sins of the fathers ought to be visited upon the children, we should have an excuse for more drastic legislation than any which the wildest reformer has ever proposed.   Thousands of hard-working, industrious, God-fearing people were driven from the lands which had belonged to their ancestors, and which for generations they had cultivated; their houses were unroofed and burnt down and they were turned out homeless and forlorn, exposed to the inclemency of the winter season, left to perish on the hillsides or to swell the full flood of misery and destitution in places overseas to which they were driven for refuge.   They suffered unbearably; very many died.   However, as time went on the descendants of those who did survive have contributed in no mean degree to the prosperity of the countries in which they finally settled.   The Highland countryside was de-populated by those clearances.   The general condition of the people left behind suffered and it has gone on deteriorating until it has become at last a matter of national concern.   If I am correct in the statement in which I have endeavoured to summarise what I have read and learned upon this subject, I ask you whether it is not time that we should submit to careful examination and review a system which places such vast powers for evil in the hands of irresponsible individuals and which makes the possession of land not a trust but a means of extortion and exaction? . . .

Thus said Joe Chamberlain only 85 years ago.   And what a statesman he was.   What carefully thought-out words; plain and simple but to the point.   *'Powers for evil in the hands of irresponsible individuals.'*   How very true; inhabitants dispossessed by unrelenting avarice, which today has been shown to be as shortsighted as it was selfish and unjust.   The Highlands is still the fairy ground of

G

legends, romance and Gaelic poetry; and the pibroch can still be heard through the sparsely inhabited regions of Shangri-La.

In a way I feel Sutherland has only itself to blame for its present condition of being a vast county with so little finance at its command; and all due to the few people living there. The number of houses and rateable property being, one might say, infinitesimal to the area covered. Only one person per 100 acres, and the entire rateable value only £195,000. Surely at the time of the Clearances there would be *some* authoritative body in every parish that could have acted as watch-dogs, taking up the cudgels, presenting the miseries then being enacted, to a level far beyond their local landowners' domain; some parish officers who would make loud protests in London, seeing the ministers would not act because of fear.

The first meeting of the Provisional Council of the County of Sutherland was held within the Courthouse, County Buildings, Dornoch, on 13th February 1890; the first meeting of the County Council of Sutherland was held at Bonar Bridge and within the Drill Hall there on Thursday, 23rd May 1890. But as I have said, there were other parish bodies having authority long before then.

A few pages before, I have quoted the incidence of the Pictou settlers, and the Captain point blank refusing to march his company of militia to suppress them, for he knew the Highland character. But were the soldiers of the 21st regiment from Fort George restrained by their commanding officer from marching to Dunrobin Castle to suppress the poor innocent people of Strathnaver and Kildonan? O dear no! and they were people living in the same land.

This Clearance adventure is not to be made good overnight; bitter feelings are deep and lasting. Think of it today if there had been no clearances; the old croft houses would be standing and occupied; there would be hundreds and hundreds more houses—those of the crofter's children—and then hundreds more; their children's children. And so it would increase; in all, thousands of men, women, children and buildings, and the vast territory thereby rich in many ways, including Faith; if only someone had stepped in and acted in those early days. So therefore I say, Sutherland must lay the blame within herself and no one else.

As to the notorious factors of the likes of Sellar, Young, Loth, Gillanders and a heap more, if they had been hanged on a gibbet,

erected in their own specific areas, and the corpse publicly displayed, draped in chains for a year or so, the bones being carefully wired together until the wind and rain had blown them away, bone by bone as a ghastly reminder of their foul deeds, *that* would have been the lesson, that terrorism in the Highlands would be met by counter-terrorism. It would have been the proper medicine to mete out, showing resentment and revenge. It would have given the landowners a shock which would not have taken them a long time to grasp, and when they had grasped the meaning, it would have put 'paid' to their barbaric methods. It would have been worse even than a military defeat.

In May 1752 there was the case of the government factor and Justice of the Peace, one 45-year-old Colin Campbell of Glenure (known as the Red Fox from the colour of his hair) who was shot and killed in the woods of Appin, North Argyll; hated because of his eviction outrages. I repeat, he was the King's factor. According to that standard Sellar and company were small fry. Why didn't they meet a similar end? And even today up in the Far North, echo answers '*why?*'

Adverting to the shooting of the Red Fox, James Stewart of the Glen was supposed to have killed Colin Campbell. But did he? There is a memorial to James Stewart on the hillock behind Ballachulish (Argyll) where he was hanged, and inscribed on it is 'In memory of James Stewart of Acharn, who was executed on this spot on 1st November 1752 for a crime of which he was not guilty.'

Who *did* kill Colin Campbell of Glenure that fateful evening? It seems it wasn't James and it wasn't Alan Breck Stewart. In justification of the sentence of death passed upon James Stewart, it is usually said that he was an 'actor' who was certainly involved in the murder on an 'art and part' basis. Alan was convicted *in absentia* of Glenure's murder on flimsy evidence. How then could James Stewart be tried as an accessory, if Alan wasn't the true assassin? Even today, the mystery and the query exist in the minds of many folk living around Appin.

*   *   *

> God moves in a mysterious way
>   His wonders to perform;
> He plants his footsteps in the sea
>   And rides upon the storm.
>
> His purposes will ripen fast
>   Unfolding every hour;
> The bud may have a bitter taste
>   But sweet will be the flower.

These are two of the six verses of Hymn No. 31 in the Church Hymnary; and as to these Clearances I have heard it said some people wonder if these happenings were *His* way of peopling the undeveloped areas of Canada and America with hardy, God-fearing immigrants of such good stock, thus ensuring their development on the right and solid lines.

I suppose these very Christian-minded people would be bearing in mind their devotion to the Bible which persuaded the recusant Pilgrim Fathers to sail forth in the *Mayflower* from Brixham, South Devon, on 6th September 1620 for a promised land? As God is Love, I, for my part, cannot equate the Almighty instigating such atrocities as the Clearances in order to populate a far-off Continent. Before these Clearances, 'Faith, Hope and Love then dwelt upon their earth, and earth by them was blest; but faith and hope must yield to love, of all the graces best. . . .'

Strathnaver, the countryside in which Sellar was free to make his fortune, is one of the most beautiful in the British Isles. Its name has vanished from modern maps, but in maps of the 17th and 18th centuries, the region comprised the greater part of the present county of Sutherland. Along the north coast of Scotland the foothills crease in ever-deepening valleys until they reach the largest and most fertile of them all, with the Naver river running through it. To the west again, Ben Loyal rears its great granite buttresses above the Kyle of Tongue. Ben Hope's half-moon summit leans towards Loch Eriboll, and beyond this long sealoch, the mountains form an unbroken chain from Cape Wrath down the west coast to the Assynt border. This is Strathnaver country; and in the days of Shangri-La the Bards used to say, 'Slow and easy; they stumble who go fast', and as I have said the Countess-Marchioness was *Ban-Mhorair-Chataibh* (the great lady of Sutherland). At the time these wrong-doings took place, Parliament was dominated by landowners. A notice appeared in an Inverness paper regarding sixty acres of land to be let in Sutherland saying that '*decided preference will be given to strangers*'. Between 1811 and 1820, the Countess invested in sheep and fifteen thousand inhabitants, consisting of three thousand (3000) families were hunted down and removed. The people had no security.

The law of the country was a disgrace to Europe.

The 'great' Countess-Marchioness-Duchess died in 1839. On the summit of Ben Bhraggie, a conspicuous landmark above Dunrobin Castle, a huge statue of the Duke of Sutherland was erected by order of his widow and her factor. Every tenant of that day had to subscribe to the cost of the erection. The back of the statue is to the glens he emptied for Lowland graziers and their sheep; and it faces the sea to which he committed thousands of people as emigrants. It is said, because he was an Englishman and knew no Gaelic, he did not hear the bitter protests and the agonising tales among his people. Yet it was all done in both his and his wife's name, under their authority and with their knowledge; certainly with their sanction. How can they be held blameless? How indeed? They became the richest landowners in Britain. Why should they have sunk to such abysmal, terrible human depths?

All through their history, the Sutherland family have had sorrows and tragedies (I recount an especial one in Chapter 14 as to the happenings at Helmsdale Castle in 1567). The one I now relate occurred in 1766; it has nothing to do, however, with the Clearances.

On an ill-fated day in Dunrobin Castle the Earl came after dinner into the drawing-room, gay and flushed with wine. He swung his infant daughter high over his head, laughing up at her. But his hold was insecure, and he lost his grip. The infant fell to the ground on its head, sustaining injuries from which it was never to recover.

The disastrous accident made the young father into a changed man. Forever brooding over the results of his careless folly, he fell into such a state of acute melancholia and physical illness that his physician came at last to recommend the arduous journey to Bath in Somerset.

His young wife, despite her pregnancy, insisted on going with him, and cheerfully undertook the exhausting journey by miry, rutty roads to the famous watering place.

On their arrival at long last, the couple barely had time to instal themselves than the Earl, a sick man already, fell victim to an infectious malignant fever. In twenty-one successive days and nights his young wife attended him while he raved in delirium, mostly unconscious of her presence by his side. The resule was inevitable, wearied out and dispirited, she herself caught the dread infection, and in a few days, death struck her down.

They kept the news from the sick man; but he knew. When his delirium had left him, he murmured again and again, 'I am going to join my dear wife'. And on the following day he died.

The bodies of the Earl and his lady were brought to Holyrood House, where they had usually resided when in Edinburgh, and there lay in state for some time previous to their interment, in one grave, near the north-east corner of the Abbey Chapel, on 9th, August 1766.

The tragic circumstances of the deaths of a pair so young, and who had stood in a distinguished position in society—leaving one female child to a disputed title—made a deep impression, and were the subject of several elegiac poems. The closing lines of one by Sir Gilbert Elliot of Minto may serve as their epitaph:

> . . . Ne'er did wedded love
> To one sad grave consign a lovelier pair,
> Of manners gentler, or of purer heart.

A further sad affair befell the present Countess of Sutherland and her husband, Mr. Charles Noel Janson, on 5th December 1969, when their 14-year-old son, Matthew (who went to Eton College in September 1968), died under tragic circumstances.

Elizabeth, Countess of Sutherland, succeeded to the Earldom of Sutherland when her uncle, the 5th duke, died in February 1963. To her went magnificent Dunrobin Castle and the sprawling estates in Sutherland But the dukedom of Sutherland went to the Earl of Ellesmere, Berwickshire, as the late duke's closest male relative. The Countess, married in 1946, has three other children. Now that Dunrobin Castle has been turned into a public school, she and her husband live at Uppat House, Brora, where she runs a 200-acre farm.

In March 1883, Prime Minister Gladstone set up a Royal Commission of Inquiry into the conditions of Crofters throughout Celtic Scotland. The Chairman was Lord Napier assisted by Sheriff Alex Nicholson and Prof. Donald Mackinnon of the Chair of Celtic at Edinburgh University. The other three members of the Commission were all Highland landowners, Sir Kenneth Mackenzie, Bart., Donald Cameron of Lochiel, M.P., and Charles Fraser-Macintosh, M.P. The Commissioners travelled through the Hebrides during June, and began their hearings in Shetland in mid July. From there, they sailed south to Orkney, and it was on 24th July they began their examination on the Sutherland estate at Bettyhill, in the parish of Farr. The Free Church minister of Farr assured the Commissioners that the native population had been left in occupation (*i.e.* those who had not been evicted overseas) only of the worst land in the area, the best pasture was *deliberately* taken for the purpose of forming sheep farms. Heaps of crofters testified to this.

The report and hearings of the Napier Commission were the trumpets which demolished the walls of Jericho that landlordism had thrown round Westminster. In 1886 the Bill was enacted, which gave to the people of the Highlands and Islands protection in the lands they occupied as statutory tenants. The power of the factor, based on the threat of instant eviction, was destroyed.

This, then, put an end to mile upon mile upon mile of desolation; league upon league upon league. But it is taking far more than 85 years to make good the damage done, and will probably take another eighty-five years before the county of Sutherland will become *the* County of Scotland with its tens of thousands happy men, women and children, so putting a stop to many dying communities in some of the out-of-the-way villages. I have seen it for myself; their pastors have spoken these very words to me—so what I write in this connection cannot be wrong or all ballyhoo.

The solution of the so-called fanciful Highland Problem of today is not just land purchase, but the resumption of the clansmen's right to occupy the Fatherland to the fullest degree. Basically, I consider there is no problem in the real sense of the word today; just make crofting to be on a broader, bigger and more attractive scale than ever before; not simply a dozen sheep and a few cattle, but sheep by the thousand—a miniature Australia in fact. Build homes for the men and their families; they will soon find happiness and the contentment as of yore and above all make it worth their while; for after all there is money in the land if properly worked. Leave Industry, with a capital I, to the confines of city overflows, only allowing the lightest of light industries into the Highlands proper. We certainly cannot tolerate seeing a steel or any other corporation in Strathnaver, nor a supersonic aircraft factory on the shores of Loch Shin, or a gasworks plonked in the midst of Altnaharra's snug community.

Further to these questions M. de Sismondi, a Swiss scholar, wrote in one of his articles in the foreign press, 'This fate has befallen the Gaelic race, descendants of the ancient Celts; the lands they had cultivated generation after generation had been handed over to foreign shepherds, their houses and villages torn down and destroyed by fire and the evicted members of this mountain race were left no choice but either to erect huts by the sea-shore and try to preserve their miserable existence by fishing (of which they knew little), or to cross the sea and seek their livelihood in the wastes of America'.

*   *   *

Napoleon Bonaparte, at one time, took 500 prisoners and was unable to provide food for them. He would not let them go, although he knew they would perish by famine 'midst the cold Siberian winter; so his idea of mercy was to have them all shot. He ordered them to be formed into a square, and two hundred French muskets with ball cartridges were simultaneously levelled at them, which soon put the disarmed mass of human beings out of pain.

As to this, and the evictions, I have this to say. All Christian nations of Europe were horrified; every breast was full of indignation at the perpetrator of this tragedy, and France wept bitterly for the manner in which the tender mercies of their Emperor were exhibited. In our Protestant law-making Britain, we should tremble at the events on our own doorstep. Under the protection of law, Colonel Gordon had consigned 1500 men, women and children to a death a hundredfold more agonising and horrifying. He and his predecessors, by invitation of his Grace the Duke of Sutherland, removed the people from the land created by God, suitable for cultivation and the use of man, and put it under brute animals, throwing the people upon by-corners, precipices, and barren moors, then exacting exorbitant rents until the people were made penniless so they could neither leave the place nor better their condition in it. And in the end the majority died of starvation or else were thrown into filthy ships to carry them—more or less as slaves—to foreign lands. Death by famine on British soil. Christian people living at ease away from the Highlands and our Christian rulers should have hidden their faces in shame before the heathenism displayed and meted out to such a Godly Highland race; and what comfort could they have in their souls when those landowners were so guilty of such deeds of inhumanity to their own species. I would say, place yourselves for a moment in their hopeless condition at their embarkation, decoyed in the name of the British Government by false promises of assistance to procure homes and comforts in Canada, which were denied to them at home—decoyed, I say, to an unwilling or partial consent—and those who resisted or recoiled from this conditional consent and who fled to the caves and mountains to hide themselves from such brigands; look at them, chased and caught by constables and other underlings, handcuffed and huddled together with the rest on an emigrant vessel; hearing the sobbing, sighing and throbbings of their guileless, warm Highland hearts, taking their last look and bidding a final adieu to their romantic mountains and glens, the fertile straths and valleys, which their forefathers from time immemorial inhabited, and where they are now lying in undisturbed and everlasting repose, in spots endeared and sacred to the memory of their unfortunate offsprings, who bid a mournful farewell to their early associations, which were as dear and revered to them as their very existence. Patient in suffering. Follow them on their many weeks dreary passage across the Atlantic in such appalling conditions. Then come ashore with them where death is in store; hear the captain giving orders to discharge the cargo of livestock 'human bondage'; hear the noise, the bitter weeping, bustle and confusion; hear mothers and their children asking fathers and husbands, 'Where are we going?'; and hear the reply, 'CHAN EIL FIOS AGAINN'—we know not.

Such is the painful picture that the English language, I am afraid, fails to adequately supply words fit to describe it all. Every tale, every incident, bears the same stereotype pattern. Fearful is the catalogue of the accursed clearing system in the Highlands of one-time Shangri-La; famine, fire, drowning, banishment, vice and crime; the unfeeling, deceitful conduct of those acting for their superiors. The duplicity and art which was used is worthy of the craft and cunning of an old slave-trader.

All the same, these old folk banded and clung together; they never isolated or disintegrated themselves one from another. In this respect there is a close analogy to what occurred in the Second World War before America threw in her lot with us.

At that time the United States were deeply concerned to find out how British morale stood. They were dark and perilous times, for the feeling in America was that Britain was doomed and that we were about to follow the way of France. So the President, Franklin Delano Roosevelt, sent one of his closest friends, Harry Hopkins, to Britain to report back to him after making a full investigation of our conditions. Churchill in particular was eager to know the intentions of America. But Harry Hopkins was not giving anything away. Moreover, he was a sick man. At a private dinner (arranged by Mr. Thomas Johnston, Secretary of State in the War Cabinet) in a Glasgow hotel for the distinguished guest, Mr. Johnston found out that Mr. Hopkins' great-grandmother had been born at Auchterarder in Perthshire; and so that was one point in favour of Scotland, and of Britain. In view of the secret nature of Mr. Hopkins' mission, it was not expected that he would speak, but after the Secretary of State had referred to Mr. Hopkins' Scottish ancestry,

President Roosevelt's special private envoy rose, slowly, paying tribute to his President as being a great man, a very great man. And then continuing, he said that perhaps he might say in the language of the Old Book to which his great-grandmother paid so much attention, he quoted from Ruth, ch. 1, v. 16, 'Whither thou goest, we go, and where thou lodgest, we lodge; thy people shall be our people; thy God our God, even unto the end'.

In saying this, he looked straight down the table at Winston Churchill. That was all; he sat down in dead silence. Churchill's eyes welled up in tears. Here was the very first news that America was to throw in its weight upon the Allied side.

What a statesman-like saying, short though it was. Surely such words should go down in history as immortal

'*Whither thou goest, we go . . .*'

That was the spirit of those that were evicted.

*   *   *

Today in these years of the 1970's we should, in our own little way, salute with deep reverence those who suffered and died. For myself, when I travel through the Sutherland glens—which I so often do—(Strathnaver in particular) I stop and I look, and I listen. When I leave, I always find myself saying, 'How on earth was it possible?' Yet, it was. The visiting public, driving through in the summer months enjoying everything to the full, are mostly unaware of what happened in those days; in fact they're not concerned; they were not involved, so why should they be concerned? Very like the wars in Vietnam, Israel, Egypt, Jordan—we're not concerned; and so little attention is paid to all the crofting ruins that lie by the wayside.

It is the way of things.

Yes, when I travel slowly through these glens of memory, the past returns; and like Ezekiel (ch. 3, v. 15) '*I sat where they sat*'.

Although unconnected with the Clearances proper, there is another foul and bloody deed which could well be embraced as being in effect an attempt at a 'shooting and butchering' Clearance. I refer to the massacre of GLENCOE on 13th February 1692, where the Campbells set about murdering their hosts, the Macdonalds; without doubt Highland barbarism at its worst.

Anyone who has been through Glencoe cannot but be struck

by its awesomeness—very like to the Torridon range—of its crowding mountains, fearsome yet inviting, menacing, yet protecting. The little village of Glencoe itself is one of the most unspoiled hamlets in the West Highlands. Going through the old village you see the knoll where a descendant of Macdonald of Glencoe, who perished in the massacre, erected nearly a century ago, a cairn topped by a tall, slender Celtic cross in memory of her famous ancestor and the other kinsfolk who perished with him on that unforgettable morning, nearly 280 years ago. There is a notice board near the old Clachaig Inn, which marks the scene of the massacre and close by is a hill, Signal Rock, where according to local belief, the signal was given for the beginning of this massacre. In the Inn itself there is to be seen a notice at the reception desk saying that hawkers and Campbells are not welcome! On top of the hill, from whatever angle you gaze, you are rewarded with many exquisite views; the towering peaks around, the Pass where the narrowing ribbon of road disappears into the uplands, and to the sea, where little boats lie at their moorings on the silver waters of Loch Leven, and Munda's Isle, the last resting place of so many chiefs of the Macdonalds of Glencoe.

The story of the massacre itself may not be well known to tourists though; the story of the glen that burned its name into Scottish history.

The accession of William and Mary in 1688 was not popular with many of the clan chiefs who still hoped for the return of the Stuarts, and looked to France for the help needed to bring this about; at the end of August 1691, a proclamation was issued by the Government threatening severe punishment for those who, by 1st January 1692, had not taken the oath of loyalty to William and Mary. Despairing of French help for the Jacobite cause, the chiefs reluctantly took the oath and so averted the threat of punitive action. But aged Alexander Macdonald of Glencoe held out until near the expiry of the day of grace. When eventually he presented himself before Colonel Hill at Fort William, it was to be told that his oath of submission could be taken only by a sheriff, and that he would have to proceed to Inveraray for that purpose. The result was that he was several days late in taking the oath, and when the certificate of oath reached the Privy Council it was rejected. This was all to the liking of Sir John

Dalrymple, who then procured letters of fire and sword against the Macdonalds. His agent for the extirpation of the Macdonalds was Captain Robert Campbell of Glenlyon who, with his troops, entered Glencoe, seeking and obtaining the hospitality of the Macdonalds. For twelve days they were entertained by the people of the Glen, and then, in the early morning of 13th February 1692, the signal for slaughter was given. Thirty-eight defenceless people, including women and children, were slain in cold blood. Others, who managed to elude their persecutors, took to the snow-clad mountains, whilst the thatched roofs of their cottages blazed from the torches of the men who had so recently enjoyed their shelter. In all, about 150 men, women and children fled, but perished in the snow-storm. All under 70 years of age were to be put to the sword, was the order.

It was a foul deed. Even allowing that the Macdonalds themselves were guilty of many misdeeds—for the times were turbulent and cruel—yet cold-blooded murder can find no justification, especially when the unfortunate victims had actually received their slayers with friendship and given them the hospitality of their homes.

This, then, is the story. It shocked Scotland at the time—and is still a delicate issue—because, as I have stated, of its ferocity and because the Campbells allegedly breached a trust of friendship and hospitality. Even today, nearly 300 years since, the name of Campbell is suspect.

Glencoe is unique to the mountaineers and the winter sports enthusiasts.

*   *   *

One can never read the story of Macdonald's journey to Inveraray to make his submission to the new monarchy without finding in it a spiritual lesson. The offer of amnesty was his, and, as he well knew, it was for a strictly limited period. Yet he dallied and brought upon himself a disaster which could have been averted. It is a pathetic story and it has many settings. For we, too, are rebels against constituted authority at times. In truth we are guilty of many transgressions of the laws of God, and although in this analogy the offers of pardon are extended to us upon condition of our timeous surrender, we are reluctant to make our submission. We do not even have the advantage of knowing, as Macdonald did, the precise date when the offer will be withdrawn. In life, we do not know the precise hour or when our opportunity will pass away for ever. We have no promise of a 'more convenient season'. There were elements of injustice in the fate of the Glencoe chief and his people. There will be none in ours if we bring Divine judgment upon ourselves.

*   *   *

Adverting to the eviction era again, I call to mind another martyr, John MacPherson—'the Glendale martyr'—a man who did much to win security of tenure for all Highland crofters. A memorial was unveiled on 25th July 1970 in Skye by Dr. Charles Ferguson of Lochcarron to his fighting crofter grandfather.

In the 19th century, every crofter and small tenant in the Highlands and Islands lived in fear of eviction, and with very good reason. The landlords had had a sniff of the profits of sheep as well as their habitual jealous protection of fishing waters and deer and grouse moors. Land was hard to hold for the poor. Improvements were sheer speculation. Year to year families lived at the tender mercy of the landlord as thousands found to their bitter cost. As I have recorded, evictions were wholesale and ruthless; whole villages, glens and hamlets were stripped of their people, left to starve or to emigrate—but all this is repetition of what I have already written; at the same time I feel there is no harm in hammering home these facts as often as one can.

MacPherson of Glendale was one of those who resisted and who had the personality to rally others around him. He was arrested and jailed in 1882 after a riot suppressed in bloody fashion by the police. Two years later he stood up to 100 marines and a frightened sheriff, averting bloodshed and stressing the people's rights. After another expedition by the sheriff he was arrested again, but shortly released without having to face trial. It was abundantly clear to all but the landlords that common human and divine justice was manifestly on the side of the crofters. The ordeal was not in vain for Parliament was eventually compelled to legislate in favour of the crofters' right of tenure. John MacPherson lived to see the crofters of Glendale receive the title deeds of their holdings in 1904; and in 1914 he saw the guarantee for the future—set up by the greatest Liberal government that has ever existed—the arrival of the internationally famed Scottish Land Court.

John MacPherson must have died a happy man in 1923, leaving behind him such glorious outcomes of his lifelong struggle—security of tenure for every crofter, and a senior and respected court to defend the poorest peasant against the wealthiest and greediest Duke in the land. However, old resentments, jealousies and fears have not been vanquished; a number of crofters are still convinced they are being oppressed. They say, 'We will see forests of trees instead of sheep, where a family steading might have been, with a landlord operating a commercial enterprise from England, instead of a crofter wresting his living from the land.' That is the issue today. The martyr of Glendale is no remote figure from an extinct past. It reminds us all that there are freedoms for which they still have to fight.

*   *   *

But this is enough for readers to realise the enormity of the offences levied against the faithful people of the Highlands. It is all as pathetic as the question of a little girl (blind from birth) asking her mother, '*What colour is the wind?*'

During these eviction days, confusion reigned and at times some voices cried, 'Forward'; others cried, 'Back', and both were drowned at intervals by mutterings of 'Sideways'. As in Balaam's day, many lost their lives trying to procure them.

During these years there were two great evils, or rather extremes, which pervaded the life of the Highlander and his family who were allowed to remain and eke out a living. First, the great gulf which divided the rich from the poor. There was not any part of the world where the good things of this life were more unequally distributed. The other extreme—the sub-tenant and the SGALLAG. The latter was a poor being who for some subsistence became a predial slave to another, whether sub-tenant, tacksman or a laird. He built his own hut with sods, boughs of trees, stubble and ferns, and if he were sent from one part of the Highlands to another, he would move off the sticks, and by means of these, form a new hut in another place. Five days a week he worked for his master; the sixth was allowed for himself for the cultivation of some scraps of land on the edge of some moor on which he raised a little kail, barley and potatoes.

Formerly these people were free, animated and bold, commanding respect from their undaunted courage and repelling injuries from whatever quarter they came by words and actions. But they had to approach even the tacksman with cringing humility, heartless and discouraged, with tattered rags, hungry bellies and downcast looks, carry their own implements of husbandry for ten or twelve miles, back and forward over hill, strath and mountain, to do the work of the tacksman; and must either sit wet in his clothes all night in a dirty kitchen, or sleep in dirty clothes. Formerly, a Highlander would have drawn his dirk against even a laird if he had subjected him to the indignity of a blow. At that time any tyrannical tacksman, in the absence of the laird—whose presence alone could enforce good order and justice—could strike a sgallag and even a sub-tenant, with perfect impunity. What degree of spirit of virtue could be expected from a people so humbled, so enslaved? What degree of courage, or even inclination, to repel an invading enemy? Not only were the tacksmen oppressors of the poor, but some of the hard-hearted clergy even practised oppression. It is recorded a minister of Barra (Rev. Roderick MacLeod), a man from the lowest origin, attained great wealth, influence and authority. He appeared to support the rich and distress the poor. As the latter had no voice in justice, they simply had to bear the yoke and keep silent. Many died and many of the older clan families became extinct; they have gone 'to the mountain of myrrh and the hill of frankincense'.

And all this in a land that the Highlanders looked upon as a contented, sacred Shangri-La.

What colour is the wind?

I would ask readers—if they will—to pause, lay aside this book, and turn their thoughts on this terrible affliction the Highlands were going through, and picture how tragic was the people's plight, and of the vendetta raised against them . . . and not all that many years either, as I have said before.

But Sutherland, O Sutherland, why did you cause such iniquity to be laid on so godly a race of people, and to hold them in such bondage; a bondage that I fear was even greater than in Egypt in the days of the Pharaohs. Human bondage in the 19th century? Human cargo, in fact.

Even the General Assembly of the Free Church of Scotland discovered there was something very far wrong and on 2nd June 1845 resolved there was a real emergency existing in the Highlands and Islands in respect of the then oppressive measures adopted against the ministers and members of the Church, and the destitution of the means of grace which prevailed against everyone; and at the Assembly meeting in Inverness on 21st August that year measures were adopted to help alleviate the evils under which the Gaelic-speaking population groaned; and they promoted a spiritual welfare revival. This had wide repercussions.

*   *   *

We must remember that before these days, there had been the '45 rebellion—Bonnie Prince Charlie's days; and that one of the results of this Jacobite intrusion had been the breaking up of the clan system. This naturally had a serious undermining effect on the whole Highland system and its people. There is no escaping this truth. The attitude of the Chief became, in most cases, totally altered. He no longer regarded himself as the father of his people, holding the land in trust for them. He now looked upon the clan territory as his personal property—as indeed it was in the eyes of the law—and he was ready to replace tenants by others who could pay a higher rent. He ceased to be a Chief; he became a landlord, and in not a few cases, an absentee landlord. The tacksman 'was a large taker or leaseholder of land of which he kept part as a domain in his own hand, and let part to the under-tenants.' He was usually of high birth, being often a kinsman of the Chief, and his holding was hereditary. He also, like the Chief, underwent a change and became a mere farmer or factor. The legislation was incomplete and one-sided. It succeeded in forcing peace on the people, but did nothing to remove poverty. It was said there was not enough work for more than half of the population of the Highlands at 3s. a week.

The causes of emigration, as I have said, were not far to seek. Rents were raised, and ambitious landlords preferred sheep to Highland tenantry. Many of the men in the Highlands joined the army. Between the '45 and the battle of Waterloo, 50,000 men enlisted in the Highland regiments. But for many, the only course which gave any so-called prospect of relief was emigration.

Between 1760 and 1783, 30,000 were said to have left the Highland and Islands for America; and the stream continued throughout the first half of the 19th century. The results, we know only
too well.

As a transfusion of blood will often bring new life to a dis-
ordered man, so by giving abundantly of its best blood to the
colonies then, Scotland rendered priceless service to the British
Empire.

It is well for all of us to remember this. . . .

It is true to say the children of those who were removed from
the hills lost all recollection of the habits and customs of their
fathers.

To every man, the hardest form of slavery is to serve as a
slave in one's own native country; there, where one was wont
to be a free lord. . . .

The Covenanters, Glencoe, the '45, the evictions . . . what a
chain of catastrophes. Hardly had the dust settled on one event
than it was blown up by another. These so-called 'acts of God'
were occasions of much perplexity to pious people, and at times
provoked the age-old taunt of the impious, 'Where is their God?'
(Joel, ch. 2, v. 17).

*   *   *

At the end of 1970 it came to my knowledge that a Government plan, hatched up about seven years ago at a secret meeting
at St. Andrew's House, was based on the principle that a selective
modern-day version of the Clearances would be the economic
answer to the Highland problem; in effect a startling proposal to
evacuate remote areas of the Highlands and Islands. I am appalled
to think that officials at the Scottish Office should even dream of
such an idea. The point at issue in this advanced age we live in,
is how do you make people evacuate from a chosen land? I
suppose it would be by making life unbearable for them in
Shangri-La! Such a callous consideration is unbelievable; unless
they regarded the Highlands as another St. Kilda where the people
themselves asked to be evacuated from such a lonely settlement.
Whilst this suggestion has not gained ground, it shows—to some
extent—what goes on in the minds of people in authority. I

suppose if those in high office were taxed with this insinuation, the answer would be that the department had no knowledge of same.

As I have told you, all these people had to go; they had no option. No precise records were kept in those days, but thousands of righteous souls must have died going the way they were ordered to go. Maybe at the End of the Road they would be comforted in the readings of their Bible, as were those early Dutch settlers journeying into the Transvaal in their covered wagons in later years; for each wagon possessed a bible. And perhaps their eyes alighted on some passages in the Book of Daniel, particularly verse 13 in chapter 12 which reads—'*But go thou thy way till the end be; for thou shalt rest and stand in thy lot at the end of the days* . . .'

How strikingly significant this should be to all of us in reading of these Clearance days. Significant as the words carved round the walls of the shrine in the War Memorial in Edinburgh Castle: '*The souls of the righteous are in the hands of God. There shall no evil happen to them; they are in peace.*' These words are from the Apocrypha, The Wisdom of Solomon, ch. 3, v. 1.

*   *   *

I feel sure all in the Highlands living today, and of real Highland stock, will ponder deeply over these final paragraphs which I have written from my heart (*de tout cœur*); words born from my sympathy and understanding for our own fellow sufferers.

The Covenanting background was *Religion*; the Clearances *Greed*; Greed—one of the seven deadly sins—played with humans as dice on the arable gaming tables of the landowners.

As the waves of fire and destruction spread, these peace-abiding folk can be likened to the people of Pompeii and Herculaneum who were constantly living under the shadow of Vesuvius belching forth molten lava. The crofters knew not when they might be snatched away from their humble dwellings; they were not oblivious though of what catastrophes might befall them in their helpless, unaided state. They looked upon any crocodile tears shed by authority (if any *were* shed) with loathsome disgust.

*   *   *

This, then, is the story of the Rape of the Highlands. The crofter and his pious family had a miserable tenancy on his earth; and earth turned out to be an unforgiving landlord.

Despite the passage of over a century, those involved in such nauseating, mercenary impositions, deserve the greatest castigation that should make their ghosts writhe and, like the viper, expire in its own poison.

*　　　*　　　*

As I have said, the Highlanders have long memories. 'Memories linger on' even today in respect of those sorrowful happenings. How could it be otherwise? You have only to travel these areas to sense the feelings and the anguish. When the hand of the Lord was open to Ezekiel, the prophet was carried out in the spirit to a valley which was filled with bones, and he was asked, 'Can these bones live?' And the answer, 'Lord thou knowest'.

So it is with the bones of those who perished and suffered unmercifully. Verily their bones live on; breath, in the fulfilment of Time, will enter into them, when they will testify in the Great Hereafter as to their innocent persecution. So be it.

Their forefathers had faith in the power they learnt about in the Bible manifested largely through right individual leadership on Earth.

In my final chapter, I poise the question 'What can I do for the Highlands; not what can the Highlands do for me?' The study of the Bible by the folk here in Shangri-La is like other studies in life, only more so; for what one gains from it, compensates many times for what one puts into it. *But one must first put something into it.*

This is the crunch of the so-called 'Highland problem'.

*　　　*　　　*

Verily this is a black chapter in Highland history. I am quite sure these godly people who perished will be rewarded in the Great Hereafter as is said in Malachi, ch. 3, v. 17, ' and they shall be mine in that day when I make up my jewels'. (This was an epitaph I saw on the tombstone of a 28-year-old girl in Melness (near Tongue) graveyard . . .)

CHAPTER 10

TOURISM
IN THE
LAND OF ADVENTURE

TOURISM now forms a major support to the economics of the Highlands. Its trade, if one may call it a trade, brings considerable benefits to hotels, guest houses, the ordinary bed and breakfast cottages, and the small shops. Although the Highlander is a Sabbath-keeping person, some who may not be so inclined concede part of their spiritual heritage in exchange for material gain.

In some communities, where only a few years ago the B. & B. notices were taken down or covered up on the Lord's Day, they are now left in position, uncovered; and the arrival and departure of guests on the Sabbath is being accepted as normal custom; even additional relaxations follow. The attractive village of Ullapool, Wester Ross, was in the news a year or so ago, over a controversy regarding small Sunday cruises round the bay, started by an incomer to the district. To the credit of the local people there was considerable opposition; but I believe these trips continue to operate on the Sabbath, but no payment is made of the passengers on their 'round the bay on the motor-boat *Dolly Gray*'.

However, it is not enough to urge by way of objection that Sunday activities are in conflict with the local way of life. That would, in essence, be a relatively small matter. What *does* matter, is that God has commanded 'Remember the Sabbath day to keep it holy'. I would like to record there are thousands of people who—even without being markedly religious—*do* like to come to the Highland countryside and villages for the tonic value of the Sunday peace and quiet. Incoming residents should recognise that.

*   *   *

Among the many curious characteristics of the British is the attitude towards the planning and arranging of holidays. It has become an almost sacrosanct ritual for a large section of the population to devote the first two or three months of each year to this subject. In countless homes, from the Shetlands to the Scillies, maps, brochures and guide books are reverently studied; travel articles in newspapers (so prolific once January comes in— like the January sales!) are ardently read; holiday programmes on TV are watched with rapturous attention, and advice of every kind sought from the ever-growing number of travel agencies. In fact, the whole sitting-room floor is strewn with leaflets, pamphlets and the like. It's truly amazing. All this certainly gives one a refresher in geography since the school days. No other nation goes about this with quite the same intensity or determination. The great thing is to go abroad, forgetting all about the uniqueness of the Highlands of Scotland, which is on one's doorstep.

By the end of February something like 80 per cent of all 'package holidays' will have been booked—despite hi-jacking! Two weeks at the Splendiferous Hotel on the Costa Plastica, or some other alluring foreign-sounding name, where the sun always shines, is seized upon as ideal in every way. All is signed, sealed and delivered; that is if the hotel is finished building in time and the 'plane gets off the ground and is not fog-bound at your time of departure; or a strike of porters (sitting down to rule) at the airport. It is really amusing to read all these spell-bound adverts, written as grey print filling up space around advertisements for cough mixtures or the removal of superfluous hair. In lots of homes the gorgeous peace and quiet of the Highlands doesn't seem to be thought of as it's too near home. Never let it be said the British have lost the spirit of adventure! Just as certain as the sap starts rising late each winter and spring in the trees, so does the latent wanderlust, hidden in most people, burst its off-season restraints. This is the time when the sap rises as I have said, and all the world becomes the traveller's oyster. However, it is gratifying to know that over six million overseas visitors came to Britain in 1970.

I have said the roads are on the narrow side in the far north, but good. Single tracks are all provided with passing places— not parking places—at regular intervals, so when two cars are approaching, one can pull into the side allowing the other to pass and carry on. These passing places should be taken advantage of by those travelling at a leisurely pace, for who knows, the car behind you may be the local doctor or the district nurse, on the way to an emergency. Sheep, too, are a bit of a hazard, especially in May when the lambs are about. If you see a sheep at one side of the road and its lamb on the other side, you can be certain the lamb will dart across to its mother immediately it sees you coming. In the road going round the Kyle of Tongue, there is a big board erected telling how many lambs have been killed up to date; all through unnecessary speeding and not taking due precautions. In September 1970, the board had chalked up on it that seventy-one lambs had been killed or maimed. That shouldn't be. Sheep and lambs come to the roadside where the grazing, for some reason or other, may be sweet; they know what they're about, but they are unpredictable animals where cars are concerned. Also, should you bring your dog with you, which is quite unaccustomed to seeing sheep, you need to keep it under control and not allow it chase them. It is a punishable offence should he kill any.

So, as regards motoring, your drive should be geared to RELAXATION speed. Keep an eye on the petrol gauge, for you don't come across garages every few miles. It is not polite to abuse uncluttered village streets by parking in the wrong place; and never park outside a driveway. Don't forget your sunglasses, for evening sunshine can be particularly dazzling up north. Remember your car, often a mere tool of transportation for much of the year, becomes up in the Highlands an exciting passport to a land of magic. Out of the seasonal months of May to late September, the roads are uncannily quiet; it's like motoring thirty years ago. This, together with all the autumnal colourings on the land and on the sea, makes the Mediterranean an 'also ran'.

*   *   *

It is well known that one receives the greatest hospitality and welcome in the Highlands; but there have been times when this inherent hospitable nature has not shown itself to the full.

I call to mind a true story of a doctor who was relieving the local doctor in a small north coast village, for a few months. He was a good, attentive, clever man, and took over the local doctor's house *pro tem.*; and lived alone, catering for himself.

One late evening a doctor friend of his from Edinburgh

unexpectedly came to see him and to spend the night with him chatting over their old days when they practised together. It was a real treat for the acting doctor to welcome him in. Not having much on hand at that hour (about 10 p.m.) to offer his friend in the shape of food, he rang up the nearby Inn to ask if he could bring his friend along to have some coffee and sand-wiches. The innkeeper's wife answered the 'phone, but quickly and rudely slammed down the receiver to say 'No' she couldn't oblige him at that late (?) hour. So that was that.

Nearing midnight, there was a loud knocking at his door, and upon opening it, he found the innkeeper's wife there, holding her hand to her mouth, obviously in great pain. She told him she was suffering a severe attack of toothache, and would he please give her something—an injection or anything—that would allay the awful pain. The doctor looked at her and without any hesitation said, 'I'll give you the same treatment for your tooth-ache as you gave me for hunger,' and slammed back the door.

Another instance I can vouch for, is the case of lady with three teenage children who were staying the day and night in a village and wanted a nice bed and breakfast place for the night; the tourist information officer sent her to a house where he knew she'd be comfortable. She went there and as her price for B. & B. was reasonable at 20s. each, she agreed willingly to stay with her. When they all came back about 9 o'clock after touring around all the afternoon, the lady of the house said, 'Well, am sure you'd all like a cup of tea and a few biscuits.' 'Yes,' said the visitor, 'that is very kind of you.' When the late cups of tea were brought into the sitting-room, and she stayed chatting with them for a little time, she said, 'and I'll bring a cup of early-morning tea up to you all; am sure you'd like that.' 'Oh, yes,' they said, and when she had said goodnight to them, they all remarked what a kindly, considerate old dear the landlady was. Next morning after breakfast and before leaving, our visiting friend asked for the bill. On it the 'dear old lady' had charged each of them 2s. 6d. for the late teas, and 2s. 6d. for the early teas; that was ten shillings extra for each lot, or £1 'extra', though they all thought no charge would be made from the nice manner in which the suggestion emanated. Our visitor and her family of three complained about all this to the tourist information office fellow, saying she'd never come back to the village again. Of course there is the other side of the picture where some tourists don't always play the game with the landlady; of cases of stealing odd things before they leave, or damaging furniture and even breaking locks on doors; going into other rooms and taking some small article of apparel from a chest of drawers that might be there.

One couple took their dog upstairs with them; it slept on the bed and was sick all over the counter-pane which the housewife had newly bought that season. She only found this out after the couple had left. She vowed she would never again take anyone in who had a dog. If they asked why, she would say she was allergic to animals.

Shop-lifting up here is also not uncommon; this is a scandalous and appalling business, and culprits should be dealt with by the heaviest of fines, if not by imprisonment.

There is no apartheid up North; anyone, irrespective of race, creed, or colour is welcome.

In my opinion the Highlands is rapidly developing into a caravanning invasion; people come north in their cars, towing their caravans behind them. Beyond Inverness, in the summer ot 1970, a tally was taken and it was found that no fewer than 16,500 tourists were in caravanettes, or bringing trailers or tents with them. It is a cheaper way of seeing the country and having a care-free holiday than staying in hotels—which latter I am afraid are fast pricing themselves out to the ordinary casual visitor. This opinion has been given me by all sorts of people, including English coach drivers; and they should know.

The B. & B. folk should also look to keeping their charges down to the minimum to encourage 'nighters' to stay awhile, and not take every advantage of small rising costs that come along from time to time just to be 'with it'; otherwise the nice old kindly landlady will be looked upon as a good old opportunist. They might take their cue from 'small profits, quick returns' which used to be the order of the day when Thomas Lipton was alive! It is more profitable to have six nighters at 20s. a night, than only three at 25s. a night.

In speaking of these landladies, there is no reason to comment on cleanliness, for everything is invariably spotless in their homes. I have already said they are a godly people, and we all know the saying 'Cleanliness is next to Godliness'.

The Earl of Cromartie of Castle Leod, Strathpeffer, made a plea in the House of Lords in 1970 for a tax on caravans, in a bid to improve camping facilities, and discourage wild, indiscriminate camping in the Highlands. The Earl is a prominent member of the Ross and Cromarty County Council. Unless, he said, such a tax was made, the necessary facilities required—such as toilets, hot and cold showers and so forth—could not be adequately met out of the relatively modest County rates. Indeed, resident ratepayers should not have to meet such expenses.

It is very necessary, especially in view of this increased mode of travel in the north, and north-west, proper facilities MUST be provided, but the caravanners should contribute towards this themselves through a modest tax arrangement. One cannot risk having outbreaks of typhoid and a such-like menace, by not having proper hygienic conditions available for these people. Expense is also incurred by the laying-out of proper camping grounds or caravan parks which will not destroy the beauty or the amenity which one would have thought was equally important to the caravanners as well as to the local community.

In the case of Sutherland, which all the year round is underpopulated and financially poorly off, there is every need to find money in financing these necessary sites, and therefore it should not be thought unreasonable to put a tax on caravans. The local authorities find it impossible—as indeed do many private individuals—to lay out the money to produce the facilities required. Countries like Canada and Switzerland have had this problem, but have coped with it properly and in a sound manner. We, in the Highlands, haven't even touched the fringe of these needs, which are yearly becoming more and more pressing.

There are estimated 180,000 caravans in Britain today; 87,000 owners belong to the Caravan Club, paying a subscription of three guineas a year. Membership rose by more than 17,000 in 1969, and by 20,000 in 1970. The Club is a kind of caravanner's A.A., with insurance and all travel facilities at home and abroad. It also operates a 'get-you-home' system.

I certainly think both Ross-shire and Sutherland County Councils should very seriously give this matter attention, before it all gets out of hand.

If these caravanners are nicely sited, warmly welcomed and looked after, I feel this offers a tremendous scope to the N.W.

Highland territory for extra tourism.   These visitors will get refreshed by the good wholesome air; by goodly neighbours and by kindly efficient management of the sites.   In short, they would become a real worth-while summer community, and stay, not just for a night, but for possibly a week, or even longer.   And such schemes would not turn away those bringing tents only, and wanting to live the real out-of-door life.   There could well be a sort of Red Indian encampment, chanting songs at night, such as

> Up in the jungle, living in a tent;
> Better than a bungalow—no rent.

And to crown everything, they would go along to the nearby farm and get milk that is *real* milk; and in bottles, not cartons, which latter to my mind affect the taste.   I have lived for many monthly periods in Sutherland each year, and the cream out of a pint bottle is terrific; about one third.   What happens to the thin milk one gets in towns is a question; the cream must go somewhere—'in suspension', I suppose.

   Up to a few years ago, every crofter and guest-house in the Highlands had its own cow, milked twice a day; and what a joy it was to have a good drink of creamy milk.   The cow was looked upon as a pet and one of the family.   Even in winter, Calum would go into its stall in the byre and speak to it like it was a Christian, and quieting it when the glare of his lamp in its eyes made the beast stamp and rattle its chain.   In the Gaelic he would talk to it, calling it the silliest names that nobody uses except to a baby.   He would cover its back with an old torn blanket if it had been raining and wipe its back and sides and with another handy cloth, rub its forehead and nose up and down.   The animal would snort and stare back at him, knowing it was Calum and that he wouldn't do it any harm.   And at the end, may be he would stoop his head and the two of them would rub their brows together.   The cow even had a name given it and both crofter and wife looked upon it as a good, and useful, pet.   And what a treat it was for mum and dad to take the children to see the cow being milked and all of them would fondly pat it on the back. Daisy would turn, and giving another snort, would mean she knew the little ones were stroking its head with loving touches. I would tell you all these animals you meet with in the Highlands have a sense that not all humans have.

I feel the real attractiveness to the Highlands—apart from its scenery—is good food and good milk; not forgetting really good fresh eggs. It is ridiculous for some cafés to be serving coffee made with powdered milk. For the hotels it is their duty to see that for breakfast, good solid oatmeal porridge is on the menu and a jug of rich milk on every table. Not just a small, paltry, insipid-looking electro-plate or chromium milk jug put on the table an hour or so before. Visitors and their children literally fall for wholesome creamy milk and they say to themselves we're coming up here again, if only for the porridge and the milk that has escaped the processing avenue. Yes, good food and Scottish food at that; for Scottish food is both tasty and satisfying. Those B. & B. folk who give an evening meal—a 'High Tea' as it is called—would do well to put Haggis before their guests. They would love it. Haggis with champit tatties and bashed neeps, is hard to resist. Continental people in particular, look for and rave over the idea of haggis. The English visitor may look rather quizitively at it, and have to be persuaded to taste the dish. Once sampled, they invariably become enthusiastic. We ought to engage a Public Relations Officer to improve the image of haggis? Further than this, there is a special Scottish soup known as 'Cullen Skink', made from finnan haddock ('haddie'), chopped onions, milk and butter; with a little mashed potatoes thrown in.

Remote hotels suffer from staffing troubles which are not lessened by the impact of S.E.T., which the new Tory Government said they were going to abolish. Of course, young people look upon coming up to the Highlands as being too drab—nothing to do in the evenings; no dance halls; no young fellows to 'neck' with; no convivial pubs and so forth. Only good Highland air and scenery. But youth cannot live on that, they say. As these hotels are not open all the year round, they succumb to the temptation of making, what the Americans call 'a quick buck', and so they charge accordingly. When a coach-load of blue-rinsed gabbling young women arrive with a few grannies and grandchildren, then the fun starts. All want their meal at once, and residents take their chance. If the latter order just soup and an omelette to make things easy for the kitchen staff, the omelette may arrive before the soup! Meantime the mini-skirted dining-room waitresses gallop around (God bless them!) snatching up a plate of bread here, a salt-shaker there, and anything else that takes their fancy, with the comment that 'grannie wants this; do you mind?' Of course you don't; you've no option. And as to their appetite, it puts you in mind of the angel's visit to Abraham, 'and he put meat before them, and they did eat'. In this case, I would make the word 'did', DID. Should there be the chance of a second helping—well, the poor residents will needs go short. However, let it be said, Scotland will not let you down and leave you hungry; not in the Highlands. You've only to ask; and biscuits and cheese is a good stand-by.

I have seen people coming up here thin, pinched and pale, bearing the imprints of inferior unwholesome food handed out where they live, and in a matter of a couple of weeks a complete change comes over their looks and in their outlook on real simple food. And what a difference it all makes to the youngsters; the results of a new life in adventurous Shangri-La. No wonder we live to a ripe old age. We don't live out of tins or soup packets, but out of the goodness this earth and the cattle provide us with, day in and day out. And on the Sabbath we wend our way to the Kirk and give thanks.

Although I have written a little plainly about charges in the Highlands, I hope it will be looked upon as constructive criticism. It is not to say any blatant exorbitancy exists as may be found in the English cities. I can quote the instance of a Scot journeying to London, and getting off the early morning train at King's Cross, went into the railway refreshment room, asking for a cup of coffee and a chocolate biscuit. The typical spectacled woman behind the still room counter said 7s. 6d. please. 'Seven and six,' the Scot roared back at her, 'if you English had charged like that at Bannockburn, you might have won!'

*   *   *

In spite of Scottish emigration, those that are still in the Highlands can be well employed making tweeds, tartan, whisky, oatcakes, and shortbread, to bring the authentic cheer of the homeland to thousands of exiles.

I am of the opinion that the many small shops up north could do far more trade in 'flogging' tartan and tweed-wear, than crowding their counters with trashy silver souvenirs, most or which are made in Birmingham, Hong Kong, Germany or Rumania. The demand for tartan and tweed is much greater than one imagines; and foreign visitors in particular are all potential buyers. Way back home, these people look upon their daughter wearing a kilted skirt, doing a Highland fling over a couple of crossed swords (or sticks), as being their heart's delight. Many countries of the world, to name but a few, South Africa, Canada, U.S.A., Australia, New Zealand, Scandinavia, are faithful customers. All these folk prefer bright colours, no matter what Clan it represents.

So here is a real hint for the small shops in Wester Ross and Sutherland—to lay in a good assortment of tweed and tartan goods; not little worthless silver or chrome trinkets that can be bought in towns and which bear no relationship at all to the Highlands.

The tartan of the Gael is a national symbol, and thought so much of that it is imitated from Paris to Peking.

> Tartan . . .
> Here's to the lightning sheen of it,
> The yellow and green of it, the white and blue of it,
> The swing and hue of it, the dark red of it,
> Every thread of it. . . .
> The fair have sighed for it, the brave have died for it,
> Men sought for it, heroes fought for it,
> Honour the name of it, drink to the fame of it:
> The Tartan!

A LAND OF ADVENTURE

Throughout this book I have taken readers through many pages of beautiful adventure in a country once styled a Shangri-La. You can come up here year after year and still not get bored or tired in finding something new to interest and attract you; the scenery, the people, the quietness is as a magnet—and a compelling one at that.

A land of adventure . . .

There are two notable 'Schools of Adventure' established up in the N.W. Highlands. One is at Applecross (Wester Ross); the other at Ardmore, near Rhiconich and Laxford Bridge in N.W. Sutherland. Both are of such inestimable value to the youth of today, that I feel proud to record—at some length—their existence and their activities.

FIRSTLY, the one at Applecross.

It is known as the West Highland School of Adventure, whose Chairman, possessing dynamic power, is Major John T. Wills of the well-known tobacco firm.

In these days it is widely agreed that our national system of formal education needs, in the case of adolescents and particularly boys, to be supplemented by the provision of opportunities for the development of character; and this applies especially to qualities of self-discipline and endurance; the capacity to face difficulties, hardship and emergencies of all kinds. Also the ability to co-operate with others. This is a school established on Outward-bound principles. The Duke of Edinburgh's Award Scheme is every year introducing more boys and girls to this type of experience. Starting with 7000 boys in 1957, the Award Scheme, even six years later, attracted 43,500 boys and nearly 20,000 girls as new entries. What progress! and it is still rising.

The Governing Body of the Dockland Settlements (which has as its Patrons, H.M. The Queen, H.M. Queen Elizabeth the Queen Mother, and H.R.H. The Princess Royal; and as President H.R.H. Princess Margaret) decided in 1963 to open this school of adventure at Applecross on the property of the Chairman, Major John Wills; and the first course started in April 1964.

Applecross, on the west coast, looks across to Skye. From where I write in Gairloch, I can daily see the mountains of the Applecross region; an area of infinite charm. It is 80 miles from Inverness and 15 miles north of Kyle of Lochalsh and the Skye ferry. The scenery around there is of a beauty and grandeur unsurpassed in the British Isles. This Applecross peninsula covers 80,000 acres and offers ideal facilities for sailing, canoeing, swimming, rock-climbing, hill and moor trekking and the like. Expeditions are not confined to this area, but range much farther afield. Excellent accommodation is available at the 'big hoose', Hartfield House on Major Wills' estate. It contains the boys' recreation rooms, dormitories, bathrooms, kitchen and pantries and various other instructional rooms and offices. The Warden and his family occupy one wing; and there is a fully equipped sick bay, and a Matron. The local doctor and District Nurse live in the nearby village. There are permanent Instructors, fully qualified in their own particular fields of training. The boys are given every opportunity to use and develop their initiative.

The normal course of adventure training is twenty-six days. These boys may be sponsored by local education authorities, schools, youth organisations, industrial and commercial firms, or indeed by anyone interested. Normal age limits are from 16 to 20.

In short, the object of this school is to encourage and foster the spirit of adventure, whereby boys may achieve strength of character through the pursuit of testing experiences and challenges under skilled supervision; to instil self-confidence, a sense of teamwork and an awareness of the individual's endurance. And to give boys the opportunity of developing the qualities of leadership and a community spirit, so that later on, it will give them a fuller interest in the way of British life. Details of the fees involved in these courses, the travelling arrangements, clothing and other equipment needed, can all be obtained from the Warden.

I have met many of the youths in the summer months here, for they often 'come over' from Applecross to Gairloch for the day, and back home again. They all appeared keenly interested in this 'adventure'.

The SECOND School of Adventure, known as the John Ridgway School, is situate in N.W. Sutherland, near Rhiconich as I have said. Its location is just as ideal as the one at Applecross; in fact I find it difficult to say which has the better scenic surroundings. Both have cliffs two thousand million years old.

It was established by Captain John Ridgway, M.B.E., in 1968. Captain Ridgway was born in 1938 and has had a great military career. He was awarded the M.B.E. after rowing across the North Atlantic from the United States to Eire with Sergeant Chay Blyth. He also sailed single-handed direct from Eire to South America. As I write these lines at the close of 1970, he is leading an expedition in South America, viz., a canoe journey from the headwaters of the Amazon to the sea.

What led him to row across the North Atlantic? In short, it was that he wanted to test himself and to establish his qualities in the face of challenge. In an open boat in mid-Atlantic he was deeply impressed by sea and sky challenge. The artificial preoccupations of the world in which most people live seemed remote; and he resolved to try and share with others his view of the world and the satisfaction his experience brought him.

The School of Adventure arose from all this. And so he

decided to create a small enclave, a corner of the world where
people could experience the same direct confrontation with the
real world which he found so stimulating and so satisfying.

He selected Ardmore, in the N.-W. Highlands where the
mountains sweep down to the empty Atlantic. Twelve miles
south of Cape Wrath, amidst sheltered sea lochs, where a thousand
years ago the Viking long ships eased through the narrow en-
trances into calmer waters.

In the lochs themselves, there are seals and otters; in the
mountains nearby nest some of the few surviving golden eagles.
On the outlying islets live thousands upon thousands of sea birds:
guillemots, puffins, razor-bills, kittiwakes and fulmars to mention
only a few.

In 1964 he found Ardmore, three miles off the main coastal
road Rhiconich to Laxford Bridge. I have been there; it is a
narrow minor road and I walked the distance. In 1968 the
Adventure took shape and the challenge which first faced him
and his family was that of building the school with their own hands
without any kind of outside capital or institutional commitment.

Today all is set fair alongside loch a' Chadh-fi. There is a
bunkhouse with dining and recreation room, hot showers, basins,
drying room and three separate dormitories. The sloop in which
he sailed from Eire to Brazil, sailing dinghies and kayaks, permanent camps in the hills and islands, are all there and 'laid on'
for the boys' courses.

The theme is like that of Applecross: to give people an opportunity of throwing off the artificial restraints, demands and worries
which pre-occupy them for most of their lives and to give them
an opportunity of measuring themselves against the sea, the sky,
and a primitive landscape of great beauty. The main experience
is a direct contact between the individual and the real world in
which he lives yet seldom sees.

Captain Ridgway's beautiful wife, Marie Christine, is the
daughter of the late Air Marshal Sir John d'Albaic, and they have
a four-year-old daughter, Rebecca.

He believes in positive thinking, not just drifting along and
accepting the easy way. He believes, too, in using one's life to
make a contribution to the sum of human endeavour to look at
one's achievement—whatever it is—and to say 'I did that; I am
leaving things a little better than I found them.'

H

Fortnight-long courses for young people, girls and boys 12-25, run through July and August taking in sailing and dinghy sailing, canoeing, hill and rock climbing, lobster fishing and expeditions with overnight stays in a moorland bothy. There is an Easter course for schoolboys, and Dunrobin school, Golspie, sends boys in relays as part of their schooling. One-week courses are arranged for business men in May and June—to get away from their wives and family!

His wife, Marie, thinks nothing of preparing breakfasts and packed lunches for up to twenty ready by 7.30 A.M.

We should bow our heads to the organisers of those two Schools of Adventure. The work done, and still being done, deserves the nation's fullest gratitude and fullest support.

Within their own confines, I look upon these two idealistically thought-out spots as depicting the Shangri-La of old. . . . May they continue to prosper and maintain the old traditions of this great land of ours.

*   *   *

There is another 'school of adventure', though perhaps not in the same category as the two I have just mentioned; it has more of a Shangri-La atmosphere—a 'school of adventurous thought' it might be termed. It is not in the real Highlands of Scotland that this book is mainly concerned with, but it is not all that far away, namely in Inverness-shire, at Fort Augustus—the abbey of the Benedictine monks. Here is a setting of unrivalled peace and contentment standing in its own 20 acres of ground in isolated beauty and charm in the mid-point of Glen Albyn, the Great Glen of Scotland. This glen is a rift valley which was formed about 200 million years ago.

The abbey's atmosphere has a gripping effect on one, and it proudly deserves mention in the realms of adventure.

The abbey stands at the south-east end of the 24-mile long Loch Ness, with the Caledonian canal nearby. It has developed from the Hanoverian Fort built between 1729 and 1742 by General Wade (the great road builder of his day in the Highlands). It was named after Augustus, Duke of Cumberland, youngest son of King George II, and it remained a Fort till 1854. The Gaelic name of the place is KILCHUIMEN—the Church of St. Chumein.

In 1867, Thomas Alexander, 14th Baron Lovat, bought the

Fort from the Government. In 1876 his son, Simon, 15th Baron Lovat, gave the Fort and surrounding land to the monks. The abbey is the successor to two ancient abbeys, that of Saints Adrian and Denys founded at Lamspring, Hanover, in 1645, and that of St. James of the Scots, founded at Regensburg, Bavaria about 1100. This latter abbey was an important centre of Scottish Catholics after the Reformation. It was suppressed in 1862 and its last Scottish monk settled in Fort Augustus Abbey. Thus the Benedictine way of Christian life led in the Abbey goes back without a break to about 1075 when the Benedictine monks first settled in Scotland at Dunfermline. The abbey is the heir to a great tradition of Christian and Scottish religious life and culture.

The dedicated life of the abbey is one of sacrifice and work, offered to God for all His human family.

The scholarship and learning given the boys who come to live at the abbey during their terms is of the highest order, and most of them qualify to go on to the universities. The school wing has accommodation for about 150 boys; and the two new wings which have been added within the last five years, provide modern classrooms and laboratories, a large hall and stage, and study-bedrooms for senior boys. The school originally opened in 1878, and over the years has given many notable men to the Scottish church and nation. There is an outdoor swimming pool, and on the loch shore, a boathouse with rowing boats and sailing dinghies. Games are played in the camp fields. The facilities include a most delightful large cricket field, looking more like a smoothly shaven bright green lawn; and an all-weather hockey pitch.

The teaching staff is composed almost equally of monks and laymen.

The general atmosphere of a Shangri-La spirit and kindness is shown to more than 50,000 visitors a year, who come from most countries in the world to see this historic and beautiful panorama. The relationship with the local community of Fort Augustus is ever cordial, and the Ecumenical reading room is open all day for the visiting public.

Seen from one part of the abbey grounds is the famous Corriegairick Pass, 2500 ft. above sea level. On 28th August, not long after he had raised his Royal Standard at Glenfinnan in the 1745 Jacobite Rising, Prince Charles Edward Stuart (Bonnie Prince Charlie) with his army of Scots and Irish marched up this Pass and saw about four miles away the ramparts and buildings of the Hanoverian Fort Augustus. On that historic day in the height of summer, those gallant Highland heroes with hearts beating high, swung swiftly up the Pass. Less than 2000 strong, later increasing to about 5000, the Prince and his loyal clansmen marched over the Pass to Dalwhinnie and Perth, down to Stirling and Edinburgh and finally down to Derby on that epic adventure which nearly toppled the Hanoverian dynasty, and which won for those clansmen and their clans undying honour and glory. After a two-day siege in March 1746 the Fort was occupied by the Jacobite forces on the Prince's way back from England, and partially destroyed. Re-occupied two months later by the Hanoverian troops, it was repaired and strengthened, and remained as a Fort till 1854.

The fine Clock Tower, standing 110 feet high and facing to the four points of the compass, lets its tuneful bells ring out at each quarter-hour to the melody of an ancient invocation, *Sanate Pater Benedicte, intercede pro nobis* (Holy Father, O Benedict, do intercede on our behalf).

The abbey church is the centre of the dedicated life here. To the right of the altar is the console of the organ, one of the finest in Britain, with its five manuals, 100 stops and 4200 pipes, ranging from the most ethereal delicatissimo to a majestic fortissimo. Many of the stops are of rare, great beauty.

This great organ, originally built in 1875 by Bryceson for a mansion house in Regent's Park, London, was removed to the old Albert Palace in Battersea Park, London, in 1884; and when the Palace was demolished ten years later, it was purchased by the Fort Augustus Abbey, transported there by rail and steamer, and stowed away for another twenty years in the largest room in the monastery.

In 1914, the building of the choir stalls of the church was begun, and a part of the organ was installed on the north side, and brought into use. In 1936–1938 the entire instrument was rebuilt and electrified by Lawton of Aberdeen, and has been in regular use ever since. Over ten miles of wire were used in the action alone. It is really a gigantic organ in a gigantic church which was finally completed by the monks themselves in 1917 after forty years' labour.   What a monumental work of dedication.

About ten years ago, I visited the monastery and its grounds for the first time, and I was so taken by everything that I never pass Fort Augustus without making a call at the abbey.   There was one visit that stands out vividly in my memory.   It was about seven o'clock one summer evening when I went into the church to admire its superb architecture, when a monk passed quietly by me, sat down at the organ's keyboard and commenced to play sacred and classical works with not a sheet of music beside him. I have seldom seen or heard an organ played with such loving affection, sweetness and delicacy of touch.   It was quite out of this world.   At the end of about twenty minutes he stopped, rose off his seat and left; just like that; saying nothing to anyone, nor looking at anyone, for he had been lost to high Heaven in his devout playing which I am sure must have ascended far above the church's lofty roof; far away into the skies orbit—and beyond. I sat on for a while, then left, and came out to the world through the big doors, feeling very humble indeed; and wrapt myself up in thought.

Later, I made enquiries as to who the talented organist was, and learnt he was the abbey's choir master and music teacher, one Father Bernard.

A 'school of adventure' did I say?   Yes;   a school of *real* adventure;   and I heard myself saying as I came away, 'This is none other but the House of God, and this was the gate of Heaven' . . .

CHAPTER II

RELIGION IN THE NORTH

SCOTLAND as a whole is a Church-minded nation to a far greater extent than England, so that in such a context, the Church of England is relatively the junior partner.

Only about 10 per cent. of the English adult population can lay claim to full Church membership; whereas the Churches in Scotland can claim 66 per cent. and more of the adult population to membership. The smaller the religious denominations, the more loyal the members. In the Highlands one can say nearly 100 per cent. are church-goers. The few that are not could be classed as incomers. In most villages there can be found three different denominations: the Church of Scotland, the Free Kirk, and the Free Presbyterian Kirk.

The fourth commandment, '*Remember the Sabbath-day, to keep it holy*', is rigorously observed. One whole day in seven was surely appointed in the scriptures. This was the seventh, or the last day of the week from the beginning of the world to the resurrection of Christ; and the first day of the week ever since, which in scripture is called The Lord's Day; and so it will continue to the end of the world as the Christian Sabbath. The Free Church and the Free Presbyterian Church set aside special dates in the year for their Communion weeks.

In the Highlands the people say the WORD must succeed where the SWORD failed. Before every verse of Holy Scripture, we should write the rubric . . . 'thus saith the Lord'.

The word CHURCH in our common talk is used in a variety of senses. Sometimes it signifies the material building erected for Divine worship; sometimes it means the people usually assembling in such a building; sometimes the aggregate body of the clergy as distinguished from the laity; sometimes the collective body of professing Christians. But the word CHURCH in scripture has but one real meaning, namely *an assembly of the people of God—a society of Christians*. The Greek word *Ecclesia* in its appropriated and religious sense means just the word CHURCH, though its primary and civil sense meant any assembly called together for any purpose.

The crofting community—the Highland life in fact—looks upon religion as of paramount importance. This devoutness is a time-honoured custom they believe in keeping; a custom as old as the hills themselves. A traditional way of life that neither time nor age will alter.

Their religion gleams with a neon sharpness; they accept the Bible in its entirety as the inspired and inerrant Word of God; and the Westminster Confession of Faith is a true representation of scripture teachings.

The Bible is the source of Christian belief; the nerve of Christian action. Faith cannot mature unless, knowing *how* to read the Bible we *make* time to read it. White-bound Bibles are sometimes carried by brides, and presented to babies. Black-bound copies are to be found in all law courts; many Scottish hotel bedrooms have a copy placed on a table.

Man's understanding of the world in which he lives is changing so rapidly that scientific text-books can be out of date before publication. But man's basic experiences—his loves and passions, hates and jealousies, his conflict of loyalties, his desires and temptations—these change not. They are to be found in the writings of Jeremiah and the Psalmist, Virgil and Homer and Milton. The truths revealed in the Bible concerning the Creator, and what is required of man, are never out-dated. One could say of the Garden of Eden story 'this never was, but always is'.

The Bible is the book which has no errata in it; neither in matters historical nor scientific does it blunder, any more than in matters theological.

*   *   *

The Sabbath in the Highlands is not deemed to be a visiting day; except at communion times (which occur twice a year).

One must not arrive or depart at a guest or Bed/Breakfast house on a Sunday. Hotels pay no heed to this tradition. The B. & B. signs come down on Saturday nights and go up again on the Monday. No letters are written and none posted on the Lord's Day, neither does one telephone, unless in cases of extreme and urgent sickness. No washing is ever left out on the line on Saturday night. The Sabbath is the spiritual market-day of the week.

For most week-days with the older generation living in a croft cottage, probably without an inside water tap and no electricity—just oil lamps—the day starts with the smell of peat and the splutter of porridge as it boils in the black sooty pan over the open fire; and when the breakfast is over, the cows have to be milked and the hens to be fed (possibly even before breakfast) and a start on some baking; scones, pancakes, queen cakes and the like. Any time you might pay a visit you'll always find there is something of a home-made delicacy available— plenty of fresh butter, crowdie (cheese) and home-made jams or marmalade.

With the approach of Saturday, things take on a very different turn; for the preparations for the Sabbath is the main objective. The peat is stacked at the back door and enough water drawn from the well to last till Monday; and before the children went to bed they would needs have a bath. Kettles and pans of hot water poured into the round zinc bath tub in front of the living room open fire, for the Sabbath is one day of the week which is meant to be welcomed with clean bodies and sparkling faces. Then late on Saturday night the vegetables are chopped, the potatoes peeled and all the ingredients for the next day's food prepared. Shoes are polished and lie gleaming by the hearth ready for the kirk in the morning. Newspapers, magazines, games and knitting all stacked away—forgotten till Monday. No dishes are washed up on the Sabbath; and when there was a change to 'Summertime', all clocks and watches were not altered to official time till the Monday morning. The kitten's small playing ball is hidden away.

This all symbolises the solemnity of the seventh day—uniquely, I would say—observed in the Highlands and Islands of Scotland as in no other area in the British Isles. And this is no over-statement. I know, for I live here; and not only do I love it, but

I look forward to this one day in the week, when everything stands still.

One can almost hear the silence, and the occasional bark of a dog is like a thunderclap. In olden days the cockerel was placed under a bucket with a heavy stone on top. Slowly, the small groups of people gather and begin to wind their ways along the paths and roads from their little cottages leading to the Kirk. Those with cars, stop and give a lift to as many as they can. Everyone is neatly dressed; the men in dark suits, black shoes highly polished as I have mentioned. The women walking with or behind their husbands, exchange casual hushed words. The children also in their Sunday best and respecting Sabbath behaviour to the full, walk quietly under their grown-up's eyes, their pockets full of pan-drops which they had bought from the sweetie-shop on Saturday. And in the Kirk, was it only the children's imagination, or *did* the Elders really have haloes above their grey heads?

At a time when the cold, withering teaching of non-Christianity spread like hoar frost over many parts of Europe, the Highlands was bathed in the 'dew of Lebanon' under many ministers of acknowledged sanctity.

On many sacramental occasions services were held outside in hollows of the moorland to accommodate the huge assembly of God-following people. Gairloch has a hollow which would appear to have been naturally scooped out for the purpose. It is situated on the small golf course near the cemetery and shadowed by a 150-year-old sycamore tree. It is called *Leabaidh na bà Baine* (Bed of the white cow).

And thither the 'tribes' came in their thousands. Here and in all such hollows was focused the ripest experience of the devout thought of the Highlands. The redeemed of the Lord went thither to give and get the marks of the children of grace. Who were they; whence came they? They were ordinary men and women of the North; trophies of redeeming love.

Eighteen centuries have passed away since God sent forth a few apostles from a remote corner of the earth to do a work which, according to man's judgment, must have seemed impossible.

He sent them forth at a time when the whole world was full of superstition, cruelty, lust and sin.

He sent them forth to proclaim that the established religions of the earth were false and useless and must be forsaken.

He sent them forth to persuade men to give up old habits and customs, and to live different lives.

He sent them forth to do battle with the most grovelling idolatry, with the vilest and most disgusting immorality and vested interests.

He sent them forth to wage war against bigoted priesthood, sneering philosophers, and an ignorant population.

He sent them forth against bloody-minded emperors. Never was there an enterprise to all appearances more Quixotic and less likely to succeed.

Those chosen few had no weapons, no worldly power to compel assent, no worldly riches to bribe belief. They merely had Faith in their hearts and the Scriptures in their hands, which they expounded and explained. The preacher of Christianity in the first century was not a man with a sword and an army to frighten people, like Mohammed. No; just one holy man with one holy book.

* * *

During one of the darkest periods of the American Civil War, a speaker of a delegation of Christian people, said to Abraham Lincoln, 'We trust the Lord is on our side' (Exodus 32, v. 26). But Lincoln replied, 'I do not regard that as so essential as something else.' The worthy visitors looked horror-stricken until the President added, 'I am most concerned to know that *we* are on the Lord's side.'

There is the story told of General Gordon when he was first in the Sudan. Each morning for a half-hour, there lay outside his tent a handkerchief. The whole camp knew the full significance of that small token and respected it. No foot dared to enter the tent so guarded. No message was carried in. Whatever it was had to wait until the guardian signal was removed; for everyone knew that God and Gordon were alone in there together.

In other books I have made references to various missionary works abroad. The Churches in Scotland have a strong field of such ardent missionaries in South America, China, Holland and elsewhere. Members of the Mission Synod have remarked how very impressive it is to see the zeal of all the foreign associates, and it would be sad if Scotland lagged behind in the exercise of that longing desire that Christ's Kingdom might soon come into its fullness among Jew and Gentile; among black and white.

There is one Welsh missionary I know who, after fighting paganism, disease and ignorance in South America for the past 37 years, retired home early in 1970 to his native land; but since arriving, the Brazilian Bible Mission has established a Rural Missionary Centre in Carmarthenshire, and Roderick Davies and his wife Blodwen are in charge. It is a large mansion house at Froodvale, Llanwrda, off the main Llanwrda–Lampeter road, and was opened on 15th May 1970.

This evangelist and his wife travelled extensively through the many Brazilian states and their headquarters were in São Paulo.

He can recount innumerable episodes in his preachings which brought him close to death in converting the die-hard bandits who thought nothing of shooting. They killed for the sheer pleasure it gave them. But battling with these trigger-happy people and working amongst primitive tribesmen was considered all part of a life for a missionary. In their attempts to reach the people, they used radio, mobile units and, where possible, house-to-house visiting. They also translated many words into native languages. They did a tremendous amount of medical and social work, but received no help from the Brazilian authorities. All their money—as with most missions—came from donations.

Here then is one story he has to tell:

Alcides Geraldo, known all over Brazil as the notorious savage bandit 'Gibi', was born in Pocos das Caldas. When he lost his father in early life, his mother with the children moved to a town. Poverty and lack of parental care saw Geraldo, when still young, a thief and a terror to the neighbourhood. At 17 he made an armed raid on a bank in São Paulo. There followed other robberies with violence and at 18 he was caught and cast into prison. In a few months time he escaped and lost his identity under the name of 'Gibi'. He joined up with another gangster called 'Seven Fingers' and there followed a series of armed raids in the State of Minas. Returning to São Paulo, he was again in conflict with the police, accused of various robberies and murder, and was sentenced to 65 years in prison. Whilst in prison he became seriously ill with T.B., and was forced to spend his days in bed, more dead than alive, paralysed in both his legs.

One afternoon another prisoner visited Geraldo's cell with a copy of the Bible that he had once bought from our missionary friend. As he was very old and his sight failing, he asked Geraldo would he read to him from the book. This he did. There followed daily visits, and each time a different portion of the Scriptures was read. One afternoon the reading was in Matthew 11 and came to the end of that chapter at verse 28, the translation of the words, 'weary and heavy laden'. Let me give in his own words what then happened: 'I was weary, weary of life, weary of stealing, weary of crime, vice and everything. These words of the Saviour produced in me a kind of great emotional shock. I felt my hard, wicked heart for the first time in my life touched by something mysterious, something which I could not explain nor understand; something which agitated my whole being. It was a ray of hope, not only in my sinful heart, but also in that cell of despair which was my life. With hope, as I read the Word of God, came faith—faith in God, and in His Word. I spent my days praying, confessing my sins, reading the Word of God. I forgot my circumstances, my sickness, my paralytic state, my sentence of 65 years (a life-time), I only knew that I, a broken-down worm of a man, abandoned by society, could come to Christ and be relieved of my weariness and load of sin. . . .'

Unable to walk because of his illness and paralysis, Alcides Geraldo lay on his bed day after day, thinking, reading the Bible, and lifting up his heart to the Lord in prayer, praise and worship. One day he had a strong impression to try and get up out of bed. To his great surprise he stood on his feet and walked a few steps. Every day he did the same, and gradually he could walk about. Five long years passed, he continued suffering from T.B., and one day due to his good conduct and T.B. condition he was released with 60 years of his sentence to run. From the day he stepped out of the State Prison every trace of T.B. disappeared from his body. Cured in heart, mind and body, Alcides Geraldo was a new creature in Christ Jesus. Coming out of prison, he sought out evangelical believers, identified himself with the Lord's people in Christian baptism and fellowship, and testified everywhere of the Lord and the Word of His Grace. At the time of writing these lines, he has already visited over 800 Brazilian cities and wherever he is announced to speak crowds flock into the evangelical churches to hear his moving testimony.

Can anything be more illuminating, more inspiring, more spectacular, more miraculous than this true story of Alcides Geraldo? It is beyond ordinary-day understanding.

Alcides Geraldo today is an evangelist, who belongs to the Prison Welfare Society of Brazil, and as he visits different cities on his evangelistic mission, the first place he visits is the local prison. No small wonder the Brazilian mission continues to pray for him, this 'Brand from the Burning'.

This is no fictional story; this is an actual fact, recorded by Roderick Davies and his noble band. Surely what I have said *must* make one think? It is really unbelievable.

John Knox was the Scottish Calvinist and Reformer. The voice of this one man was able in one hour to put more life into human hearts than a thousand trumpets. So it was said. In 1559 John Knox returned to Scotland after ten years exile. The country faced a religious and political crisis. Protestant power was growing but was not yet strong enough to overthrow the Catholic rulers. Knox provided the '*lion's roar*', and within a year the Reformed faith was established in Scotland. Dr. Martin Luther standing antagonised but defiant before his ecclesiastical accusers declared, 'Here I stand; I can do no other.' He carried crisis on his back. The effects of the Reformation which resulted in the two parts of Europe continuing their development along different cultural, philosophical and political lines, still remain the most important in the world today.

For a considerable time after the Reformation there was a shortage of ministers and as a result, in some places, the common people, lacking spiritual guidance, fell into pagan ways. This was especially the case in the north of Sutherland. The images of saints, which were generally carved from stone, were often regarded as idols, and as such were treated with great reverence. Naturally this was a source of worry to the ministers of the new religion. They preached strongly against it, but that did not have much effect. There was a minister in the far north who felt compelled to take more decisive action. It was in 1613 that he began to go here and there about the county, and everywhere that he found one of those idols, he smashed it to atoms.

There were people of the N. West who had one of these, which they called Saint Fergus. In due time, the devout minister came along. He sought out the treasured image and broke it up.

There was an immediate and natural outcry among those who were in the habit of worshipping this 'golden image of stone'. They gathered and threatened violence against the Godly man. The magistrates of the day came to his rescue and he was taken into the safety of a Christian house. There he stayed till darkness fell. He thought that he could then slip out quietly and make for his home, some 10 miles away. He had miscalculated. A number of the more determined were hanging about, on the watch. They followed, and when he was clear of the village, they fell upon him. Into the river they pitched him—and there he drowned.

The murderers put the story around that their Fergus had helped them and that they had actually seen him holding the minister down in the water in his final struggle.

The story I now record can be classed, to my mind, an *Inspirational story of the highest order*. It was told me when I was young; and many times have I tried to find out its origin. But no one seems to know:

Centuries ago a great artist was engaged to paint a mural for the cathedral in a Sicilian town. The subject was the life of Christ. For many years he laboured diligently and finally the painting was finished except for the two most important figures; the Christ Child and Judas Iscariot. He searched far and wide for models for those two figures. One day whilst walking in the old part of the city, he came upon some children playing in the street. Among them was a 12-year-old boy, whose face stirred his heart. It was the face of an angel—a very dirty one perhaps, but the face he needed. The artist took the child home with him, and day after day the boy sat patiently until the face of the Christ Child was finished.

But the painter still found no one to serve as a model for the portrait of Judas. For years, haunted by the fear that his master-piece would remain unfinished, he continued his search. The story of the unfinished work spread far and wide, and many men, fancying themselves of wicked countenance, offered to pose as models for the face of Judas. But in vain the old painter looked for a face that would serve to show Judas as he envisioned him— a man warped by life, enfeebled by surrender to greed and lust.

Then one afternoon as he sat in the tavern over his daily glass of wine, a gaunt and tattered figure staggered across the threshold and fell upon the floor, 'Wine, wine,' he begged. The painter lifted him up, and looked into a face that startled him. It seemed to bear the marks of every sin of mankind.

Greatly excited, the painter helped the profligate to his feet. 'Come with me,' he said, 'and I will give you wine and food, and clothing.' Here at last was the model for Judas. For many days and parts of many nights, the painter worked furiously and feverishly to complete his masterpiece. As the work went on, a change came over the model. A strange tension replaced the stuporous languor, and his bloodshot eyes were fixed with horror on the painted likeness of himself.

One day, perceiving his subject's agitation, the painter paused in his work. 'My son, I'd like to help you,' he said. 'What troubles you so?'

The model sobbed and buried his face in his hands. After a long moment he lifted pleading eyes to the old painter's face. 'Do you not remember me?' he said. 'Years ago I was your model for the Christ Child . . .'

The face of Judas Iscariot.

And one can hear him saying, 'I am a dying man; all before me is unseen; the world to come is a harbour unknown.'

*   *   *

The old Scottish theological principles date from John Calvin (the French Protestant reformer, 1509–1564) and John Knox (1505–1592, the Scottish Calvinist reformer as I have just said); and these teachings are for the most part observed. It is true you cannot hold fast a mist or a fog; but you *can* hold fast to religion. And up north, this religious outlook and upbringing gives everyone a generous heart.

In the early pages of the first chapter of this book, I remarked upon each morning being looked upon as a new 'Christ risen' day. This brings to my mind two significant stories.

One is of a little boy who had never been in a train before. Suddenly, the lights of the carriage went out as the train dashed along through a tunnel. When the train emerged from the tunnel, and everything was bright again, he said excitedly, 'Look, Mummy, it's tomorrow, a new Christ risen day.'

Then again, the lamplighter of olden days going along the

solitary streets putting out the gas lamps. As he extinguishes them, he looks back into the dark, seeing in retrospect his past life; as he carried on to the lamps ahead, his mind turns to the future. And when the last lamp was snuffed out, it was daylight; it was morning; The Risen Christ day.

From one post to the other post (MEN AMOOD LÉ AMOOD YAATIK EL FARAG, as they say in Arabic). The light changes; the old gas lamps were only a short distance apart, so anything can happen to change life quickly. MAKTOUB, 'for so it is written'.

*   *   *

At 9.17 p.m. on Sunday, 20th July 1969, man first landed on the moon. This prophetic day was hailed as a veritable triumph; and so it was. But is all this necessary? What is to be the real progress of MAN if wars and hunger persist and worsen; if we cannot trust each other? Assuredly Man's ingenuity fascinates us —perhaps to the point of madness? Man jumps over the moon; but look what the old cow did! We need to affect a strict balance over our scientific ideas, and use the fullest possible common sense for all occasions. We should remember that Voltaire said in the 1700's, 'Common-sense is not so common.'

There is a piece of Eastern (Chinese) wisdom which says: 'If there is righteousness in the heart, there will be beauty in the character. If there is beauty in the character, there will be harmony in the home. If there is harmony in the home there will be order in the nation. Where there is order in the nation, there will be peace in the world.'

We are here, not on a freehold, but on a tenancy . . . terminable at any time, with or without notice. 'Thus saith the Lord.' The Highland folk look upon dying as an important part of living.

*   *   *

Two thousand years ago we were shown the way; but the realisation is further away than ever. . . .

In the pristine annals of Britannia the blessèd Book was the stable foundation of her pre-eminent splendour, but alas, the glory that was has seemingly departed. As a nation we have drifted by degrees from our moorings. The decline and fall of ancient Rome can be seen in our own mirror. In 1970 there were

160,000 abortions in Britain; and 80 per cent. teenage girls were already pregnant before they married teenage boys. Bedroom talk of Victorian days (so closely guarded), gradually became table talk between the two world wars, and now it has become classroom talk in the form of sex education. There are over 50,000 persons behind prison bars, which we taxpayers have to keep. Murder, embezzlement, day and night robberies, divorce, alcoholic and drug addicts continue to increase at an ever-alarming level. All this, rushing through the flood-gates of our society.

The spire of a church is inspiring; a sign of beauty and of holiness. Today, when new churches are built in so-called New Towns, this spire seems to have been forgotten, maybe on account of expense in the building of such a specialised piece of architecture. This is to be regretted, but I suppose it tends to modern art, modern planning; for Planners seem to have no soul.

The following lines may be applicable to our day and age:

> . . . Man builds a monument, graceful high
> With pinnacles reaching to the sky
> Some a masterpiece of Art—;
> Others simple, but they serve their part
> Each and everyone He gave
> A symbol that his soul doth clave;
> To thank his God for blessings kind
> For gifts He gave to all mankind.
> A grateful token is this noble sign
> To crown an edifice—a Holy shrine.

All the same, I look to a church's spire to signify an in-spire-ation.

The Queen's responsibility for maintaining the Protestant religion in Scotland was laid on her as a result of a Cabinet conflict —which took place when she was only ten years old. With the publication of pre-war Cabinet papers, they show that when the late King George VI was about to be crowned, Scottish Secretary of State, Walter Elliot, fought in the Cabinet for a special mention for the Protestant faith of Scotland and Northern Ireland. Prime Minister, Stanley Baldwin, and the Archbishop of Canterbury, Dr. Lang, had decided that no change was needed in the Coronation Oath. But Walter Elliot warned that this would lead to strong criticism and feeling, and at his insistence the Oath was reworded. King George VI had to affirm his reply to the question: '*Will you, to the utmost of your power, maintain in the United Kingdom, the Protestant reformed religions established by law?*' And this rewritten Oath was also used in the 1963 Coronation. Documents show that P.M. Stanley Baldwin and his Cabinet thought that the 1911 Oath covered the position of the Established Churches; but it made no mention of any Church other than: 'The settlement of the Church of England, and the doctrine, worship, discipline and government thereof as established in England.' After long discussion it was left to Mr. Elliot and Defence Minister Sir Thomas Inskip to re-draft the Oath. Mr. Elliot was later to become the Lord High Commissioner of the Kirk's General Assembly.

I may remark here as to Britain's religious implications in joining the Common Market. The population of the Common Market, if Britain and Ireland joined, would be 142 million Roman Catholics and 80 million Protestants. It was quoted in the news magazine *Torch* that a Rome correspondent had written that the Vatican Council considered the Common Market 'the work of Divine Providence'.

*   *   *

Christmas time is not generally accepted up in the north as a calendar date of significance as in most other countries.

Elsewhere in this book I have mentioned the white stag and a white camel.

In legend, in the hearts of children, the animals have always shared the joyousness of Christmas. Were not the first witnesses to the Holy Star, sheep, goats and the dogs of the shepherds? According to an apocryphal tale, the baby Jesus lay in warmth between an ox and an ass in a cow's manger. From the Holy Land comes a sacred legend of the littlest white camel which accompanied the caravan of the Wise Men. This little beast fell to its knees before the Holy Child, exhausted and weary from trying to keep up with the older camels. The child Jesus was so moved by this devotion that He took pity on it and blessed it with immortality.

And so it happens that each year the littlest camel repeats its

journey, and the Christian children of the Holy Land believe it is
he, and he alone, who brings their gifts and their joys.

> Faith came singing into my home
> And other guests took fright;
> Grief, anxiety, fear and gloom
>   Sped out into the night.
> I wondered that such peace would be
> When Faith said gently, 'Don't you see,
>   That they can never live with me?'

To this I would add: 'I know not where His islands lift their
fronded palms in air; I only know I cannot drift beyond His love
and care.'

As a rule, a Highland family is a devoted family. Their faith
binds them together as nothing else can. In this connection I give
the following Latin lines which I seem to remember years ago
(when I used to get minus marks in that language at school!) . . .

SIVE AD FELICES RADEM POST CAMPOSSEN FERAT ARDENTUM
RAPIDI PHLEGTHONTIS AD UNDEM NIC SINE TE FELIX ERA NEC
TECUM MISER NUNQUAM . . . and the translation,
'Heaven would not be Heaven were thy soul not with mine;
nor Hell be Hell were our souls together'.

Just as a particular disease in the world is treated by various
medical methods, so there are many religions to bring happiness
to human beings and others. Different doctrines have been
introduced by different exponents at different periods and in
different ways. Where I lived most of my life, in Ceylon,
Buddhism was the principal faith—or should I say, philosophy.
And I think there was nothing wrong with it if one lived up to
all Buddha's thoughts and principles. I believe all these philo-
sophies fundamentally aim at the same noble goal in teaching
moral precepts to mould the functions of mind, body and speech.
They all teach not to tell lies, or bear false witness, steal or take
another's life. All embody love, for 'Love is a many splendoured
thing'.

*   *   *

'*The day the sun stood still.*'
I have to bring to notice an amazing matter that happened

in 1971 to a group of astronauts and space scientists at Green Belt,
Indiana, U.S.A. They were checking the position of the sun,
moon and planets out in space as to where they would be 100
years and 1000 years from now. They have to know that, in
order not to send up a satellite should it collide with something
later on in Time, on one of its orbits, so that nothing will go
wrong. They ran the computer measurement backwards and
forwards over the centuries when suddenly the computer stopped,
showing a red signal indicating there was something wrong either
with the information fed into it or with the results compared
with the standards. They found there was a day missing in space
in elapsed time. Puzzled, there seemed to be no answer.

Then one man in the team remembered from his Sunday
School days, of the 'sun standing still'. The reference was found
in the book of Joshua, chap. 10, verses 12–14 . . . namely, 'the
sun stood still, and the moon stayed, and hasted not to go down
about a whole day'. 'There is the missing day,' the space man
said; and when they checked the computer going back into the
time it was written, the answer was close, but still not close
enough. The elapsed time missing back in Joshua's day was 23
hours, 20 minutes—not a whole day. Forty minutes had to be
found because it can be multiplied many times over in orbit. It
was then that the scientist who had some Biblical knowledge
remembered at some place or other in the Book, 'the sun went
backwards'. In searching the Bible, they found how King Hezekiah on his death-bed was visited by the prophet Isaiah, who told
him that he was not going to die, and Hezekiah asked what the
sign should be. And Isaiah said, 'This sign shalt thou have of the
Lord, that the Lord will do the thing that he hath spoken: shall
the shadow go forward ten degrees, or go back ten degrees?'
And Hezekiah answered, 'It is a light thing for the shadow to go
down ten degrees; nay, but let the shadow return backward ten
degrees.' And Isaiah cried unto the Lord, and He brought the
shadow ten degrees backward, by which it had gone down in the
(sun) dial of Ahaz (2 Kings 20).

Ten degrees is exactly forty minutes. Twenty-three hours
and twenty minutes in Joshua, plus forty minutes in 2nd Kings
made the missing twenty-four hours. So the scientists in Indiana
in 1971 had to log in the log book the cause of the missing day in
the Universe.

The Bible is the chart of history. It affords a panoramic view of the whole course of events from the Creation and the fall of man, to the final judgment, and the inauguration of the new heaven and the new earth. It gives us, not events only, but their moral character; events being shown in relation to their causes and their effects, and the judgment of God as to their character being revealed.

Without the Bible, history would be a spectacle of unknown rivers flowing from unknown sources to unknown seas. Under its guidance we can trace the complex currents to their springs, and see the end from the beginning.

In its reading, *we never walk alone. . . .*

When Gladstone was Prime Minister, he once had occasion to call THE BOOK 'the impregnable rock of Holy Scripture', but went on to say that it was becoming evident not only to have ceased being impregnable, but ceased even being a rock. Those words were said towards the closing years of Queen Victoria. Indeed they seem to be even truer today.

> To each is given a bag of tools
> A shapeless mass, and a book of rules
> And each must make ere life has flown
> A stumbling block, or a stepping stone.
> Is it not strange that Princes and Kings
> And clowns that caper in sawdust rings
> And ordinary folk like you and me
> Are builders of Eternity?

CHAPTER 12

ARDVRECK AND MONTROSE

. . . After the Marquis of Montrose and his Royalist army were defeated by the Covenanting troops at Carbisdale on 27th April 1650, he fled, and coming into the country of Assynt, was arrested by a small party of men acting under orders from Neil Macleod XI Baron—an ardent Covenanter and Sheriff-Depute of Assynt—and brought to Ardvreck Castle. A few days later, Montrose was duly handed over to the Scottish Government, by whom he was sentenced to be hanged and dismembered as an 'attainted rebel'. The capital sentence was carried out in the Grassmarket, Edinburgh, on 21st May 1650. Eleven years later, the remains of James, Graham, 1st Marquis of Montrose, were buried in St. Giles', where a monument was erected in 1888. . . .

THUS is linked the Castle of Ardvreck with the 'Great Montrose'; but there is more to it than that, for upon Montrose's execution baseless defamatory accusations were circulated by his partisans, and a 'cloud of witnesses' against Macleod, and in 1660 when the Royalists came to power, these accusations broadened and exploded into legal charges alleging that Neil had *betrayed* Montrose, and that he should be classed as a villain, a Judas and the like . . . 'The Shame of Ardvreck'. This entirely false image was further stirred up by Bishop Wishart of St. Andrews, an ultra-royalist, and has been carried down for over three centuries by historians and writers alike.

Once in a while, history is rewritten; once in a while those engaged in historical research come across mistaken dates and facts which need correcting and straightening out so that the rising generation may have a more truthful account, even though

238

the time-lag is a few hundred years . . . 'for men to come into the knowledge of the truth' (1 Tim. ch. 2, v. 4).

In April 1970, I produced a small Treatise on this matter recording the many distortions of facts, putting them right, so as to wipe out this shame cast upon Neil Macleod. This I did at the request of the Misses M. L. and E. A. Macleod of the Cadboll (Easter Ross) branch, who with their brother Colonel Roderick Macleod, D.S.O., M.C., are the direct descendants of the second wife of Neil's grandfather. Over many years they have collected evidence from a mass of authentic, musty documents, including those discovered from exhaustive study of all the Acts of Parliament and Register of the Privy Council records made by the late Dr. Donald Mackinnon. The Misses Macleod and their brother trace their ancestry as far back as the Kings of Norway and the Isle of Man, to LEOD, son of Olaf the Black and 1st Baron of Lewis (d. 1282). So it can be judged Neil Macleod of Ardvreck was not a 'petty lairdling' as has so often been alleged.

I was honoured in being asked to write the text for these distinguished gentry-folk, and in giving hereunder the main substance of the Treatise—much of which had never seen the light of day before—I am adding further interesting notes and comments as after-thoughts; for in the original I was very limited to space.

I may add that Col. Macleod, D.S.O., M.C., is one of the few eminent military personages left of the two world wars. He was a personal friend of Field-Marshal (later Lord) Ironside, who on the outbreak of the Second World War became Chief of the Imperial General Staff (C.I.G.S.), and Colonel Macleod was brought in as his Military Assistant; and when Ironside became Commander-in-Chief Home Forces, he appointed Col. Macleod as his representative on the Home Defence executive.

(In 1962 Col. Macleod was senior editor and produced with his co-editor barrister-friend Denis Kelly *The Ironside Diaries, 1937–1940*, a 434-page book. Lord Ironside died in 1959.)

From 1944 onwards Colonel Macleod was attached to General Eisenhower on the Intelligence side of S.H.A.E.F. to perform an operation connected with D-Day; the actual work involved is a State secret which cannot be released until around the year 2000.

*　　*　　*

Here then, is an abridged version of the Text bearing upon Ardvreck and Montrose. It was titled, *3 Centuries of Falsehood Exposed*. The booklet is still available.

. . . Few people know where Assynt is, or where Ardvreck Castle is situated. It is not everyone who may know everything about Montrose, and even less about Neil Macleod; and few will be acquaint as to how the great Macleod family came to lose their country. It is hoped this treatise will provide absorbing, electrifying and poignant reading to students of history, as well as to the great body of Macleods, whose wings are spread out all over the world, and whose forebears' sympathies have been, I feel sure, with Neil Macleod over the past 300 years. There are 25,000 MacLeods in North America alone.

Assynt

The district known as Assynt, comprising 100,000 acres, is in north-west Sutherland, centred one might say around Lochinver.

There are several interpretations of the name Assynt, the most likely, I think, coming from the Norse 'ass' meaning 'rocky'. The Gaelic name is 'as agus int' . . . ('in and out'), and this well describes the uneven contour of the area. Long ago the whole district was one vast forest of the Thane of Sutherland and was originally Suderland (the south land) of the Vikings, who raided the Scottish coastal regions. The Earldom of Sutherland dates from 1228. The Norsemen were ousted by the MacNicols who inhabited the coast near Ullapool, and for this aid they were given the lands of Assynt in vassalage. But the Vikings, smarting under this blow, returned, burning down the forests. The MacNicols remained for a few centuries, when the aged chief's daughter, Margaret, married in 1343 Torquill, 4th Baron of Lewis, and with consent of the Thane, the lands were made over to the happy couple. King David II (1324–1371), only son of King Robert the Bruce, granted a charter to Macleod in 1346 that he would possess Assynt for all time. His younger grandson, Tormod, became 1st Baron of Assynt (1406–1437).

About 1585 Donald Bain Mor Macleod (c. 1565–1646) became 9th Baron of Assynt, his chief residence being Ardvreck Castle, a tower-house stronghold on Loch Assynt, situate about a mile from Inchnadamph. One stone in the outer wall of the Keep bears the date 1516; so the castle was probably built by Donald's father or grandfather. In 1642 Donald Bain (or Bàn) obtained a charter for the whole estate *direct* from King Charles I. By his marriage to his first wife, Marian (aunt of 1st Lord Reay), his son Neil X Baron of Assynt who married Florence (5th daughter of Torquil Coinneach Macleod) begat Neil XI Baron—whom I refer to as Neil Macleod of Ardvreck.

Donald Bàn Mor was a heavily built man, of giant stature, with fair hair.

ARDVRECK

The Macleods of Assynt were one of the three great families of Sutherland (the others being the Sutherlands and the Mackays). The castle in its time bore a distinctive style of architecture, but today it is rapidly crumbling away, and is merely a shell of its former grandeur, filled with an atmosphere of gloom and despair. The Castle as it now stands, is shown at the head of this chapter.

MONTROSE (1612–1650)

James Graham, fifth Earl and 1st Marquis of Montrose, was a poet, statesman and soldier. He succeeded his father to the Earldom in November 1626, and in the following January was admitted to St. Andrews University, where he became a great friend of the Earl of Sutherland.

When 21 years of age he left Scotland in 1633 to travel on the Continent, returning in 1636 when he sought an interview with King Charles I to offer his services, for trouble had arisen because Charles and Archbishop Laud were resolved to impose Episcopacy upon the Scots Kirk, by force if necessary. This put all Scotland in a ferment, and its leaders, including the Earl of Seaforth, drew up a National Covenant to unite all those determined to resist this imposition. But Montrose was received with coolness. The next year, 1637, he voluntarily signed the National Covenant drawn up by the Earl of Seaforth and other nobles. A copy of this document can be seen in the Council Chamber of the Town Hall, TAIN (Easter Ross), with Montrose's signature twice as large and florid as any other.

Neil Macleod was then only ten years old.

Montrose became a brilliant Commander-in-Chief of the Covenanters' army; but because of much dissension amongst their leaders —particularly Argyle—after five years, in May 1643, he went over to the Royalists and proceeded successfully to wage war on his former comrades-in-arms, and became the foremost champion of the Crown.

To the Covenanters, quite naturally, Montrose was thus looked upon as a traitor to their cause; and this was officially proclaimed by the Scots Parliament on 14th September 1644. He was deprived of all his titles, and a price put on his head.

After many victories his clansmen melted away and he was defeated at Philiphaugh (September 1645) by Lt.-General David Leslie. Montrose withdrew to Morayshire, and it was then the Earl of Seaforth entered into secret negotiations with him, and at the siege of Inverness (April 1646) openly went over to him. Seaforth then began to besiege Ardvreck Castle, but when news came of King Charles' surrender to the Scots army the siege was lifted. On 31st May 1646, Montrose received a letter from the King to disband his forces. He and four others were expelled from Scotland, and on 3rd September that year, accompanied by Bishop Wishart, set sail for the Low Countries. Wishart was made chaplain to a Scottish Regiment at Schiedam in Holland, and did not return to Scotland until after the Restoration in 1660. Seaforth also left Scotland.

In 1649 when the English Parliament had beheaded Charles I, Montrose was commissioned on 4th March 'to recover Scotland' and given the Order of the Garter. He crossed over to Orkney late February 1650 after issuing in December 1649 from Gottenburg, Sweden 'an impudent Declaration' requiring all loyal Scots to join him. In reply, having publicly burnt this 'scandalous pamphlet' at the Market Cross, Edinburgh, by the hand of the common hangman, the Committee of Estates (the Scots Parliament) issued on 24th January 1650 a Declaration . . . 'discharging all persons from aiding or assisting that ex-communicated traitor, James Graham, under pain of High Treason'. . . . Such a peremptory, punitive command would make one seriously think; çela donne beaucoup à refléchir.

In April 1650 Montrose landed in Caithness; few men rallied to his Standard.

On 27th April 1650 he was finally defeated at Carbisdale (Culrain), a few miles south of LAIRG and opposite INVERSHIN in Sutherland. He was subsequently captured and suffered execution on 21st May 1650, as recorded already.

NEIL MACLEOD (1628–1696)

From the day of Montrose's execution Neil Macleod, XI Baron of Assynt, lived and died under the stigma of a Judas in that he was supposed to have betrayed Montrose—and for money too—after his defeat by the Covenanters at Carbisdale.

The Treatise is especially designed to absolve Neil of these iniquitous charges, as well as other 'shames' that have persisted for over 300 years, and particularly those by his enemy, the 3rd Earl of Seaforth, who needed an excuse to dispossess him of the Assynt Estates, wrongfully accusing him of unpaid debts and so on; these allegations being followed through by a long line of historians, writers and romantic novelists, such as Bishop Wishart, Hume, Burnet, Napier, John Buchan, the poet Aytoun and even Sir Walter Scott, all of whom (and many others in later years) can be named as some of the 'cloud of witnesses'.

The main issues involved were:—

1. Neil was said to have *betrayed* Montrose to the Scottish Government, and so deserved all the abuse heaped on him.
2. That he did it for money.
3. That Bishop Wishart was the originator and prime instigator of these false images and fully substantiated the accusations in his *MEMOIRS* published in Scotland 70 years later.
4. That Neil was a bosom friend of Montrose.

Now for real facts:—

BETRAYAL

(a) Some writers have said that Montrose went to Ardvreck, knocked on the castle door, revealed himself and was accepted as a guest; a sort of *ecce homo*. I find myself asking the question how ridiculous can some stories be hatched up, and if repeated often enough, believed? Also that he went into the Assynt country thinking he would there meet up with other Royalists, when in point of fact there were no royalists within miles.

(b) No ordinary person of sane mind would cross over to a hostile territory without knowing full well he would be met with anything short of ARREST. He could not—as we hear so often today—seek political asylum in his own country, as he could if he had fled to the Continent. Neil, as Sheriff-Depute of Assynt, appointed early in 1650 by the Earl of Sutherland, Sheriff of the County, had received a direct command through his brother-in-law, Sir Andrew Munro, 'to apprehend' any stranger that should come into Assynt, especially James Graham. Everybody was constantly on the alert, and it so happened that two of Macleod's herd-boys on 30th April 1650, came across Montrose in a bothy, and took him to Ardvreck as a prisoner, for Neil happened to be away at the time in DUNBEATH (16 miles north of Helmsdale where there was the Castle and village) in Caithness. This alibi was proved in the Edinburgh courts later when Neil was on trial. In the *Scotsman* newspaper of 6th September 1910, there appeared a letter signed '*Historicus*' in which the writer said he had in his possession a letter written by Neil from Dunbeath the day Montrose was captured. It would seem Macleod went to Dunbeath, Montrose's base, to prevent reinforcements and supplies reaching him, and so to cut off his retreat. No doubt he was again hoping for a ship to take him back to the Continent, or even to Orkney.

(c) As Neil was away, those left in charge would naturally send off a message to the Covenanting High Command, General Leslie, who forthwith despatched a party of Government troops and arrested Montrose.

If Neil's wife was present when Montrose was brought to the castle, then by Scottish law in those days, a man was responsible for his wife's deeds, but it was not until after 1660 that such an action as 'arrest' was deemed a criminal offence. Neil's wife was Christian Munro, whom he married in 1647 (two years before he came of age), daughter of Col. Sir John Munro of LUMLAIR, who was Sheriff-Depute in SLISH-CHILES, part of the country north of the Dornoch Firth as far as the Oykel. It was the Colonel's son, Sir Andrew Munro, whose reconnaissance and suggested stratagem led to Montrose's defeat at Carbisdale. Christian's mother's father was GRAY of SKIBO, Sheriff-Depute of Sutherland; so who can say that Neil was not encompassed on both sides by a noble family?

(d) Some of the 'cloud of witnesses' are not slow to state Neil and his wife had no children. This is another terminological inexactitude, for if there was no issue how could Neil's *son-in-law*, John McConnell (who had married their daughter) be in command of the garrison of Ardvreck Castle when Seaforth laid siege to it in 1672?

(e) Later on, I mention the court trial of Neil in Edinburgh in 1674 in which this all-consuming betrayal point had to be abandoned for lack of proof, even though he was tried at the time, not by his own party, but by Royalist judges and a packed Royalist jury. Fourteen out of the fifteen jury-men acquitted him.

(f) Five years ago my co-partners put the whole question to Lord Migdale, a Premier Scots Law Lord, who told us (I quote) 'I can see no justification whatever for calling this a *betrayal*. It was a perfectly normal arrest of an enemy of the Government by a properly authorised Magistrate'. In 1968 the historian Sir James Fergusson (Keeper of the Scottish Records) wrote to us saying, *inter alia*, 'I am sure that "arrest" is the correct word'. Lord Migdale is now Lord Lieutenant of Sutherland.

THE QUESTION OF MONEY

Although the Scots Parliament in September 1644 (when furious public indignation was rampant over Montrose's desertion from the Covenanters) announced in general terms in agreement with a Proclamation by Argyle that a price of £20,000 Scots—£1700 sterling—be put on his head, it was not until AFTER his capture and execution (in 1650) that the Committee of Estates met in calmer atmosphere to consider what sum *might* be given to Neil (in his capacity as Sheriff-Depute acting under orders from the Sheriff of the County) and his household for his past services.

It is true, as recorded in an old Government document of 25th May 1650, that Neil Macleod be 'satisfied' with a sum (unspecified) to be paid out of the estates of Montrose and his other 'accomplices' in connection with the late invasion of the Kingdom. The document is signed by one A. Henderson. But it turned out later there was no money available from such sources; so any chance of award never materialised. However, Neil was made a Captain of the garrison at Strathnaver, additional to his Assynt Estate. There was also proposed a sterling ex gratia award of £1000 and a gold chain be given to both Colonel Hackett and Colonel Strachan for their services at the battle of Carbisdale.

This proposed award to Neil has so often been confused with another, as it could well have been—indeed it is definitely likely—*i.e.* for his good services at the age of seventeen in exposing the defections and machinations of Seaforth (a despicable affair), as well as some compensation for the devastation of his lands by the Mackenzies who made havoc upon the Assynt Estates, carrying off over 10,000 cattle and burning down nearly two hundred homes of his people. This payment *in kind* was duly given him for the relief of his starving clansfolk, namely 400 bolls (2400 imperial bushels) of meal, though half arrived sour—a mess of pottage as it was termed by his enemies. It might have been more suitable to have called it a 'sop to Cerberus'.

This question of meal-award was only first mentioned some thirty years later at Neil's trial in 1674.

We can therefore blot out this burning question of bringing in the misnomer 'betrayal-for-greed' and substitute 'DUTY' which was plain and specific. Any other loyal Covenanter would have done the same. If not, and had Neil assisted Montrose to escape, he would have been guilty of Treason and swiftly found himself on the block.

Records show Neil was in great financial straits the years following 1650, so that if he had received any honorarium of a substantial nature, how could he have been poor? Also, in 1654 Seaforth made a further invasion of Assynt with dire results, again impoverishing Neil.

Assynt was never at any time linked with Montrose's name, personally or impersonally. Even if there had been any ties, the fact that Montrose having betrayed his party and gone over to the King's side would be no reason why Macleod of Ardvreck should do the same. And as mentioned earlier the betrayal charge was—or rather had to be—abandoned at the Edinburgh trial for lack of evidence.

It is true Neil did not capture Montrose in the field of battle, nor did he lead a search party in pursuit of him; he did not risk his life, nor was he put to expense in his capture, since Montrose was in such a state of despair and starvation that he was only too relieved to allow himself to be apprehended—even by herd-boys. So that at the time, coupled with Neil's absence from the scene, the point as to capture for gain (other than gain for Scotland) would not have been uppermost. Rather it would have been the spirit of adventure to lay low the 'Great Marquis'. So the more one examines this matter, the more it becomes patently clear this was a capture of circumstances; of a high-ranking commander wandering about a country known to be hostile.

It is recorded later in that self-same year of 1650 that Neil was taken by his kinsman, the Earl of Sutherland, to Edinburgh in an endeavour to seek *some* recompense from the authorities, for the Earl considered some recognition, however small, should be given Neil Macleod; but as I have indicated no monetary award came his way.

BISHOP WISHART, who was an ultra-royalist, and certainly not a Highlander, was expelled from Scotland for his beliefs in 1646 along with Montrose (when in May of that year Charles I escaped from Oxford and surrendered himself to the Scots army) and Wishart did not return from Schiedam in Holland until after the Restoration in 1660—ten years after Montrose's execution. He was therefore absent during Montrose's last campaign. His version of the whole affair given in his *MEMOIRS* was thus written (originally in Latin) several years after the event by a man 700 miles away at the time; and most certainly concocted from hearsay and biased imagination. Nothing more, nothing less; and as said before his allegations have been built up with added embellishments by subsequent writers in order to glorify their hero, Montrose, and to blacken the reputations of his enemies. What else? It is also significant that in 1651 Neil's enemy George, 2nd Earl of Seaforth, was also in Schiedam and had not followed Montrose to Scotland.

Is it not strange that no English version of his Memoirs was pub-lished in Scotland until 1720? Wishart's work can only be regarded as a receptacle of all the malignant Royalist calumnies showered upon the honourable Laird of Assynt; and this supposedly authentic account has been copied *ad lib.* by all and sundry, even down to guide books. His M/S copy in Latin can be seen in the Advocates' library in Edinburgh.

At the time of writing his MEMOIRS, I suppose Wishart would think all he had to say would never be questioned as to whether it was right or wrong; for as a bishop he would be looked upon like Caesar's wife 'above reproach' and his clerical robe would appear as a Banner of Truth to everyone in England and on the Continent. And so he wrote *sans peur et sans reproche* in that era of intrigue. By all means let us admire and pay homage to the brilliant Montrose, but do not let any so-called blind hero-worship affect the scales of justice. It might be well here to make an all-round recapitulation of Montrose. He deliberately signed the Covenant in 1637 and at the early age of 26 was placed in command of the Covenanters' army; a wonderful distinction. Later, with differences arising, he entered into negotiations with the King, and in doing this he broke the oath which he swore when putting his signature to the Covenant. Now, in the cool judgment of the 20th century, we can, in a way, understand Montrose's justifications for this, but in the furious passions of the 17th century when their own commander—the most brilliant they had—deserted their cause and went over to the other side, naturally feelings ran high; and made more so when he began smiting them right and left. One can therefore appreciate they found no adjectives strong enough in their condemnation. I find the Highlanders, under the Earl of Sutherland's command, were not as rabid as those following Argyle. Montrose expected 20,000 men would join him immediately, but this proved wishful thinking. Only three of any outstanding bearing came to him in Caithness. One was Robert Munro of Achines, who was his chief intelligence officer; but his failure to locate more than one troop of horse in Col. Strachan's army (Andrew Munro's stratagem, mentioned earlier) was the cause of his defeat at Carbisdale.

Many of the Scots in the pre-Restoration years remembered Montrose had burnt their homes, crops and slain many of their relatives, so they would not think of him as a hero. To the deputa-tion from the Scots government, which went to see Charles II in Holland around 1650, the King declared he had never given 'any commission to James Graham or any other, to invade Scotland'. With this assurance is it surprising that Montrose was considered to have acted on his own initiative? But of course in those days many stories were handed around; even Charles was rather good at double-talk. In fact, broadly speaking, one might ask 'who was on whose side, and who was chasing whom?'

Neil's Relationship with Montrose

As to Neil being a bosom friend and companion-in-arms of Montrose, as writers have said so often, this is quite untrue. Neil, like his grandfather Donald Bàn, was always and steadfastly a staunch and loyal Covenanter. His own parents died when he was still a child, and before that Donald had married again. He probably spent part of his boyhood staying with his mother's second cousin, the 2nd Earl of Seaforth, for until 1645 the Earl was head of the Covenanting army beyond the Spey. It must be remembered that Neil was very young during those early turbulent years.

When Montrose signed the Covenant, Neil was but a child, and only fifteen when Montrose changed sides, and seventeen years of age when the Marquis was banished. It should be remarked that seventeen in those days was not the enlightened age of seventeen in this day and age.

Neil came of age on 12th September 1649 (three years after Montrose went into exile), when he succeeded to the title and Estates of Assynt; so it becomes blatantly clear he could never have been a companion in friendship, let alone 'in arms', of Montrose. In fact, in research, we have not come across anything that even says Neil ever *met* Montrose.

Macleod's Loss of Assynt

I come now to the last episode of this lamentable drama, as to Neil being constantly persecuted after the Restoration, and how finally on 14th January 1698, some two years after his death, the Estates and debt claims were made over to the Mackenzies.

In 1651 the Earl of Seaforth died abroad and was succeeded by his son, a Roman Catholic, who continued the feud with Assynt. Seaforth was heavily in debt, for it appears his father had spent something like one million pounds in helping Charles I.

The Restoration of 1660 gave Seaforth the opportunity for which he had longed. At his instigation, the Lord Advocate (a Mackenzie) charged Neil with betraying Montrose, and other crimes. Macleod was kept in prison in the Tolbooth, Edinburgh, for three years without being brought to trial. There were, however, reports on the matter in the Privy Council, and a number of preliminary examinations, consultations and so forth between Assynt's counsel and the prosecution. All this time Neil vehemently protested his innocence, and rightly so; and, 'he having proved he was (at the time when Montrose was captured) no less than 60 miles distant from his countrie, was by an assize assoilzied as innocent of the said process', *i.e.* having proved an alibi, the case was dropped.

Early in 1663 he pleaded the Act of Indemnity under the Treaty of Breda, 1650, but was still not discharged, but as his health began to suffer he was released on condition he remained in Edinburgh; and bail of £20,000 Scots enforced. Two friends stood surety.

It was not until 1666 that King Charles II wrote a special letter to the Privy Council (20th February) ordering Neil Macleod be set free as there was no evidence upon which to convict him; and *no further proceedings were to be taken against him*. Neil then returned to Assynt from where he had been absent six years.

Although at liberty he had little or no money (the Mackenzies having been all this time in control of his estates and rents) so he therefore exercised the ancient rights of Highland Chieftains to levy dues on all shipping using his waters. Admittedly he made them rather higher than previously, but except for a Capt. John Kerr, the merchants and fishermen made no complaint. Neil's traducers, however, alleged that this was 'piracy', and it was for this reason the Earl of Seaforth obtained the Commission of Fire and Sword against him—one of his many imaginary accusations.

Now to the question that Neil was supposed to have been heavily in debt.

In this connection we have recently been given the privilege of access to some family papers belonging to the GEANIES McLeod branch (pronounced Gay-knees), who are direct descendants of John —Neil's younger brother—and Donald, Neil's nephew who was his lineal heir, from which much valuable detail is brought to light for the very first time. The following records culled from these papers, loaned us by Mrs. C. McLeod Morley of Beaconsfield and now given publication, are of tremendous interest to the Macleod clan in particular, as much of the material was compiled by Donald McLeod 3rd of Geanies, who was the renowned Sheriff of Ross and Cromarty for over sixty years; a man who had a trained legal mind.

After the Macleods of Lewis lost their lands by forfeiture in neglecting to obey a Royal Proclamation to produce their charters or Title Deeds by a certain day, George, 2nd Earl of Seaforth, in 1635 obtained by favour of the King a charter of the Barony of Lewis and

I

its dependencies. By such a grant he obtained right to the superiority of Assynt. About 1640 Seaforth, in order to further his avid design to add the Estate of Assynt to that of Lewis, purchased a claim against Assynt from his brother Thomas Mackenzie of Pluscardine in Morayshire. This was during Donald Bàn's time, and Seaforth, on the security of this claim and the title founded thereon, granted a mortgage (a *wadset*) on the estate for 40,000 merks to Kenneth Mackenzie of Scatwell, although this had been discharged by 1643 and receipts given. The Mackenzies did not inform the Macleods of such a transfer and this debt was ever after held against the Estate. (20,000 merks is roughly £13,333.)

A 'Decreet of Apprising' was obtained on this claim, and on expiry of the Court order, Seaforth, believing that the Wadset could not be redeemed, invaded Assynt and inflicted great damage. For this illegal invasion he was prosecuted and Donald Bàn Mor was awarded £40,000 Scots damages; and the sum was applied to paying off part of Seaforth's claim, the remainder being paid off by Donald Og (elder son of Donald Bàn by his second wife) as already said in 1643. Donald was then managing the estate for his aged father.

Adverting to the Seaforth 'claim', Kenneth Mackenzie of Scatwell conveyed the claim over to his son John; by him it was conveyed to Sir George Mackenzie, later Lord Tarbat, and by him re-conveyed to John Mackenzie, Seaforth's second son to whom he was Guardian. So the claim passed into and through many channels.

In 1656 a new plan was envisaged, namely, Sir William Sinclair of Mey, Caithness (whose sister was married to Sir George Mackenzie) lent to one Ross of Little Tarrell the sum of £154/10/- on a bond for which Neil Macleod and Mackenzie of Scatwell stood Cautioners (*i.e.* surety).

Towards the year 1667 Neil became suspicious of the good faith of the Mackenzies, and took legal steps to discharge the debt himself, but was dissuaded from doing so by his first cousin, Sir George Mackenzie of Tarbat (just named) on the grounds that Seaforth had other plans; and in this web of intrigue there were many 'plans'. Sir George said it would 'irritate' Seaforth!

The debt by then had amounted to about £202 with interest on the principal sum together with the Sheriff's fee of £10/12/-. Sir George also promised the debt would never be used against Neil or his Estate. Promises and intrigues?

In 1670, during Neil's absence from Ardvreck, Seaforth summoned him to pay and when this was not forthcoming, he sent the Sheriff of Sutherland to eject him from Assynt. After Neil's tenants had violently opposed the Sheriff (September 1671), Neil was denounced as a rebel, and so Seaforth obtained a commission of Fire and Sword against him in July 1672.

With 2300 men Assynt was ravaged, and the Castle (in which Neil's household were) was besieged, being defended then by Neil's son-in-law John McConnell—previously mentioned. After fourteen days Neil decided to escape to Edinburgh by sea, taking with him his charter chest containing his charter to Assynt, the charter Donald Bàn had obtained in 1642 under the Great Seal of Charles I confirming to him and his heirs the Barony, title deeds with many unrecorded vouchers of payments, and also of partial payments of debts affecting the Estate; but the ship was driven by contrary winds to take shelter in the Orkneys, where he and his precious chest were captured by the Laird of Mey (acting under Seaforth's orders) and taken to the Castle of Mey where he was imprisoned in a vault. Neil was now truly stripped of all his earthly possessions. From here he was taken under escort to TAIN, and finally to Brahan Castle, Seaforth's seat. He was kept there for many months in the most miserable of circumstances, being threatened with worse usage if he did not agree to sign a blank paper designed to dispose of all his estate to Seaforth. This he refused to do. His charter chest and all his title deeds were never seen again by him. His family and many of his friends were also imprisoned and cruelly treated.

Thus was Neil originally turned out of possession of an estate of £300 rental a year and upwards (which would be worth thousands nowadays) for a paltry sum of an original debt of £154 sterling. Never afterwards did he touch a penny of these rents.

At the instigation of Seaforth, Neil Macleod was put on trial before the Justiciary in February 1674, the outcome of which I have briefly recounted—viz. Neil being honourably acquitted.

But the Mackenzies were still in possession of his estates, and having kept Neil out for some thirteen years decided on another 'plan' to give better colour to their unjustifiable proceedings. Being in possession of Neil's charter chest and all the deeds, it was easy for them, without going to a farthing of expense, to claim the rights to some old debts which had definitely been discharged, and to 'secrete' the receipts. Two merchant bills were used totalling about £750, which Neil declared had been fully settled prior to 1672; but how to prove it?

In 1678 our 'hero' tried to regain his rights by bringing a charge of theft against Mey, Seaforth and others, but, the old Earl of Seaforth having died while the Process was 'in dependence', the young Seaforth declared he knew nothing about the charter chest, and so the case was consigned to *avizandum*.

Neil made a further attempt to regain the property in 1690 when he was challenged to produce evidence of ownership. In 1692 he did succeed in obtaining about £166 damages for the theft of his charter chest. After that he had no alternative but to abandon his efforts. Eventually death overtook him whilst living in Edinburgh in 1696, wretched and in abject poverty—the victim of cruel ill-usage in life and malicious defamations after death.

As though this was not enough, in January 1698 the estates and debt claims were legally assigned to Roderick Mackenzie of Preston-hall. However, in 1715 his son Alexander, having been engaged in the rebellion of '15, was convicted of High Treason, and the Estates were forfeited to the Crown, the King gifting them to Lord Lovat who had married a Mackenzie. After the '45 rebellion they again reverted to the Crown. Captain Hugh McLeod 2nd of Geanies went to much expense in 1753-1755 in trying to establish his claim, petitioning both the Commons and the King; but with no satisfaction.

At the public auction early in 1757, the Earl of Sutherland stepped into the arena, and on bidding £12,000 (£1000 more than the Geanies family) deprived the rightful owners of their property yet again—so that at this point ownership had turned full circle, and the lands of Assynt came back to the Sutherlands who, centuries before, had given them to the MacNicols of Ullapool.

I doubt if any such treacherous parallel can be unfolded in Scottish history as this.

Thus it is proved beyond all shadow of doubt Neil was not heavily in debt. The total amount of debts fraudulently claimed was the surety on a bond for some £202, together with £750 for 'alleged debts' to merchants, all involving an estate worth thousands of pounds with £300 yearly rentals. In 1740 the Rental of the Assynt Estates, from all sources, was some £3800.

Coming back to Neil's trial in Edinburgh in 1674, all those that have dwelt on the trial have been guilty of quoting the charges against him as though they were facts, whereas of the seven indictments, two were dropped for lack of proof, two were declared not relevant, and he was honourably acquitted of the other three.

At the outset records plainly show the Privy Council recognised it was at the Earl of Seaforth's instigation that Neil was incarcerated. The first two charges concerned the alleged betrayal of Montrose, and the accusation that in 1654 Neil had assisted the 'English rebels' under General Morgan. These charges were withdrawn by the Lord Advocate at the first hearing, for no proofs could be brought and so both these accusations were an 'aggravation' inserted to raise a clamour against Neil.

The other indictments were, briefly:—

1. Imposing taxation on all ships which anchored in Lochinver. (The 'piracy' catchphrase.)
2. Kidnapping and holding to ransom Captain John Kerr because he refused to pay the dues.
3. Of twice resisting the Sheriff of Sutherland sent to eject Neil from Ardvreck for alleged non-payment of a debt to Seaforth, and of uttering treasonable words.
4. For convocating men, placing them under officers, drilling them and paying them, and for garrisoning and provisioning his castle *after* the Commission of Fire and Sword had been granted against him—which was treason, and carried capital punishment.

Of the Lord Advocate's four witnesses, two could not speak English, and all the four failed him by testifying that they had seen Neil's men training and drilling about Whitsun, which was *before* the Earl of Seaforth marched into Assynt to execute the Commission of Fire and Sword in July. The Lord Advocate was so disgusted with the inexpertness of his witnesses that he wanted the jury to go back and reconsider their verdict. But the Judges took no notice of this unorthodox request.

Neil's advocate very successfully combated all the malicious charges, and also proved that as soon as Neil had been shown the Commission's Order (about August) he instructed his son-in-law to surrender Ardvreck. It will be remembered Neil tried to escape by sea. It was really the last charge (4) that the prosecution was so earnest to prove. Under the clouded circumstances this was most difficult, for in the Highlands people had often to defend themselves against robbers and suchlike. In this case the Convocation was only to defend themselves against the Letters of Ejection raised at a private person's instance, and the Commission of Fire and Sword was of the private person's procuring. And unless the prosecution could prove, without all manner of doubt, the alleged crime was designed to resist the King's Majesty and Government, it was quite impossible for the Judges to rate Neil as a rebel and traitor.

Regarding the charges named in 1, 2 and 3 above, I would embrace them together by saying he was entitled to charge dues if he wished as a heritor of the Barony of Assynt; that he had an alibi and that he was not at Ardvreck at the times the ejections by the Sheriff were resisted; so it could not have been himself who had uttered treasonable words.

Finally, as I have said, the verdict was NOT PROVEN and he was acquitted by all but one of the fifteen (royalist) jury-men, after the (royalist) judges had given their summing-up. The Lord Advocate was furious and accused all the persons of the Inquest of wilful error, except Mr. Robert Blackwood, the one dissentient voice!

The curtain must now fall on the unwarranted 'Shame of Ard-vreck', 'midst righteous applause for Neil Macleod. Evidence given herein is incontrovertible so we can rub out these three centuries of heaped-up calumny and abuse on this man's good name for merely having done his duty; a man who can be described as, in appearance and manner, the *Beau Ideal* of a Highland Gentleman—Neil Macleod XI Baron of Assynt. And surely too, we are entitled to substitute a new caption, and now salute the 'Hero of Ardvreck'.

Too long have the *real* facts remained untold; too long has all this abuse been bandied about and woven out of fantasy. This Treatise therefore comes as a corrective. All evidence has been marshalled and combed with special care. 'For whom the bell tolls . . . it tolls for thee' (of the mid/late 1600s) and it can now be said *payment has been made in reverse.*

Now for Further Comments

(i) ASSYNT

The Assynt estate remained in the hands of Mackenzie of Seaforth until 1715, when—after thirty years' ownership by Lord Lovat—it was bought at the public auction in 1757, on behalf of the infant Countess of Sutherland. Captain Hugh McLeod, 2nd of Geanies, was eventually given an indemnity by the Government of £2000 sterling, in recognition of their being convinced of the justice of his claims. Justice at last? At this point the circle was complete; the lands of Assynt had reverted to the Sutherland family who, as indicated earlier, had centuries before given them to the MacNicols of Ullapool.

The MacNicols were considered to be of Pictish or Gaelic origin. They can be identified with the KAIRINOI of Ptolemy's *Geographia*, who lived in the Mormaorship of Ness, *i.e.* the districts of Durness, Eddrachillis and Assynt which were forest lands belonging to the ancient Thanes of Sutherland. The first individual of the tribe to be mentioned in tradition or document is GREGALL or Krycul, who held the coast of Coigach, near Ullapool, and who was regarded as the founder of the Clan. It was a Norse clan coming originally from Norway about the 10th and 11th centuries. MacNicol is sometimes pronounced as Macreacall. Other groups of the same name took up their abode in the Hebrides and in districts further south. As the north-west of Scotland was under Norse domination at the time of these settlements, there was every reason for parties of MacNicols to select the mainland, as well as the islands, for a place of residence. As mentioned in the Text, the Thane made over the district of Assynt in vassalage to the MacNicols in grateful recognition of their keep and in particular when a gang of marauders driving a large herd of his cattle raided from the north of Sutherland were severely trounced and driven off and all the animals recovered. This established the MacNicols as a powerful clan.

(ii) Montrose

(*a*) There is no doubt the great Marquis *was* indeed a 'Great Marquis', and looked upon as a hero. In culture and outlook he was in advance of his day and time; even today a large part of Scotland still regards him as such. But of course to the Covenanters he was a traitor; for although he was their brilliant Commander-in-Chief for five years he turned over to the King's (Royalist) side in May 1643. In so doing we cannot but be left with the impression that he was unprincipled despite the apparent breach between himself and the leading Covenanters. Just think what a staggering blow this must have been to them. After his defeat at Carbisdale and his capture near the Covenanting stronghold, Ardvreck Castle, he was executed all in a matter of days.

(*b*) Although I set out at great length in the Treatise to disprove the word 'betrayal' for 'arrest', to my mind this could well have been boiled down to a few lines. For instance, suppose it were Israel's brilliant Defence Minister, General Dayan, who completely brought Egypt to her knees, and then crossed over the Suez Canal to help the Egyptians on account of some differences he had with his own countrymen; and later, in leading the Egyptians against Israel, was defeated, captured and brought back to Israel, how would he be treated? He would be branded as a traitor, as an outcast, put up against a wall and shot at once.

(*c*) As Montrose went to his execution in Edinburgh on 21st May 1650, he conducted himself with regal dignity; calm, serene and confident; for he had always said, 'I do but follow my conscience'. His horse-drawn cart stopped for a moment outside Argyle's house, where the crowd was at its thickest.

No man had lifted a hand against him; in fact, instead of hurling stones, filth, and insults at his person, they *sobbed in pity*. (I must, however, mention that on his way south to Edinburgh, and passing through the Aberdeen area that he had twice sacked, the fury of the people was turned on him.)

Argyle looked out from behind his half-closed shutters, and Montrose, tied to his chair in the hangman's cart, looked up and saw him. Argyle quickly drew back, and Montrose went onwards, slowly to his death. What a spectacle of History? In due season Argyle was to follow him. As I have said, Montrose's greatest victory was in his death.

After the Restoration of Charles II, Montrose's son took part eleven years later, on 1st January 1661, in the State funeral of his father at Holyrood; but at the trial of the Marquis of Argyle in April 1661, he declined to vote, admitting that he had too much resentment to judge in the matter.

It was universally acknowledged Montrose went to his death proudly. Perhaps he thought if he stage-acted in a princely manner he might avoid the downward stroke of the axe, before his head bit the dust.

We say history repeats itself; I firmly believe it does, even to some extent in our own lives.

We have a similar personage a hundred years later in Bonnie Prince Charlie when he landed in Scotland and hoisted his standard at Glenfinnan on 19th August 1745. He appeared as a young romantic figure to everyone, with his hair a lovely deep golden colour and his eyes brown, and continued as a hero throughout his exploits until at Culloden, 16th April 1746, when his troops, like those of Montrose, melted away, sullied and discontented, and he was utterly defeated. Though he escaped to France, avoiding capture and death, he conducted himself as became his royal parentage; and when he knew all was lost, he made his historic gesture, '*Gentlemen, I have flung away the scabbard*'. I think if we had then been present, we too might have sobbed 'midst our applause!

(*d*) Regarding Montrose's capture, he, with Major Sinclair and the Earl of Kinnoul, escaped after Carbisdale and wandered towards Assynt. The three finally split up; Kinnoul could go no further, being wounded; and later died of fatigue and hunger among the hills. The Major—from Orkney—went off to find help and food, but nothing further is known as to what became of him. Montrose continued on alone, trying to find his way to the Reay country. This was on the third day after the battle. Later that day, he came to a small hut or bothy which was occasionally used for dairy purposes on the hillside by one of Neil's tenants at a grazing farm called Glaschyle. Montrose had put on the short woollen coat of a countryman before escaping from Carbisdale, and he now approached the hut and modestly asked if a stranger who had lost his way could be given some food. The tenant farmer was quite unsuspicious, but the only sustenance he had in the hut was some whisky, for it was not a place of residence. Montrose drank some, and asking the name of it, said he had never tasted anything so good and so refreshing. He had another drink, and then appearing more active and alert, asked the way to the Reay country. The farmer pointed out the direction to him, but said no stranger could find it on his own. Montrose said he was too poor to pay for a guide. However, by this time the farmer's suspicions were aroused, because whilst Montrose was drinking the whisky, the front of his coat had opened a little and the farmer caught a glimpse of either a star or rich metallic embroidery on his waistcoat. Montrose then set out, but the man followed him at a distance. As Montrose was going up GLAS BHEINN, a hill a few miles north of Glaschyle, he met another herdman who had been sent out from Ardvreck to search for strangers wandering through that part of Assynt. Montrose tried to go in another direction, but finding it impossible to escape, sat down until both men overtook him, having previously scattered all the money in his possession among the heather—some of these coins were picked up by chance about 200 years later.

In answer to the question of Macleod's servant, Montrose again said he was making for the Reay country but had lost his way, and asked to be guided there. The men seemed to agree, but speaking in Gaelic to each other, decided the best plan would be to take him to Ardvreck instead. When Montrose saw the castle, its peculiar situation on a peninsula almost surrounded by water (and called by old chroniclers 'The Isle of Assynt'), Montrose became convinced he had been betrayed and was now in the power of Macleod of Assynt. He anxiously enquired if it was Ardvreck Castle, and the men telling him it was, said he would observe Macleod's lady at its gate waiting to receive him. He hurriedly asked her father's name, and was told that she was the daughter of Black John of the Breast. Montrose hearing this, stood for a while motionless and aghast, and then exclaimed that his destiny was now fulfilled and his fate certain. The two men who captured Montrose were named Angus Macleod and Neil Macleod, both of whom were outlawed in 1663. The fact that one of these men was called Neil might well have caused confusion at the time with the Laird's name, Neil Macleod of Assynt.

It is recorded that early in life Montrose had consulted a witch and asked her to tell his fortune. She had answered angrily that he was to beware of a black lake and the daughter of a black-featured man, for if he were to come in contact with the little black loch of Drum Carbisdale and the daughter of Black John of the Breast, his ruin and his downfall were at hand.

Montrose's fears now, could simply be accounted for because he knew that Black John had been fighting against him, and that Macleod was also opposed to his allies, the Mackenzies and the Mackays.

Upon arrival at the castle, he was immediately carefully guarded, and a message was sent to Col. Strachan. No doubt he was offered fair words along with good food, whilst the secret message was on its way. This action was undoubtedly legally correct; but in the context of 'Highland hospitality', this would have been termed 'treachery' by Neil's enemies; which then led to the word 'betrayal'.

In my travels I have heard it said that Neil's wife had made amatory advances to Montrose some years before, but had been rejected. I rather doubt this.

There was a day of public thanksgiving when news came through that Montrose was captured; and on the day the great Marquis was elevated on the scaffold, the Covenanter's cry was 'Today, by the Grace of God, Montrose dies'.

(e) According to the sentences passed upon Montrose, his body was cut down from the thirty feet high gibbet after three hours of execution and dismembered. The limbs were distributed among the towns of Aberdeen, Perth, Stirling and Glasgow. The trunk was buried beside the public gallows in Edinburgh. His head was placed on a spike on the west face of the Tolbooth, and eleven years later taken down to make place for Argyle's head. How disgustingly revolting, gruesome and barbarous it is to us today to read of such execution methods. One leg in Aberdeen; one in Glasgow. One arm in Perth; one in Stirling. One arm had first been offered to the town of Dundee, to be placed over the city gate, but Dundee had the good taste to refuse. Such was the fate of a man whose military and other genius shone forth beyond any that ever appeared during those civil disorders.

I have mentioned the name of John Graham of Claverhouse, Viscount Dundee (1648–1689)—the 'Great Dundee'. Claverhouse admired Montrose's career, whose exploits he endeavoured in after life to emulate. He looked upon Montrose as one who had a singleness of purpose. He, like Montrose, was a Graham of course. In Claverhouse's library at Inverpaffray, is preserved the pocket bible of the great Marquis, which has the owner's signature; and there is also written in Montrose's hand, '*Honor mihi vita potior*' (Honour to me is better than life). This sentiment, too, was the ruling principle in the life of Claverhouse, who was a firm believer in Episcopacy.

(iii) DUNBEATH

(*a*) It will be recalled from the Text, that at the time of Montrose's capture and arrival at Ardvreck Castle, Neil Macleod was away on the east coast, at or near Dunbeath in Caithness (16 miles north of Helmsdale, which Sutherland village almost borders on Caithness).

Dunbeath Castle is unlike that of Ardvreck in that it is not in ruins; in fact over the many centuries it has been more or less continuously occupied. Even two hundred years ago it was recorded that it was 'one of the few such ancient edifices still inhabited'.

Mr. Harry E. Blythe, Jr., of Chimney Rock Ranch, Paso Robles, California, U.S.A., is the present owner of the Castle and Estate, purchasing it in September 1967. He and his wife look upon the Castle as unique. And so it is.

The accompanying illustration shows the approach avenue, lined with trees and bushes, with the ivory-looking Castle in the distance. It is situated on a narrow, precipitous rock projecting out into the North Sea, which surrounds it on three sides. The neighbouring cliffs are from eighty to a hundred feet high, and when the sea is roughened by a breeze, the scene produced by the waves dashing against them, and boiling at their feet, is exceedingly wild. When I saw the castle in all its autumnal glory in September 1970, it reminded me of Walt Disney's castle in the film 'The Wizard of Oz'.

The castle has been often renovated, but the frontage has been left unaltered as to its Norman aspect. The present owners have only preserved the general structure so as to make it safe and secure for future decades.

There are many secret stairways built into the castle's walls, as one can expect; and it would have its own dungeon to be sure in those far-off times. There is a cave coming up from the sea to a dark, dreary vault which in turn connects with the castle by a narrow twisting stairway. Most probably this arrangement served as an easy exit to the sea to escape in boats when the castle might have been besieged by an enemy. It would also be admirably adapted for concealing contraband goods. In 1650, the castle was surrounded by a moat filled from the sea.

(b) Montrose, coming over from Sweden, landed in Orkney as I have said before, and made his headquarters at Noltland Castle on the island of Westray; and there spent his time in raising more troops. In April (1650) all his followers mustered at Kirkwall to be embarked for Caithness. The whole force was about 2000 men. Major Sinclair, of Orkney, accompanied the Marquis. The whole contingent was transported across the Pentland Firth, disembarking at Duncansbay (Duncansby) near John o' Groats. There Montrose—making Dunbeath-ways—at once displayed three banners, one of which was made of black taffeta, in the centre of which was exhibited a representation of the bleeding head of the late King as struck from the body, surrounded by two inscriptions, 'Judge and avenge my cause, O Lord', and '*Deo et victricibus armis*' (To the glory of God and the victory of arms). Another standard had this motto, '*Quos pietas, virtus, et honor fecit amicos*' (with whom Piety, Courage and Honour made friends). These two banners were those of the King. The third, which was Montrose's own, bore the words '*Nil medium*' (all or nothing)—a motto strongly significant of the stern and uncompromising character of the man.

The news of the landing spread like wildfire through the country greatly alarming the inhabitants, many of whom fled from their houses, and hid themselves among the rocks.

Soon the report reached Dunbeath, and Sir John Sinclair (no relation to the major mentioned earlier) took horse and posted off direct to Edinburgh to communicate this news to the Scots Parliament—the Convention of Estates—leaving the castle to be defended by his lady and servants.

Montrose advanced to Thurso, and lodged in a house near the old church. It was a mean, thatched hovel. His appeal to the patriotism of the people of Caithness to join him fell on deaf ears for the call to arms met with little response. Everyone was indifferent or lukewarm in the cause, as the proprietors (landowners) made no efforts to induce their tenantry—little more than serfs at that time—to join Montrose. In this respect they acted very differently from those in Orkney.

Montrose decided to leave Thurso and marched south by the eastern route making for the Ord of Caithness. Passing through Latheron, he came to Dunbeath and laid siege to the castle and vigorously attacked what small garrison was there. Sir John Sinclair's wife, having no real means of defence, after holding out for a few days, surrendered on the condition that persons and property should be respected. This was readily granted. The possession of this stronghold was of the utmost importance to Montrose in case he should meet with a reverse (as he did eventually at Carbisdale) and be obliged to retreat back into Caithness. A garrison was left behind at Dunbeath, a Major Whitford being in charge. Marching on towards the Ord, he entered Sutherland, where the Earl of Sutherland was in arms against him. The Earl found himself unequal to the contest at the formidable defile of the Ord, although a few of his brave men (such as Leonidas at Thermopylas) could have held out against a host. The Earl was summoned to attend a Council of war at Tain.

(c) Meantime when the Scots government heard of Montrose's invasion, they ordered General David Leslie to proceed north with 4000 men. Colonel Strachan was sent on before with a strong body of cavalry to check Montrose's progress. The latter met with no serious interruption until he reached Carbisdale. Here he was unexpectedly attacked by Col. Strachan, and having no cavalry worth mentioning to oppose the far superior cavalry force of the enemy, his raw and undisciplined foot soon gave way, with disastrous defeat as already recorded.

After the battle, Captain William Gordon of Dunrobin was despatched to Caithness in pursuit of Montrose's brother, Henry Graham. Just as he arrived at Thurso, Graham, who had been apprised of his brother's defeat, was setting off in a vessel from Scrabster for Orkney, and from there he made good his escape to Holland.

General Leslie soon after, accompanied by the Earl of Sutherland, entered Caithness and laid siege to Dunbeath Castle, which was bravely defended by the few adherents of Montrose that had been left in charge. They were only taken at last by cutting off their supply of water. Leslie summoned all the principal landowners of the county before him, sending some of them to Edinburgh to be dealt with by the Convention of Estates. Sir George Drummond of Balloch, who was apprehended in Orkney, was brought over and shot at a post in Caithness. The church then took into her own hands the punishment of the ministers, who, with the exception of the Rev. William Smith of Bower, were all summarily deposed by the General Assembly —punished for their compliance with Montrose excommunicate, in his rebellion and shedding the blood of the country. The whole of the ministers of Orkney were also deposed. Patrick Balfour, the possessor of the castle of Noltland, was fined £2000 and forced to fly to Holland for complicity in his loyalty to the great Marquis. All these people had subscribed under intimidation to the written oath or bond which Montrose had tendered them. There is no doubt, Orkney suffered severely for the assistance which it had given to Montrose.

Immediately after the defeat of Montrose at Carbisdale, a Captain Collace, by warrant of General Leslie, came to Orkney and violently quartered his troop of horse and men throughout the land, destroying and eating, trampling and abusing the growing corn in the fields, and threatening for money, would not remove their quarters till they got 500 merks or so from each person owning land; and this amounted to the sum of £5000 Scots. The following year, 1651, Orkney suffered greatly by many English men-of-war which plundered many houses and islands to the value of 10,000 merks, and also uplifted and violently took sheep, cattle and other victuals.

Such was the aftermath of Montrose. After the Restoration the poor islanders were refused any compensation for the plunder committed. This was quite in keeping with the careless and ungrateful character of Charles II. The islanders gave Montrose 2000 men and £40,000 Scots. Again, they raised more men and contributions to Charles II in 1651; and he rewarded their loyalty and their sufferings by a further exaction of £182,000 in 1662. They were indeed reduced to great want. The ex-minister of Reay, after acknowledging his guilt, was allowed to preach, as he might be of use in the Gaelic language.

(d) In September 1651, Sir John Sinclair of Dunbeath, who had taken such an active part against Montrose, died. His wife, who defended the castle in his absence, was a daughter of Lord Lovat and sister of the Countess of Sutherland. Her name was Catherine Fraser, and she was his second wife. After Sir John's death she married the first Viscount Arbuthnot. As Sir John had no male heir, the estate was divided between his brother Alexander's son and his own daughter's children, which daughter was married to the Baron of Kilbrace. His nephew, William, succeeded to the title, and became laird of Dunbeath.

(iv) MACLEODS OF ASSYNT

(a) Twice was Neil accused and brought to trial; twice were the charges withdrawn or not proven. Why? I have given the answers, yet even today, 320 years later, there are many writers—some of renown—who still stick to this question of guilt, either through ignorance or not bothering to sift the inner and essential details. Once a lie is let loose, and its unjust flame fanned by a so-called 'host of witnesses', it is sometimes difficult to catch up with it, let alone smother it. And so it goes on its way, just as a snowball does, gathering more; in this case, more baseness; or like a phantom funeral procession picking up more mourners (witnesses) on its road through the Corridors of Time. One seldom meets a lonely lie. Lies go in droves, whereas Truth can stand alone; but a lie needs a brother on the right and another on the left, to prop it up.

(b) In the following paragraph (c), extracts are given from just two of many letters I received, showing that however lucidly one may present authentic, cast-iron references which leave no question as to conclusiveness, doubts still exist in some minds.

Memories linger on . . .

Not only doubts, but quite a large number of Scottish people are unconcerned as to what happened hundreds of years ago; and in regard to ancient buildings, some landowners don't seem to care a tinker's cuss or a tuppenny legend what happens to a Chieftain's castle, an early historic broch, or such like. This, obviously, is not the age for 'thinking on these things'.

However, come what may, what is written in this chapter is gospel truth, and should help dispel any feelings of scepticism so that the verdict of all clear-thinking, unbiased persons should be that to have stigmatised Neil Macleod of Assynt with that odious word 'betrayal' was the most unjust imaginable. The alleged 'betrayal' can be termed a classic fabrication.

But as I have said, memories linger on . . .

Of course in politics, wars and anything of national importance, if anything goes wrong, a scapegoat has to be found; and when Montrose was delivered up from Ardvreck and duly executed, it would only be a matter of hours before whisperings went around in the manner of the grape-vine (which is surprisingly active in the Highlands), and what better or easier than to say it was all due to Ardvreck and the Macleod Clan? This, together with that distortionist (I might even say, 'contortionist') Bishop Wishart was enough to fire the imagination of hero followers; and through the years they solidly held on to this accusation. All too simple. And so, Neil Macleod, after 1650, bore the mark of Cain to his death. To my view Neil's history rather reminds me of that of the prophet Job.

(c) Referring to the previous paragraph, (b) the first extract is from a titled lady, who before her marriage was a Mackenzie. Whilst thanking me for the complimentary copy of the Treatise

I had sent her, and saying what a great deal of research had been involved, she went on to say (and I quote), 'Macleods and Mackenzies were hereditary enemies; and having been brought up to revere the 'Great Marquis', I remember that as a child I used to spit whenever coming face to face with a Macleod, to the great embarrassment of my nurse. Though my husband has Macleod blood, he is not really interested in these old controversies, but even now, I cannot thole the idea of any attempt to whitewash Macleod which blackens Montrose, and therefore would rather not accept your gift as such, and so enclose a cheque in payment for the copy and for another one which please be so good as to send, as I think I know a Macleod who would enjoy it.'

Doubts; still doubts. In all these scepticisms, I am reminded of the ancient writings, 'Can the Ethiopian change his skin, or the leopard his spots?'

The other letter is from a very cultured friend of mine (also a Mackenzie) in the Durness area of north-west Sutherland.

He wrote saying: 'I am sure every Macleod in general and those of Assynt in particular will feel grateful to you for clearing Neil's name even at this late date. The majority of the inhabitants of Assynt are Macleods and Mackenzies, and probably all the Mackenzies have a strong mixture of Macleod blood. When I was going to school at Stoer, ninety per cent. of the 150 pupils (there are only 9 now!) were either Macleod or Mackenzie. What battles we used to have! Sometimes the Macleods were victorious, sometimes the Mackenzies. I often think of how those Macleod boys reacted to the slander. Perhaps sometimes when they were almost routed, some fool of a Mackenzie would shout, "Macleods of Assynt sold Montrose for 400 bolls of rotten brose". Like fury they would surge back into the attack and invariably had us running. We soon learnt not to hurl that abuse until the enemy were well scattered. Our headmaster, a MacIver from Tongue, frequently said, "Can you young ruffians never forget Ardvreck?" Of course I am not going to try and condone the actions of the Mackenzies in Assynt. Those were wild times, when Might was usually Right. That the Macleods were no paragons of virtue and Neil was not the lily-white gentleman either. Ask the Mackays of Eddrachallis, when the Macleods, led by the famous Neil, would raid their lands and drive their cattle into Quinag's Byre—a valley on the top of the mountain with a loch in it. There is one thing I do hope will come out of your Treatise, that Ardvreck would be at least partially restored; and perhaps be converted into a museum. . . .,'

Memories still linger on. . . .

(v) THE FAMILY TOMB

This was built in the little graveyard of Inchnadamph, about the year 1450, adjacent to the wee parish church. I found the graveyard tidy—though the small iron gate to the vault had been wrenched off I was told some 15 years ago—and the whole picture, with the water's edge of beautiful Loch Assynt close by, presented an atmosphere of restful simplicity; and as I looked at the big vault where Donald Bàn, IX Baron of Assynt, had been interred centuries ago, I took off my hat in reverence to this ancient monument which this tomb portrays. I can well describe this sacred plot as 'where the sound of living waters never ceaseth; God's quiet garden by the loch'.

However, I felt aggrieved that no plaque or inscription of any sort had been fitted into the stone-walled vault to let visitors from all over the world—particularly the great clan of Macleods —see where the historic Assynt branch lie buried. This surely is the least that should be done. Even the commonest of a common grave, has a name chiselled on its stone. This unheard-of omission on such an illustrious resting place should be made good right now.

As you enter this cemetery, on the right of the small gateway is a memorial stone to R.A.F. personnel who lost their lives on the nearby hill in 1941. The inscription is plain and simple, viz., 'R.A.F. Flying Officer J. H. Steyn, D.F.C.; Pilot Officer W. E. Drew; Sergeants J. Emery; T. B. Kenny; C. M. Mitchell; H. A. Tompsett. Here are commemorated the crew of an aircraft crashed on Ben More 13 April 1941, whose bodies rest where they fell. . . .'

(vi) PRESERVATION OF THE RUINS

I have already commented upon the ruinous state of Ardvreck Castle; how the centuries have caused it to be looked upon as a bygone relic, instead of being revered. Sooner or later the last stones will crumble, and falling apart, leave only dust; a tragic reminder where loch and land intertwined, and proclaimed the Highland spirit—an independence born of solitude. In the spring, golden broom brightens the land, often grey with clouds. Even so, the very dust will be dear to the Macleods of Assynt; though when that happens, I am sure those who may still be living will be quoting, through tears, the words the Book of Proverbs, ch. 22, v. 28 has to say, 'Remove not the ancient landmarks which thy fathers have set'; and they will bow their heads and curtsey like a Hindu paying his devotions to the Ganges.

A few pages back I have said some people don't seem to care a tinker's cuss what happens to some of our ancient landmarks in the Highlands. The Ancient Monuments Society and the Ministry of Public Buildings and Works seem to skate around this category; and whilst the principal provision in the various Acts (dating from 1882) designed to protect ancient monuments is known as 'scheduling', it appears to me that in most cases the onus is put on the owner. I am left wondering if we are to dig up Neil Macleod, the last Chief of Ardvreck, himself? Urquhart Castle on Loch Ness is 'preserved' and impeccably kept. Is this castle of any more significance than Ardvreck? What has Urquhart Castle got that Ardvreck hasn't? *Qu'est-ce-que Ardvreck?* Surely to see the castle crumbling away before their very eyes, ought to rouse and urge the Assynt Macleods (at home and overseas) to immediate restorative action before Miss Anno Domini and her sister, Miss Tomorrow, finally step in. These two worthies have the tools and will finish the job ere long—the job of complete disappearance.

(vii) FURTHER HISTORICAL DATA

Previously in the Text proper, I have expressed thanks to Mrs. C. McLeod Morley for permitting the Macleod family (of Cadboll) and myself to make use of certain documentary evidence from the unique Geanies Papers in her possession. Many of the extra details now recorded for the first time are also culled from that source, and from the Public Record Office, London. Coupled with all this, I would wish to thank the present Countess of Sutherland for allowing various items in this chapter being brought to the notice of my Macleod friends.

In reading through some of the following addenda it may doubtless rouse the most fervent interest in the great family of Macleods wherever they may be—as well as reputed 'Historians' —to realise that Neil Macleod, XI of Assynt, must have handled some of these documents referred to, himself.

One of the most valuable is an Inventure (Inventory) dated 19th November 1662, of the 'Writs and Evidents' in Neil's Charter Chest. They were tied up in bundles according to subject, charters, receipts for land tax, loans from various individuals, each marked by a cryptic sign. Lord Migdale and Dr. A. L. Murray, Assistant Keeper of Records at H.M. General Register House, Edinburgh, helped in interpreting many of the old legal terms, so making it possible to identify the documents mentioned; e.g. the wadset, which was used so unscrupulously by Neil's enemies, and the bond for which he stood cautioner. As early as 12th June 1656, the Laird of Mey began putting pressure on him for payments.

One of the many stories handed down through generations concerns Neil, the eldest son of Donald Bàn Mor by his first wife. According to this, he was *not* the father, but the uncle, of the 'traitor'. He became engaged to a cousin, a certain Jessie Macleod, but went away to fight in a war on the Continent. After some time an old tramp arrived in Assynt with a message that Neil was a captive and expected to be executed next day. He then directed his nephew to marry his sweetheart, Jessie. The nuptials were duly celebrated, but a year later Uncle Neil turned up again! Jessie died within a week of a broken heart, her lover disappeared and was never heard of again, and his nephew Neil was ever after hated by his relations as a traitor. Perhaps one should check on this story, by going into facts. First, there is no mention of a Jessie Macleod in any of the genealogies investigated. Secondly, the first mention in the Inventory of Neil 'feare of Assint' (*i.e.* heir having title to an estate during his father's lifetime) is on 15th December 1610, in a marriage contract between himself and Florence McCleod—who was the 5th daughter of Torquil Conanach. Two days later she was granted the lease of five properties in Assynt. There is no mention of any children by the union until 31st July 1623, when Neil 'assigned Island Handa to his spous and daughter'.

Neil's name appears frequently until 1633. His last act was to grant a Charter to his father 'donald mcCleod alias Neilsone and Christian Ros his spous on the haill lands of assint daitit the threttene day of Junij 1633 yeiris'. His three younger brothers seem to have been ignored.

At this time the younger Neil would have been about five years old—a little young, one would think, to take over anyone's deserted sweetheart in marriage! But the date *does* confirm his own statement that his father died when he and his brother John were infants.

The contract between him and his spouse Christian Munro is dated 24th November 1649, the same date that his uncle Hugh granted him a Charter of the lands of Assynt. One doubts if much money came with this Disposition, because his father-in-law, Sir John Munro of Lemlair, on the same date granted him a mortgage on the lands, which gave him possession for about three years. The lands were renounced in favour of Neil on 15th October 1652; so it would seem that in 1650 Neil would have been very much under the influence of Lemlair.

In the case of the wadset the original creditor appears to have been a Mr. James Browne 'marchant burges of Bruntisland'. In those days a creditor could obtain a 'Decreit of Apprising', which gave him title to a debtor's lands subject to redemption on payment of the original debt, interest and legal expenses. A third party could, however, buy up the Apprising and take over the right. A creditor could even obtain a 'Decreit of Removing' which enabled him to eject tenants from lands as a means of asserting ownership. Mr. Browne obtained his 'Decreit of Apprising' on 2nd September 1634 'against donald McCleod alias neilsone for 3083 merks and 152 merks expenses'.

On 6th February 1636 he assigned this to Sir John Munro of Lemlair, who on 21st December that year transferred it to Thomas MacKenzie of Pluscardine, with consequences already recorded. By 18th February 1640 the 'soume' was stated to be 26,950 merkes.

Donald Bàn's wife, Christian, seems to have taken over the management of the estate about 1642. On 26th January that year the aged husband resigned it, nominally, into the hands of their eldest son, 'Donald younger'. Christian used the rents of Assynt to buy up Pluscardine's Apprising (and other debts), putting the bonds in the name of *her* son. She also bought Cambuscurry for her younger son, Hugh. The 'Inventure' confirms that the balance of the debt was paid off in two instalments—on 20th December 1642 at Edinburgh, and at Stornoway, Lewis, on 23rd September 1643, when Pluscardine legally disponed the Apprising in favour of Donald Og.

In 1683 Neil brought an action against his uncle Hugh for having failed to deliver to him all the 'Writs & Evidences' of the Estate of Assynt when he came of age in 1649. True there is a gap of five years, 1643 to 1648, in the lists of documents. During this period both Donalds died, the son before the father. It is known that old Donald was alive in May 1646, when he defended Ardvreck Castle during the Mackenzies' vicious raid on Assynt. The missing documents were not in the Charter Chest when it was stolen in 1672.

Seaforth's raid on Assynt in 1654 is the subject of the latest document to be discovered amongst the Geanies Papers. In a 'Suplication' addressed to General Monck, Neil complains of his lands of Assynt 'having been about the last of July invaded by the Lord Seafort now in arms against the Comon Wealth', and describes how 'they did burn and destroyed my lands in taking away our horses, kows and sheep to our outer rouine'. The signature is probably in Neil's own hand. On the reverse side there is a note certainly in General Monck's, dated from Dalkeith 20 Nov. 1654, which reads as follows: 'I desire Col. ffitche Governor of Inverness or Lieut.-Col. Blunt (in the Collonel's absence) to consider of the within peticon And to doe therein as hee shall thinke fit.'

The MacKenzies, in the 2nd indictment at the 1674 Trial, accused Neil of having led General Morgan and the 'rebels' to attack their territory, but in reality it was General Monck himself who had marched through Kintail in June/July 1654 in pursuit of General Middleton's Royalist troops. His despatches to Cromwell (at Worcester College, Oxford) prove that General Morgan was nowhere near Assynt at that time and so the indictment was dropped.

The charge of 'betrayal' was also abandoned. Later on Neil claimed that this was because he had already been assoilzied by an assize, as he had proved that he was 'alibi' on the day of Montrose's capture. Till recently there had been no legal proof of his statement, but now a document has been located amongst the State Papers in the Public Record Office in London, which provides valuable evidence. It is entitled 'Informatione Agst Assint' and consists of the arguments which Neil's lawyers put forward when he was arraigned in 1663, and the Lord Advocate's replies. (The extracts quoted are by permission of the Controller of H.M. Stationery Office.)

It begins: 'This is ane summonds of treasone exhibited at the instance of his Maties advocat against the sd assint wherein he is accussed for having not only denyed the Marquis of Montroes protectione but lykwayes gave intelligence to his father-in-law Limlair, or Hollburne, the Marqueis was at his house.'

The defence's case is that 'the lybell is not relevant because the day & place is not condescendit upon . . . and that if circumstances wer condescendit upon the defendar wold prove he was alibi.'

It is noteworthy that the defence did not deny the second charge, but claimed . . . 'the giveing nottice to Limlair was noe cryme becaus . . . anything that was done at that tyme was by violence & force quod excusat a crimine'.

A further proof that Neil himself was away from home is the Lord Advocate's accusation that the act was done 'at his own house by his own brother and servants'. His wife is not mentioned.

Lastly, the Lord Advocate declared that the indemnity that Assynt claimed under the Treaty of Breda did not apply in his case. Charles II, however, thought differently, though he took more than two years to answer the letter which the Privy Council wrote to him. Perhaps this document accompanied their letter to London, for there seems to be no record of it in Edinburgh.

After the Mackenzies, not content with robbing Neil of his lands, made a second attempt to deprive him of his honour and of life itself, he may well have exclaimed with Othello:

> . . . Who steals my purse steals trash.
> But he that filches from me my good name
> Robs me of that which not enriches him,
> And makes me poor indeed! . . .

The family, however, did not enjoy for long their ill-gotten gains. The Hon. John Mackenzie, in whose name so many of the unjustifiable deeds were perpetrated, failed to pay off a loan,

and was ejected from the property by his uncle, Roderick Mackenzie of Prestonhall. But Roderick's son, Alexander of Fraser-
dale, lost not only his lands but his life also after he was involved
in the 1715 rising.

As already mentioned, the Estate of Assynt was eventually sold
by the Government to the Sutherland family, in spite of the
protests of Capt. Hugh McLeod, 2nd of Geanies, who emphasised
that *he* and his ancestors had always been loyal to the Crown; he
had in 1745 raised 110 men from that very same Estate (snatching
the 'colours' from a MacDonald who was trying to recruit men
for Prince Charlie).

It is gratifying to be able to finish this paragraph by quoting a
letter from his son Donald, 3rd of Geanies: 'My father was at
one period very persevering in prosecuting his claims to the
Estate of Assynt, and so satisfied was the Government of the day
of the justice of those claims that on the sale of the Estate by the
Crown after discharging various debts and claims on it, the
residue, being a sum of £2000, was assigned and paid to him.'

(viii) A MACLEOD STORY
(unauthentic—of course!)

It is said that a Macleod and a Campbell—pronounced
'camel' very often in the Highlands—met, and had a hot argument as to which clan was the older. Said the Campbell, 'Man,
the Campbells were before the time of Abraham, Isaac and Jacob,
for do we not read in the Bible that when Isaac lifted up his eyes
he saw the Camels coming?'

'Ah! well,' said the other, 'the Macleods were afore the flood.'
'How could that be,' asked the Campbell, 'when we do not hear
of a Macleod coming out of Noah's Ark?' 'Noah's Ark,' said
Macleod, 'what would the Macleods be doing with Noah's
Ark? Whoever heard of a Macleod who hadn't got a boat of
his own?'

(ix) CONCLUSION

I fear there is little more I can usefully add in vindication of
Neil Macleod, the 11th and last Chief of Assynt, whose name has
borne the sinister reputation of being a betrayer of Montrose.

In delving into all the scattered documentary papers over the centuries and in attempting to unravel so much conflicting theories and views—to say nothing of untruths, which in those days seemed of little account to the chroniclers—I am hopeful readers interested in this historical chapter will appreciate the endeavour to make a fairly connected narrative coupled with some traditional allusions. All told, I feel it was as difficult as the Egyptian task of having to make bricks without straw. As far as I am aware this is the very first lengthy and serious documentary attempt ever made since 1650 to uncover the incredible lies made with such apparent pleasing nonchalance by so many people in those far-off days. But public opinion then was more gullible than it is today. I have said many of the extracts appear for the *first* time in these pages. *They should be of incalculable historic value.*

If history has ever heaped defamation and slander on any man's good name for having merely done his duty, it has surely done so on Neil Macleod; a man whom I described in the Text as the *Beau Ideal* of a Highland gentleman. Under the circumstances, I think he should be classed one of the Great Men of Scottish history.

*　　*　　*

I have said doubts still exist.

It is strange, doubts are the things that appear to unite mankind; whereas strong beliefs or convictions seem to separate them.

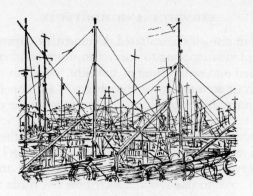

CHAPTER 13

HIGHLAND FISHERIES

*T*hey *that go down to the sea in ships.* . . . A town lives—and dies—by the sea. *Fishers also shall mourn and they that spread nets on the waters shall languish.* . . . And so one could carry on these apt quotations relating to the cruel sea; for such are the hazards of deep-sea fishing, and later on in this chapter I will be unfolding the sad side to the happy fishermen and their wives.

But first of all, some information of a general nature.

The people of the west coast of Scotland are specially interested in fishing, and by that I do not mean just fishing for salmon or trout, but for sake of a better name, I mean 'the catching fleet' or the fishing boats that are manned by men from the east coast, and fish the Minch from Gairloch, Ullapool, Lochinver and Kinlochbervie.

You can spend many an hour on a Highland pier just watching and watching, and being interested all the time at the various activities going on; the boats coming in with a majesty of their own and with a perfect sweep to tie up alongside the pier or alongside another boat. No fuss or bother; everything sails in with smoothness and precision. There is much to occupy you in all this. And what of the names of these tidy ship-shape boats? *Ocean Dawn, Flashing Stream, Morning Star, Guiding Star, Silver Cord, Coral Strand, Pilot Me, Harvest Moon, Dewy Rose, Guide Us, Amber Queen,* to name but a few; and all with their identification marks as from where they came.

Its part of the holiday people will tell you, to take an evening stroll down to the little grey harbour to see these boats dock as gulls scream greedily overhead, and the men in blue jerseys or vivid coloured oil-skins swinging the heavy fish boxes on to the quay; boxes laden with the finest quality fish in the world, taken only a few miles off-shore.

Over the past few years striking developments of the white fish industry have taken place particularly in LOCHINVER and KINLOCHBERVIE harbours. It is barely 25 years ago when only two fishing boats were working out of Lochinver, from Culag pier, and the value of the landing was about £6000. Today there are upwards of forty boats in daily service and landings now amount to over £500,000. Nowadays, prawns and lobsters are playing an ever important part in the landings, and providing a very lucrative business as a side-line to the white fish catchings. A lot of pioneer work has been involved in attaining the present position at both Lochinver and Kinlochbervie, and great credit is due the fishermen from the east coast who worked there under primitive conditions for years. The co-operation received from them and from buyers from the east coast helped to overcome the difficult conditions under which they worked. The same may be said or the other west Highland ports. Very ambitious boat-building schemes are on hand and in any success resulting, the staff, including the long-distance drivers, share in the credit.

In all these matters, every endeavour is being made to entice the fishermen and their families to live in the ports from which they fish by building houses for them, instead of the men having to go home the many miles involved each week-end (which is generally from late Thursday to 6.0 a.m. Monday). How much better this would be. Of course all this takes time, but as the years pass, we will see Lochinver and Kinlochverbie a much bigger fishing community than ever before. The Culag pier has been enlarged and strengthened and has an up-to-date ice plant. New oil installation plants envisaged will greatly increase the efficiency of these ports and make them very much self-contained. The Royal National Mission for Deep Sea Fishermen have a mission station at both these places named and this is an amenity much appreciated by the men using these harbours, and fixes in fishermen's minds the idea that these are solid ports.

The fishing port of KINLOCHBERVIE consists of two landing

jetties placed on each side of the isthmus of a small peninsula. Loch Clash, to the north, is the old landing place and behind the jetty are the offices, ice plant and chandler's shop owned by Pulford (Scotland) Ltd. who are the local fish salesmen and operate the nightly auction. The boats generally come in around 6.0 p.m. This pier is open to the north-west and so is often not a safe anchorage. Loch Bervie nearby to the south is completely land-locked. According to the fishermen it is the safest harbour in Scotland, and is sometimes referred to as *Loch Safety*. Over the years more and more of the heavy landings of prime fish have been sold from Loch Bervie and fewer from Loch Clash. I have seen as many as 50 boats resting safely round the pier in Loch Bervie. The whole harbour makes a beautiful picture as you look down upon it from the main road to Oldshoremore. The entrance channel to Loch Bervie has been deepened recently, after the sad loss of the Banff fishing boat *Refleurir* on 3rd January 1968 with a crew of five on board, to which I allude later in this chapter. Before this deepening, at low spring tide there was only four to five feet of water in the channel and even the small boats could neither enter nor leave. A covered market in which to sell the fish has been erected. One has only to think of one black January night a year or so ago, and the grim conditions with sleet rolling in from Cape Wrath, and 1500 boxes of fish to be sold, iced and loaded without a scrap of cover for the men who did not finish till midnight.

Messrs. Pulford are doing a great job at Kinlochbervie and taking every opportunity in development. Already four new families, from as far apart as Gloucester and Orkney have come to live at Kinlochbervie in consequence. Pulfords are also interested in backing fishermen in acquiring new boats, especially if this means more fishermen living in the West.

To give some idea of the importance of this picture-postcard fishing port, it should be realised that with the sister port of Lochinver and the herring port of Ullapool and some smaller landing places in the north-west, these districts have the second highest landings in Scotland, behind only Aberdeen district where the deep-water boats land.

Surely this is of exceptional significance. Landings here vary between a million and a million and a half stone of prime one-day fish each year. To sum up, progress will become spectacular, and all set to encourage more locals to fish and to encourage established fishers to come and live up in the north-west, introducing new methods and techniques. And above all, not to be afraid of change.

In all this I would mention the name of Mr. F. B. Drakard, head of the Sutherland Transport and Trading Co., who has now transferred his headquarters from Lairg to Kinlochbervie in order to be constantly on the spot to lend his special genius to all the improvements required to this fishing industry.

*   *   *

I now turn to four other fishing items; one of lighter vein, the other three, however, bringing sad memories of very recent times.

The first is about the *Politician*—the wreck of the *Politician* in 1941, the time of the Second World War.

A bell stands outside the church on a small island in the Outer Hebrides, the island of Eriskay. But the ship is not the *Politician* (the whisky galore vessel I am about to relate) which foundered nearby. The bell comes from the German battle-cruiser *Derfflinger*, scuttled in Scapa Flow at the end of the First World War.

The *Politician* was a British merchantman of 12,000 tons, registered at Liverpool. On a February evening in 1941, this vessel went ashore upon a rock immediately at the east of Calvay, an islet in the shallow Sound of Eriskay. It is a mystery how any ship of her size came to grief at this spot even under the black-out conditions of war-time then prevailing. It is supposed her navigator mistook the Sound of Eriskay for the Sound of Barra. The latter separates the south end of Eriskay from Barra; the former intervenes between the north end of the island and South Uist, is much more constricted and is so shallow that when crossing it by small boat at low water even on a moderately calm day the eye has to closely follow the sandy sea-floor all the way—merely a dozen feet below.

An island fisherman said as to the shipwreck, 'Och, well, it would be the whisky aboard that would be putting her off course.'

Thereby hangs a tale of orgy and drunkenness surpassing any in the history of the islands. The boat was affectionately called 'The Polly'.

Little mention of this wreck was made public owing to

wartime secrecy. There was a slight reference in the press in the autumn of 1941, when a few of those who had helped themselves too liberally to the 'Polly's' cargo were brought before the sheriff at Lochmaddy, and sentenced to varying terms of imprisonment up to two months for offences against the excise laws. Otherwise one knew little of what had occurred except that the Islanders were said to have enjoyed the most convivial spell in living memory.

The first indication the inhabitants of Eriskay had that anything unusual had happened was given by the steamer's siren, the constant blare of which rudely disturbed the peace of this historic and romantic isle, and even filled many of them with fear. Young and old hastened in the direction from which the blare was coming. They arrived at the beach opposite Calvay to find a great ship firmly aground, roughly 100 yards off shore. Soon the crew were landed in Eriskay and there they remained for some days receiving at the hands of the inhabitants the hospitality for which that isle has long been renowned. The 'Polly' meanwhile lay stranded and completely abandoned. For several weeks no one came near her. Soon it began to be whispered among the islanders that whisky comprised the bulk of her cargo. This prompted verification!! Some of them now visited her at high water in small boats and found her full of whisky. Cases of it lay partly submerged in her enormous hold. With this discovery there now began what some have described as 'the greatest saga of the Outer Hebrides in modern times'; but which certain members of the clergy in the locality said was probably one of the most disastrous episodes in which the islander had ever been involved.

News of this palatable treasure spread like wildfire throughout the Isles. People arrived on the scene from as far north as Lewis, and from as far south as Mull. They came armed with ropes, rods, hooks and all manner of contraptions for the fishing out of the ship's interior as much as possible of the whisky she carried. Rumour had it that the vessel contained a million bottles. In point of fact, she had 20,300 cases or 243,000 bottles, there being a dozen bottles to a case. The whisky—the best Scotch, and overproof at that—was on its way to the American market. The unloading of the cases continued day and night. The unlawful removal of the intoxicating cargo went on unceasingly. In the dead of night, fifty or so men, black beyond recognition with oil, might be seen in the hold with their bright Tilly lamps, standing up to their thighs in oil and sea water probing, tugging, hauling and slinging cases of whisky to the upper decks.   You couldn't visit the 'Polly' without meeting someone you knew; you would meet people there from all the other islands that you hadn't seen for years.   Cases were removed from her by the hundred, and in Eriskay and also in Barra and South Uist, whisky was now so plentiful that the islanders thought nothing of sprinkling half a bottle of it over a fire to make it burn more vigorously.   They were using it as a substitute for paraffin.   The 'Polly's' whisky revived many a sluggish peat fire.   Never had liquor been so ubiquitous.   Young and old made merry on it. In Eriskay life became a perpetual revelry.   Nearly everyone fell under the influence.   Little work was done without liberal potations.   'Thou shalt not dilute whisky' (the 11th Commandment as it is called in Scotland) was strictly observed.   Whisky and plenty of it must be 'Knocked ower' neat.   The very poultry were drunk in Eriskay; while pecking about the crofts or on the sands of the machair, they would come upon dregs or broken bottles.   And so it went on.

   Gradually, stories of this era of abounding hospitality began to filter through to the mainland.   In due course the attention of the Ministry of Shipping and of the Customs authorities was at last directed to Eriskay.   A night watchman was now placed aboard the 'Polly' and the island invaded in large numbers by police and excise officials.   This intrusion occasioned great alarm. No one had come near for weeks, and since the war was still raging, it never occurred to the revellers that anyone would ever land to claim the wreck and its contents.   The method of the ancient fiery cross was now resorted to, lest any inhabitant should be caught unawares.   In attempts to conceal the great quantities of liquor still unconsumed, every imaginable deception was adopted.   Bottles hung up in chimneys; stuffed into the thatch of cottage, barn, byre or henhouse.   Like Achan of old they buried their treasure in the ground, deep down among the potatoes and the sown corn of Eriskay, of Uist and of Barra the bottles went. Never had there been such digging for Victory!   Cases buried on the moors, or on the shore.   Burying became second nature. Everyone cunningly hid their treasures from the dreaded excise officers. With the good weather, there came a spiritual resurrection.

Every stack of corn or peat concealed the amber bottles. Spring mattresses were found very serviceable. Elderly natives, though hale and hearty were bundled off to bed, surrounded by a heap of bedclothes, so bamboozling the prying officers. Hot water bottles filled with whisky; water tanks emptied and filled with the precious stuff. The search continued unabated. Not even a dung-hill escaped attention. The silver sands upon which Bonnie Prince Charlie disembarked from the French frigate just two centuries earlier, were probed with the prying appliances. Bottles were buried in places which the natives, 'midst their subsequent confusion, afterwards failed to locate. Even a year later the ferryman salvaged clandestinely no fewer than 2000 bottles.

Some of the whisky carried by the 'Polly' was contained in firmly corked decanters, labelled 'Highland Nectar'. In course of time a salvage tug reached Eriskay and dragged the 'Polly' off the rocks; she was then cut in two. The fore-half of her was towed into Lochmaddy to await suitable weather for the long voyage to Rothesay. The stern half got stuck beyond recovery on a submerged sandbank between Eriskay and Calvay, and there she sank deeper and deeper, taking with her hundreds of cases of the precious liquor.

Whisky was not the only cargo the ill-fated *Politician* had aboard her; she carried thousands of yards of shirting. Dozens of bicycles were also taken off her unlawfully; some had never seen a bicycle before. Scores of bottles of perfume; children brought them to school, and the schoolroom became scented like a beauty parlour. Toothpaste also; hundreds of tubes were taken from the wreck. The children found diversion in squirting the paste at one another—smeared upon everything, clothes, hair, limbs, seats and school-books.

Some of the elderly actually died following such excessive drinking orgies.

Sure, the 'Polly' had a popular cargo!

*   *   *

I commenced this chapter with a quotation from Isaiah, ch. 19, v. 8 . . . '*The fishers also shall mourn, and all they that cast angle into the brooks shall lament, and they that spread nets upon the waters shall languish*' . . . and now I turn to relate three sad sea disasters. One,

the loss of the Banff fishing boat *Refleurir* off Kinlochbervie on
the 3rd January 1968 with a crew of five on board; the other, the
loss of the Fraserburgh lifeboat on 21st January 1970 with a crew of
six aboard, five being drowned; and the third, the loss of the Longhope (Orkney) lifeboat crew of eight men on 18th March 1969.

First, the *Refleurir*. Although I referred to this disaster in
Highland Pearls, I feel I must detail some of that sad story again,
in order to build up to the poem given later.

The disaster happened just outside the harbour during a gale-
driven blizzard in the North Minch. It was a tragedy that swept
over the entire district. The *Refleurir* lies wrecked at the bottom
of the sea. The 58-feet boat made her last radio call when she
was only ninety minutes from harbour, where she was due at
1 p.m. Then there was silence; and as darkness fell, fears
mounted for the 50-year-old skipper, George West of Gardenstown, and his crew. The boats that had already berthed in harbour
were virtually locked in from going out to help, for the tide was
then too low for their boats to sail through. The Lochinver
lifeboat was launched in the gale. The R.A.F. said they would
send an aircraft to help search at first light if weather permitted.
The *Refleurir* put to sea at 5 a.m. on the 3rd January, when the
North Minch was described as being like a mill-pond. Subsequently the weather became violent and atrocious and it was
thought the boat would have sought shelter in one of the many
bays around the coast. The following morning grief was tinged
with frustration when all hope for the crew was abandoned. As
the boats were unable to get out, the men felt they were robbed of
at least a slim attempt of saving their fellow men; and for the
time being, until the tide was suitable, they could only wonder
frantically if some or all of that crew were hanging grimly on to
life. Twenty-five boats were in harbour, because the rocky
entrance was so shallow for them to get out. The next morning
there was still a little armada of twenty-five boats, and a Shackle-
ton aircraft from Kinloss combing the area, and coastguards and
volunteers, some sixty in all, were searching the rugged coastline
—but in vain. Oil flecks and bubbles were spotted five miles
west of the entrance to Loch Inchard. It was the *Refleurir's* first
trip of the New Year. Wives and sweethearts mourned behind
drawn curtains all along the Banffshire coast. The disaster left
six sons and daughters fatherless. Two young women who were

K

married only a year have been made widows; a pretty girl who was to be married six months later lost her fiancé. This heartbreak story—so common with fisherfolk—was shared by all along the north-east coast. Over a hundred fishermen together with a host of people of the district, attended the memorial service for the drowned men, which was held in the Church of Scotland; Mr. Mathew Hopper, their present missionary at the Loch Clash Deep Sea Mission, conducted the service; and the local organist, Mr. John A. Morrison, rendered appropriate sacred music. Most of these fishermen belong to the Close Brethren, the religious sect whose members keep their own counsel and hide themselves and their grief behind closed doors. At this sad time in Gardenstown, a little village clinging to the side of a huge black cliff like a limpet, the streets were empty and silent. No dogs barked, no youngsters shouted. Only the sound of grey waves pounding on the jagged rocks provided a link with reality. One old man at the harbour stood facing the cruel sea, and said, 'Fisherfolk expect this sort of thing. God gives, and He takes away.' That was all; he said no more. Doors remained closed to any knocking. The small fishing fleet from this wee place is the most modern of fleets, and earns nearly £1 million in the course of a single year. Yet in Gardenstown, they show the world no joy when times are good—and no sadness when tragedy strikes. Another old man there said he hoped the men would be found, but, he added, 'they are in God's hands'. Like the old man at the harbour, he had nothing more to say.

In connection with this disaster, I record below a poem given me through the widow of one of the crew members, which was composed by someone in Gardenstown in memory of the five men. The seven verses have been a comfort to many who were related to the crew, and I feel privileged to print them. They were—more or less—for private circulation and so have not been publicised before. The poem bore the caption, 'In loving memory of crew of M.B. *Refleurir* lost at sea 3rd January 1968'; and is titled SAFELY ANCHORED.

> Lord we are waiting for the morning,
> For the brightest and the best,
> We shall hail its glorious dawning,
> And shall join our Lord—at last;
> Yes—their warfare's sooner over

And their triumph's sooner won,
They are safely over Jordan,
They are with the Lord—at Home.

Many loved ones sadly miss them,
Here their fellowship was sweet,
And their presence cheered life's pathway
With their radiant smile to greet;
No—they did not want to leave us,
Earthly ties were sweet and strong.
God Himself did plan and twine them
So secure—until He come.

Now their stormy voyage's over
And their anchor safely cast,
They have found a place of refuge,
Safe from every stormy blast;
With their loving Lord and Saviour,
He who knew their work was done,
Called them up to Higher Service;
They have heard the glad—'Well Done.'

Waiting, watching, soon to meet them
With His own He'll come again.
Balm of Heaven to spirits wounded
Soon with Christ and them to reign.
This our hope the Lord has given
While as Pilgrims here we roam,
We shall meet again in Heaven
When our work on earth is done.

Pondering o'er their youthful service
Gladly spent, dear Lord, for Thee,
Telling forth the wondrous Story
Of Thy Love upon the Tree.
Truly they have left their footprints
On the fleeting sands of time,
Truly they were oft with Jesus
Searching out His Holy Mind.

Till then Lord still keep us faithful,
Lamps all trimmed and burning bright,
Waiting, watching for the Bridegroom,
For He just may come tonight;
And He'll call them from the ocean

And from the quiet silent grave,
For it was the Lord who took them
And it was the Lord who gave.

No more watching the horizon,
No more waiting for the tide,
They have cast the Heavenly Anchor
On a fairer, calmer side.
Lord we leave them in Thy keeping,
Blessed thought, with them 'tis well,
Anchored in the Heavenly Harbour,
Safely Home—with Christ—to Dwell.

*   *   *

When a town lives—and dies—by the sea.

I come now to the sad loss of the Fraserburgh lifeboat on 21st
January 1970.

Scottish lifeboat crews live one call away from tragedy. A
truth given terrible emphasis by the fate of these five men. They
put out to sea to answer a distress signal. The boat overturned.
Normally this means total disaster, but on this occasion, because
of the proximity of a Russian ship, one man is saved to prevent
the raging cruel seas from winning a total victory. Seamanship
and good fortune saved him.

That Wednesday night they mourned quietly in the Aberdeenshire fishing town of Fraserburgh. Demonstration is not in
their character when such a shock hits them. They live by the
sea, which gives them their daily bread, and they are prepared
to die by the sea. They never pause to question their fate, these
people whose faith and courage mark them out in the category
of very special human beings. (There was a similar disaster one
winter's day in 1953, when seven men lost their lives—and their
boat. When a meeting was called the following week to recruit
a new crew, it was at once filled; for the men who go down to
the sea in little ships do not stop to count the cost. The lifeboat
duty is a mission of mercy, which they themselves, as fishermen,
may need tomorrow; so they go to help save the lives of men
from home and foreign ports who would do the same for them.
Just as they did on 21st January 1970, and just as they did all their
yesterdays. Just as they went in 1940 when they sailed away from

Fraserburgh and Peterhead with their small fishing boats to rescue men from the beaches of Dunkirk. It is the way of things.) Truly the action of these brave lifeboatmen redeems our society and restores our self-respect.

The coxswain of the boat was John Stephen, who left a wife and two daughters. In all, five wives were left and fifteen children.

Ten thousand people answered the call when the lifeboat maroons went off in the heartbroken fishing town. Shoulder to shoulder they encircled the centuries-old greystone parish church. They lined the streets, 10-deep in places, and when at 3 p.m. the twin bang of the maroons shattered the stillness, they went with the lifeboatmen of Fraserburgh on their last voyage. Men and women wept unashamedly, as parish minister the Rev. Andrew Mitchell spoke of their heritage from the sea: '*It appears to be the destiny of this community that, time after time, we have to bear the brunt of sacrifice.*' The voices of a thousand people in the church were relayed by loudspeaker to the square outside where another 9000 mourners joined with them in singing one of the great seamen's hymns—'Jesus, Saviour, pilot me, over life's tempestuous sea . . .' Then led by the tall figure of the Duke of Kent, president of the Royal National Lifeboat Institution, the huge cortège moved slowly through the town to the Kirkton cemetery. For the Duke it was a poignant moment. Sixteen years ago, his mother commissioned this Fraserburgh lifeboat, naming it *Duchess of Kent*, after herself. Lifeboatmen from all over Britain walked behind in the half-mile procession, which took twenty-five minutes to pass through the town. But it was at the graveside that full pathos of the occasion came. Widows and children broke down. Outside in the town every shop was closed and blinds drawn at every window. In the harbour the fishing fleet was tied up, the crews ashore to mourn their friends in time of need—the lifeboatmen. The maroons signalled the last voyage of Coxswain John Stephen and his gallant crew. The lifeboatmen took their last trip on a calm day with little wind and good visibility.

The memorial address was delivered at the funeral by 80-year-old Lord Saltoun of Cairnbulg, known throughout Scotland as the lifeboatmen's friend. He commenced by saying, 'We are here today to commend to the mercy of God the souls of our comrades recently lost; and to thank Him for the example of their lives.' Carrying on, he said some trenchant things about our present society and that one did not feel very civilised about same. But then he said, 'One learns a lifeboat has put out to help some vessel in distress, encountering all hazards, with no thought of reward, just because the men are those kind of men. It is true to say that these men by redeeming our society from its petty unworthiness have followed, as well as men can, the footsteps of our Master.'

*   *   *

The third tragedy is that of the loss of the Longhope lifeboat crew of eight men on 18th March 1969, when their boat was swamped and overwhelmed by heavy seas in the Pentland Firth off the island of Hoy in the Orkneys. Seven of these gallant men were buried in the cemetery of Osmondwall; the eighth man was never found. On the 9th August 1970, the Queen Mother flew across the Firth to unveil two memorials to the former lifeboat crew. One was a plaque set into the outer west wall of Walls Old Kirk, and given by the Coastguards of Orkney. At the cemetery the Queen Mother unveiled a life-size bronze statue of a lifeboatman standing on a stone cairn looking out to the Pentland Firth from which lifeboatmen of Longhope have saved more than 600 seamen in the past 96 years. More than 500 travelled to Longhope by ships large and small to attend this tear-stained ceremony. The Queen Mother stood near the widows and families in the old stone church and sang with them Hymn 84, 'Fierce was the billow wild.'

There is more to all this though, for behind almost every lifeboatman (or for that matter every man who sails the seas) stands a woman; for it is hers to wait, to hope, and to pray standing by the shore. And all the time knowing that possibly one day she will wait in vain. Surely there is heroism here? Words fail me in expressing my realisations of all this involves in those that go down to the sea in ships; those who when joining a lifeboat crew are put the question, 'Are you prepared to die?'

All you and I can do, is to commit these brave souls to the care of the Lord, saying with the prophet, 'The souls of the righteous are in the hands of God; there, shall no torment touch them.'

So ends my tribute to heroes in cockleshells.

*   *   *

Over the past four years, the Highlands and Islands Development Board has invested over £1½ m. in the fishing industry in the Highlands. When there is added to this the grant aid contributions made by the statutory fishing authorities for the purchase of new boats, the total public investment is of the order of £2 million—an all-round demonstration of faith in the future of fishing.

*   *   *

Since writing these lines, I have to record a further sad event in the loss of the seine-netter *Rosebud II*, which foundered on the Torran rocks off the south coast of Mull on 14th December 1970 with all its crew of seven. This fishing boat came from the Morayshire port of Burghead (pop. 1400).

Once again a small village was plunged into mourning. The sea which God created, makes all equal; and equally the sad bereavement is shared by the people. 'They cried come soon, come soon,' yet the cruel sea, without horizons, swept o'er them. It is a strange coincidence that when Robert Louis Stevenson wrote his book *Kidnapped*, the shipwreck depicted was on these same Torran rocks.

In the days before radar giving weather forecasts for shipping and such like, every fishing boat carried a barometer, which, as we all know up in the Highlands, is a very handy thing to have about the house and gives a clear warning of weather changes.

The fishing boat I have in mind was out in the Minch when a storm blew up, and the ship was getting a real tossing and all looked ominous; visibility was down to nil. So the captain, who was having a hot drink, told one of the crew to go along and look at the barometer reading. Reeling backwards and forwards, old Hughie struggled manfully to the wheel-house, only to find the barometer had fallen off its hook and was broken in two, the needle having dropped down past the 26 mark. Stormy did you say, 'Chust that and more, chust that,' said Hughie to himself. In all alarm he rushed back as fast as his reeling steps would allow him to the captain who said, 'Well, what's it reading, Hughie?' Hughie spluttered out, 'Cap'n, it's chust terrible; in fact I think we're in for an earthquake; chust that, chust that!'

CHAPTER 14

DORNOCH AND EASTERN SUTHERLAND

WHILST I realise the towns of the east coast of Sutherland
—embracing Dornoch, Golspie, Brora and Helmsdale
—are not strictly within the orbit of the west's Shangri-
La territory (for the environments have not the majestic scenery
as the west, nor the complete peacefulness)—yet it seems fitting
to devote a little of this book to drawing readers and visitors attention as to what they may find in that area, especially if they
have sporting inclinations such as golf.

DORNOCH, delectable Dornoch, has only a population of 1000,
but this figure increases two or three times that number during
the summer months by reason of being such a favourite resort.
It is known as the Cathedral city; the St. Andrews of the North
to golfers; the historic County capital of Sutherland; and is a
Royal Burgh. It is 14 miles away from Bonar Bridge. One of
the charms of Dornoch is its sequestered squares, making the town
very open, and is a great centre for many interests. The illustration
at the head of this chapter is a striking view of the Cathedral
which dates back to the early 13th century and is still in use; so
we may term Dornoch an Ancient Cathedral town, small and
tranquil, lying by the sea in the mild, dry south-east corner of
the county.

It is one of the fourteen ancient cities of Scotland. It was an
ancient settlement of the Culdee Church dating from the 6th

century A.D. and remains of kitchens denote a history of settlement going back perhaps to 3000 B.C. Dornoch was elected into a Royal Burgh by Charter of Charles I, dated 14th July 1628.

The town is noted for its golf course; it is the third oldest course mentioned in history still in use—a championship course rated by Americans as one of the six best in the world; 'The Royal Dornoch Golf Links' of International standard. The six historic links with date of first mention are St. Andrews, 1552; Leith, 1593; Dornoch, 1616; Montrose, 1628; Aberdeen, 1642; Musselburgh, 1672. Many 'open' events take place from June to September.

Close to the Cathedral stands what remains of the Bishop's Palace, now called Dornoch Castle, a stately turreted pile which contributes largely to the venerable appearance of the Burgh. Though only one of the towers and the Bishop's kitchen chimney have survived, they suffice to indicate the original extent and importance of the building. This interesting old pile to which has been added a large modern wing, has served successively as the Bishop's Palace, the residence of Sir Robert Gordon (the great benefactor of Dornoch in early days), the Tolbooth, the County Court House, the Prison; and after the renovation, the residence of the local Sheriff. It is now an hotel.

I must make mention of the WITCH STONE. In a garden close by the golf course on the lower links, a simple slab of rough, bluish whin-stone bearing the date 1722 marks the spot where the burning of the last witch in Scotland took place. The charge against her was the ludicrous one of transforming her daughter into a pony to ride to the witches' meeting place, and having her shod by the devil!

Miles of golden sands afford excellent and safe bathing. There are facilities for tennis and bowling; good fishing may be had locally.

Reverting to the Cathedral, it was said to have been erected by Bishop Gilbert in the first half of the 13th century as I have just said; one source gives the date as A.D. 1224, but it was burnt down in 1570 by the Master of Caithness and Mackay of Strathnaver, and the ruin was further destroyed by gales in 1605. A certain amount of reconstruction was undertaken in the year 1616, otherwise the building remained in a ruinous condition until 1835, when it was rebuilt from the foundations with the exception of the central tower resting on lancet arches springing from shafted pillars, the old windows being more or less preserved. The church contains the tombs of the Sutherland family, relics of Sir Richard de Moravia, brother of Saint Gilbert, and a statue by Chantrey of the first Duke of Sutherland. This imposing statue stands at the west end of the nave. The full size monument in Carrara marble is a wonderful specimen of Sir Francis Chantrey's sculpture.

During the years succeeding the Reformation, the cathedral entered on a new phase of its history, and for the past four hundred years it has continued its spiritual function as the parish church of Dornoch. On entering the church the atmosphere is one of simple dignity. Its fine proportions give the building a suggestion of more space than it actually has. There are twenty-three stained glass windows. One on the south wall by Francis Spear of London erected in 1952, commemorates the life and service of Brigadier General Sir George Paynter, K.C.V.O., C.M.G., D.S.O., Lord-Lieutenant of Sutherland. The main subject is St. George, patron saint of soldiers, slaying the dragon. Also in the window are St. Andrew for Scotland, St. Peter for fishermen, St. Hubert for huntsmen and St. Gilbert for Dornoch. An organ was installed in the north transept in 1893.

This cathedral has a clear power of communication that tells better than recorded history, 'here surely has been the cradle of religion in the north'. In fact Dornoch itself is a corruption of the Gaelic for 'the holy place'. In its present state the cathedral is still a beautiful edifice, endowed with beautiful proportions. For over seven hundred years now, it has withstood the ravages of time, an abiding witness to the glory of God and of the permanence of things spiritual amid the transience of all things earthly.

* * *

Meikle Ferry crosses the Dornoch Firth near Dornoch, and it was across this ferry that a major disaster took place in 1809 when the overcrowded ferry-boat sank in mid-stream with the loss of 98 people on board. It was carrying 110 men, women and children. As to ferry regulations in those days, none existed, and so the public were obliged to submit to the caprice and humour of the ferryman. This of itself was an evil of the first magnitude, particularly as the ferrymen were permitted to sell whisky. Irregularities of many natures were of frequent occurrence; in fact, at some times, mere boys were left to manage the boat if the ferryman had other and more lucrative work on hand; and these boys sometimes sought the assistance of passengers. In this sad disaster, the boat was very much overloaded; a sudden squall encountered across the Firth caused panic, and the boat capsized with, as I have said, ninety-eight people (including the Sheriff-Substitute of Dornoch) losing their lives. Twelve only were saved. It struck a fearful blow to the community as can well be imagined. The Great Ferry Disaster of 1809.

Dornoch offers excellent opportunities for the study of ornithology, zoology, botany and archaeology 'midst an unspoiled country.

It may not be generally known, but Dornoch's most valuable asset is its extraordinarily dry and sunny climate; and this is no tourist propaganda message. The strip of the east Sutherland coast which extends from Dornoch at the mouth of its great Firth northwards by Golspie to Brora is one of Scotland's dry areas. On fine dry days one can see north up to the Ord of Caithness (beyond Helmsdale) with Brora, Golspie, Dunrobin and Embo as landmarks. Then ten miles to the east is Tarbet Ness with its lighthouse; Tain to the south across the Firth; Struie. And on a very clear day, the Cairngorms and Braeriach—seventy miles off; and when the sky is blue and the sea deep blue with the hills and moors purple, the fields green and gold, one can realise what colours are presented. And as I have remarked of Shangri-La on a clear day one can *see for ever*.

Both Norsemen and the Danes recognised Dornoch as a delectable area at which to beach their ships, to land and to settle —as did they on the western seaboard. The Norse were defeated in the 9th century, and the later-coming Danes in the 13th. Strange how often these fierce raiders and invaders from Scandinavia picked on what are now favourite holiday places; like Rothesay in its sheltered bay, and the Isle of Man.

It is a long way from Dornoch to Iona (off the isle of Mull), but there is something I should say about Iona here. It was *not* the first Christian community in Scotland; Dornoch can prove that, for St. Fiunbarr (with whom St. Columba had a grievance) had a settlement here before ever St. Columba was banished from

Ireland. The monastery was over-run later by the Norse invaders. Later on, Dornoch academy was built on the site.

*   *   *

I cannot leave this account of Dornoch without paying tribute to one of its greatest men of the 20th century, namely, the Rev. William MacLeod, D.L., J.P., M.A., who was the senior minister of Dornoch, who preached the Gospel in the Free Church there for over forty years—from 1928 until his death on 15th December 1969. He was mourned, not only within the bounds of the Church he served for so long, but by a multitude of friends he had made during his many years of public life. He was held in the highest esteem and affection by young and old alike for he was a minister of quite outstanding ability.

He was born in Arnol in the favoured Isle of Lewis, which has given us many eminent ministers, and received his early education in the Nicolson Institute, Stornoway. He died at the comparatively early age of 76.

Mr. MacLeod's administrative abilities came to light when, in his early ministry, he was Clerk to the Presbytery of Glasgow. After serving as Junior Clerk of Assembly, he was elevated to the Principal Clerkship in 1949, retiring from that position in 1963. He took more than his share of Standing Committee work, and at some time or other he was Convener of almost every Committee of the Church. Shortly after coming to Dornoch, he saw fit to place his talents at the disposal of the people of Sutherland through the medium of the County Council on which body he served for 36 years; and for the last six of those years he occupied the Convener's Chair. Concurrently with his last years on the County Council, Mr. MacLeod was Provost of Dornoch, of which he was made a Freeman in 1964. He was elected Moderator of the General Assembly in 1940. What a history to be sure— and one to be proud of too. The sanctity of the Lord's Day was near to his heart and he fearlessly asserted its claims. His wife predeceased him by ten years. He is survived by one son, Dr. Alan MacLeod, who is a psychiatric consultant in a Northampton hospital.

*   *   *

In the light of what I have just written I would say there has been a tendency on the east coast to lose respect for the old ways of life, and a desire to become more up to date and give religion the go-by. Whilst the older generation keep up the old traditions, the younger folk in this age of ours are no longer so interested. T/V I think has much to do with this slant of life. Dornoch folk used to deplore the number of visitors who rushed in and out of the burgh by car on the Sabbath making it a week-day tour to the north or the west coast; and to go off to play golf at Tain, or even farther away. Due to pressure from hoteliers and such like, about six years ago Dornoch also 'fell' and there is now Sunday golf on the links. I am afraid to think with the passing away of such a godly man as the Rev. Mr. MacLeod, the Sabbath will fast become an ordinary week-day.

GOLSPIE, population 1600, lies eleven miles up the coast from Dornoch. It is an attractive small town in the shadow of Ben Bhraggie (1256 feet) on whose summit is a monument, 105 feet high, erected in 1834, to the 1st Duke of Sutherland. This monument can be seen for miles around. Building, agriculture and estate work provide local employment. There is also a small gasworks opened in 1862 and close to the golf links. Sutherland County Council have their main office here. (The Council Chamber is in Dornoch.) A school hostel for girls, named 'Mackay House Hostel', and another one for boys called 'Mac-Leod House Hostel' are provided in Golspie village for girls and boys attending the High School. It also has the general hospital for the county, known as the Lawson Memorial Hospital.

Golspie, by long association with the Sutherland family, maintains the character of a ducal village, necessarily growing as a complement to Dunrobin Castle, now a Public School in the Gordonstoun tradition, opened in September 1965. The school is controlled by a Board of Governors, of which the Countess of Sutherland is a member; and it caters for boys from 13 years to university standard. It is able to provide accommodation and facilities for at least 200 boys.

Dunrobin Castle, the historic home of the Dukes and Earls of Sutherland, stands on the coast one mile out of Golspie. It is a lovely castle with impressive towers and turrets which give it an almost foreign appearance. The original Keep is said to date from the early 12th century and was built by Robert, 3rd Earl of Sutherland, the name Dunrobin meaning the mote or hill of Robert, and it commands a magnificent view over the Moray

Firth; and the gardens modelled on Versailles present a striking contrast to the rugged background of the surrounding country-side.

Golspie, as I have mentioned in another chapter (on Printing), houses the county weekly newspaper *The Northern Times*, owned by Elizabeth, Countess of Sutherland, and was first printed and published in 1899. It has a wide circulation among Sutherland folks living in the south and overseas.

I have mentioned the Lawson Memorial Hospital. It is beautifully situated in its own grounds as you enter Golspie from the south and serves the county as a whole. Essentially it is a surgical hospital with an up-to-date operating theatre. The number of beds is twenty-five. Due to the generosity and public spirit of Mr. A. B. Lawson, of Clynelish in the neighbouring parish of Clyne, the building of the hospital was undertaken, and the first wing was opened in 1936. A further addition was made in 1946, and in 1949 a dentist's surgery was added. It is interesting to record that Dunrobin Castle was used as an emergency hospital during the two world wars.

The countryside surrounding Golspie has often been the scene of interesting archaeological discoveries. There is evidence that the district was once a site where Stone Age weapons were manufactured. A few ancient iron furnaces have been found on the Links, along with saws, knives and scrapers. Many of these objects, as well as other county antiquities, are kept in the Sutherland Museum in the park at Dunrobin Castle.

The Mound, south of Golspie, conceived and designed by Thomas Telford, was built by Lord Gower in 1818. It is an earthen mound 1000 yards long across a shallow tidal estuary which resulted in the reclamation of 400 acres of land. Before the building of the mound and the bridge at Bonar Bridge, the crossing of Loch Fleet and the dangerous Meikle Ferry near Dornoch had for long been formidable hazards for man and beast. Alongside the bridge over the Golspie burn, there is the historical interest in the Sutherland Clan stone built into the parapet on the crown of the bridge. It was to the head of this bridge that the chief of the Sutherlands called the clan by messengers who carried a wooden cross with its tips burnt and dipped in blood. The war-cry was 'To the head of the little bridge'—the Rallying Stone. The Mound railway station, the junction for

Dornoch, was closed in 1960 and the branch line to Dornoch was lifted in 1962 (constructed in 1896). The railway from Bonar Bridge to Golspie was completed in 1868 by the Sutherland Railway Company. The railway from Golspie to Helmsdale was built at the expense of the 3rd Duke of Sutherland, and completed in 1871. In 1884 the Duke sold his undertaking to the Highland Railway. The Dukes of Sutherland retained running powers for their rolling stock over the lines of the L.M.S. right up to the time of nationalisation of British Railways after the Second World War. The locomotive and saloon coach were sold in 1950 and were in the museum of the Romney, Hythe and Dymchurch Railway, but were sold and transported to Canada in 1965. The large saloon, an example of the finest British coachwork in existence, was built in 1899 and became the prototype for the royal train used between 1903 and 1941.

The 3rd Duke of Sutherland presented to the fishermen of Golspie, in 1865, a barometer which was built into the wall of a house in Shore Street. This barometer may be seen to this day, and the house is known as 'Barometer House'.

One of the most memorable occasions in the history of Sutherland and of the east coast was the visit in 1866 of the Prince and Princess of Wales to Dunrobin Castle via Ardgay, Bonar Bridge, and Golspie. The future King Edward VII and Queen Alexandra had come from their Highland residence at Abergeldie, near Balmoral. From Bonar Bridge the royal party, with the Duke of Sutherland, had travelled in an open carriage drawn by four grey horses, with an outrider, and when they arrived at Golspie they were saluted by the firing of a battery of guns, which was answered by two 24-pounders sited near Dunrobin pier.

'The Prince wore a plain Highland dress, consisting of a kilt of the Stuart hunting-tartan, with a jacket of heather mixture, a Glengarry bonnet, dark hose and brogues. The Princess was attired in a dress and jacket of light blue trimmed with velvet and buttons, with black straw bonnet trimmed with blue.' (So goes the official description.) Arches were erected of trees and heather at varying intervals from Bonar Bridge to Dunrobin with *Ich Dien* and heraldic devices, banners and such like interwoven in the framework. Three huge bonfires were erected on commanding heights near Golspie; great preparations had been made, and rockets shot up into the air at night. Torch-bearers also lined the route from the outskirts of Golspie to the Castle. It all reminded the spectators, who numbered many thousands, of the gorgeous Arabian nights era. All this in 1866.

BRORA, population 1700, is five miles north of Golspie and also on the coast, is a busy town with wool mill, brick and tile works, distillery, and the most northerly coal mine in Britain. It has a golf course, and safe sandy beaches. The centre of a compact community, Brora continues to grow, and unobtrusively it has become the industrial centre of the county. There are facilities for bowling, tennis and golf. The golf course was laid out by James Braid in 1924. Over-run by the Norse and the frequent battleground of the Sutherlands, Sinclairs and Mackays it has little recorded history. The existence of coal here was known as early as 1529 and its working began in 1598. It has been in continuous operation since 1872, and is now operated by the miners themselves as a co-operative enterprise. On an adjacent site there is a rich deposit of Dover Clay and the brick-making industry here has been revived. I often wonder why official guides and press adverts stress the fact of there being a a coal mine and a brick-works in Brora. I would have thought most tourists would want to by-pass such an 'industrial town' on their tour of those parts.

There is something far more attractive in Brora than coal and bricks, and that is the woollen mills of international repute; that of Messrs. T. M. Hunter Ltd. making tweeds and yarn. Brora tweed never seems to wear out, and these tweed skirts are very popular with ladies. Large numbers of visitors are shown round the mills each year. The mill provides employment for about a hundred people, engaged in all stages of woollen manufacturing. Much of the raw wool comes from the Highlands and Islands, but the mill serves a much wider area than that. For example, yarn is spun for handloom weavers in all parts of Britain and a large part of their production comes back to Brora for the finishing process. Much of the mill's output is for the export market.

In 1901, the building—originally built by the 3rd Duke of Sutherland as an engineering shop—was taken over by Mr. T. M. Hunter (the father of the present chairman) and enlarged. Mr. Hunter was brought up in the woollen trade in Galashiels. While part of the output was for sale as tweeds, blankets, travelling rugs, knitting yarns and weaving yarns, the chief trade was the manufacture of wool into products to meet each customer's specific requirements. This wool came from Shetland, Orkney, the mainland of Scotland and the Western Isles as I have said. In 1916 Mr. Hunter, senior, died but the business continues to be carried on by the Hunter family. The present chairman has been associated with the company for over fifty years. In 1963 he was awarded the M.B.E. for his service to industry.

Brora also sports a distillery, the Clynelish distillery, founded in 1817 as a brewery by the Marquis of Stafford (later created Duke of Sutherland); but two years later the buildings were converted for distilling purposes and 'Clynelish' Highland malt whisky came into being.

In the small square in the centre of this little town is an old-type Queen Victoria Jubilee Fountain, bearing the dates 1837–1897. The Queen's head appears to be kept a brightly painted gold colour whenever I chance to pass through Brora.

HELMSDALE is twelve miles north of Brora, and on the way there you pass the small villages of LOTH and PORTGOWER.

I have told you of the burning of the last witch in Scotland in 1722. At Loth on the right of the road is a stone marking the spot where the last wolf in Sutherland was killed by one Peter Polson around the year 1700. The inscription reads: 'To mark the place near which the last wolf in Sutherland was killed by hunter, Polson, in or about the year 1700. This stone was erected by His Grace the Duke of Portland, K.G.; A.D. 1924.' . . . As so many visitors stop to look at the stone just at the roadside, it is to be moved to a new site nearby, off the busy trunk road.

Helmsdale is a village which formerly enjoyed the great prosperity that accompanied the herring fishing boom that came to an end early in the 1900's. Now, some twenty boats, mostly seine-netters, are engaged on white fishing. Overlooking the village from a hill to the south, is the ruined Helmsdale Castle, originally square in form, with sharp angles and had been the hunting seat of the Sutherland family, adjoining the old deer forest that extended to the Ord of Caithness, a few miles to the north. It was built in 1460 and reconstructed in 1616. The sea has been sapping the bank on which the castle was built, and now the castle is being demolished, not only on account of this but by reason of new road and bridge construction works.

Helmsdale Castle has a tragedy within its walls to unfold.

About the year 1560, John, Earl of Sutherland, bought the Estate of Dounreay from the Bishop of Orkney. Set up there on the north coast, it was remote from his main possessions, divided from them by the Earldom of Caithness and some of the Mackay country.

Earl John's sister was married to William Sinclair, Laird of Dunbeath, twelve miles away to the north, who was a vassal of the Earl of Caithness. Earl John gave the tenancy of Dounreay to this brother-in-law. Isabel, a sister of the Laird of Dunbeath, was married to Gilbert Gordon of Garty, who was an uncle of the Earl of Sutherland. Should anything happen to the Earl, and to his only son, Alexander, a lad of fifteen, then Isabel's oldest son, John Gordon, would fall heir to the Earldom.

So the stage was set. One stroke might make the Garty boy Earl of Sutherland, and also secure his uncle in possession of Dounreay.

In July 1567, Earl John, his Countess and son Alexander, came to spend a few days at their castle at Helmsdale and Isabel of Garty was there with them. Isabel prepared a poisoned drink. The butler bungled the instructions and the drink was taken by the Earl and his Countess. The Earl realised what was happening. He pulled the table cloth, and the cup intended for son Alexander was spilt. Then the Earl had Alexander hurried away to Dun-robin Castle.

Meantime, Isabel's son, John Gordon, came into the castle, and being thirsty called for a drink. A maid unwittingly gave him a cup of the poisoned wine. He drank it and died seemingly before the Earl and Countess, who lived for five days.

Isabel Gordon was taken to Edinburgh, tried, found guilty and sentenced to death; but she died on the morning of the execution, supposedly by taking poison. A bad time followed for Sutherland; six years of continual trouble until the young Earl, Alexander, attained his majority and took over the reins of power.

*   *   *

The great headland known as the Ord of Caithness (750 feet) mentioned in the Dornoch paragraphs, lies some five miles north of Helmsdale. In 1513 the Earl of Caithness and 300 men crossed the Ord on their way to Flodden. None returned. The local superstition is therefore that it is unlucky to cross the Ord on a Monday, particularly if you are a Sinclair and wearing green.

There is a deserted village perched on a cliff's edge just north of the Ord, called BADBEA. A solitary shaft of stone rises from the rubble of ruined thatched cottages and garden dykes on a bare heather-clad moor. On its sides are displayed four plaques which give a list of the inhabitants who emigrated to Wairappa, New Zealand. They had struggled in vain to wrest a living from the wind-swept slope. They had perished in the surging waves that washed below. But to this 'land tribe' the sea and the tides had remained a mystery. The last inhabitant moved out in 1910, and on that site of erection was the home of John Sutherland— known as 'John Badbea'—a moving spirit in the Disruption of 1843.

If you have ever eaten lobster in a fashionable Paris restaurant it most likely came from Helmsdale. This little fishing village has a thriving export trade to France and other parts of the continent.

*   *   *

In the old days these villages I have named from Dornoch to Helmsdale (for they were only villages then) suffered much from the marauding Vikings. Later, when feuds between the men in the north and the Sutherlands were frequent, these parts, lying across the route from Reay and Caithness to Dunrobin and Dornoch, were often traversed by raiding forces, and the henwives must have had reason to bewail their ravaged roosts!

A mile north of Helmsdale is the hamlet of Navidale where I have often stopped and found the hotel there—a family concern of the Mackays—to give hospitality and service of the highest order 'midst its unrivalled position facing the sea. Shortly after here comes the Ord of Caithness and the Sutherland/Caithness boundary line.

*   *   *

I have mentioned the village of LOTH, in Sutherland between Brora and Helmsdale. The Rev. Alexander Pope was ordained minister of Reay in 1734. He was a native of Loth. He was a young man and of great strength, and by all accounts he needed to be, for the Reay people of that time had the roughest of reputations. He was determined to subdue them, and when he went his rounds he carried along with him what he called his *bailie*, a stout cudgel which he was wont to use to good effect on anyone unruly.

But on one occasion early in his ministry it was his fists that he used. A man who lived far in the interior of the parish bragged that he wasn't to knuckle under and be driven to church by such a one as Mr. Pope. This reached the minister's ears, as it was doubtless intended.

Since, so far, Donald knew the minister by reputation only, Mr. Pope took advantage of this, and one day he put on the garb of a poor layman. He arrived at the man's house towards nightfall. He was accepted as what he seemed to be, a simple traveller, and as was the hospitable custom in those days he was invited in, and shared supper with the family. Later on the goodwife prepared a shakedown on the floor for him, of heather and deerskin. 'The man of the house will be putting up a prayer before we retire,' said the disguised minister.

The man of the house, Donald, looked in amazement at the guest who made such an unlooked-for suggestion. 'That's a thing I can't do; that's a thing I never do.' 'You are going to pray,' the other insisted gently. 'And who's going to make me? You're not the one. Even Pope the minister himself—and they say he's a strong fellow—couldn't make me.'

'I am Mr. Pope. I see you are an obstinate sinner. Go down on your knees at once, or I'll make you sorry in every bone in your body.'

That was enough; Donald jumped to his feet. Not even his acceptance of the rules of Highland hospitality was to make him suffer such an insult as that.

Mr. Pope was up as quickly. The fight was on at once. Donald was strong; but the minister was stronger and he had some science behind his blows. It wasn't long before Donald gave in. 'You're a better man than me, minister. I'll do what you want'; he yielded.

'On your knees then,' said Mr. Pope quite pleasantly. Donald got down. His prayer must have been the shortest on record. 'Oh, Lord, you know very well that I can't pray.'

'That will do for a beginning, Donald. I'll finish off now with a few words, and then we can go to bed with our minds at

ease.' His wife, who had been looking on in shame and amazement whilst the fight and uproar had been taking place, also
kneeled.

That wrought a wonderful change in Donald and his wife;
he became a different man altogether; a regular attender at the
church (with his wife) and a zealous admirer and supporter of the
minister who, in time, was happy to make him an elder.

*   *   *

In these few pages relating to the east coast, I have told some-
thing of the last witch, the last wolf, coal and bricks, poison and
greed, tweeds and whisky; and of the Prince and Princess of
Wales'—later King Edward VII and Queen Alexandra—visit to
Dunrobin Castle in 1866. As well as how the Rev. Alexander
Pope 'fought a good fight'.

And that, from Dornoch on a clear day, *you can see for ever.*
Can one ask for more, within a few pages?

*   *   *

HELMSDALE (contd.)

Excitement reached fever point in this little village on Saturday 16th October 1971 in connection with the home-coming
of 25-year-old Alison Rapson (daughter of the Rapson family,
drapers and house furnishers in Helmsdale) upon her winning the
premier award—the gold medal—for her singing in the National
Mod at Stirling on the previous Thursday. It was the first time
for 71 years that a Sutherland girl had achieved such distinction.
Alison had previously won the learners silver medal in 1966 at
the Inverness mod.

The Gaelic piece which won her this high award was 'My
brave dusty lad'. Alison, a very pretty girl, is a hotel receptionist
in East Kilbride.

Congratulations, my dear!

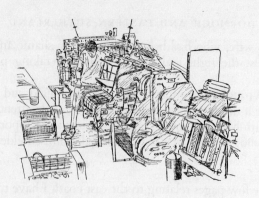

CHAPTER 15

PRINTING IN THE HIGHLANDS

ALTHOUGH this chapter deals with printing operating in the Highlands and Islands, I am interweaving same with a reference to Orkney and Shetland.

After leaving Dingwall, where the well-known weekly *Ross-shire Journal* is printed, and which provides an excellent coverage in its news, articles and letters, I am inclined to think the average tourist believes there is no printing works, let alone newspapers, in the Highlands and Islands, save the national papers. This is not the case; for there are the following weeklies, which deserve mention, viz.:

The Northern Times—Golspie
The Shetland Times—Lerwick (Shetland)
The Orcadian—Kirkwall (Orkney)
The John o' Groat Journal—Wick (Caithness)
The Caithness Courier—Wick (Caithness)
The Stornoway Gazette—Stornoway (Isle of Lewis)

I am more particularly *au fait* with the first- and last-named papers.

The Northern Times, and their associated company Method Publishing Co. Ltd. (which came up from the South in September 1968), within recent years embarked on a costly programme of modernisation, and today—1971—in its seventy-second year of service to Sutherland, the works contains some of the most modern and versatile plant in the whole country; the operating machinery now provides greatly increased floor-space to accommodate the growing activities of the company. Apart from the

weekly 8-page (sometimes 12-page) newspaper which has sub-
scribers all over the world, the works turns out all kinds of commercial material, booklets, pamphlets, etc., in the most modern
and sophisticated print design as can be obtained anywhere else
in Britain. In fact Fleet Street has a very competitive, progressive
firm in the Highlands in the shape of *The Northern Times* (also
known as The Sutherland Press).

The Method Publishing Company was a young publishing
firm; it had been formed in the South by a native of Argyll who
was anxious to get back to the Highlands; and the marriage of
the interests between the companies appeared to be of benefit to
both in the pooling of skill, experience and machinery. The
main production difference between the two companies was the
method by which printing was done. The *N.T.* had the latest
machinery for letterpress printing (*i.e.* printing direct from metal
type) whereas Method Publishing was equipped for offset litho
printing, where the image is transferred from a metal plate,
engraved by a photographic process, on to a rubber blanket, and
from there to the paper.

The average weekly circulation of the *N.T.* is around 6000.
The permanent staff and operatives number 21, including part-
time workers.

The paper is owned by Elizabeth, Countess of Sutherland
(of Dunrobin Castle) who lives at Uppat House, Brora. She took
over after the death of her uncle and at once appreciated the vital
need for expansion.

Mr. Iain Gordon Carmichael is the Managing Director of
both Method Publishing Co. Ltd. and Northern Times Ltd.

Mr. David Bruce-Weir is the genial Editor and Director of
The Northern Times. He joined as editor in 1949, prior to then
he was with *The Glasgow Herald* from 1932. During the war
years he served in Army Intelligence at home and abroad.
Bruce-Weir, M.A., was brought up in the old school of factual
and comprehensive reporting, and his editorial policy has always
reflected this. It is true to say he has throughout kept the *N.T.*'s
readers better informed on council affairs than in any other
Highland county; and the same might well be said of other local
news and opinion.

I know from personal contact the whole establishment has a
fine loyal team of workers; there being no clock-watchers.

Above all they have surrounded themselves with bonnie lassies!
The company also houses in its building The Highland Welcome
Shop where visitors can spend quite a little time finding many
articles of local interest to take away as mementoes of their
Highland holiday. In 1970 the firm published its first coloured
Tourist Supplement; a splendid, comprehensive 24-page pro-
duction.

The Shetland Times is printed in Lerwick and has a circulation of some 7000 copies a week. In 1968 the company embarked
on a programme of modernisation costing over £21,000;
business people are taking courage in both hands and investing
in their faith in the future of Shetland.

The paper was founded in June 1872 by C. & A. Sandison
and in 1894 was bought by Basil Johnson and Peter Greig. It
then had a circulation of 1700, which soon increased to over 2000
when the paper was enlarged to 8 pages in 1897. The paper was
suspended for nine weeks due to an unfortunate fire which
gutted the whole building. In 1942 the firm became a limited
company.

Whilst there is a decline in the island's population, there is
widespread belief that this tide will turn. What grounds have
they for this belief? They are the same grounds that motivated a
big Manchester industrialist to buy land in Shetland; the belief
that the United Kingdom must develop its empty acres to create
breathing space for those now crowding the old industrial centres,
partly because a nation bereft of its lucrative overseas possessions
must exploit its other assets. There is the evidence of increased
productivity in Shetland's industries, new and old. In fishing,
agriculture, textiles, tourism; and in new and unfamiliar ventures
ranging from mink and trout farming to stone polishing and
jewellery manufacture there is an upsurge of activity and a
response to opportunity. In all these matters there is recognised
the importance of communications in a modern society and the
role of a weekly newspaper in the infra-structure of the islands.
In retail trading and service industries there has been a vast
improvement in standards in the islands in the post-war years.
For its size, Lerwick (pop. 6000) caters very well for island
requirements and in the rural areas too there are better facilities
than ever before. Meanwhile plans are on foot to make Scalloway, on the west coast some 6 miles from Lerwick, the town it

ought to be, not the village it is at present. And justification for Scalloway's expansion can be found in its industrial expansion with two fish processing plants, a crab and lobster plant, knitwear units and ship repairing. In the island's field of public works there has been much progress; Shetland's roads are of a high, and constantly improving, standard and reach once remote townships, as do water, drainage and electricity services, the latter coming from the largest diesel generating station in Scotland. They count their blessings in the island in the form of amenities; well planned and attractive schools, a magnificent new hospital, eventide homes and community centres. At their own firesides the folk enjoy comforts that few knew of in the days when Shetland wore a false air of prosperity for a few weeks of each summer herring season. Private investment in housing is particularly encouraging for each new house and each improved or enlarged house represents an investment in the community by an individual —an investment he would not make were he not fairly confident that it would appreciate in value. Although the County Council has built a considerable number of houses fairly evenly disposed over the isles, the transformation in rural housing is most significant in the private sector, where trim bungalows or modernised croft houses have replaced many a 'but an' ben'.

Today Shetland is still catching up with the developed world. Tomorrow it may well forge ahead of many places that today seem better endowed. Then population statistics will commence to show not merely a reduction in the outflow of people but a healthy two-way traffic with the balance in the favour of the Shetlands; with the people's opportunities to live the good life, as well as just to make a living.

The SHETLAND ISLES, known officially as ZETLAND and deriving their name from the old Norse HJALTLAND, meaning 'high land', number a hundred or more, of which twenty-four are inhabited. They lie about 53 miles north of the Orkneys. The largest island, named MAINLAND, has a coast line so much indented by long fjord-like 'voes' that, although it is nearly 500 miles in length, there is no spot on the island more than three miles from the sea. Shetland is noted for its tiny, shaggy ponies, and for its sheep, which produce a fine wool that is knitted into exquisite shawls.

There are steamer services from Kirkwall (in the Orkneys) to

Lerwick in 8 hours, and from Aberdeen direct in 14 hours. Also daily air services from Glasgow and Aberdeen or Inverness via Wick and Orkney.

Halfway between Orkney and Shetland is FAIR ISLE, meaning a sheep island, famous for its jumpers, hand-knitted in traditional design.

Lerwick—meaning Clay Bay (pronounced *Ler-wick*) is the capital of Shetland and is situated on the south-east coast. The broch of CLICKIMIN, a mile west of Lerwick, is considered to be the best extant specimen after Mousa (pronounced *Mooza*)—which is famous for its possession of the only perfect broch in Scotland, 158 feet in circumference and 45 feet high. It is constructed of dry stone, without cement, and bulges out below and again towards the top to prevent its being scaled. The doorway, low and narrow, gives on a passage leading to the open area inside. The North Isles of Shetland, served by steamer from Lerwick, are Whalsey, Yell, Fetlar and Unst. The latter deserves a visit, for it has good fishing and shooting, wild coast scenery and numerous antiquities. Its sheep produce the best wool in the Shetlands. The lighthouse on Muckle Flugga, a rock off Herma Ness, is the northernmost habitation in the British Isles.

*   *   *

As to **The Orcadian, The John o' Groat Journal** and the **Caithness Courier,** I am sorry to say I have no details to give of these paper's activities; but a few words about the Orkneys and John o' Groat may not be out of place.

The ORKNEYS—the name is probably a Celtic–Norse derivation meaning 'whale islands'—are divided from the mainland of Scotland by the Pentland Firth. It has an evil reputation for its swift tide-race and its storms. The Orkneys are composed of old red sandstone and number about 70 islands, twenty-nine being inhabited; apart from countless rocky islets and skerries, *i.e.* rocks awash at high tide. The largest island is again called MAINLAND, and except for the west coast of HOY and Mainland, are deeply indented with rugged cliffs. The islands are somewhat bare and treeless and of low elevation. The Orcadians, largely Norse in origin, are practically all farmers. The Orkneys and Shetlands were conquered in the year 875 by Harold Haarfager

('Fair Hair') and remained Norse until 1468, when Christian I pledged them to his son-in-law, James III of Scotland, as surety for the payment of his daughter's (Margaret) dowry.

The mail route to Orkney is by steamer from Scrabster (near Thurso) to Stromness in 2½ hours. The steamer from Scrabster crosses the Pentland Firth, passing Dunnet Head, leaving the islands of Stroma and Swona well to starboard. To port are Hoy and the pasture-holm of Switha. The steamer then enters Scapa Flow, which was the anchorage of the Grand Fleet during both World Wars. The German fleet, surrendered at the Armistice in 1918, was interned there, but on 21st June 1919 nearly all the ships were scuttled by their crews. Of the seventy vessels, thirty-nine were raised between 1924 and 1947. At the narrowest part of MAINLAND, which is only two miles wide, lies KIRKWALL on a land-locked bay (the name means Church Bay), the chief town. The main thing to see at Kirkwall is the Cathedral of St. Magnus, an impressive red sandstone building in a plain Romanesque style. Now used as the parish church, it was founded in 1137 by Rognvald, or Ronald, Jarl (Earl) of Orkney in honour of his uncle and predecessor St. Magnus, treacherously slain on Egilsay, an island east of Rousay off the north of Mainland. Their bodies were found inside two pillars during a recent restoration. The Cathedral was not completed until the 15th or 16th century. On the south side are the ruins of the Bishop's Palace, where King Haakon IV, King of Norway, died of a broken heart after the Battle of Largs, and his remains rested in the cathedral until their removal to Trondhjem. The roads on the island are exceptionally good. Stromness, the only other real town in Orkney, is about 16 miles from Kirkwall on the western coast side. Close to this roadway one comes across *Maeshowe*, a great conical mound containing stone chambers, and further on, the famous Standing Stones of Stenness. About seven miles due north of Stromness is the Bay of Skaill, on the south side of which is *Skara Brae*, a well-preserved Stone Age or Pictish village (excavated about 35 years ago) dating back to 1500 B.C. and consists of huts, equipped with stone beds, dressers and other fixtures, and opening on narrow-covered alleys. Further on is Marwick Head, with a memorial tower to Lord Kitchener who was drowned close by on 5th June 1916, together with his staff and 700 officers and men of H.M.S. *Hampshire*, when the cruiser struck a mine, as it was journeying to Archangel in Russia. This, at the time, was looked upon as a mortal blow to England.

The southern Orkneys can be visited by local steamer from Stromness; they include Burray, South Ronaldsay, Flotta, and Hoy. This latter is the second largest of the Orkney Islands and has the finest scenery. The Old Man of Hoy is an isolated column 450 feet high and pierced with arches.

The north Orkneys are served by steamers from Kirkwall, Shapinsay, Rousay (pronounced 'Rowzy'), Egilsay ('Church Isle') where St. Magnus was murdered. Between Rousay and Mainland is the uninhabited island of Eynhallow, with the remains of a Cistercian abbey. North of Rousay is Westray where the ruins of Noltland Castle can be viewed, which is assigned to the 16th century. Papa Westray, another island N.E. of Westray, derives its curious name from the hermits that once lived there. The other islands, Stronsay, Sanday, and North Ronaldsay are of less interest.

As I write these lines (1971) the people of Stronsay are very proud of their oldest inhabitant, Mrs. Margaret Lennie, for she cleans her house, does her housework, her washing, cooks her meals and she is 97 years old. In her youth she says Stronsay had a population of over a thousand and was the principal base of the herring fleets. Today the population is a little over three hundred. In those days the harbour used to be filled with the fishing boats, sometimes as many as three hundred of them, and it was possible to walk from one to another for miles, so closely were they anchored. Every day Margaret and her friends sat side by side from six in the morning until bedtime, as they worked at the gutting, and they managed to fill 50 barrels a day, for which they received eight pence (8d.) a barrel. No strikes for higher wages then? She married when she was fifty. Fourteen years ago her husband died. He was eighty-six. Have I not told you they live almost for ever in Shangri-La?

With the passing of Time, however, the hands that had once been so swift became stiff and her eyes began to fail; but she can still see to do her housework as I have said. She is ending her days sitting in her old rocking chair talking to her visiting friends, and gazes out across the now almost empty harbour, but seeing once again in her mind the ships that were her life. Surely one must take off one's hat in salute of such a wonderful person.

I have mentioned THURSO and JOHN O' GROAT. Thurso was a favourite landing place for the Viking invaders. They gave it the name of THOR'S-A, which means the river of the God Thor. Thurso is in Caithness. The river Thurso which flows through the town and into the bay is a popular stretch of water with salmon and trout fishermen. Caithness, like Sutherland, suffered from a long series of raids by the Norse Vikings, but eventually Norse and Gael learned to live together in peace. The Dounreay Atomic Station (commenced building in 1954) is near Thurso, and this has turned from what was a small town at the beginning of the Second World War into a thriving community with a population nearing 10,000.

John o' Groat is always looked upon as the most northerly point of the British Isles, as is Land's End in Cornwall the most southernly. But strictly speaking Dunnet Head, twelve miles away to the west, is more northerly. It is a very popular place for visitors to go to, but like Land's End there is really nothing to see—but the sea! Many tales exist about John o' Groat, but the the historians say that 'a green mound near the hotel marks the site of the famous "Johnny Groat's House" and that the original story tells how, sometime before 1500, three brothers, Malcolm, Gavin and John de Grot, natives of Holland, arrived in Duncansby nearby, with a letter of protection from King James IV. They prospered and multiplied and annually celebrated their arrival in Caithness. At one of those gatherings a dispute arose as to who was the head of the clan, which now numbered eight families. Old John promised by the time of the next assembly he would settle the point to the satisfaction of all. This he did by building a house with an eight-sided room having an eight-sided table, then all were equally head of the table.'

The Grot family tombstone dated 1568 and with some quaint lettering can be seen set in the wall of old Canisbay church, originally placed in the churchyard by 'Donald Grot sone to Jhone Grot'. About 1568 too, William Sinclair, second son of the Earl of Caithness, built the Castle of Mey, which is now the Caithness home of the Queen Mother, and is six miles from John o' Groat.

*   *   *

The Stornoway Gazette publishes a weekly paper of some 12,000 copies and its circulation area covers Lewis and Harris,

North and South Uist, Barra, Isle of Skye, Wester Ross, Inverness-shire and Glasgow. The staff of the *Gazette* numbers
twenty-one members, and in addition to producing the newspaper, commercial printing, school magazines, booklets, pamphlets are also undertaken. The newspaper is a bi-lingual one,
Gaelic/English, and the Gaelic found in its columns reaches a very
high standard of presentation.

Peculiarly enough the *Gazette* does not have an editor, but a
Managing Director, Mr. Samuel Longbotham, who has the day-
to-day responsibility of running the paper; as help he has an
editorial adviser. I think this is more or less a unique set-up.

The Stornoway Gazette was founded in 1917 by the late
William Grant, an Inverness man, who came to Stornoway in
the early 'nineties as a reporter for the *Highland News*. He was
the *Gazette's* first editor. He became a naturalised Lewisman
and in 1906 married Johanna Morison, a teacher on the staff of
the Nicolson Institute. His wife was associated with him in
founding the *Gazette*, and she became proprietrix after his death.
She was the youngest daughter of Roderick Morison, a retired
ship's captain and coxswain of the first lifeboat stationed at
Stornoway by the Royal National Lifeboat Institution. Both the
founders of the *Gazette* were closely associated with the Nicolson
Institute in the exciting early days of W. J. Gibson's rectorship
when this institute was one of the pioneer schools in Scotland;
for instance, photography was taught as a science subject; then
original research on bee-keeping was carried out in the school, a
new observation hive invented which was called after the school,
and a disease which was worrying bee-keepers throughout
Britain was first identified. Later on a commercial department
was established at the school, largely by Mr. Grant's suggestion.
William Grant died in 1932 at the early age of fifty-nine. His
younger son, James Shaw Grant, became editor, and he continued to edit the *Gazette* until his appointment as chairman of
the Crofters' Commission in 1963. The present Managing
Director, Sam Longbotham, already named, came to the *Gazette*
from the staff of the *Daily Express* in Glasgow.

On 7th January 1967, the *Gazette* published a special 4-page
'Jubilee Supplement' which made interesting reading.

*   *   *

It is true to say:

> . . . All history records the past
> What was and is no more;
> But not a line of type is cast
> To tell what lies before.
>
> The glories of an ancient age
> Are plain for all to see;
> But no one now can print a page
> Of glories yet to be. . . .

CHAPTER 16

THE DECLARATION OF ARBROATH

. . . for as long as but a hundred of us remain alive, never will we on any conditions be brought under English rule. It is in truth not for glory, nor riches, nor honours that we are fighting, but for freedom—for that alone, which no honest man gives up but with life itself. . . .

*   *   *

THE above inspiring paragraph taken out of the Declaration has, I think, been quoted and re-quoted *ad lib* over the last 650 years. By any standards this is quite one of the most extraordinary documents, considered, endorsed and published of all time. The Declaration is widely regarded as one of the world's most eloquent statements of a nation's freedom and independent spirit. Parts of this lengthy declaration for nationhood were incorporated in the American Declaration of Independence more than 400 years later. I would say its thoughts and its meaning stand to this day in the highest esteem; for all Scots and English alike hold the banner of Freedom high. Whenever there is talk about the Declaration of Scottish Independence, one cannot separate—or indeed single out—the personalities that dominated these epoch-making events in this interesting war of Scottish liberation, which had begun in 1297, since all of them in one way or another played an important part in it. In general, one can say that Liberty is indebted to bad Kings

312

It was on the 6th April 1320 that this Declaration was signed with all pageantry and solemnity—embodying these ideals of freedom and addressed to Pope John XXII. It would not have been inscribed in Gaelic (with which it is most improbable the Pope would be familiar) but it breathes the spirit of the Gael and is truly the Celtic Magna Charta. There is no doubt of this. This famous document was drawn up six years after Bannockburn, in the 14th year of Robert the Bruce's embattled reign, and nine years before his death. The Declaration was to be the first great appeal for recognition of National independence in modern history. It was to the Pope, recognised as the Supreme Pontiff by the community of Scotland—and of that day a sort of one-man United Nations—that they appealed to arbitrate between their King, Robert the Bruce, and England's headstrong Edward II.

After Bannockburn, Edward escaped to Dunbar where he got a small boat to take him to Berwick; an ignominious end to his boast to wipe out 'Robert de Brus, who calls himself King of Scotland'. The victory of Bannockburn made all Scots feel they really were one Nation. This Arbroath Declaration and the Treaty of Northampton which followed gave formal recognition to the bravery of the men who fought and the freedom they won. It is remarkable to find a medieval leader so versed in the principles of war as was Bruce, though numerically so inferior and lacking the decisive arms of the period—heavy cavalry and archers—he was so victorious, because he adhered to principles, later to be en-coded by Napoleon and practised by successful commanders.

Robert Bruce was profoundly dedicated to the freedom which in twenty-four searing years he fashioned and brought to perfection and acceptance. It is against this backcloth that this Declaration was written—not by Bruce, although not one word therein could have been written without him. This is what makes the references to Bruce so startling, so utterly electrifying and so poignant. Only when this is understood can the full meaning and vision of the Declaration be recognised.

What produced the need for this Declaration was the fact that the Earls and Barons had brought the Pope in on their side. This was not new, for though the Church in Scotland itself had all along been Bruce's most faithful support, Holy Church as represented by the Holy See had always been against him—the ex-communicate murderer of John Comyn ('The Red Comyn' who claimed the Scottish throne, murdered in 1306).

Today, as I write in 1971, this century echoes much of that early ache for recognition and freedom; it sees a reassertion of similar demands all over the world . . . self-determination.

*   *   *

The story of Arbroath Abbey goes back in its origin to Poitier and Tiron in France. Here Abbot Bernard, in 1109, founded a new Benedictine monastery, and fame of this order spread rapidly through the Christian world. To Scotland, Benedictine monks were brought firstly to Selkirk in 1113, and later to Kelso by the Earl of Huntingdon, later King David I. Sixty-five years later William, King of Scots (on his return from captivity in Normandy, to the glory of God and St. Thomas the martyr, Archbishop of Canterbury, *apud Aberbrothock*), founded a new Benedictine monastery—Arbroath. In this most magnificent and powerful abbey, Abbot Bernard de Linton, Chancellor of Scotland since 1307, an excellent diplomat, '*suaviter in modo, fortiter in re*'—gentle in manner, resolute in deed—drafted this famous Declaration.

The Earls and Barons, about fifty of them, had arrived two days before at this great-stoned abbey on the brink of the North Sea. Their King Robert I, the Bruce, was there too—standing apart with Scotland's Chancellor, who was also Abbot of Arbroath. All were there with a common purpose . . . for it was 6th April 1320. That day the monks, writing laboriously and artistically in the abbey's writing room, were to complete the document known, as I have said, 'The Declaration of Arbroath'. That day the noblemen were to sign it, and one after the other, add their seals—not just their signatures—to complete a festoon of witnesses, for six years earlier had been the military triumph of Bannockburn, and since then they had come to believe in their rights and new sovereignty above the Border. Now was the time; now was the hour, to seal this with universal recognition of their nationhood.

While they met and talked and were guided by the wise abbot in the chapter house within a cross-bolt's reach of the sea, their King kept apart. He fretted in the Abbot's House on the other side of the abbey; and we can well imagine his feelings, his anxiety—his mounting anxiety. What was to be done FOR him, because they chose that he should remain the people's leader. They would, he felt sure, appeal to the Pope that he would recognise The Bruce and that he would counsel Edward, the English King, to do likewise. What else could happen but this. For after all one man, and one man only, had come to set them free— King Robert. But even *he* had to respect the common wish, and so, too, should those outwith Scotland, especially the King of the English. Couldn't he, the Supreme Pontiff, prevail?

The monks copied the finished document. One was taken down the passage-ways, past the kitchens and the cloister to Robert in the Abbot's House. The principal copy was despatched to the Pope at Avignon. Another went to Edward in England, a courtesy copy. This copy has never been seen since.

Even to this very day, we can picture the tremendous overwhelming tension that would hold the entire abbey in its grip.

Four years later the Pope deigned to address Bruce as King. Another four years later King Edward III (Edward II had died the year before in 1327) formally recognised Scotland's King and her independence. Bruce died the following year, 1329; but he had seen his dream come to reality.

The fighting went on, but the manifesto written at the abbey was to become more than just an historic relic of a strange meeting of Church, State and commonalty. It was a declaration of a people's faith, undying in its expression—and wonderful in that no nation had ever done the like before. . . .

To give the full text of the original document would take up at least five pages of print; therefore I am not producing it in detail. However, what I have already written gives the essence of this historic occasion.

*   *   *

The year of grace 1970 saw a service of remembrance enacted in the Abbey grounds on Monday, 6th April, commemorating the 650th anniversary. It was an impressive occasion. A large procession of dignitaries, including one of the most representative gatherings of local churchmen to be seen in Arbroath since the Reformation; nearly 2000 people attended the ecumenical service. The procession made its way through the ruined west door and the short introduction was opened by the Rev. T. Gemmell

Campbell, Minister of the Old Parish of Arbroath, with the words, 'I said to the man at the gate of the year . . .' He went on to say:

. . . The Deathless Declaration of Scottish Independence was a worthy successor indeed to that made by the Church ten years before at Dundee—the very first assertion of nationality in the entire history of modern Europe. It was said at the time to be 'the noblest burst of patriotic feeling, the finest declaration of independence that real history has to show'. Not even Magna Charta was more auspicious in its significance. This matchless manifesto is only to be equalled in respect of its consequence with the great Declaration of American Independence. It is not merely an assertion of rights and privileges, but rather it is a Confession of Faith—a proclamation of where Scotland stood then, and still stands—in the age-long struggle for human liberty.

This 650th anniversary serves to remind us that the price of Freedom is Eternal vigilance. But above all it reminds us that where there is no feeling for eternal things, any strutting upstart tyranny can devastate the world. Once again from the great 'Round O', there goes forth a clarion call to the freedom loving peoples of the world. And never more needful than today.

For all too long we have been taking our liberty for granted. What we could get out of it; not what we should dedicate to it, has been uppermost in our thinking.

Where, today in our soft flabby hands; where in our easy and comfortable lives; where in our prosaic and unadventurous souls are the marks of that old robust independence upon which our fathers built their greatness? It is the sheerest folly to think that we can preserve our freedom by living in a fool's paradise with loose morals, disintegrated family life, licence and self-restraint thrown to the winds.

Nothing worth having, least of all freedom, can be achieved save as the cost of it is paid in self-discipline. And if we do not discipline ourselves from within, we are going to have discipline imposed on us from without. The roots of a self-disciplined character are profoundly spiritual—faith that there are values worth being dedicated to Faith; that there are ends worth being disciplined for; faith that by God's grace there is a possible world founded on four essential freedoms—freedom of SPEECH and of WORSHIP; freedom from WANT and from FEAR, that self-disciplined men and nations can build.

To such a Faith we must dedicate ourselves afresh. . . .

After the service a 'Flame of Independence' (Remembrance) was lit by the Countess of Errol, Lord High Constable of Scotland. The flame, contained in a pedestal on the raised lawn at the north side of the door, was kept alight during the six-month season of commemoration. The flame pedestal was encircled by Saltire flags and the Burgh flag, which were broken by members of Arbroath's Youth Organisation when Lady Errol lit the flame.

To mark the occasion a special 5d. postage stamp was issued by the G.P.O. and a special cancellation was designed by Jan Zbigniew Raschke, a member of the Arbroath and District Philatelic Society. This special cancellation is the one the P.O. authorities decided to use to give letters first day cover. The design is unique in that it includes the word SCOTLAND—the first time ever, since the introduction of postage stamps, that the name of a home country has been included. First day cover envelopes are regarded highly by philatelists.

The 5d. stamp itself was designed by Fritz Wegner (from Vienna, a lecturer in graphic arts) and is composed of nine different colours, with the Queen's head embossed in gold, on a predominantly orange-red background. Seated behind an olive-green table is presumably Abbot Bernard de Linton, dressed in Archiepiscopal robes (red and gold) wearing a mitre. On his right stand three Scottish nobles and on his left two Scottish Barons discussing the text of the Charter. According to some historians the Declaration was discussed and drafted in the chapter-house of the Abbey. The front of the table is decorated—among other motives—with the St. Andrew's Cross, the patron saint of Scotland, whose bones were supposed to be brought in the 7th century to St. Andrews. The mitre headdress was worn by High Priests in the ancient Jewish church. In the Christian church the mitre was worn by Archbishops, Bishops and more important Abbots from the 10th century upward, as a signal of Episcopal dignity.

*　　　*　　　*

THE STONE OF DESTINY is probably the oldest relic of Scottish royalty. It was kept at SCONE (SKOON) near Perth, and Scottish kings, when they were crowned stood up with one foot on the stone (in the attitude of a toast being drunk) and one foot on the table.

The Stone (which has a link with Arbroath Abbey) is nothing

much to look at; just a rough, rectangular, three-hundredweight block of black basalt, 26 inches long, 16 inches broad and 10½ inches in depth. The top is flat and bears on it the marks of chiselled hieroglyphics. The theories concerning the origin of the Scots Coronation Stone are almost as complicated as the legends which cling to it. A general notion prevails that it is of Irish origin and that it is actually '*Lia Fàil*', or Stone of Destiny spoken of in Irish tradition which was brought to Scotland by conquering Irish Scots from the Hill of Tara. This Stone, as we know it, can most definitely be proved to have been situated in the Royal Scottish demesne at Scone in the 13th century, until it was removed to Westminster Abbey by Edward I in 1296. When Edward annexed Scotland then, he seized both the Stone and other symbols of Scottish nationality and had it placed in the Coronation Chair, specially made to contain it, at Westminster Abbey, on which English kings have since been crowned.

Scotland, regarding the Stone as sacred and the symbol of her independence, saw its going as her greatest humiliation.

I gave a very lengthy and first-hand account of this Stone of Destiny in my very first book (written several years ago) woven particularly around the plot to remove it from Westminster Abbey on Christmas Day 1950. This daring exploit was carried out by three Scots students and a Scots girl—a Ross-shire girl whom I know and who lives not far from me. After the exciting, hectic removal and transportation back to Scotland, the Stone was finally taken to Arbroath Abbey in April 1951. It was carried through the abbey gates in great secrecy, across what is now a carpet of green turf, placed in front of the High Altar and covered with the blue and white of the St. Andrew's Cross. As the bearers turned away, the leader seemed to hear the voice of Scotland speak as clearly as it spoke in 1320:

> For so long as there shall be but one hundred of us remain alive we will never give consent to subject ourselves to the dominion of the English. For it is not glory; it is not riches, neither is it honour, but it is liberty alone that we fight and contend for, which no honest man will lose but with his life. . . .

This *voice*, though not exactly word for word as the monks wrote out on that memorable 6th of April 1320, is substantially the same; and no matter what our views or what our nationality may be, I think it must be agreed the diction is as simple as it is superb.

Later the authorities took the Stone back to Westminster Abbey, one hundred and nine days after its disappearance.

*   *   *

Then, on Christmas Day 1970—the 20th anniversary of that dramatic removal of the Stone of Destiny from the Abbey— there suddenly appeared a lump of stone outside Parliament House in Edinburgh, with the claim that this was the REAL Stone, and so stirred afresh one of the great romantic dramas of modern Scottish history. This simple act brought to mind those headlines of the world twenty years ago, namely of Scottish independence. It was indeed a gargantuan ploy. Police and other authorities made equivocal comments as to whether or not it was the genuine article. Experts said there were three 'stones' in existence; and shrugged their shoulders, treating this incident as a hoax. Many laughed at the consternation, as another generation did twenty years ago. Scots were thus made to think, by this small act, of their nationhood; and this is no bad thing indeed.

A note on the stone read: 'A Christmas present to the people of Scotland. On the 20th anniversary of the return of the Stone of Destiny to Scotland, we feel it only right that the people of Scotland should know that the real Stone of Destiny was never handed back. Now, 20 years since, the demand that Scotland should be a self-responsible and self-governing nation, has grown. Let us keep this Stone in Scotland as a symbol of the new nation which, together, we are building.'

Whether this hunk of stone deposited outside Parliament House, Edinburgh, was meant as a giggle and no more, it vividly brought back, like a fiery cross, the tremendous excitement of that day in 1950 which upset the gaitered glory of Westminster.

As to legends surrounding the Stone which I have given, there is still another one which has a strong following; that is, it is the Stone on which Jacob rested his head when he saw the vision of the angels ascending and descending the ladder. It is believed it was brought to Scotland by *Scota*, a daughter of one of the Pharaohs. King Edward First's motive was to deprive the Scots of this symbol of their independence and to show where authority over Scotland lay.

At the time (1950) the then Secretary of State for Scotland—the late Hector McNeil—made no secret of the anxiety of the late King George VI, who regarded the Stone's disappearance as a bad omen. In the thick of that plot was Dr. John MacCormick, then Rector of Glasgow University. He was one of Scotland's most fervent advocates of Home Rule. He died in October 1961 aged but 61 years. He was a lawyer by profession and one of the greatest orators Scotland has produced this century; he might conceivably have become Prime Minister of Scotland, for he had a country marching behind him. Gradually the dream faded and his lieutenants melted away, just like Montrose and Bonnie Prince Charlie; in short, he was a *Wallace of the Word*. Of this, there is no question.

Sometimes we hear the comment, that if it was bad for Edward I—the Hammer of the Scots—to steal it from Scone, was it not equally wrong for some far-wandered Scot to whip it from the land of Jacob?

Since it seems there is more than one Stone of Destiny, there was a light-hearted poem some bard wrote many years ago as to there being the possibility of a whole heap of 'stones' being systematically turned out—each one claiming to be the true and original one.

The poem went something like this:

. . . the fellow that was turning them off on a belt
At the peak of production was so sorely pressed
That the real one got mixed up along with the rest.
So if ever you come on a stone with a ring
Just sit yourself down and appoint yourself King,
For there's none would be able to challenge your claim
That you'd crowned yourself King on the Destiny Stane. . . .

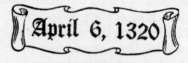

April 6, 1320

Freedom? We have only to cite the Second World War after Dunkirk, when Britain, the Commonwealth and the Empire were quite alone; the flame of the world's freedom extinguished except for a rich glow at the end of Churchill's cigar. Yes freedom is precious.

CHAPTER 17

GOODBYE SHANGRI-LA

FROM all that has gone before, I feel it will be agreed the Highlands form a striking landscape merging in with Clan loyalty; that it is indeed a *real* country. In fact I cannot help repeating in regard to Sutherland its vastness *is* a reality— an unspoiled paradise. The pity is so few in the British Isles know what they are missing.

Readers may find in this, and all my writings of the Highlands, there is much detachment in the narrative; much involvement. But who cares; for once you are in the Scottish far north, things 'crowd' upon you, and your thoughts are led away into numerous channels, all of which affects one's outlook on life. This seems to resemble my full life for twenty-five years in the East and Far East which was like an adventure story; and writing about the Highlands *is*, in a sense, a story of adventure into unknown pearls of beauty and life; a life in some areas resembling Shangri-La.

Scotland is not merely an area, but a great nation—a nation to be proud of in many ways; a nation that in this century alone has given no fewer than six Prime Ministers, Balfour, Campbell-Bannerman, Bonar Law, Ramsay Macdonald, Harold Macmillan and Sir Alec Douglas-Home. In discovery, there were David Livingstone and Mungo Park (of Nigeria's fame). In science, the stars are many and indeed brilliant; to quote but two, Sir Alexander Fleming, discoverer of penicillin, and John Logie Baird, pioneer of TV. As for religion, the names of famous ministers are legion. All such have come from a nation, few in numbers; for Shangri-La is a chosen land, small in extent rarely to be found.

When the busy man and his family come north, for the first few days there is always the apprehension about having nothing to do—as if leisure was a crime. But gradually the old instincts of primitive man reassert themselves. Birds, beasts, fish and all the sights and sounds of nature begin to lure one away from the thought of the old routine, lying in the heather (when in mid September it all looks like a carpet of spilt claret) in lazy contentment with a seeing eye and a hearing ear; and a heart beating in unison with that of mother earth—the Good Earth. This Highland continent is Britain's tranquilliser, the bromide of the North, for it can offer everything that Europe has, in a nutshell. What does one come to the Highlands for, but to re-live the age of leisure? And when you laze on one of the secluded stretches of beaches, you will get the feeling the world is passing you by.

In this fickle age today, the era of pop, cannabis, and permissiveness, all things change and pass away in time; even true love, they say, may grow cold. 'Happiness is hard to find, yet shall Fate too long unkind, bring you peace of mind when you grow old.' This was the philosophy spoken by the Emperor Franz Josef of Austria in the *White Horse Inn* musical, staged at Drury Lane theatre in the 1930's. Today, man is stretching out his hands to catch the stars; he forgets the flowers at his feet. And when you have spent a glorious day in Scotland's Shangri-La, you may perhaps gratefully muse over the following lines . . . if not, then you should do.

> Ere evening's golden shade is spilled
> O'er flower and tree and moorland way,
> There comes that muted moment filled
> With thanks, for such a lovely day.

For the voice of the glen is like a soothing dream as one strolls amid the trees; there's always a song from the rippling stream, and laughter from the breeze. You have left the hurly-burly of what is called 'life' in the towns and cities of the south.

*   *   *

I hope throughout these pages I have made clear that the whole Highlands of Scotland is a countryside where you're not jostled about or knocked off the pavement as you are in a town; and for two reasons. Firstly, as the area is so vast, there are no crowds in sight, even the beaches are so spacious that even with hundreds of visitors they appear empty. There is none of this crammed 1s. deck-chair business up North. Secondly, there are no pavements! This Highland territory is another country, another world. Many north-west and east coast villages live and die by the sea. They live by the sea which gives them their daily bread; they mourn quietly. It is true that formerly busy home-steads are now crumbling memorials to a populous past; the country has not yet caught up with the Clearances, yet the people show an all-round kindness. In this respect, I quote from the TALMUD (the body of the Hebrew laws), 'He who shows kindness to those who are seen, but cannot see, will be rewarded by Him, who sees, but is not seen'.

The enormous area has an indented coast line, beaches and sandy bays galore, and the sea rolling in across the Minch (LA MANCHE, the sleeve) is always an attraction and gives one an exhilarating feeling. In the pioneer days of old, the Greek warriors of Alexander the Great's time when they first caught a glimpse of the sea, rushed towards it, and in their excitement called out THALASSA, THALASSA; the sea, the sea. And on a sunny calm day and with quietness all along the sands, you speak in whispers to break the silence of the sea.

As you travel carefully along the roads of Wester Ross and Sutherland and the many bends and corners at leisure (remember-ing there are always sheep about, for it is *their* home and *we* are the intruders), not by appointment do you meet delight and joy, for they heed not your expectancy; but round some corner or other—as in the streets of life—all of a sudden they clasp you with a smile and you glory at Creation's masterpiece. If you are not mindful of this, and do not acknowledge the existence of a supreme architect, then I would say the end of a Christless life is a useless life.

Once I find myself in Sutherland and the north-west near Ben Loyal (which I have called the Queen of Scottish mountains), the drawbridge winds up, with me inside, so to speak—and there I remain for as long as I can, locked in the moorlands and glens. God made the country and man made the towns, and even in this moon-age no one has yet found a way of reversing this process. It can only go one way. There is much courtesy and kindness shown by the folk in the old-time villages, and such a welcoming air (Highland air, at that) is displayed towards strangers. We must see to it our Planners preserve the way of life up north, for it is so precious, so worthwhile that we simply cannot let it be thrown away in this, or even next, century. The bulldozer must not be tolerated to uproot the trees, the hills or the mountains; if so we shall rapidly become a lost Atlantis; a lost Shangri-La. Should this come about, and these planners showed face up here, I would have a longing to shoot them at high noon, just as they did in the Western films.

It is well known of course the people choose what form of government they like, and can alter or recall it when they please. Our policy of late years seems to have been propelled by events instead of controlling them, with the result that positions become more entrenched and divisions deeper.

In this age we don't need white-collared fellows in togas fiddling around with ideas of planning for the sake of planning (as per those Glasgow students of May 1968 in *Toga Virilis*, producing such a laughable, childish and altogether preposterous £4½ m. 'plan' for Wester Ross). We need experts who possess plain commonsense and sure instincts for the Highlander's wishes; not theorists. This may be plain speaking—but true. As to the 'Plan' mentioned above, we in Shangri-La have heard nothing further since my 'broadside' against them throughout the Highland and national press. The instigators have gone to earth like the midges in the winter.

It is true a great deal of useful improvement work has been done in the Highlands since the establishment of the Highland and Islands Development Board in 1965, but no one can expect its formation to overcome in six years the neglect of a hundred or more years. If, as we may well assume, there was some satisfying social and economic system operating before the Jacobite rebellion, then it has taken five, six or seven generations to run it down to its present state. Well, nobody can run it up in less than a generation or so; and the five years just closed is far short of one generation. A certain amount of damage to the Highlands was done by men who treated it as a hostile land, although it is one-fifth of the land surface of Great Britain.

In another fifty years, if planning and development proceeds at an intensive pace, then the land up here will see yet another revival—a revival of the Clearances; a disappearance of everything characteristically HIGHLAND. This is no empty statement, but rather a prophecy. Sir Robert Grieve was the Board's first chairman. Resigning the post in 1970 he gave place to a 60-year-old Lowlander, Sir Andrew Gilchrist, an ex-diplomat who was recently (1970) ambassador to Eire. The post carries a salary of £8250 a year. With all due respect, I find myself asking what such a distinguished personage knows of the Highlander and his life's requirements. At any rate the Board must not function as 'Development' for development's sake, as I have said for planning. However, if it comes to pass and planners *had* full scope 'regardless', the cost would be as hair-raising as the cost of wigs on the National Health Service!

In the past, Whitehall has appeared to stoop to any means in their cunning psychology, to infilter into well-contented areas, all kinds of ideas and policies calculated to lower the moral standards of indigenous populaces. *Divide et impera* (Divide and Rule) seems to be their self-satisfied, conceited methods. The advent of so-called attractions to the far northern Highlands would put money into the bank balances of the developers to be sure, but nothing in the way of riches to local inhabitants; and further, thousands of those seeking peace and contentment would then keep well away from such spoliation of God's own country. And to crown all, in December 1969, a Welshman was made Director of the new Scottish Tourist Board!

In the fourth annual report (June 1970) it is reported the Board and private enterprise invested just over £11 million, including £6 million by the Board itself in 1134 projects. Out of 458 such projects given loans, 26 went broke. So quite a considerable amount of money has had to be written off covering these loans and interest.

In October 1970 it was sensationally disclosed that the Board had poured £87,000 (of taxpayer's money, remember) into a small firm which started up a factory in Barra (Outer Hebrides) and Campbeltown (Mull of Kintyre) to make spectacle frames and which crashed into liquidation; and only weeks before the crash, the Board was offering to advance another £12,000. The firm's total deficiency was put at £127,000. The lawyer for some of the creditors was alleged to have said that no commercial finance house would have considered this proposal in the first case; and he went on to say (I quote), 'Some of the members are babes in arms when it comes to the hard economic facts of business.' In the tiny island of Barra, the work started up in a converted school-house; and in Campbeltown in a factory built by the Board of Trade with the help of the Highland Board. The business only lasted three years. In the first year of operation in Campbeltown the factory made a loss of £30,000. The champagne bubbles that heralded in these two optical ventures have now burst and gone flat.

This makes sad reading for both Barra and Campbeltown; and for all those who are suddenly thrown out of their work.

Students? to say nothing of what Education is costing this country—millions of pounds *a day*. It is fantastic; it is appalling. And what have we in the ultimate product? Pretty poor, taken by and large.

Only at the general election time, June 1970, I had a report from a Cambridge lady who, whilst at the polling station there, got into conversation with some of the University students; and here are some of their illuminating comments given her in broad daylight: (*a*) 'The Queen is the richest woman in Europe. The government give her £7 million a year to spend on herself!' (*b*) 'There are far better people who should occupy Buckingham Palace. I wouldn't mind if all that lot were lined up against a wall and shot.' Just imagine that, readers. (*c*) 'In Education, accuracy is not all that important.' (*d*) 'Jesus Christ would never have prayed for the Queen.' What on earth are we coming to; what will our rising generation think out next in this age of unity, permissiveness, free love, comprehensiveness and comprehensive schools and colleges, and a host of other '-ivenesses'? During the French revolution the *vox populi* was 'Liberty, Equality, Fraternity'. Now the teenagers in this country cry, 'Liberty, Equality, Maternity'.

* * *

The men who built this nation
Are the envy of the world
Their courage and creation
Maintained our flag unfurled.

But now the modern planners
Are wont to sweep away
The old and solid banners
Deep underneath the clay.

We must hold in mind our past
As a guide for cultures new
Stand firm, be true, 'Hold Fast'
On which our greatness grew.

The whole point in all this planning should be to create, not to destroy. I repeat they must preserve our way of life, so fostering a better understanding. There is all the difference in the world between Improvement and Development.

The late King George the Sixth, broadcasting on Xmas Day 1950, said 'Our motto must be whatever comes or does not come, I will not be afraid. If our world is to survive in any sense that makes survival worthwhile, it must learn to love, not to hate; to create, not destroy.'

Invariably in all these development matters, with the local people making objections, it all ends up in a compromise. Indeed, today, all industrial disputes seem to be resolved by compromise. This boils down to the art of dividing a cake in such a way that everyone believes he or she has got the biggest piece; the biggest slice.

*   *   *

I stopped one day to speak to a shepherd along the Tongue/ Lairg road near Ben Loyal. He was standing with two lovely grey ponies, looking wistfully towards the mountain. I asked what he was looking for; what was he expecting, and he told me he was looking for a fire. 'A fire?' 'Yes; you see my superiors are up the hillside stalking, and when they kill a stag or two, they light a small heather fire, and that's my signal for the spot where I should go. Then I ride up the hillside with the ponies, strap the stags to them, and bring them down.' I remarked you seldom, if ever, come across such an out-of-the-world setting as two lovely horses and a weatherbeaten venerable shepherd gazing at the mountain waiting for such a cue. 'No,' he replied, 'now there are no horses but plenty of cars for people to look at; but then, ah! then, there were no cars but plenty of ponies which caused folk to stop, admire and pat them.' Should there be no stags or deer to collect he would just quietly walk back to the Lodge about two miles away with the ponies untethered, walking casually by his side, ambling slowly along.

Later that day after coming back from Lairg, I met up with

him again and the lovely beasts—homeward bound, all as quiet as you please. There had been no kills that day. I stopped and chatted with him again, and the two animals allowed me to stroke them. I left the trio to journey on their way; it was obvious they loved their shepherd and he loved them. This was Shangri-La at its best. Not a soul in sight; just the four of us alone, with nature around us, as far as the eye could see. Mutual love, mutual trust, mutual understanding. It made my day. Truly a hill without a shepherd is a barren place. Raising my hat in salutation, I sped on feeling something fine amongst those moorlands and mountains—miles from nowhere—had emerged in that encounter. It reminded me of watching the potter moulding the clay in the Eastern bazaars. A flaw in the vessel he was making did not mean discarding the clay, but a new beginning, till something finer emerged; and as I have just said, something finer than the flaws of the ordinary work-a-day had emerged in my 'Brief Encounter'. The theme of Shangri-La was again ringing in my ears. You may know some dumb animals can be very appealing and lovable and are a source of great company; you can even get to like a cow and give it a pet name. As they say up north, all these animals 'are as wise as is necessary'. And as for the sheep-dogs—the collies—they have an intelligence that is quite uncanny.

*   *   *

Have you ever had the sensation that a certain moment snatched from Time is of tremendous significance and of importance to you? That you must savour it slowly and to the full. Many parts of Sutherland and Wester Ross give you that sense and feeling, and you will be grateful for the good fortune, and never allow the stresses and pressures of a working time-table stop you using your eyes to appreciate the manifold splendours of the Universe, and to think of the handed-down glories of the Highland folk and of their heritage of the past. Science is making immense strides; a trip to the moon will become as straight-forward an expedition as an Olympic airway ticket to Greece and Istanbul. Man, said Socrates, must think and make up his mind for himself, but leave time for contemplation. Time? Well there's plenty of it in Shangri-La; praise be to Allah the merciful! Time? No bustle here, no hurry. Not everyone is even

aware of current events. At the last general election, some of the
old generation asked if William Ewart Gladstone was still alive!
And as to calling in the plumber for any emergency—well, you
need to have patience. (Not that this applies to where I live, in
Gairloch, for 'Percy the plumber', will come at a minute's notice.)
The story goes in another village, of the plumber being 'phoned
to come as soon as he could; but he arrived days late. Asking
how the good lady of the house had managed, she said, 'Oh! well,
since you've been so long in coming, I've taught the children to
swim!'

As I said earlier, the language spoken in the Highlands was
'the Gaelic'. Nowadays it is mostly to be heard amongst the
coterie of ageing folk, not the young; but there are indications
the balance is being redressed and that the younger generation is
playing an increasingly realistic role in Gaelic cultural activities.
When conventional codes and accepted values are being questioned on a universal scale, it is important that the voice of
Gaeldom's youth should not only be heard, but encouraged.
However, when these youngsters scramble to join the southward
drift for money, and having sampled *La Dolce Vita* of urban
civilisation, quite a few of them return; but during their maybe
short absence, the Gaelic touch was apt to have been laid aside
and so forgotten. Certainly those who remain here lead full and
happy lives, more so than their more sophisticated expatriate
contemporaries. What a wonderful country the Highlands would
be if *everybody* only spoke Gaelic! Surely that would hold something of a spectacular nature—a magnet indeed—to anyone visiting these two counties. Then I am sure strangers would un-
hesitatingly say, 'This is truly Shangri-La right over from far
Tibet itself'; either that, or they would think they were in
Jugoslavia or Rumania.

As to the Gaelic language, why should Scotland, with its
reputation for justice and independence, be seemingly reconciled
to let the language, which distinguishes it from other nations,
pass into oblivion through neglect and lack of support? Gaelic
should be given more official status.

I must say some Gaelic people write laudable articles, and
like most advocates of Gaelic write and write, and talk and talk,
putting forward no new ideas, whilst all the years past, Gaelic
has withered and died on the vine. The root of the dry rot of

M

decay in the future of Gaelic is the old enemy, the English Educa-
tional system in Scotland. The days for writing nice things are
past, and the time for talking and talking like chattering magpies
is also past. It is time for action, positive action. Scotland should
take over its own education. There is no choice; we either have
a truly Scottish Education—or we die as a nation.

A cumail na Gaidhlige beo (keeping the Gaelic) is a common
phrase with people lamenting that Gaelic is dying out. But far
more than just lament is needed if Scotland is in dead earnest over
its native language. After all, Gaelic was spoken even in the
Lowlands in the days of Wallace; let alone in the Garden of Eden.

A giant statue should be erected at Bonar Bridge and at Garve,
indicating to travellers that they were coming into the Highlands
of Scotland, showing a *real* Highland welcome; one which
nobody could fail to notice; a statue of a Highlander in prayer
for his country, not just an ordinary plain, common, unattractive
board lettered CEUD MILLE FÀILTE (a 100,000 welcomes) which
means nothing. I called in at one small hotel up north once, for
the board said, 'This hotel bids you a hearty welcome.' All I
wanted was coffee and a biscuit. The former came stone cold,
the latter melodiously soft! I called for the proprietor and told
him what I thought of his notice board, politely indicating where
he should put it—and stumped out. I suppose if I had lingered
and listened to him, he would have blamed S.E.T. or transport
difficulties or some other parrot-phraseology.

It was Cromwell, I believe, who was once looking at some
statues of great men, and turning to a friend remarked, 'Make
mine kneeling, for by that I have risen.' Significant, surely?

Sutherland, I must repeat, is vast. All it needs is like Arizona,
bordering on Mexico, in America, with its giant cacti-like sign-
posts to Eternity, bursting in a fabulous fashion with flowers of
every shade of violet, orange and pink. You are not on a Saturday
afternoon in The Casbah of Tangier that I know so well, with
soft-eyed, shaggy-haired donkeys treading their patient way
through the narrow cobbled alley-ways in the Arab quarters,
with the natives smiling in flowing *fellabas* jostling each other on
every side and the plaintive reedy notes of Arab music mingling
with the cries of the traders calling their wares through a hundred
doorways, where you glimpse a wealth of exciting merchandise.
No, you are far away from your package tour abroad; you are

in a country—your own country too—not so distant from your
home, that is not yet spoiled; with a population in so far as
Sutherland is concerned, of only seven per square mile. For
Ross-shire the figure runs to eighteen per square mile and will be
more when the big Invergordon complex gets going; so Sutherland can well afford to accommodate more people; people of
the right sort; people who will honour the natives' ways, and
pay respect and homage to their religious beliefs.

Readers; you may not have paused to think what your idea
of paradise may actually be? It is not an easy thing to visualise,
and most of us never get much further than the prospect of gentle
sun and a blue lagoon. I have lived for years in those tropical
surroundings but I wouldn't say it was all paradise. Some people's
idea might be the KERGUELEN islands, deep in the frozen wastes of
the Antarctic, inhabited only by penguins. But then perhaps a
lack of human beings is the *sine qua non* of paradise for some folk.
Again, in earlier days, natives of Papua where humans did dwell
in *their* paradise; they were half or completely naked, with
beautiful brown or black bodies. Then there are the Cameroon
Highlands in Africa, with their gentlest and most joyful of marriage ceremonies. Or Ceylon? where every prospect pleases and
only man is vile. All the same the people there are for ever
smiling 'midst the waving of the ubiquitous palm trees. I used to
call Ceylon, where I lived for twenty-five years, 'The Isle or
Delight', for there is no other land in the East or West to compare
with its exotic beauty. Moslem legend has it that after Adam
and Eve were cast out of the Garden, they had the choice of all the
world's loveliest places for their earthly Eden. They chose Ceylon.

LANKA is the old Sanskrit name for the island (which hangs like
a pear-drop from Southern India) brought down twenty-five
centuries ago by the Sinhalese from North India. Another name
for it was *Serendip*. Horace Walpole in 1754 coined the word
'Serendipity', the faculty of making happy, chance finds, from
the title of the fairy tale, *The Three Princes of Serendip*, whose
heroes were always making discoveries by accident and sagacity
of things they were searching. In this respect, Ceylon in the very
old days could be likened to this book's title. The earth in
Ceylon is of a reddish colour, and when some 500 years ago the
Portuguese and Dutch soldiers first stepped ashore, they cried
'THAMBAPANNI'—copper soil. This, in later years was changed

to TAPROBANE (*Tap-ro-banee*) as another name for Ceylon.

Finally, paradise could be Shangri-La, where the birch trees are like tall, straight cathedral columns brooding in silence, and stretching illimitably?

For myself, despite my travels in exotic countries, I plump for Wester Ross and Sutherland as a Paradise hard to beat.

In truth, *Chaqu'un son Paradis*.

In all these thoughts, I am reminded of a small boy (who had never been out of Glasgow) sitting just behind the driver on his very first coach tour, leaving Glasgow one morning; a circular tour which his 30-odd passengers were bent on enjoying. After leaving the crowded city streets and suddenly coming out into the open, with moorland and mountains looming up in the distance, he said excitedly, though timidly, to the driver, 'Please mister, is this the country?' for that would be *his* paradise. And the driver's reply, 'Aye, laddie, this is the country; God's own country.'

Even today there are some people who have the queerest ideas about the Scottish Highlands, and that anyone going from the South to live even around Inverness, is going to live at the back of beyond; that they'll be freezing cold, although of course they will certainly be able to live on next to nothing! One widowed lady down in Middlesex who, with her two children, was shortly changing house to come up to live outside Inverness wrote telling me her twelve-year-old daughter's headmaster (a Lancastrian) asked her if she thought she'd be all right up there; would there be decent schools, school dinners, free milk, entertainment and so on? She ended her letter saying folk down south seem to think Highland people live in igloos and chase haggis over the hills! Another Scottish lady on holiday in Holland went into a post office to purchase some stamps for a few picture-postcards she was sending off to her friends at home. She was met with the puzzled stare, 'Scotland, Scotland,' said the P.O. clerkess, 'is that in Europe?' It looks as though our government controlled Tourist Board is sadly lacking in its propaganda efficiency.

Another incident came to my knowledge of a couple who went into a Yorkshire village shop for some gramophone records. They wanted to buy some records of Scottish songs. Not being able to find them in the racks, they asked the young assistant where such records were, and she said, 'Oh, they'll be under the foreign records section.'

All in all, we should not overlook the splendid vacational opportunities which exist here under our very noses. I believe in course of time, holidaymakers *will* retain their allegiance to the British Isles, having become fed up on the grounds of foreign costs, so much travel formalities, inoculations, visas, language difficulties (should we join the Common Market perhaps we'll all be talking with a Common tongue?), and continental food, bringing in its wake 'continental tummy'. We are not accustomed to food being cooked in oceans of spicey fats, or strange-sounding dishes; spaghetti Bolognaise, sauce Finisterre, Hungarian goulash, coq au vin and other equally queer named tasty concoctions. And believe me, a tummy upset the first few days you are away in the glorious sun-baked resort can very easily mar your whole two weeks stay. However, in time, such continental-bent travellers will begin to feel with much regret the absence of moorlands abroad.

As to one form of boosting tourism to the Highlands, I think school holidays should last for ten full weeks in the summer, and be cut to one week at Christmas, and a couple of days at Easter. This I put as a serious suggestion to ease the holiday congestion, so extending the holiday season to take in the usually sunniest and warmest month of the year, June. American and many of the European schools close for a period of around three months in the summer, and it would seem the education of their children does not suffer. After all, the last few weeks following the May exams are spent in generally relaxing from their taxed brains. This suggestion is not meant to undermine the nervous tension of the nation's mothers of course! During July and August there are crowds, queues and traffic jams up and down the country. Overcrowded and under-staffed hotels and restaurants literally crumble under the onslaught; and tempers fray. And the situation can only get worse as more and more people get increased holiday benefits. At anyrate this is an idea which our government should do well to consider; and in June the Highlands offer plenty of room. There is infinite delight in the colours of the moorland landscape. Those who are of an indifferent nature may call all this boring and monotonous; yet can the keen eye discover anything richer? Even in winter there is variety and a gorgeousness about the moors and hillsides when late autumn turns the bracken to a rich brown and the sun casts blue shadows everywhere. Often too, at high summer noontides, there comes along a blue Italian sky; then the sea is turned to a deeper azure flecked with the whitest foam where it swirls unceasingly against the cliffs. And the crofters' patience? well, this is humorously illustrated by the following lines, which a crofter was moved to utter:

> Oh! that the peats would cut themselves
> The fish slump on to the shore
> And that we all in bed might be
> For aye and evermore. . ..

Och aye! These people have their own ways and customs.

Let us think a little further of the great counties of Wester Ross and Sutherland. America goes in for National Parks in a big way, and I understand these parks were visited a year or so back by 150,000,000 visitors. Just imagine that figure. True, the U.S.A. is much bigger than our Highlands, but all the same 150 million people is 'some people', and the income derived from these visitors was forty times the annual maintenance sum allowed by Congress.

We have no National Parks, but we have a Countryside Commission, and perhaps there is a lesson here to be learned for Scotland, with so much variety of unvarnished scenery and wild life compressed into small space. Making, say, the far north-west into a sort of National Reserve, boosting it as such, the Commission could sell these regions of the Highlands without any loss of scenery and wild life, and still hold, and maybe increase, its resident population to add to the natural beauty which crofting agriculture gives the landscape? For believe me there is nothing on this earth today which will yield such a reward—without any gambling speculation—as the proper management of scenically fine landscape coupled with wild life.

I think there is no doubt that in the matter of a year or so, visitors will look upon the Highlands as well fitted for a caravanning holiday; and as such, what better than a Natural Park, well organised. This could serve some purpose to the rest of Scotland. Far better this, and not the emotional wails of some sort of industrial and social rejuvenation. Silly, little, heavy industrial schemes have no place in the *real* Highlands.

As to beautifying our villages more, a great deal has been

done by Highland schoolchildren in certain neighbourhoods under a scheme organised by the Crofters' Commission and the Scottish Civic Trust. 'Highland Village Project, 1970' was made possible by a generous gift of £5000 by Lord Dulverton. This money is to be used to encourage schoolchildren to take in hand to beautify in crofting areas in whatever manner took their fancy. This has 'taken on' with much enthusiasm and success; and I would record the following that have really been outstanding; at Ullapool a lovely garden has been created on the foreshore; at Bowmore, on Islay, a piece of derelict ground was cleared and terraced as a playground; a park and nature trail was laid out in a glen behind Portree by children of Portree High School; a garden was created by Oban High School from rubbish-strewn ground near the main road at Kilmore village; a view indicator, overlooking the site of the two battles of Inverlochy, was built by Lochyside School, Fort William; an ancient Norse mill was reconstructed by pupils of Shawbost Secondary School, Lewis, and they converted a disused church into a folk museum; at Helmsdale in Sutherland two gardens have been constructed by the secondary school pupils. Such projects as these are surely of immense importance; bringing and training Youth into the foreground with worthwhile ideas.

In regard to wild life, the Royal Scottish Society for Prevention of Cruelty to Animals, the R.S.S.P.C.A., performs a most useful and extensive task in Scotland; and I know from personal contact their many inspectors are kept busy all the year round. The Society collaborates closely with the Royal Society for the Protection of Birds, and particular attention is paid to investigations of the capture of wild song-birds in small cages by use of bird-lime; it also extends to the protection of the eggs of common wild birds. If any person is suspected of taking or destroying eggs illegally, a constable is empowered to stop and search the person and his vehicle without a warrant. There was a case not so long ago of two men coming up from the south staying at an Inn in Wester Ross, and going out very early one morning in search of eagle's eggs in the mountainous range near Dundonell, close to Gruinard Bay. They had all the latest equipment for the job. I believe one of the men was an American. Their haul was quite big; about 30 or 40 eggs. But word got around and the police soon had them charged at the Sheriff's court. Tackle and eggs confiscated; but the poor eagles and their eggs?

It may surprise some people that, in the small district where I live, there are nearly one hundred different species of wild birds.

Deer is another problem, for there is quite a lot of illicit shooting and peddling of the carcasses in the Highlands; and the close season for all species is not always observed. There is reason to believe the snaring of roe deer continues undetected owing to the wide areas in which it can be practised. The Forestry Commission has forbidden this in its woods.

Something over 30,000 red deer, stags and hinds, are killed each season in the Highlands (and at the correct season too) with the rifle. Exploitation at this level is dictated by sound management, as it leaves the herds at roughly 180,000 head. The killing is humane and efficient.

I was very sorry to know that a legend died on 1st December 1970, when a single rifle shot killed the famous white stag of Arran. It was a 16-stone beast that was put down by the head gamekeeper on the instructions of Lady Jean Fforde of Brodick.

The legendary stag was born some 13 years ago, the same year that Lady Jean's mother, the late Duchess of Montrose, died; and many villagers claimed the stag represented the old lady's spirit on the island. (Arran—Lochranza—was the first place I ever came to know of in Scotland many years ago.) It appears the stag was frightening old people and children in Lochranza. Legend has it that when the head of Lady Jean's family dies, a white stag is seen on the hillside. Recently, due to the stag's age, his teeth were worn almost right down, and he was then dependent on the villagers to feed him. Many old folk were afraid to leave their homes at night because he would follow them along the road; and during daylight, he became a danger to children. He only had one very long antler, but that could well prove lethal. The mysterious stag—whose colour resulted from a freak genetic strain—died in the garden of a Lochranza cottage.

I believe a stag's life would be about 20 years. Surely someone, somehow, somewhere in its Lochranza haunts could have taken him into their fenced garden as a pet, seeing it was growing old and looked to people for its food, so enabling this noble beast to enjoy its remaining life in its own majestic, quiet way.

Although the killing of such an animal was unkind, there are of course times when one has to be cruel to be kind. It would perhaps have been against the white stag's nature to be fenced in, as it might have caused it to try and run wild, so endangering the public more, yet I have seen quite a few stags becoming used to being 'petted', and in this particular instance I think some attempt might have been made to fence him in, and see how he reacted to being fed and petted daily.

We must not forget the grouse, pheasant, and the renowned salmon, which every year brings a great number of Sasunnachs up north, with all their guns and paraphernalia—and in regard to the salmon, a wealth of tackle, to 'tackle' the wily princely fish.

The tenacity of purpose of salmon ascending a river is a thing at which one must marvel. In almost every river, they have to pass difficult places, which in Scotland are called 'loups' and 'linns'; and there they can be seen leaping into the falling waters, then, with violently-wriggling body and flailing tail, striving to force themselves up and over the final water-washed rocks into the easier stream above the falls. Many make effort after effort and fall back exhausted; but the salmon is a fish of power and spirit, and after resting for a while, it will then spring into the air in a final successful leap.

The salmon was named by the Romans 'the leaper' from the Latin *salio*, 'I leap', on account of this characteristic trait; for it can leap four or five feet—and more—into the air, often clearing what would seem to be impassable obstacles. I believe the record stands at just over eleven feet.

Salmon leap up waterfalls for the simple reason they can't help it! The fishery department design costly fish-ladders on rivers in the belief that fish like to swim upstream; but they don't. They much prefer to jump, and the jump is made easy for, when water drops into a pool, it creates an upthrust known as a 'standing wave', and it is this thrust which makes the salmon leap so helping it upstream to the spawning ground. Salmon ascending a river don't feed because they can't. Their stomachs shrink to nothing; they exist on their own tissues, and may lose as much as twenty-five per cent. of their weight on their way upstream.

There is no more perfect movement to be witnessed in any other species than the coiling (head touching tail) and sudden springing of this silvery fish, which can be likened to a taut strongbow suddenly released. At certain salmon-leap falls, you will come across crowds of visitors literally hypnotised, watching this spectacle for long enough.

Poaching, of course, is a very 'catching' habit in the Highlands; any housewife will tell you, poached salmon (in the true culinary sense!) is very tasty.

There's not only the salmon, but the whisky! An old Highlander used to tell me that whisky was one of the two gifts God gave to Scotland. The other was the scenery; and he made it clear that in his estimation, whisky—or usquebaugh to give it its true Gaelic name—was by far the more important. For, he said, a drink like this could never have been discovered or invented; it had to come from Heaven. Throughout the world, whisky is the most popular spirits drink of all. Today, there are so many brands about, it is difficult to keep count. There must be many hundreds.

Two crofters were talking, and one said to the other, 'there's nae better cure for the toothache than whisky'. 'Am surprised at you,' the other said, 'that's the first word I've ever heard in praise of it.' 'Aye,' came the reply, 'there's no mony that speak weel o' the toothache.'

Peat plays an increasing part in the making of whisky. The green malted barley grains contain a large amount of moisture, and are dried out in the smoke arising from a peat fire some ten or fifteen feet below, till it only contains about three per cent. of moisture; for peat can soak up many times its own weight of water, and hold on to it for long periods.

*   *   *

The Countryside Commission are now being interested in so-called wildernesses, and in preserving them against development, and so I hope this region of north-west Scotland *will* be so preserved. In this connection certain areas have been suggested; Loch Hope to Loch Loyal, 50 square miles; Sutherland and Ross border, Loch Lurgainn (near Stac Polly) to Loch Assynt—Lochinver ways—90 square miles. The Cuillin of Skye, 50 square miles; the great region north of Loch Maree (Wester Ross) 200 square miles, and a few others not coming within the scope of this book.

We all know whatever Government may be in power, they love to bring in new departments, a commission for this, a commission for that, with new staffs to be housed; and when all is said and done most of them sitting pretty with little work to do —for they've little money to spend. However, we seem to muddle along, and of course up here as I have said we have *Time on our hands*, and we make haste slowly. There is an Eastern proverb which says, 'Hurry is of the devil, but slow advancing comes from God'. What is done hastily is seldom done well; and being ill done, it has to be undone; and this wastes time. With eager feeding, food will choke the eater.

A propos of this, there is the story of the American tourist being annoyed at the scheduled (skeduled) time of the *Loch Seaforth* leaving Kyle of Lochalsh for Stornoway at 2.30 p.m., and it then being after three o'clock, and no sign of the ship sailing. He was strutting about the deck impatiently, and with holiday guide book in one hand, and a gold watch and chain in the other, went up to the seaman at the gangway, intending to let out on him for this unheard of delay, which never happened in the U.S.A.; but the canny Highlander forestalled his wrath by telling him, 'she never leaves *before* 2.30 p.m.'.

Things do get mixed up sometimes by overseas tourists. Aunty and her companion were making for Melbost in the Outer Hebrides, and her textbook said when they got off at the Uist port after coming across the ferry service from Uig (Skye), they were to turn right. This they did, but after a few miles there seemed to be no signpost or anything to say Melbost was round the corner. Stopping and asking a local with his sheep dog trailing at his feet, he told them this was Lochmaddy. They should have taken the boat from Uig to Lochboisdale in South Uist, not Lochmaddy in North Uist.

Then again, I was once told some experiences of an English couple visiting Tiree (a small island off MULL, and south of the isle of COLL), who took a caravan over there; it appeared to be the only one on the island. Upon arriving they asked for milk at the Co-op shop, and were asked, 'Have you ordered it?' 'No,' they said, and therefore there was no milk available. Asking for bread they were again asked, 'Have you ordered it?' Therefore, 'no bread'. They then went on to the Harbour Master's store. The Harbour Master was away with the pipe band on the mainland and would not be back for a few days. They thought they would be sure to get a carton of Long Life milk there. The assistant gave them a sympathetic hearing to their plight, but said she hadn't a single carton on hand, and couldn't split a case of L.-L. milk. So they had to settle for a whole case. They told me that they and their relatives were using L.-L. milk for months afterwards!

Whilst they were talking to the one and only island's policeman near the signpost at the harbour, they congratulated him on there being at least two road signs on the island. He immediately replied, 'Two? where's the other one?' They enlightened him by saying it was outside the airstrip. He went off to locate it. They spoke to him as to where they could park their car and caravan, and toilet tent, and he said, 'You are most welcome to put them anywhere you like on the island.' 'A fabulous welcome to strangers on an enchanting island,' they said. Just himself and his wife as visitors. An event of a lifetime they told me, adding that they were going back there, again and again—'so long as their tackle held good', grandpa said upon their return home.

As motoring is now of such a problem in which sitting behind a wheel makes everyone more or less ill-tempered, a trip to Shangri-La should improve these city tensions; for it is perhaps the only area of Britain where drivers are polite to each other; due no doubt to the fascinating system of 'passing places' on our single track roads; for every few hundred yards on these narrow winding roads is a bulge just wide enough for a vehicle or two to move off the roadway to let another car or lorry pass. Often invisible from a distance, these bulges are marked by a white-painted diamond-shaped piece of iron plate on a post. Many hundreds of miles are like this, and so motorists pull into these places as soon as they see another car approaching, and flash their headlamps indicating they are stopping, and giving them the cue to come on. This is relaxed motoring to a fine art. The remote realms of these passing places are mostly in the west, where mountains, the broken coast-line and the scattered settlements have resulted in narrower roads.

In the middle of the last century, the Highlander and his way of life were brought very much into focus by Queen Victoria, when she led the way after purchasing and rebuilding Balmoral. Then arose the question, if the Queen had her summer residence in the north why shouldn't the aristocracy from Belgravia, or industrialists from the midlands do the same? So the Highlands

became fashionable; historic tartans were devised and new traditions invented, almost daily. And so Shangri-La became even
more historic. Queen Victoria called her estate on Deeside,
'*This dear Paradise*'.

Emigrants from the British Isles, more than those from any
other land, have been in the habit of calling settlements and
natural features in the countries to which they moved, after
place-names at home. The Scots undoubtedly seek to keep a
nostalgic link with their homeland. A part of the New World
which particularly appears to bear out this impression is Nova
Scotia—New Scotland (ACADIA was the ancient name, the
country being renamed in 1622); although those other than
Scotsmen settled there; French, German and English. In Nova
Scotia there is quite a preponderance of Highland place-names,
such as Appin, Argyle, Arisaig, Gairloch, Glencoe, Glengarry,
Kinloch, Knoydart, Loch Broom, Morar, Moidart, Oban, and a
heap more. There are Hebridean names to be found as well.
Personal names also crop up as place-names, *i.e.* Abercrombie
(General who was killed at Bunker Hill in 1775); Claverhouse
(Viscount Dundee); Elgin (James Bruce, 8th Earl of Elgin,
Governor-General of Canada, 1847–1854). There is also a settle-
ment named Dingwall, after Robert Dingwall, a shopkeeper;
and there is Culloden, so named when a ship called the *Culloden*
was wrecked there in 1859. I find no settlement named Shangri-
La; it would of course be centuries before any of those emigrants,
emigrated!

I have already mentioned that Greek figure-wizard who said
the straight line was the shortest distance between two points.
He would have laughed at the men who tramped the drove roads
between John o' Groat and Inverness, for over the centuries they
had to trudge with their cattle round mountains, ford streams and
so on. When the early road builders came along, they too, more
or less, kept to the 150-mile track in its contours, gradients and
dykes. But even when those roads were made, the drovers still
kept to their own hillside tracks, for they said the hard-surfaced
roadway wore out the cattle's feet. Soon, I suppose, we shall see
another M1 motoring road from Inverness to Wick and Thurso—
a straight Euclid-lined hundred mile an hour roadway, spanning
the Beauly, Cromarty and Dornoch Firths; spot on, dead on to
Scotland's 'Land's End'.

In olden days, there were often many hazards facing these drovers, least of which was being intercepted by attacking marauders, who ran off with a score or so of cattle. There is one narrow defile, admirably placed for these highwaymen, between Achnasheen and Loch Luichart on the Gairloch–Garve road. I think it must have been called 'The Cumberland Gap'.

In the early 18th century (1739 in fact), a well-known Sutherland drover and his men, were taking a 'golat drove' of cattle to the Crieff sales. As usual they took the old-fashioned drove road route, crossing fords and going through glens and moorlands. Later on their journey they forded a river at Loch Ness— long before the Caledonian Canal was constructed. A few miles farther on they and their cattle rested. During the early night a small band of men rode up demanding some of the herd. This, in local dialect, was termed 'road collop'; and it was the bandit's custom in returning to their village with the booty, to give over a few animals to those Clan Chiefs through whose land they were travelling in payment, so to speak, for the privilege of passage.

These men were nothing less than robbers; and the drover's chief was in no mood to accede to their request although he had no weapons to withstand an assault. He suggested as it was dark, and not to stampede his herd, they could conveniently wait until the morning to take what cattle they wanted. And this was agreed.

As I have said, the drover and his company had no weapons due to an oversight; for the Disarming Act of 1716 made an exception in the case of drovers for they could get the necessary licence to carry pistols. However, this noted drover had friends in Inverness, five miles away, and he sent one of his men to tell them of his predicament. His messenger returned at daylight with many fire-arms and pistols. In due course, the robbers, who had camped nearby, came along to claim their 'reward'; but they were met with pistols at the ready. They quickly made off! The whole drove reached Crieff safely and the cattle sold. However, the precious pistols—to be returned to the Inverness friends on the way back home—were discovered by a patrol of militia near Kingussie, who thought there was something peculiar in the bulges of the drover's men's trousers. The weapons were discovered, and there being no covering licence, confiscated.

No doubt this great Sutherland worthy would in future see to it that he obtained a licence to carry firearms on his next voyage of adventure south.

* * *

One of the few generalisations that can be made about the Highlands is that one cannot make generalisations about the country! Differences between the east and west coasts are greater, racially and ethnically, than between independent nations. Even in the western area local conditions vary from glen to glen; from village to village. During the troubled years following the '45, clansmen, as I have told you, were driven out of their glens and forced westward. Later, clearances of hill land for sheep pushed crofting families to the coast. Disease, and all its dire results, made havoc with the normal death rate; however, the introduction of the potato allowed more people to live on less land. Then came crop failure and famine, and the exodus again took shape and has continued. In Gairloch in 1861 there were nearly 6000 inhabitants. Today, the figure will be around 1500 In Sutherland, only the voice of the wind answers a man in some of its empty expanses. A lone house clings tenaciously to fields turned green by frequent rain. Crofters' snug homes once filled, and over-spilled, the land. But that was before the sheep arrived, causing wholesale evictions. It all makes sad reading as I have described earlier. But the long Highland evenings, extending to well after midnight in the summer (the land of the midnight sun?) helps to repulse the darkness of those years. Indeed there would be no darkness, no despair at all really, for the first light of dawn soon silvered their sky. Although the Highlander still has one foot planted in the past, he continues to feel with the other, a foothold in the present. The old years do not die; they are reborn in the life ahead. His Faith, and his banner of Truth, El estandarte de la verdad (Peruvian Spanish, not Gaelic this time!) has been his shield, and will be so for all Time to come.

* * *

I have written of *Autumn* at the beginning of this book. What about *Spring*? Spring is the most therapeutic thing in the natural world. Always, at that irksome, restless time between Christmas gone and summer still-to-come, it arrives in a multitude of green shades to revitalise every living thing (even Love!).

It does one good to feel it in your bones, let alone see it from one's Shangri-La fortress. So a visit to the Highlands during that season of the year can do you a world of good. In fact it is a spare holiday for those who may be saving their sterling (or decimal) allowance, and looking for something different abroad.

Here you find the blissful quiet; no milling crowds blotting out—with their litter too—the unique scenery you've travelled up to see and admire; no anxiety to obtain accommodation; there's plenty of room for everyone, dog included. And prices below the peak season. There is plenty of daylight in the spring; there's a tang in the air, the trees become green again after their winter nakedness, and the hills and straths have an infectious serenity and glow. You can forget all about strikes; and with your car, you can take it all in, with plenty of time to spare. The Scottish Highlands have something to suit all ages and all pockets. In autumn and early spring you can find some passes full of hill mist so thick you could cut it up and sell it for briquettes! . . .

John Knox and Mary, Queen of Scots, are Edinburgh's most famous ghosts. Somehow or other, in recent writings, I have found my mind drawn to Mary, Queen of Scots, whose mother was Mary of Lorraine, wife of James V; for I look upon her with a certain amount of romanticism—as I do with Bonnie Prince Charlie. I feel touched by the tragedy of the young Queen, the *reinette*, or little Queen, as she was called in France, who was betrothed when she was only five years of age to the Dauphin of France. She was much beloved at Court. Mary arrived in Paris in 1548; she was Queen for a few months only, as her husband Francis II died soon after his accession.

She set sail from France on a summer's day in 1561, arriving at Leith in August that year to the initial joy of her Scottish subjects, but to the lasting grief of the friends she had left behind in France. The day she set sail for Scotland she lingered late on the ship's deck and rose early in the morning so that her eyes might rest upon the beloved shore of France until it vanished for ever from her sight. She was three times married before her imprisonment when she was only 26 years old. Few public lives have been more intriguing. Was she involved in Darnley's murder; did she marry Bothwell of her own free will?

Some people have us believe she was just a flighty piece;

others look on her as a martyr, others just as a warmly human woman. Many think of her as being a wicked woman. Probably there was a bit of all these things in her make-up. She had a great trust in people and in humanity and she was forever being disappointed when even her friends let her down.

What little we were taught about her from English history at school, was very much glossed over, and all the concentration was on Elizabeth; though the two Queens never did see each other.

Mary had a magical quality that touched everyone she met. Some real clue to her character is shown by one heart-tearing gesture. The night before she was executed, she sat up for hours making a kind of Will which ensured that all her servants would be provided for after she was dead. That she could do such a thing, knowing the axe was waiting for her in the morning, tells us more about her than almost anything else.

Her mysterious life was set against the religious and political squabbles of an age of violence. She was truly a Prisoner of Power, and when she went to her execution to the Great Hall of Fotheringay Castle in February 1587, she prayed there might be a beginning; for in her latter days she constantly used the enigmatic motto, '*In my end is my beginning*' . . . and at the close, 'my end *is* my beginning'.

The end is my beginning?

These five simple words, with a question mark, will doubtless produce an impact on each one of us, the immensity of which is difficult to grasp; it is beyond our ken. None of us can predict when our end may be; nor where our end will lead us to after death.

> . . . The Clock of Life is wound but once
> And no man has the power
> To tell just when the hands will stop
> At late or early hour.

*　　　*　　　*

Although I have likened the Far North to the mystical EVERLASTING Shangri-La country, many of my friends, to my grief, have faded and passed over to the other side. This, we must expect.

In the first book I ever wrote about the Highlands some years ago, I concluded with these words: '*as the years multiply, the milestones become gravestones, and under each a friend*'. This is a truism that all of us, one time or another, have to painfully experience. All the same we must carry on in our quiet way to the end of the road.

I have lived for many years in Gairloch, overlooking the bay, the Torridons and Skye; but I, too, in the fulfilment of Time will be taking a journey at the turn of the tide and at the going down of the sun; though not on the *Loch Seaforth* to Stornoway, but on the *Loch Henceforth*—a very different journey and one of Great Adventure to another Shangri-La.

All my life I have regarded myself as an apprentice in that one has never done learning; and I suppose I will still be an apprentice upon entering the next Shangri-La.

There is a Gaelic saying, MA'S MAITH LEAT DO MHOLADH FAIGH BAS . . . 'if you wish to be praised, die'.

The gold medal winning poem at the Gaelic 1970 Mod held in Oban, was by Donald John MacDougall; and the rough English translation comes very fitting for this paragraph. 'I'm old and tired. A ship will one day come for me. White visionary sails will leap across the rim of the horizon and stiffen to the breeze and bear down swiftly towards me. I shall say Goodbye to all my friends . . . and step aboard.'

This book is not by any stretch of imagination meant to be melancholy, but all the same—sooner or later—we must come to grips with the realities of Life from which none of us can escape.

Frequently in these chapters, I have touched upon the Timeless atmosphere up north, which is never dreamt of anywhere else in Britain.

> What is Time? a river flowing
>   To Eternity's vast sea
> Forward, whither all are rowing
>   On its bosom bearing thee.
>
> What is Life? a bubble floating
>   On that silent, rapid stream
> Few, too few, its progress noting
>   Till it bursts, and ends the dream.

Lives of great men all remind us we can make our lives sublime, and departing leave behind us footprints on the sands of Time; footprints that perhaps another, sailing o'er life's solemn main, a forlorn and a shipwrecked brother, seeing shall take heart again.

> ... And quietly the waves of our fast-ebbing tide
> Resolve to return to where all must abide. ...

*   *   *

To live in the Highlands is to know why exiled Highlanders save and save in the far distant countries of the outside world, or the more luxurious, coddled in hot climates, to return home perhaps with fading eyes, but a Celtic longing to this land of lochs and peat; stags and eagles; castles and corries; of mountains and glens; of wild seas and endless moors; and why I, a Colonial Englishman, deign to raise a glass and toast 'The Highlands'.

When the Supreme Architect created the Highlands, he made it for himself originally—a vast country full of space and majesty; a great loneliness and incomparable beauty. Today the Highlands brood dramatically over their yesterdays; their moments of shining greatness, the glories and the sorrows and the despairs etched indelibly in the stones, the mountains and the moors; reflected in the sightless eyes of lochs. Who but a Scot would have thought of placing a timely stone to commemorate that spot in Sutherland where the last wolf was killed around 1700, and how it fires the imagination—a wolf and a hunter. Or who, on that road to the Isles from Invermoriston, would not be stirred by the bravery of Roderick Mackenzie who fought a battle single-handed against soldiers seeking Bonnie Prince Charlie (whom he resembled) to allow Charles Edward to escape, and fell at last mortally wounded at the spot the cairn commemorates. To follow the escape route of the Prince is an exciting experience, and to attempt it on foot is to wonder and respect anew how it was ever accomplished with greedy redcoats on his heels. . . . And at Culloden where the last battle on British soil was bloodily and murderously enacted, one stands with bowed head at the mute clan stones bearing witness to the Highland dead.

The wildness of the past is echoed still in Nature. The mountain sheep, independent and self-sufficient drop their lambs . . . far from the midwife hands of shepherds; and here and there, the Highland cattle graze like shaggy horn-helmeted Vikings of old, moving on all fours for camouflage. How can we allow planners to desecrate or destroy the general way of life here? How indeed?

Sometimes the coming of modernity brings the crofter unexpected bonus along with aesthetic disadvantages.

The dead of winter brings its own transformations; the grass in the snow standing rumpled as unmade beds; the lochans frozen gun-metal grey with their winter armour of ice. The deer, desperate for food, return to the valleys and the ways of man.

And the islands? they are so different; some with enchanted Mary Rose landscapes. The wide variety of Lewis with its magnificent coastline; the sturdy boats and fishermen of the nations in Stornoway, and the stately *Loch Seaforth* resting at anchor after butting its way to and fro across the Minch which at times can be as still and calm as a pail of milk, and at others, produce waves tall as cathedrals, so much so one is almost surprised to land eventually at Kyle of Lochalsh in a dark cold morning and not to have been dining with Neptune in the deep, cold salt water.

And Skye? So near the mainland yet so far off in Time; and so different. To see the Old Man of Storr (as I do every day from my bungalow in Gairloch), the Quirang and the bare precipitous awe-inspiring Cuillin, is to be aware of Eternity— and a sense of limitlessness. It is all so real.

Early summer brings its own delight of almost endless daylight when the sun dips down and returns again almost immediately. And the dawn chorus is under way long before 3 a.m. Once in the north at Tongue in Sutherland I saw, one evening, a primeval battle waging between the rising moon and the setting sun. Can you see that anywhere else in Britain? The Highlands take the palm, the crown, the heart. There is greatness here, and everything is king-sized and would even bring delight and applause from any Texan or Patagonian.

Highland hospitality is larger than life, like the views, the landscape, the people and their history. One American visitor once said to me that he didn't know this gracious kind of living existed any more. 'You Scots,' he said (he didn't know he was speaking to an Englishman!) 'are so polite and civilised.' People living in this Shangri-La territory should ask themselves, 'What can I do for the Highlands?' not 'What can the Highlands do for me?'

Here one can live with legends in the past, in this land of *Tir-nan-Òg*; the land of the ever young as I remarked upon in the first chapter.

What a beautiful sounding name is Tir-nan-Òg? And here are a few poetical lines eulogising its significance. They were written by Ian MacLeod who, for only a few weeks until his sudden death, held the high office of Chancellor of the Exchequer in the Tory Government of 1970. They were given me by a personal friend of his.

There's a land amongst the sunsets set amidst the Western
    main,
Where the dead are done with dying and are once more
    young again
And the sun streams gently downwards like the fall of
    endless rain
        In Tir-nan-Òg.

There they live, the lovely women and the bravest of the men
There the chiefs of Siol Torquil go out to war again
And the pipes of the MacCrimmons are awaiting in the glen,
        In Tir-nan-Òg.

There the sands go dancing downwards to meet the shining sea
There the great hills rear triumphant heads disdainfully and free
And all my dreams are haunted and are ever calling me
        To Tir-nan-Òg.

*   *   *

There is the same sense of Timelessness which has permeated the Highlands, as with the Spanish, namely, 'tomorrow, I'll do it' . . . and of course tomorrow never comes. I remember as a boy, my uncle who lived outside Sheffield, and where I used to spend many of the summer months, telling me of a Spanish proverb that was very apt. For many years he was on a sailing ship trading up and down the west coast of South America from Cape Horn to Valparaiso and Antafagasta on the Chilean seaboard, and he picked up a smattering of Spanish. He was a godly man, and when he retired, became a lay preacher. Here then is the Chilean proverb, 'never be in a hurry except when catching fleas'. Some truth in this?

*   *   *

Out of the holiday season, the sense of quietness can not only be felt in the far north—but touched. 'Anything for a quiet life,' said the young mother of three infants, as she set off with them to hear the pipe band!

'Timelessness.' No sense of hurry; only a sense of great holiness, for the land is hallowed near to God's feet. In their own language they will tell you *Chan'eil ni sambith do-dheanta do Dhia* . . . 'you cannot do anything without God'.

Surprisingly though, life in the Highlands is very often lived—in its own sweet way—more fully than it is in busy cities. The influx of the B. and B. guests provide a continued variety of interest; and the incomers (people whose jobs have brought them from afar to the lonely villages and people who have retired from town life, as well as those from foreign lands) all come to enjoy the peace of the Highland life. They, as a rule, blend in well, and have something to give each other. Whilst the locals have a strong background foundation (they know each other's history as far back as can be remembered) the incomers bring a freshness which can enrich community life. The village shops can provide almost everything and the store-keeper or his assistant can switch from English to Gaelic without blinking an eye-lid. Then, there are the 'van days', when neighbours meet and news (like in the post offices) is exchanged whilst purchases are made. The driver always has news which he has gathered on his way, so that people know more about friends who may live 20 miles away, than they would know of somebody who only lived a distance of yards in the city's suburbs; and all news is received so sympathetically that they wonder how they can help if there is trouble, or what to buy for a wedding present or for a new baby.

The folk who inhabit the far north are truly the right people for the right setting; proud, strong, characterful and delightful . . . and the night shall be filled with music, and the cares that infest the day, shall fold their tents like the Arabs, and as silently steal away.

* * *

We hear so much about the Highlands and its problems. But the Highlander is capable of tackling every thing, if given the opportunity and the incentive to do so. If they are able to plant and grow trees in the Sahara (or Great Desert) of sand, through which I have travelled, where only camels and their tribes journey from one oasis to another; if they can now cultivate 260 acres and acclimate 100,000 trees, fruit and vegetable crops and join up green belt by green belt at these oases, what is to prevent new ideas, new developments to help the sparse Sutherland county? This Sahara scheme is fascinating, and could convert the oceans of sand into a land flowing with milk and honey. Eucalyptus and acacia trees are being planted, and a ten-year project is in hand. The Algerian forestry depts. are interested, and more acres are being planted; in fact, there seems to be no limit to this exploration—save the sky; the hot, burning, scorching sky.

*   *   *

Many of the places and islands off the western coast here can be termed as 'Dreamlands'. I think I have given readers this impression through these many pages. I call to mind one in particular, the little island of Raasay, not far from Gairloch. It is shown in the small map given at the heading of the Gairloch chapter, and lies between the Isle of Skye and the mainland. One lady wrote me saying, 'I would willingly spend the rest of my days here, looking over the water to Skye, with the Applecross hills at my back.'

In such a place as Raasay and to such an atmosphere, the absence of cinemas, bingo and other present-day amusements and entertainments gives an air of tranquillity (as I have remarked upon throughout this book) hard to equal in today's noisy world. The number of cars is less than the miles of road; you feel the road is your own, as you do in the beautiful Strathnaver valley in Sutherland. Apart from the small village post office, only one shop serves the community. There, the inhabitants will gather daily, for small talk and news, when the soft lilt of Gaelic sweetens the air. The district nurse, the postman, the policeman are all important members in this very small community, which is entirely self-supporting and which survives the march of progress. Raasay has a wealth of untamed vegetation. The magnificent Raasay House, once a mansion which contained a most extensive library when I was there some years ago, is to be converted into an hotel. This, and other small changes are happening slowly enough not to mar the island's natural loveliness. All this is being watched by DUN CAAN, the island's mountain. Raasay is not rich in worldly goods—few of these 'Highland Pearls' are—yet those who are attracted and fascinated by such a little haven from modern society will return there, time and time again.

There is beauty in the sunlight and the soft blue heavens above; oh! the world is full of beauty, when the heart is full of love.

What next? as the tadpole said when his tail dropped off! I am afraid there will be no 'next', for I think I have let the world outside Shangri-La know enough of the breathtaking variety of scenery, beaches of fine sand lapped by a gentle sea, the tranquil beauty of a mountain-guarded loch, and the joy of living up in Wester Ross and Sutherland. Anything further would be idle repetition, for I have written over half a million words extolling this great northern territory.

So this book may be read 'as a tale that is told', quoting Psalm 90, v. 9.

Have you ever seen Heaven? Of course not, but if you have read through these pages and pondered over the many thoughts expressed, I think I may have shown you something of this side of Heaven in the Highlands. Over a hundred years ago, a great American writer and political leader, Horace Greeley (born in New Hampshire in 1811, d. 1872) used the phrase, 'Go West, young man', presumably to find the epitomy of human desire. For myself, I would say, 'Go North, young man, far north of the border, and grow up with the country there'.

To be happy you need to find yourself. To find yourself you must first lose yourself; and this can be a deeply rewarding experience if gone about in the right way. To lose oneself is to lose one's inhibitions, and one cannot even know what those inhibitions were until they have been lost. The same old sameness of life is an eternal process. How, then, can we escape into a totally different dimension to look at ourselves? Where can such a place be? It is in Shangri-La; that means, go to the Highlands of Scotland.

Scotland sings of a past which was born of a kind of freedom which is indestructible. The secret lies in journeying, as I have indicated, to the Highlands; she will tell you her own story, her own song—a story without words. Its story is grandeur, its awesome starkness, its frightening beauty; its limitless wonder is such a vast storehouse of treasure that to dare attempt to relate it, is to scratch merely the surface of infinity.

The plot of the Highland story unfolds the farther north one goes. It is a story of why and a story of what, which, even though heard many times, is one you'll want to hear again and again. 'Why and what?' you may ask. Well, why are the hills and mountains so majestic; why is nothing spoilt, as it is elsewhere? Why is one attracted to the magic arena of life? What makes it all so staggering in its wild splendour? And many more like questions.

Here, Time stands aside to allow you pass. Highland drama, to a perceptive and receptive beholder, is quite gripping and complicated. Complicated in its varied scenes and history, as I have endeavoured to expound. Only a fool can return from this fairytale land unmoved by what he has experienced. One will, on being enraptured by all this drama, become swiftly and irrevocably aware of one's own feeble attempts to find contentment, for here there is no mad struggle to be on top; no time factor . . . there's enough Time for everyone and anything. And it is quite true, as I have said before, on a clear day *you can see for ever.* You can see what matters, you can see what is ideal; and you can also see what loneliness is. You need to see all this to understand it; see the endless moorland as yet untouched; see the imposing majesty of a rock outcrop mountain-size.

You must look through the mist and the Corridors of Time; you must look as far back as the ancient Kingdom of Dalriada (now Southern Argyll). Then later on, look to the Kingdom of Shangri-La—and Peace.

One of my favourite readings in The Book, is that of the Prophet Isaiah. I believe it was written by two distinct Isaiahs; but that is beside the point. The whole of its sixty-six chapters are full of realities, and remind me of a jeweller's-window ablaze with gems; and none rarer than the 3rd verse of chapter 26 . . . 'Thou wilt keep him in perfect peace, whose mind is stayed on Thee'. Perfect peace, as known in this Highland territory, is one of the loveliest settings ever; not just the peace of some ancient churchyard, sleeping half-forgotten in its solitude but a peace whose rare quality only emerges when it is set within the turmoil and grind of a work-a-day life. There may be pebbles or shells by your doorway, that you've brought back home from your

holiday, but they are now dull, drab and lifeless, whilst from the
seashore they appeared so bright and so attractive when picked
up wet from the restless sea in Shangri-La's land of Peace.

Of course life would be unbearable if it did not change.
Everything changes; our circumstances and our fortunes. The
years bring changes in our very outlook, and Time bleaches the
colours of our earlier enthusiasms. 'Thou wilt keep him . . .'
Albeit this thought, like the lovely gem it is, needs the perfect
setting as all gems do. I can only tell you, this can be discovered
in the Far North's glory.

The north-west and middle-west areas of Sutherland and of
Wester Ross have a strange uniqueness. Unique inasmuch that
all things *are* unique, strangely so because of the magic of it.
Have you ever been in such a state of isolation as to be out of
range of any sound; literally any sound? Before you answer
'yes', think again. I could almost guarantee you'd be wrong.
There'll always be a rustling zephyr to intervene, a distant car—
however hushed; a train, the rain, a fly or something. I have sat
on a hillside far away looking on to the Kyle of Tongue, with a
superb distant sunset for company, and heard—nothing; just
silence. A silence which can be touched; and it is uncanny,
unreal—yet real. It is magic all over again. A glowing sunset
over the still blue sea will cast a spell to haunt you, and continue
to haunt you; so near, yet so distant you'll want to touch it.

I think there will be few people who, in watching the sun
going down and shooting its swords of gold, ever notice that
as it just slips below the water's edge, there is in that split fraction
of a second, a gorgeous flash of green colour; the sun's refraction
(not reflection) through the ocean's water. You can see this
almost every night in the tropics; you can see it along the
western seaboard of the Highlands. Wander where you will,
you will want to come back; it will draw you like coming home
does. You will feel like running to a hill-top in this Utopian
State, and shouting out aloud, 'of course I'll come back; I *must*
come back'. The call of the North, once heard, is incessant; for
who but God could make the day, and gently tuck the night
away. As in the Gothic world, Shangri-La embraces a world of
chivalry, courtesy and romance.

This is the land of black-faced sheep, the collie dogs, sleeping
cats, and General Wade's hump bridges (just like the cat stretching

its back after sleeping). Here you don't need a house that looks like a palace, but a palace with a house of contentment inside it; and a loyalty to your fellow Highlander.

In Exodus, ch. 34 and verses 30 and 35, you will read that 'Moses' face shone'. I venture to say of all I have written respecting the Shangri-La country, readers faces too will shine upon seeing such great beauty the Highlands can unfold. Let there be many windows in your soul, that all the glory of the Universe may beautify it. Not the narrow pane of one poor creed can catch the radiant rays that shine from countless sources. Tear away the blinds of suspicion and let the light pour through fair windows, broad as truth itself, and high as Heaven. Tune your ear to the music of the stars and to the voice of nature, such as you can see—if you have the wish to see—in the Far North. If you do this, you'll be thrilled as never before, and your general outlook will turn to truth and goodness, as a plant turns to the sun.

The Highlands of Scotland, I would have you know, is no place for the juke-box and the hamburger crowds; or kiss-me-quick car labels. It's calm, relaxing and civilised in a way that most countries have forgotten how to be. It is—so far—an unspoiled outpost of Britain. Make no mistake about this.

However, following the waves of emigration during the last decades of the 18th century and the early 19th century, the glens and the clachans at that time lost most of their hereditary SEANCHAIDH—reciters of tales of the brave days of old—at the happy ceilidh circles gathered round the peat fires on long winter nights, after the day's work had finished.

But yet, there is still humour to be found; dry Scottish humour that the crofter comes out with unknowingly. He doesn't create a situation for humour, but takes the humour out of the situation. Sometimes that humour comes out of ordinary sayings that could be phrased differently as the two following remarks will show.

There were twin boys, and after a lapse of a few years, one of them came back to the village for a week's visit. One of the old inhabitants, accosting him in the street, said, 'Hello! son; was it you or your brother that was killed in the war?'

Two other men talking of their wives, and one wanting to make out how much his wife and he loved each other said,

'There's nothing I wouldn't do for my wife and there's nothing she wouldn't do for me. That's how we get on so well together, doing nothing for each other.' And they are good at casually making up little rhymes and verses. There is one that has always amused me:

> Ma Grannie made a dumpling
> She wrapped it in a clout;
> She boiled it in the kettle
> And couldna get it oot!

In some of the out-of-the-way villages in the N. West the locals will tell you they clip all their cats' tails, so that on cold days they can shut the doors more quickly behind them and so conserve the heat!

They will reminisce about a grand feast and dance they had in the village hall after the war, and everyone was asked to turn up and bring something. One person brought a chicken; another a duck; another wine; another fruit. One man brought his brother.

The Scots are well-known for their thriftiness. For instance, the wee boy asking his father for a penny to go next door to see the moon through the shepherd's telescope; and the reply 'it's only a half-moon tonight, son; wait a week and then you can see the whole thing for the same money'. And of the tombstone in the churchyard bearing the inscription, 'Dr. Macleod, Surgery Hours 9–11 a.m.' because the widow refused to pay extra for lettering when there was a perfectly good door-plate going begging. And again, of the husband who fell off the roof of the house, and as he passed the kitchen window called to his wife, 'Annie, no lunch today!'

I remember staying at a Highland hotel once, and noticed that my own cake of soap (that I usually take with me in travelling) was missing off the wash-basin. On calling for the young mini-skirted Highland lassie and in a way almost accusing her of stealing my nicely scented soap, she opened the bathroom window and showed me where she had put it—on the ledge; for she said putting it out there hardened it and so it lasted longer. She was in fact demonstrating 'thrift'; later on I tried the idea myself, only to find the wet cake slid off the ledge, falling two floors below into a heap of empty beer bottles in the bar courtyard!

Should you be talking to a crofter by the wayside on a very windy day, he may point to his fence posts, telling you they were at least two inches higher when he first drove them in; the wind had driven them that much into the ground.

For the many years I have lived in Gairloch, I have often said that when a man is tired of the Highlands, he is tired of life. This is all too true; for there is up here all that life can offer and afford. Here you can recognise to a unique degree the worth of the people and the goodness of their lives.

This, in a way, is a short book of only 360 pages. One always tends to overpraise a long book because one has got through it at long last! However (like all my others) it is not written to a formula for any material gain it may bring about albeit we are living today amongst a materialistic society; but rather it is written springing from the roots of faith in the Highlands of Scotland. It is not born of imagination; it is homespun from the loom of my own feelings and my own beliefs. Love for the Highlands and the Islands, and the real Highland people, is not seated on heights far above us; it is seated at our own level, accessible to our own trend should we care to embrace it. In an ever shrinking world, it is good to know there is still the Highlands.

It's not only now, this moment, that's important; it's to-morrow when you, readers, have returned home from visiting this Far North, and the next day, and the days after when, in remembrance, you'll find in your thoughts the peony is growing by the cabbage patch.

Reluctantly do I come to the end of this saga, for space is running out, and I must say goodbye to Shangri-La. Much rather would I say *sin un adios* (without a goodbye). However, in the Africana language of farewell, I bid you all *hlalani kakuhle* (stay well) and *hambani kakuhle* (go well).

> Farewell to the mountains covered with snow
> Farewell to the straths and the valleys below;
> Farewell to the forests and their stately woods
> Farewell to the waterfalls, majestic in floods.

When I leave the far north of Sutherland, I leave overburdened with its riches Scotland has showered on me over the years; in a soothing dream as Tennyson would call 'the honey of delicious memories'. . . .

Concluding, I proudly quote the words specially given me some time ago by a fair and lovely maiden of Lewis: deep peace of the toppling wave to you; deep peace of the flowing air to you; deep peace of the quiet earth to you; deep peace of the shining stars to you; and deep peace of the Son of Peace to you . . .

With these words I bring to a close these pages of the *Land of my Love* and the *Land of my Joys.*

This small corner of Scotland holds its broad shoulders firm and strong against the sky. Its personality is as varied as its people. The country rolls and tosses and pitches, and the unwavering miles flow out in cosmic poetry. It is lavish in space and distance; and its bigness can at times be overpowering and formidable. Nothing in its make-up has been done in half measures, nor do you find the conventional frills of picture-book scenery tacked on as an afterthought. The mountains don't fade into a nothingness here; the suspense you experience is beyond words. Surprises in the scenery round many corners result from the Creator's careful planning and careful timing. *Tediousness is not one of its vices.* The country is wide, open, and limitless. The Highlander and his family obey the mandates of their consciences and the precepts of God—and above all this, they are free.

How foreign to this land are ideologies drenching the outside world of Shangri-La with blood today. Democracy, boiled down, is good neighbourliness and the breaking down of false pride. Their way of life was created by its people long, long ago; a very simple life. Sunrise and sunset are little daily miracles you will always remember up here. All this is a little part of Scotland, called 'wonderland'. Room enough, as I have said earlier, to breathe in; big enough to move about in; space enough to be alone in, to think; should you wish to think. A land full of poetry, legends and romance.

LAND of my LOVE,
LAND of my Joys . . . *where one never walks alone.*

THE END

RAPTURE IN THE HIGHLANDS